T0235692

Communications
in Computer and Information Science   1382

More information about this series at http://www.springer.com/series/7899

Sule Yildirim Yayilgan ·
Imran Sarwar Bajwa · Filippo Sanfilippo (Eds.)

Intelligent Technologies and Applications

Third International Conference, INTAP 2020
Gjøvik, Norway, September 28–30, 2020
Revised Selected Papers

 Springer

Editors
Sule Yildirim Yayilgan Ⓘ
NTNU
Gjøvik, Norway

Imran Sarwar Bajwa Ⓘ
The Islamia University of Bahawalpur
Punjab, Pakistan

Filippo Sanfilippo Ⓘ
University of Agder
Kristiansand, Norway

ISSN 1865-0929   ISSN 1865-0937   (electronic)
Communications in Computer and Information Science
ISBN 978-3-030-71710-0   ISBN 978-3-030-71711-7   (eBook)
https://doi.org/10.1007/978-3-030-71711-7

This Springer imprint is published by the registered company Springer Nature Switzerland AG
The registered company address is: Gewerbestrasse 11, 6330 Cham, Switzerland

Preface

The present book includes accepted papers of the 3rd International Conference on Intelligent Technologies and Applications (INTAP 2020), held in Gjøvik, Norway during September 28-30, 2020, organized and hosted by NTNU, Norway and IEEE Norway. The conference was sponsored by the Research Council of Norway and EuroAI and was supported by IEEE Norway.

The conference was organized in eight simultaneous tracks: Image, video processing and analysis [3 papers], Security and IoT [4 papers], Health and AI [3 papers], Deep Learning [4], Biometrics [5], Environment [2], Intrusion & Malware Detection [5] and AIRLEAs tracks [8 papers].

INTAP 2020 received 117 submissions, from 27 countries and districts on six continents. After a blind review process, only 34 papers were accepted based on the classifications provided by the Program Committee, resulting in an acceptance rate of 29%. The selected papers come from researchers based in several countries including Albania, United Kingdom, USA, New Zealand, Australia, France, China, Malaysia, Denmark, Norway, Finland, Germany, Greece, Hungary and other countries. The highly diverse audience gave us the opportunity to achieve a good level of understanding of the mutual needs, requirements and technical means available in this field of research.

The selected papers reflect state-of-the-art research in different domains and applications of artificial intelligence and highlight the benefits of intelligent and smart systems in these domains and applications. The high quality standards of research presented will be maintained and reinforced at INTAP 2021, to be held at the University of Agder, Norway, and in future editions of this conference.

Furthermore, INTAP 2020 included five plenary keynote lectures given by Prof. Ole-Christoffer Granmo (University of Agder, Norway), Prof. Sokratis Katsikas (Open University of Cyprus, Cyprus and Norwegian University of Science and Technology), Serena Villata (Centre National de la Recherche Scientifique, France), Ibrahim A. Hameed (Norwegian University of Science and Technology, Norway) and Prof. Frank Dignum (Umeå Universitet, Sweden). We would like to express our appreciation to all of them and in particular to those who took the time to contribute a paper to this book.

On behalf of the conference Organizing Committee, we would like to thank all participants. First of all, the authors, whose high-quality work is the essence of the conference, and the members of the Program Committee, who helped us with their eminent expertise in reviewing and selecting the quality papers for this book. As we know, organizing an international conference requires the efforts of many individuals. We wish to thank also all the members of our Organizing Committee, whose work and commitment were invaluable.

The proceedings editors wish to thank the dedicated Scientific Committee members and all the other reviewers for their contributions. We also thank Springer for their trust and for publishing the proceedings of INTAP 2020.

October 2020

Sule Yildirim Yayilgan
Imran Sarwar Bajwa
Filippo Sanfilippo

The original version of the book was revised: the book's subtitle was revised. The correction to the book is available at https://doi.org/10.1007/978-3-030-71711-7_35

Organization

General Co-chairs

Sule Yildirim Yayilgan	NTNU, Norway
Imran Sarwar Bajwa	The Islamia University of Bahawalpur, Pakistan
Filippo Sanfilippo	University of Agder, Norway

Program Co-chairs

Raghavendra Ramachandra	NTNU, Gjøvik, Norway
Ferhat Ozgur Catak	NTNU, Gjøvik, Norway
Athar Khodabakhsh	NTNU, Gjøvik, Norway
Imran Ghani	Indiana University of Pennsylvania, USA

Organizing Committee

Sule Yildirim Yayilgan	NTNU, Norway
Filippo Sanfilippo	University of Agder, Norway
Mohamed Abomhara	NTNU, Norway
Marina Shalaginova	NTNU, Norway
Linda Derawi	NTNU, Norway
Javed Ahmed	NTNU, Norway
Ogerta Elezaj	NTNU, Norway
Doney Abraham	NTNU, Norway
Blend Arifaj	NTNU, Norway
M. Taimoor Khan	University of Greenwich, UK
Irfan Hyder	Institute of Business Management, Pakistan
Riaz Ul Amin	University of Okara, Pakistan

Program Committee

Adel Al-Jumaily	University of Technology Sydney, Australia
Adina Florea	University Politehnica of Bucharest, Romaina
Adriano V. Werhli	Universidade Federal do Rio Grande, Brazil
Agostino Poggi	Università degli Studi di Parma, Italy
Aleš Zamuda	University of Maribor, Slovenia
Alexander Gelbukh	National Polytechnic Institute, Mexico
Amin Beheshti	Macquarie University, Australia
Anand Nayyar	Duy Tan University, Vietnam
António Luís Lopes	Instituto Universitário de Lisboa, Portugal
Anna Helena Reali Costa	University of São Paulo, São Paulo, Brazil
Álvaro Rubio-Largo	Universidade NOVA de Lisboa, Portugal

Asif Baba	Tuskegee University, USA
Athar Khodabakhsh	NTNU, Gjøvik, Norway
Barbara Ongaro	Liceo Alessandro Greppi, Italy
Bahram Amini	Foulad Institute of Technology, Malaysia
Bernard Moulin	Université Laval, Canada
Bill Grosky	University of Michigan-Dearborn, USA
Bujor Pavaloiu	Universitatea Politehnica din Bucureşti, Romania
Carl James Debono	University of Malta, Malta
Carlos Filipe da Silva Portela	University of Minho, Portugal
Costin Bădică	University of Craiova, Romania
Chrisa Tsinaraki	Technical University of Crete, Greece
Cyril de Runz	Université de Reims Champagne-Ardenne, France
Dan Cristea	UAIC, Romania
Daniel Rodríguez García	Autonomous University of Barcelona, Spain
Di Wu	North Dakota State University, USA
Dion Goh Hoe Lian	Nanyang Technological University, Singapore
Elias Kyriakides	KIOS Research Center, Cyprus
Eric Matson	Purdue University, USA
Emanuele Principi	Università Politecnica delle Marche, Italy
Farshad Fotouhi	Wayne State University, USA
Ferhat Ozgur Catak	NTNU, Gjøvik, Norway
Francesca Alessandra Lisi	Università degli Studi di Bari, Italy
Filippo Sanfilippo	University of Agder, Norway
Gazi Erkan Bostanci	Ankara University, Turkey
Gerald Schaefer	Loughborough University, UK
Gianluca Reali	University of Perugia, Italy
Gianluigi Ferrari	Università degli Studi di Parma, Italy
Giuseppe Boccignone	University of Milan, Italy
Grigore Stamatescu	Politehnica University of Bucharest, Romania
Hichem Omrani	LISER, Luxembourg
Harald Kosch	University of Passau, Germany
Haralambos Mouratidis	University of Brighton, UK
Hazrat Ali	COMSATS Institute of Information Technology, Abbottabad, Pakistan
Isabel De La Torre Díez	University of Valladolid, Spain
Imran Memon	Zhejiang University, China
Jan Platoš	VŠB-TU Ostrava, Czech Republic
Jan Muhammad	BUITEMS, Pakistan
Jamal Bentahar	Concordia University, USA
José Carlos Martins Fonseca	University of Coimbra, Portugal
José Moreira	Universidade de Aveiro, Portugal
José Torres	Universidade Fernando Pessoa, Portugal
Juan Carlos Nieves	Umeå Universitet, Sweden
Juha Röning	University of Oulu, Finland
Jurek Z. Sasiadek	Carleton University, Canada

Weronika T. Adrian	University of Calabria, Italy
Wei Wei	Xi'an University of Technology, China
Yap Bee Wah	Universiti Teknologi MARA, Malaysia
Yasushi Kambayashi	Nippon Institute of Technology, Japan
Zbyněk Raida	Brno University of Technology, Czech Republic

Invited Speakers

Ole-Christoffer Granmo	University of Agder, Norway
Sokratis Katsikas	NTNU, Norway, and Open University of Cyprus, Cyprus
Serena Villata	Centre National de la Recherche Scientifique, France
Ibrahim A. Hameed	Norwegian University of Science and Technology, Norway
Frank Dignum	Umeå universitet, Sweden

Contents

Deep Learning

Biometrics

Image, Video Processing and Analysis

Classification and Segmentation Models for Hyperspectral Imaging - An Overview

Syed Taimoor Hussain Shah[1], Shahzad Ahmad Qureshi[1(✉)], Aziz ul Rehman[2],
Syed Adil Hussain Shah[3], and Jamal Hussain[4]

[1] Pakistan Institute of Engineering & Applied Sciences (PIEAS), Nilore,
Islamabad 45650, Pakistan
drsaqureshi@pieas.edu.pk
[2] National Institute of Lasers and Optronics (NILOP) College, PIEAS, Nilore,
Islamabad 45650, Pakistan
[3] Comsats University, Wah Cantt, Pakistan
[4] Ghulam Ishaq Khan Institute of Engineering Sciences and Technology, Topi, Pakistan

Abstract. An advancement in Hyperspectral Imaging (HI) technology is creating important attraction among the researchers to develop better classification techniques. This technology is well known for its high spatial and spectral information due to which the discrimination of materials is much more accurate and efficient. The useful information is extracted in Hyperspectral Imaging technology after applying it in agriculture, biomedical, and disaster management studies. A review comparison has been carried out for air borne images using hyperspectral acquisition hardware for classification as well as segmentation purpose. Numerous approaches that have been focused for implementation namely semi-supervised technique used for hyperspectral imaging using active learning and multinomial logistic regression, Generalized Composite Kernels (GCKs) classification framework, classification of spectral-spatial based data on loopy belief propagation (LBP), multiple feature learning of HI classification, and semi-supervised GCKs with classification accuracy on AVIRIS dataset (59.97%, 92.89%, 81.45%, 75.84%, and 95.50) and segmentation accuracies using α-expansion method as (73.27%, 93.57%, 92.86%, 91.73% and 98.31), respectively.

Keywords: Semi-supervised hyperspectral image data cube · Classification · Loopy belief propagation · Multinomial logistic regression · Active learning · And AVIRIS dataset

1 Introduction

A conventional RGB image consists of three colors namely red, green, and blue images, but a hyperspectral image usually can have many colors across the whole electromagnetic spectrum. In hyperspectral imaging, spectral and spatial signatures are combined to create a 3D hyperspectral data cube. Every pixel of the image carries some spectral signature. The hyperspectral image, which is formed by the reflection, of light from sample contains quantitative diagnostic information. The idea of the hyperspectral image

© Springer Nature Switzerland AG 2021
S. Yildirim Yayilgan et al. (Eds.): INTAP 2020, CCIS 1382, pp. 3–16, 2021.
https://doi.org/10.1007/978-3-030-71711-7_1

initially developed for remote sensing [1, 2] and Hyperspectral Imaging technology provides useful information when used in real life applications such as agriculture, biomedical, disaster management studies, etc. Applications of hyperspectral imaging include agriculture [3–7], eye care [8, 9], food processing [10, 11], mineralogy [12, 13], detection of environmental pollutants [14], chemical imaging, astronomy for space and surveillance [15, 16] and medical in-vivo and in-vitro diagnostics [17] in surgical marking of tumors [18–20]. Remote sensing technology is getting much improvement due to advancement of sensors. Now-a-days, these sensors are capturing a large number of images having different wavelengths [21]. For this reason, hyperspectral imaging (HI) is getting reputation and arising in the shape of major domain among the researchers for classification and segmentation on the basis of spatial and spectral information [22]. NASA's Jet Propulsion Laboratory first time introduced AVIRIS sensor. These days, this sensor is in its much advanced shape and having capability of capturing the same area with much information by storing more than 200 bands against each pixel [23]. This kind of HIs helps the classification models to identify each object in the pixel efficiently on the basis of their unique spectrum [24]. HI-based dataset exhibits different kinds of problems during classification. One of these problems is Hughes phenomena. It states that with increasing the number of spectral bands or dimensions, classification precision increases and after a point this begins to fall dramatically with further increase of spectral information. This effect is caused by the existence of strong correlation and redundancy in the dataset [25–28]. Ma et al. [25] has introduced a solution namely principal component analysis (PCA) for this kind of problem. Before classification, features should be reduced in a manner that there should be less correlation and redundancy. This work showed that usually strong correlation coefficient exists among the features. Bruzzone et al. [29] showed that capturing the labeled samples is a computationally expensive task. The exploitation of large ground truth information for this kind of field is not so common. Scholkopf et al. [30] addressed the solution for this kind of problem as the utilization of kernelized methods, i.e. multinomial logistic regression (MLR) [27, 31–34] and support vector machine (SVM) [29, 35, 36] utilize kernel methods. Their output precision can be enhanced by giving them less dimensional data.

There are different machine learning based classification methods which have been addressed for HI based datasets such as SVM [29, 35, 36] MLR [27, 31], and deep learning based methods [37]. Some of them are conditional random field (CRM) and Markov random field (MRF) which utilize spectral information with spatial information. Due to Hughes effect, traditional classifiers are not that much efficient for classification. Li et al. [27] has solved this problem by introducing semi-supervised technique with active learning (AL). On the basis of AL, few samples, which are having much prominent classification information are selected from the dataset and passed to the classification method. Classifier learns the knowledge and develops the boundary on the basis of these selected features. Chapelle et al. [35] introduced a semi supervised approach emphasizing that similar features, on the behalf of their similarity, should belong to the similar class. This causes to either shrink or stretch the decision boundaries usually towards a low density area. Such kernelized methods are used on spatial and spectral information due to having the capability of tackling curse of dimensionality. This technique has good generalization power and produced good classification results.

Benediktsson et al. [38] introduced two more problems which come to face during classification. One is about the spectral information and the other is about spatial information. Against each pixel spectral information is usually abundant with mute spatial information. In an image of HI, usually spatial information is abundant having less spectral information. Fauvel et al. [22] has given an overview on the importance of using spectral as well as spatial information which improves the classification accuracy. Pesaresi and Benediktsson [39] exploited the morphological profiles [26, 28, 38–42] using opening and closing mathematical operations for classification of features. The series of these opening and closing operations produce a large features set from the original dataset having more discriminant information for classification and result in much improved classification accuracy. Li et al. [43] has introduced a novel approach in which few samples are required for training the classifiers. Similarly, this approach also solved another issue namely the over fitting which is caused by the existence of abundance of spectral information. On the basis of bias-variance dilemma, the proposed solution mainly handles high dimensional and inadequate training samples. Tan et al. [44] has introduced a novel idea of active learning using quasi-Newton multinomial logistic regression (MLR) algorithm. This idea helped in fast MLR classification using quasi-Newton algorithm for developing the logistic regressors and the selection of unlabeled samples which has much dominant information for classification in less computational time. In the present overview, we have compared five approaches for classification- and segmentation-accuracy computation: namely dynamic semi-supervised learning with multinomial logistic regression [27], classification based on GCKs framework [26], spectral-spatial classification using LBP [45], multiple feature based classification using various sources [28], and semi-supervised GCKs [46]. Methodologies are described in Sect. 2, results and discussion are given in Sect. 3 followed by conclusion in Sect. 4.

2 Methodology

The four basic hyperspectral imaging techniques (Spatial, Spectral, Snapshot and Spatio-Spectral scanning) acquire a three-dimensional (X, Y, λ) dataset. X and Y represent the spatial coordinates while the λ coordinate corresponds to the spectral dimension and can have any value across the whole electromagnetic spectrum depending on the availability of light source, detectors and the particular application.

The main theme of this work is to develop a comparison among four different approaches for hyperspectral data analysis acquired using any of the four above listed methods and are discussed in the following sections:

2.1 Semi-supervised Technique Used for Hyperspectral Imaging Using Active Learning and Multinomial Logistic Regression

In this approach [27], a semi-supervised learning based technique is applied on the data for segmentation. For unlabeled data, a graph-based technique is used. This graph-based technique promotes the regressor vector, so similar labeled and unlabeled features should have to be in the same class to guess the best regressor. This whole mechanism is bounded in an algorithm named Gauss-Siedel Algorithm with the goal to improve the precision of the regressors assigned to the unsupervised dataset. In the next steps, the posterior class distribution is built through the MLR and Markov random fields (MRF). The MRF is modeled by using Multilevel Logistic (MLL) technique. The segmentation is finally given by [27]:

$$\hat{y} = \underset{y \in L^n}{arg\,min} \sum_{i \in S} -log\left(p(y_i)|\hat{\omega}\right) - \mu \sum_{i,j \in C} \delta\left(y_i - y_j\right) \qquad (1)$$

Where $\hat{y}$ is the MAP estimation of label y, L is a set of class labels, i represents every image pixel where i ∈ S, a set of integers indexing n pixels of an hyperspectral image, p(yi|$\hat{w}$) represents posterior distribution of regressors, μ is the smoothness parameter, C represents set of cliques over the image with ith and jth adjacent vertices, and $\delta(y_i - y_j)$ is the unit impulse response with higher probability for equally neighboring pixels. The least confident points of unsupervised nature are subject to classification using corresponding class label entropy. Prior to image labels is an MLL model which enforces segmentation. MAP is determined using the algorithm of α-expansion and the optimization algorithm defining threshold for minimum correspondence energy.

2.2   Classification Based on Generalized Composite Kernels Framework

In this work [26], generalized composite kernels framework is applied on the HI based data for classification. For classification, the broad spectral information exists the remotely sensed HI data cube, which allows for distinguishing similar objects [48]. So, kernels can be applied in a linear fashion and also in different combinations (spectral, spatial, spectral-spatial and spatial-spectral) for HI data set. Since a probabilistic framework is used, it allows a perfect blend of the composite kernels along with the generalization capacity with the help of logistic regressor. Further a Laplacian prior, a regularization technique, can be used in the proposed algorithm with the result of ensuring problem convergence is ensured [47].

MLR technique is used to calculate the posterior class probabilities on the basis of trained regressors by inputting the features. Regressors are computed by using the MAP estimation.

Further, attribute profiles (APs) and morphological profiles (MPs) are computed on spectral and spatial details that helps in classification [38–40]. APs are computed by applying attribute filters (AFs) to gray level image. In this technique, the whole feature (spectral band) extracted from the original pixel is not considered. So several principal components (PCs) are taken for this technique and the remaining components are ignored yielding extended attribute profiles (EAPs). In this paper, only the first three PCs are considered having maximum of the variance. When EAPs are compared using stack of attributes, it results in extended multi-attribute profile (EMAP). It transforms the HI data in a better format for training. The maximum-a-posteriori (MAP) is optimized for regressors as given by:

$$\hat{c} = \arg\max_{c} \left\{ l(c) + \log p(c) + \sum_{i=1}^{L} \sum_{j=1}^{L} \left(\begin{array}{c} c_{j+1}^{(y_i)} K^{\omega}\left(x_i^{\omega}, x_j^{\omega}\right) + c_{j+L+1}^{(y_i)} K^s\left(x_i^s, x_j^s\right) \\ + c_{j+2L+1}^{(y_i)} K^{\omega s}\left(x_i^{\omega}, x_j^s\right) \\ + c_{j+3L+1}^{(y_i)} K^{s\omega}\left(x_i^s, x_j^{\omega}\right) \\ - \log \sum_{k=1}^{K} \exp c_1^k + c_{j+1}^{(k)} K^{\omega}\left(x_i^{\omega}, x_j^{\omega}\right) \\ + c_{j+L+1}^{(k)} K^s\left(x_i^s, x_j^s\right) + c_{j+2L+1}^{(k)} K^{\omega s}\left(x_i^{\omega}, x_j^s\right) \\ + c_{j+3L+1}^{(k)} K^{s\omega}\left(x_i^s, x_j^{\omega}\right) \end{array} \right) \right\} \tag{2}$$

Where spectral and spatial kernels $K(x_i, x_j)$ have been represented with superscripts ω and s respectively, $l(c)$ is the log-likelihood function of logistic regressors, $p(c)$ represents probability of regressors with respect to Labelled and Unlabeled data and L represents number of samples in the labelled training set.

Logistic regression via variable splitting and augmented Lagrangian (LORSAL) algorithm is used to deal with large kernel sizes [45] and also to have less complexity for the computation of the repressors. These computed regressors are passed to the GCK algorithm which outputs classification posterior probabilities. Maximum-a-posteriori (MAP) is used over these probabilities to get the classification map. The final thing about MLR is LORSAL that plays a key role in this work. For comparison, we have done an extra work of segmentation by using α-expansion algorithm.

2.3 Spectral-Spatial Classification Using LBP

In this approach, a new framework of spectral-spatial classification is proposed for HI based dataset [49]. Supervised HI based data is limited, expensive, and difficult to obtain by the help of remote sensors in real scenarios. The important contribution from the proposed framework is the use of marginal probability distribution (MPD) which uses the whole (spatial and spectral) information of the data where MPD is based on joint probability distribution (JPD). JPD is a table that shows the joint probability among random variables. The sum of each individual variable shows its marginal probability while the sum of all variables shows the MPD. The posterior class probability is computed with a discriminative random field (DRF). DRF is a combination of MLR classifier and MLL. MLR computes association potential by the help of regressors while MLL computes interaction potentials by the help of MRF. MLR computes the posterior probabilities and regressors for each feature. Gaussian radial basis function (RBF) is used in MLR due to its wide use in the classification of HI based data problems. RBF is a nonlinear function while the current problem is also nonlinear and shows some kind of symmetry. Isotopic MLL prior work helps to get spatial information to and belongs to MRF class and encourages segmentation and leads to a solution according to which adjacent pixels should belong to the same class. We can estimate the final solution by means of posterior MAP marginal for node i, which is given by:

$$\hat{y}_i = \arg\max_{y_i} q(y_i|x) \tag{3}$$

Where $q(y_i|x)$ is the marginal density of $p(y|x)$ with respect to y_i. MAP estimation, for getting the most suitable label, is used to minimize the Bayesian risk which is associated with zero-one loss function. Bayesian classifier chooses the class that has a greatest posterior probability. Here MAP marginal (MAPM) is computed with the help of LBP technique because the marginal density in MAPM is very difficult to compute. For LBP computation, first a square lattice is built in which pixels are connected with both hidden nodes and labeled nodes neighboring pixels. In square lattice, hidden nodes and labeled nodes both are given. In this technique, margin is computed by the help of interaction potential and association potential. Interaction potential finds every similar pair of neighboring labels and then association potential computes the probability against given evidence. The basic idea of LBP technique is that every node propagates message to its neighbors and in the response of message a belief is developed at each node. This is done for each node and all the incoming messages' power is estimated. The margins are computed which help in the computation of MAPM.

2.4 Multiple Feature Learning of HI Classification

Since, the kernels are managed in a linear manner due to which the approach is more flexible and computationally less complex, so new framework is proposed which carries out the combination of multiple features for learning [28]. Moreover, a new technique is introduced with GCK, in which APs are generated by the help of AFs. The dimension of HI based data is high, so it is named as multi-APs. In this technique, all the features (spectral band) extracted from the original pixel not considered; hence, limited PCs are taken into account to yield EAPs. The logistic regressors' ω are given by the input features h(x) as given by:

$$\hat{\omega} = \arg\max_{\omega} \sum_{i=1}^{L} \left(h^T(x_i)\omega^{(y_i)} - \log(\sum_{k=1}^{K} \exp(h^T(x_i)\omega^{(k)}) + \log p(\omega) \right) \qquad (4)$$

Where ω represents regressor for label y, h(x_i) is a feature obtained by a linear/nonlinear transformation and p(w) is the Laplacian prior. The stack of EAPs is called EMAP. These EMAPs are used in the classification process. However, these approaches mainly focus on kernels, which might cause redundancy or information loss. MLR technique is used to calculate the posterior class probabilities on the basis of trained regressors by inputting the features. The features are extracted in MLR by using the linear function [27] applied to the original spectral information) and nonlinear function applied to the EMAPs function. The linear function extracts linear features (original spectral) from the linear kernel to deal with linear class boundaries while the nonlinear function uses a nonlinear kernel which has some kind of symmetry. This nonlinear kernel uses mapping to map the high dimensional data to a high dimensional space for better discrimination as different features have different characteristics as well as orientations depending on the complexity level of source data-distribution. MAP estimate is used at the end to guess the best regressor and finally to compute the segmentation score, classification map is fed to α-expansion algorithm.

2.5 Semi-supervised GCKs

In this method [46], a new framework is proposed which is a combination of two different techniques namely semi-supervised HIS using active learning [27], and generalized composite kernels framework [26]. To begin with, the dataset is divided for training and testing samples. On all samples, attribute profiles are mapped in the form of gray level images for the calculation of EMAP with several PCs. Then, a semi-supervised technique is used on these extracted training features. LORSAL Algorithm [31] is used to train the regressors thanks to its lower complexity. Further, posterior probabilities are computed by passing these trained regressors to MLR technique enclosing composite kernels. Each feature vector is taken from the training sample without replacement scheme and fed to the MLR, having linear and non-linear kernel functions; which produces output in the form of posterior probabilities. A logical hypothesis for image segmentation is that the contiguous pixels mostly lie in same class. For image modeling, isotropic multi-level logistic (MLL) prior has been used. Piecewise smooth segmentations are encouraged by this prior by using Markov random fields (MRF). In MRF, the Gibbs energy distribution is computed.

The maximum-a-posteriori (MAP) is computed for regressors as given by:

$$\hat{c} = \arg \max_{c} \{l(c) + \log p(c|X_{L+U})\} \tag{5}$$

Where c represents regressor which is dependent on the maximization of its log-likelihood with the incremental effect of posterior probability of labeled and unlabeled data X_{L+U} For the calculation of classification accuracy, similarity-based measure is used on maximum-a-posteriori (MAP) by the help of trained regressors with comparison of ground truth map. Finally, segmentation process has started with α-expansion algorithm enclosing Markov random field (MRF) functionality. Similarly, similarity-based measure is used again on the final segmentation map in comparison of ground truth map.

2.6 Alpha-Expansion Algorithm

This algorithm permits to minimize the energy E on a finite set of classified labels L and a class called penalty metric. The notion behind alpha-expansion algorithm is to successively segment all α and non-α pixels with graph cuts and the algorithm will change the value of α at each iteration. The algorithm will iterate through each possible label for α until it converges. At each iteration, α region can only expand. This changes somehow the way to set the graph weights. Also, when two neighboring nodes do not currently have the same label, an intermediate node is inserted and links are weighted so they are relative to the distance to the label. The prior model for segmentation is given by:

$$p(y) = \frac{1}{z} \exp\left(-\sum_{k \in K} P_k(y)\right) \tag{6}$$

where z is a normalizing factor and P_k is called prior potential and k is a set of cliques over the image. The potential over cliques is computed by:

$$-P_k(y) = \begin{cases} v_{y_i}, & if \ |k| = 1 \ (for \ single \ clique) \\ \mu_k, & if \ |k| > 1 \ and \ \forall_{i,j \in c} \ y_i = y_j \\ -\mu_k, & if \ |k| > 1 \ and \ \exists_{i,j \in c} \ y_i \neq y_j \end{cases} \tag{7}$$

where $\mu_k \geq 0$ It is clear from Eq. 7 that the contiguous pixels have the same labels. The Eq. 6 becomes flexible by introducing $\exp(v_{y_i}) \propto p(y_i)$ and it may be given by:

$$p(y) = \frac{1}{z} \exp \left(\sum_{i \in P} v_{y_i} + \mu \sum_{(i,j) \in K} \delta(y_i - y_j) \right) \tag{8}$$

where μ is used to control the level of smoothness and $\delta(y_i - y_j)$ determines the higher probability towards label assignment.

2.7 Hyperspectral Imaging-Based Dataset

In this hyperspectral dataset [3], the region namely Indian Pines, Northwestern Indiana has been captured by AVIRIS sensor in 1992. As hyperspectral data usually contains a 3-D shape. So, in this dataset, spatial 2-D matrix contains 145×145 samples and against each pixel, its third dimension contains 224 channels. In this dataset, there are total 16 classes which have been captured by AVIRIS sensor. In these experiments, the dataset is first preprocessed by removing few bad channels.

3 Results and Discussion

We have produced results on the basis of five different techniques. In each approach, we have used 10-fold cross-validation and ten independent Monte Carlo runs for more reliable results from the point of view of biasness and variance. Finally, the results with dataset were explained below.

Overall Accuracy (OA)
This term is defined as the probability of correctly classified instances reported on percentage basis [27].

k Statistics
This is an unbiased estimator to find the agreeing amount occurring on chance basis [50]. The independent Monte Carlo simulation has been run 10 times on the dataset for finding OA and κ statistics.

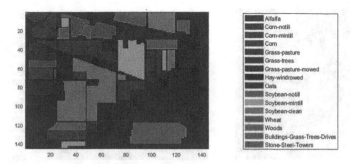

Fig.1. Ground truth map: 2-D matrix [46]

3.1 Produced Results Through Proposed Method

In these experiments, the dataset is first preprocessed by removing few bad channels. After this initial trimming, its dimension becomes $145 \times 145 \times 202$. The machine used for this work has been 8-GB RAM with 3.00-GHz processor. The ground truth [46], the direct information rather than inference, is shown in Fig. 1 for AVIRIS dataset.

The classification and segmentation results of different techniques are displayed in Table 1. It can be observed that semi-supervised GCKs methodology provide over all accuracy of classification accuracy of 95.50%. The κ-statistics has been found to follow the same trend as for OA (94.52%) for classification purpose (maps shown in Fig. 2 [46]).

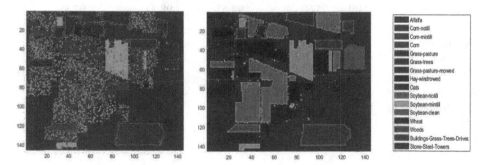

Fig. 2. Classification map (front image dimensions: 145×145): Semi-supervised using active learning's classification map is on left (worst case), Semi-supervised GCK's classification map is in mid, and labels are on right (best case).

For segmentation performance, semi-supervised GCKs methodology has shown improved accuracy of 98.31%. The same methodology dominated in segmentation because each methodology uses classification map for the development of segmentation map. α-expansion algorithm is used in each methodology. So, the dominated classification performance map has produced better segmentation map using expansion algorithm as shown in Fig. 3 [46].

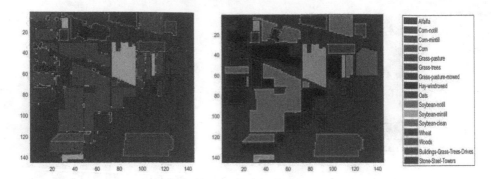

Fig. 3. Segmentation map (front image dimensions: 145 × 145): Semi-supervised using active learning's segmentation map is on left (worst case), semi-supervised GCK's segmentation map is in mid, and labels are on right (best case).

Finally, we have shown in Fig. 2 and 3 the compared graphs of classification and segmentation. In left image of both figures displaying the worst case of namely semi-supervised using active learning technique [27].

Table 1. Comparison of classification and segmentaion accuracies amongh different techniques

Methods	Ref	Classification accuracies		Segmentation accuracies	
		OA (%)	k-statistics	OA (%)	k-statistics
Semi-supervised GCK	[46]	95.50	94.52	98.31	97.88
Generalized composite kernels framework	[26]	92.89	90.11	93.57	90.89
Spectral-spatial classification using LBP	[45]	81.45	78.19	92.86	89.12
Multiple feature learning	[28]	75.84	71.76	91.73	90.54
Semi-supervised learning using active learning and multinomial logistic regression	[27]	59.97	76.10	73.27	80.11

Similarly, in right image of both figures displaying the best case of namely semi-supervised GCKs technique [46] from Table 1, it is concluded that Composite kernels technique [26] is the next rival to semi-supervised GCKs technique. The worst case is semi-supervised using active learning technique which is showing the less classification- and segmentation-scores.

4 Conclusions

In this paper, we have provided a brief review with comparison of semi-supervised technique used for hyperspectral imaging using active learning and multinomial logistic regression, Generalized Composite Kernels (GCKs) classification framework, classification of spectral-spatial based data on loopy belief propagation (LBP), multiple feature learning of HI classification, and semi-supervised GCKs techniques for hyperspectral imaging based on remote sensing data Most of them are based on MLR for posterior class probabilities. MAP is used to calculate the best label for classification map. For segmentation, α-expansion algorithm is applied on the classification map. The best found method has shown 95.50% overall accuracy and 94.52% κ-statistics. The better classification has resulted in outclass segmentation map (OA- and κ-statistics have been found to be 98.31% and 97.88%, respectively). In future, further improvement in the results by introducing a hybrid of compressive sensing technique and evolutionary computation procedures is to be expected.

References

1. Johnson, W.R., Wilson, D.W., Fink, W., Humayun, M., Bearman, G.: Snapshot hyperspectral imaging in ophthalmology. BIOMEDO **12**(1), 014036–014037 (2007)
2. Thenkabail, P.S., Lyon, J.G.: Hyperspectral Remote Sensing of Vegetation. CRC Press (2016)
3. Pierna, J., Baeten, V., Renier, A.M., Cogdill, R., Dardenne, P.: Combination of support vector machines (SVM) and near-infrared (NIR) imaging spectroscopy for the detection of meat and bone meal (MBM) in compound feeds. J. Chemom. **18**(7–8), 341–349 (2004)
4. ElMasry, G., Kamruzzaman, M., Sun, D.-W., Allen, P.: Principles and applications of hyperspectral imaging in quality evaluation of agro-food products: a review. Crit. Rev. Food Sci. Nutr. **52**(11), 999–1023 (2012)
5. Tilling, A.K., O'Leary, G., Ferwerda, J., Jones, S., Fitzgerald, G., Belford, R.: Remote sensing to detect nitrogen and water stress in wheat, p. 17. The Australian Society of Agronomy (2006)
6. Lacar, F., Lewis, M., Grierson, I.: Use of hyperspectral imagery for mapping grape varieties in the Barossa Valley, South Australia. In: Geoscience and Remote Sensing Symposium, 2001 IGARSS'01 IEEE 2001 International. IEEE (2001), pp. 2875–2877
7. Shanahan, J.F., Schepers, J.S., Francis, D.D., Varvel, G.E., Wilhelm, W.W., Tringe, J.M., et al.: Use of remote-sensing imagery to estimate corn grain yield. Agron. J. **93**(3), 583–589 (2001)
8. Li, H., Liu, W., Dong, B., Kaluzny, J.V., Fawzi, A.A., Zhang, H.F.: Snapshot hyperspectral retinal imaging using compact spectral resolving detector array. J. Biophotonics **10**(6–7), 830–839 (2017)
9. Shahidi, A., Patel, S., Flanagan, J., Hudson, C.: Regional variation in human retinal vessel oxygen saturation. Exp. Eye Res. **113**, 143–147 (2013)
10. Dacal-Nieto, A., Formella, A., Carrión, P., Vazquez-Fernandez, E., Fernández-Delgado, M.: Common scab detection on potatoes using an infrared hyperspectral imaging system. In: Maino, G., Foresti, G.L. (eds.) ICIAP 2011. LNCS, vol. 6979, pp. 303–312. Springer, Heidelberg (2011). https://doi.org/10.1007/978-3-642-24088-1_32

11. ElMasry, G., Sun, D.-W., Allen, P.: Non-destructive determination of water-holding capacity in fresh beef by using NIR hyperspectral imaging. Food Res. Int. **44**(9), 2624–2633 (2011). https://doi.org/10.1016/j.foodres.2011.05.001

12. van der Werff, H.M.A.: Knowledge-based remote sensing of complex objects: recognition of spectral and spatial patterns resulting from natural hydrocarbon seepages. Universiteit Utrecht (2006)

13. Holma, H.: Thermische Hyperspektralbildgebung im langwelligen Infrarot. Photonik (2011)

14. Rickard, L.J., Basedow, R.W., Zalewski, E.F., Silverglate, P.R., Landers, M.: HYDICE: an airborne system for hyperspectral imaging. In: Optical Engineering and Photonics in Aerospace Sensing: International Society for Optics and Photonics, pp. 173–179 (1993)

15. Hege, E.K., O'Connell, D., Johnson, W., Basty, S., Dereniak, E.L.: Hyperspectral imaging for astronomy and space surviellance. In: Optical Science and Technology, SPIE's 48th Annual Meeting: International Society for Optics and Photonics, pp. 380–391 (2004)

16. Rafert, B., Sellar, R.G., Holbert, E., Blatt, J.H., Tyler, D.W., Durham, S.E., et al.: Hyperspectral imaging Fourier transform spectrometers for astronomical and remote sensing observations. In: 1994 Symposium on Astronomical Telescopes & Instrumentation for the 21st Century: International Society for Optics and Photonics. pp. 338–349 (1994)

17. Fischer, C., Kakoulli, I.: Multispectral and hyperspectral imaging technologies in conservation: current research and potential applications. Stud. Conserv. **51**(sup1), 3–16 (2006)

18. Zonios, G., Perelman, L.T., Backman, V., Manoharan, R., Fitzmaurice, M., Van Dam, J., et al.: Diffuse reflectance spectroscopy of human adenomatous colon polyps in vivo. Appl Opt. **38**(31), 6628–6637 (1999). https://doi.org/10.1364/ao.38.006628

19. Tuchin, V.V.: Editor's Introduction: Optical Methods for Biomedical Diagnosis, pp. 1–15 (2016)

20. Calin, M.A., Parasca, S.V., Savastru, D., Manea, D.: Hyperspectral imaging in the medical field: present and future. Appl. Spectrosc. Rev. **49**(6), 435–447 (2013). https://doi.org/10.1080/05704928.2013.838678

21. Chang, C-I.: Hyperspectral Imaging: Techniques for Spectral Detection and Classification. Springer, New York (2003). https://doi.org/10.1007/978-1-4419-9170-6

22. Fauvel, M., Tarabalka, Y., Benediktsson, J.A., Chanussot, J., Tilton, J.C.: Advances in spectral-spatial classification of hyperspectral images. Proc. IEEE **101**(3), 652–675 (2012)

23. Goetz, A.F., Vane, G., Solomon, J.E., Rock, B.N.: Imaging spectrometry for earth remote sensing. Science **228**(4704), 1147–1153 (1985)

24. Thompson, D.R., Boardman, J.W., Eastwood, M.L., Green, R.O.: A large airborne survey of Earth's visible-infrared spectral dimensionality. Opt. Express **25**(8), 9186–9195 (2017)

25. Ma, W., Gong, C., Hu, Y., Meng, P., Xu, F.: The Hughes phenomenon in hyperspectral classification based on the ground spectrum of grasslands in the region around Qinghai Lake. In: International Symposium on Photoelectronic Detection and Imaging 2013: Imaging Spectrometer Technologies and Applications: International Society for Optics and Photonics, p. 89101G (2013)

26. Li, J., Marpu, P.R., Plaza, A., Bioucas-Dias, J.M., Benediktsson, J.A.: Generalized composite kernel framework for hyperspectral image classification. IEEE Trans. Geosci. Remote Sens. **51**(9), 4816–4829 (2013)

27. Li, J., Bioucas-Dias, J.M., Plaza, A.: Semisupervised hyperspectral image segmentation using multinomial logistic regression with active learning. IEEE Trans. Geosci. Remote Sens. **48**(11), 4085–4098 (2010)

28. Li, J., Huang, X., Gamba, P., Bioucas-Dias, J.M., Zhang, L., Benediktsson, J.A., et al.: Multiple feature learning for hyperspectral image classification. IEEE Trans. Geosci. Remote Sens. **53**(3), 1592–1606 (2014)

29. Bruzzone, L., Chi, M., Marconcini, M.: A novel transductive SVM for semisupervised classification of remote-sensing images. IEEE Trans. Geosci. Remote Sens. **44**(11), 3363–3373 (2006)
30. Schölkopf, B., Smola, A.J., Bach, F.: Learning with Kernels: Support Vector Machines, Regularization, Optimization, and Beyond. MIT Press (2002)
31. Cao, F., Yang, Z., Ren, J., Ling, W.-K., Zhao, H., Marshall, S.: Extreme sparse multinomial logistic regression: a fast and robust framework for hyperspectral image classification. Remote Sensing. **9**(12), 1255 (2017)
32. Böhning, D.: Multinomial logistic regression algorithm. Ann. Inst. Stat. Math. **44**(1), 197–200 (1992)
33. Li, J., Bioucas-Dias, J.M., Plaza, A.: Spectral–spatial hyperspectral image segmentation using subspace multinomial logistic regression and Markov random fields. IEEE Trans. Geosci. Remote Sens. **50**(3), 809–823 (2011)
34. Li, J., Bioucas-Dias, J.M., Plaza, A.: Semisupervised hyperspectral image classification using soft sparse multinomial logistic regression. IEEE Geosci. Remote Sens. Lett. **10**(2), 318–322 (2012)
35. Chapelle, O., Chi, M., Zien, A.: A continuation method for semi-supervised SVMs. In: Proceedings of the 23rd International Conference on Machine learning, pp. 185–92 (2006)
36. Mountrakis, G., Im, J., Ogole, C.: Support vector machines in remote sensing: a review. ISPRS J. Photogramm. Remote. Sens. **66**(3), 247–259 (2011)
37. Zappone, A., Di Renzo, M., Debbah, M.: Wireless networks design in the era of deep learning: model-based, AI-based, or both? IEEE Trans. Commun. **67**(10), 7331–7376 (2019)
38. Benediktsson, J.A., Palmason, J.A., Sveinsson, J.R.: Classification of hyperspectral data from urban areas based on extended morphological profiles. IEEE Trans. Geosci. Remote Sens. **43**(3), 480–491 (2005)
39. Pesaresi, M., Benediktsson, J.A.: A new approach for the morphological segmentation of high-resolution satellite imagery. IEEE Trans. Geosci. Remote Sens. **39**(2), 309–320 (2001)
40. Dalla Mura, M., Benediktsson, J.A., Waske, B., Bruzzone, L.: Morphological attribute profiles for the analysis of very high resolution images. IEEE Trans. Geosci. Remote Sens. **48**(10), 3747–3762 (2010)
41. ElMasry, G., Sun, D-w.: Principles of hyperspectral imaging technology. In: Hyperspectral Imaging for Food Quality Analysis and Control, pp. 3–43. Elsevier (2010)
42. Lu, G., Fei, B.: Medical hyperspectral imaging: a review. BIOMEDO **19**(1), 010901 (2014)
43. Li, F., Xu, L., Siva, P., Wong, A., Clausi, D.A.: Hyperspectral image classification with limited labeled training samples using enhanced ensemble learning and conditional random fields. IEEE J. Sel. Top. Appl. Earth Observations Remote Sens. **8**(6), 2427–2438 (2015)
44. Tan, K., Wang, X., Zhu, J., Hu, J., Li, J.: A novel active learning approach for the classification of hyperspectral imagery using quasi-Newton multinomial logistic regression. Int. J. Remote Sens. **39**(10), 3029–3054 (2018)
45. Li, J., Bioucas-Dias, J.M., Plaza, A.: Spectral–spatial classification of hyperspectral data using loopy belief propagation and active learning. IEEE Trans. Geosci. Remote Sens. **51**(2), 844–856 (2012)
46. Shah, S.T.H., Javed, S.G., Majid, A., Shah, S.A.H., Qureshi, S.A.: Novel classification technique for hyperspectral imaging using multinomial logistic regression and morphological profiles with composite kernels. In: 2019 16th International Bhurban Conference on Applied Sciences and Technology (IBCAST), pp. 419–424 (2019). https://doi.org/10.1109/IBCAST.2019.8667162
47. Zhang, L., Wei, W., Tian, C., Li, F., Zhang, Y.: Exploring structured sparsity by a reweighted Laplace prior for hyperspectral compressive sensing. IEEE Trans. Image Process. **25**(10), 4974–4988 (2016)

48. Plaza, A., Benediktsson, J.A., Boardman, J.W., Brazile, J., Bruzzone, L., Camps-Valls, G., et al.: Recent advances in techniques for hyperspectral image processing. Remote Sens. Environ. **113**, S110–S122 (2009)
49. Li, J., Bioucas-Dias, J.M., Plaza, A.: Spectral–spatial classification of hyperspectral data using loopy belief propagation and active learning. IEEE Trans. Geosci. Remote Sens. **51**(2), 844–856 (2013). https://doi.org/10.1109/TGRS.2012.2205263
50. Tezuka, F., Namiki, T., Higashiiwai, H.: Observer variability in endometrial cytology using kappa statistics. J. Clin. Pathol. **45**(4), 292–294 (1992)

Exploring Circular Hough Transforms for Detecting Hand Feature Points in Noisy Images from Ghost-Circle Patterns

Frode Eika Sandnes[1,2]([⊠]) [iD]

[1] Faculty of Technology, Art and Design, Oslo Metropolitan University, Oslo, Norway
frodes@oslomet.no
[2] Faculty of Technology, Kristiania University College, Oslo, Norway

Abstract. Several applications involve the automatic analysis of hand images such as biometry, digit-ratio measurements, and gesture recognition. A key problem common to these applications is the separation of hands from the background. Color based approaches struggle to detect the boundaries of the hand and the background if these have similar colors. This paper thus describes work-in-progress with a spatial approach for finger feature point detection based on the circular Hough transforms. The main challenge is to interpret finger feature points in the patterns of circles amidst noise. The approach was implemented in java and tested on a set of images. The results were assessed using manual visual inspection. Such spatial approaches hold potential for more robust and flexible hand related image analysis application. Moreover, these approaches could also give faster algorithms as there is no need for image binarization and threshold optimization.

Keywords: Finger feature points · Hand analysis · Image analysis · Hough transform

1 Introduction

Hands are used in a variety of applications including detecting gestures [1], biometry [2] and digit ratio measurements [3]. Certain gesture applications employ cameras to capture the movements of an individual and thereby interpret the actual motions of the person and hence his or her gestures. The person can therefore use gestures to control computers. The approaches often involve sophisticated image analysis algorithms for detecting arms, hands and fingers for the orientation and location of the individual fingers [4–6]. Similarly, several biometric applications, that is, the detection of an individual's identify based on his or her unique human features, rely on hand information such as fingerprint [7], the shape and texture of the hands [8] or palmprints [9–11]. Common for these is that overall hand features must be detected before the detailed information can be analyzed, that is, the fingerprint location, or the palm location and orientation, etc.

Automatic digit ratio measurement [12–14] is another area that requires the accurate detection of hand feature points. The purpose of digit ratio measurements is to find the

© Springer Nature Switzerland AG 2021
S. Yildirim Yayilgan et al. (Eds.): INTAP 2020, CCIS 1382, pp. 17–26, 2021.
https://doi.org/10.1007/978-3-030-71711-7_2

length ratio between the index finger and the ring finger of a person as this is an estimate of exposure to certain hormones early in life. To measure finger lengths, it is necessary to identify the feature points of such fingertips and the joining of two fingers.

Applications requiring hand feature points typically attempt to first separate the hand from the background. Several general binarizing techniques have been proposed [15]. However, the problem is challenging, and the problem is often solved for a specific domain. The detection of skin versus non-skin is no exception [16, 17]. A problem with the pixel-based approaches that use the pixel color to classify a pixel as skin or not skin is that they often fail if the background has a similar color as the skin. The proposed method thus does not rely on a binarization step. Instead, the spatial characteristics of features are analyzed. For this purpose, the classic circular Hough transform is employed [18].

2   Related Work

There is a vast body of work on finger tracking, especially in context of gesture-based interaction where the hands are moving. Several studies have used RGB-depth cameras, usually the widely available Kinnect device. Liang, Yuan, and Thalmann [19] used a Kinnect depth camera to track fingers and palms using a Kalman filter and particle filter. Maisto et al. [20] also used a Kinnect depth camera and identified fingertips by extracting the hand contour which were transformed to piecewise linear contours to compute the center of mass. Next, the fingertips were detected using the convex contour. A similar approach using a Kinnect camera and convex hull was reported by Alamsyah and Fanany [21]. Lin et al. [22] used a Kinnect with kernelized correlation filters, principle component analysis and extended inscribed circles to detect the fingertip locations. Other fingertip tracking approaches utilizing Kinnect include Silanon and Suvonvorn [23].

Wu and Kang [24] extracted fingertip locations based on the curve of the hand silhouette by using a combination of temporal and spatial features, using optical flows to combine tracking and detection. Higuchi and Komuro [25] detected the location and orientation of a single finger with complex backgrounds. Li et al. [26, 27] proposed a two-stage tracking process using discriminative correlation filters that first tracked at a course grained level followed by tracking at a fine-grained level. A discriminative correlation filter was also applied by Liu, Li, and Tang [28]. Grzejszczak, Molle, and Roth [29] focused on tracking hidden fingers folded inside the hand by recognizing hand landmarks through distinctive gestures. Wu and Kang [30] detected the hands using optical flow and a skin color model and then detected the fingers based on the resulting region using distances to the centroid. A similar approach was reported in [31]. Bhuyan, Neog, and Kar [32] proposed a hand pose recognition method based on a probabilistic model of the geometric features of the hand.

Several approaches have also applied circular Hough transform for fingertip tracking. Do, Asfour and Dillmann [33] used a Hough transform to extract fingertip locations for moving hands. The movements were tracked using a particle-based filter. Hasan and Mishra [34] employed circle templates. Although similar to circular Hough transforms, circular templates are not strictly speaking a circular Hough transform per se. The circular templates are fitted within the area of the and their positions were used to detect fingertip positions. Alam and Chowdhury [35] used a circular Hough transform to detect potential fingertip locations and then selected the most probable candidates using color features. Boswas [36] used a combination of the line Hough transform and the circle Hough transform to find fingertip locations. The circular Hough transform indicated the fingertip contenders while the Hough lines were used to select the most probable alternatives.

3 Method

3.1 Assumptions

A manual inspection of numerous images confirms that the silhouette of hands has rounded features. The roundedness is caused by the equal forces that act on all areas of the human skin filled with soft tissue. Both fingertips and finger-hand joints occur as arcs (see Fig. 1). Given a method for detecting circles, such as the one offered by the circular Hough transform, it should be possible to detect such features. In reality, the circular shapes are inexact, aliased and fuzzy, and one is likely to observe additional ghost circles, that is, smaller circles inside the larger circles (see Fig. 2). Moreover, one is likely to see ghost circles between fingers, across fingers and across hands when enough pixels across the silhouette points appear in circular shapes. The method explored herein is thus based on exploiting not only the main circles, but also the patterns of the ghost circles. R_{max} denotes the maximum radius of the Hough transform circles. As shown by Figs. 1 and 2 it is important to select the radius R_{max} such that it is sufficiently large to capture fingertips, yet sufficiently small not to trigger ghost circles across fingers assuming that the widths of the fingers are wider than the gap between the crevice fingers.

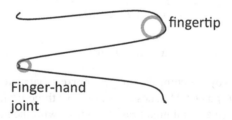

Fig. 1. Optimal situation with one circle per fingertip and finger-hand joint

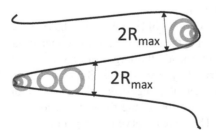

Fig. 2. Realistic situation with ghost circles.

3.2 Preprocessing

Hand images captured by flatbed scanners are input to the system. Current image capturing hardware usually have a high resolution. It is assumed that the hand is occupying
most of the image view. Next, the images are down-sampled such that the new width
is 100 pixels. The down-sampling is effectively a low-pass filter that removes irrelevant high-frequency image noise while maintaining the low-frequency hand features.
Moreover, the smaller down-sampled images are faster to process in subsequent steps.
The system then applies edge detection to the resulting images. In this study, a simple
convolutional edge detector was used with a 5×5 Laplacian kernel given by:

$$
\begin{bmatrix}
-4 & -1 & 0 & -1 & -4 \\
-1 & 2 & 3 & 2 & -1 \\
0 & 3 & 4 & 3 & 0 \\
-1 & 2 & 3 & 2 & -1 \\
-4 & -1 & 0 & -1 & -4
\end{bmatrix}
\tag{1}
$$

3.3 Circle Detection

The fingertips and finger-hand joints have the visual appearance of half circles. The
idea is therefore to detect areas of interest using a Hough transform [18]. The Hough
transform is a general method that has been used for identifying basic geometric shapes
such as lines, circles, and ellipses. The Hough transform represent circles using three
parameters the coordinate (p, q) of the circle center and the circle radius r, namely

$$
x = p + r\cos(\theta)
\tag{2}
$$

$$
x = q + r\sin(\theta)
\tag{3}
$$

The transform works by searching the image for pixels that matches the two equations
for different values of p, q and r. Matches are stored in a three-dimensional accumulator
array. Circles are detected as accumulator array entries with the most hits. The circular
Hough transform is applied to the edge-detected image and the result is a list of circle
candidates. The Hough transform is limited to circles with maximum radii related to the
maximum expected finger width.

Figures 3 and 4 show examples of Hough circles based on a very basic hand contour.
As can be seen circles occur at the fingertips. Some fingertips also have multiple circles,
where smaller circles occur inside the larger circles. Similarly, the finger-hand joints
are also clearly characterized by circles. Figs. 3 and 4 show that these fall into one of
two categories, the ones where the fingers are close and the ones where the fingers are
more spread. If the fingers are spread the finger-hand joint appears as a clear circular
shape with larger radius. These are observed as larger circles with smaller circles inside.
The cases where the fingers are closer together are characterized by circles with smaller
radii.

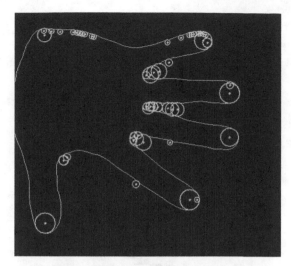

Fig. 3. Example Hough circles for the left hand.

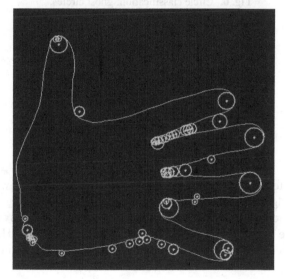

Fig. 4. Example Hough circles for the right hand.

There are circles also circles extending out along the gap between the fingers. These circles to not actually touch the finger-hand joint. However, the radii increase with the distance to the finger-hand joint.

Note that the contours in Figs. 3 and 4 are the result of hand binarization and tracing the edge of the hand. Next, color fill was used to separate the two hands, that is, a filling algorithm was used till in the areas of the two hands with green and blue to separate the two hands. The resulting edges are thus free from noise such as scanning artefacts and uneven backgrounds.

Fig. 5. Circle classification: arc circle.

Fig. 6. Circle classification: ghost circles.

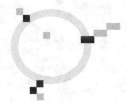

Fig. 7. Circle classification: noise.

An edge detected image based on a convolutional edge detector will thus contain many additional edges and the hands will not be separated. The Hough transform will thus report many more circles not related to the hand outline, as well as circles occurring across hands if the hands are separated by a distance related to the Hough transform radius range. This example was generated with the author's own java image processing library.

3.4 Overlapping Circle Detection

To detect fingertips and finger-hand joint contenders, sets of overlapping circles need to be detected. Two circles a and b are overlapping if

$$(p_a - p_b)^2 + (q_a - q_b)^2 < (r_a + r_b)^2 \tag{4}$$

That is, the circles are overlapping if the distance between the two circle centers are smaller than the sum of the two radii. If the circles are overlapping, the smallest circle is kept and the largest is discarded.

3.5 Circle Classification

To make an overall decision of whether it is a fingertip or finger-hand joint the proposed method depends on defining the image as a half arc (see Fig. 5), a ghost circle occurring between two fingers (see Fig. 6) or simply noise to be discarded (see Fig. 7). The classification is simply performed by exploring the pixels lying along the lines of the circle in the edge detected image. To detect whether a pixel x, y is on the circle given by center p, q with radius r, the distance d between x, y and p, q must satisfy $r - \delta r \le d \le r + \delta r$. That is, instead of considering the exact circle, a flat donut shape with width $2\delta r$ is used.

Once the pixels on the circle are detected, the angular distribution is used for classification. That is, if most of the pixels are grouped in one area the circle is classified as an arc, if the majority of pixels are located in two groups it is classified as a ghost circle, otherwise the circle is classified as noise.

4 Results and Discussions

The proposed approach was implemented in Java and tested on a selection of hand scans and the results were visually inspected. A visual inspection approach was chosen due to a lack of a reference dataset with ground truths. Moreover, the manual visual inspection method was practical, quick, and informative. Clearly, the quality of the results varied with the quality of the images analyzed. For some images, a clear set of hand feature points could be detected, while with other images many ghost circles remained leading to ambiguity in what constitutes the actual hand feature points (see for instance Figs. 3 and 4). It was easy to decipher this through the manual inspections, but quite hard to do automatically by machine. On a few occasions the approach detected too few feature points, while in most other situations too many feature points were detected. Therefore, it seems unrealistic to end up with exactly 9 feature points for each hand (5 fingertips and 4 finger cervices). Moreover, the approach does not determine the mapping from a specific Hough circle to a specific finger feature. Therefore, a second step is needed to perform such mappings and filter the remaining ghost circles. Obviously, Hough circle post-processing cannot compensate for missing circles.

One weakness of the Hough circle approach is that features are extracted at micro level, that is, all identified circles trigger a potential feature point. This approach thus introduces the second challenge of assessing the relevance of the contenders. It is possible that a global approach may be a more fruitful direction, such as the methods based on hand silhouettes. Instead of using all detected circles as feature point contenders, the contour of the hands can be traced, and its overall features used to detect the finger points. Although this approach may seem straightforward, there are challenges with identifying the actual tip of the fingers and the crevices as detecting a point slightly offset to the middle of the finger will render inaccurate measurements. Moreover, with high resolution images it is necessary to focus on the global turns and ignore the small but frequent perturbations on the finger contours. However, a global contour-based approach relies on successfully binarized images. On the other hand, the Hough transform does not require the input image to be perfectly binarized. Note that the test performed herein where all using binarized images. It would have been relevant to also have tested the approach by bypassing the binarization step. One would expect that noisy backgrounds also would yield many additional ghost circles that could be challenging to separate from the actual hand feature points.

The hand feature detection approach described herein is quite different to most of the approaches to finger tracking described in the literature. First, most of the finger detection approaches described in the literature were intended for tracking moving hands, for instance for the purpose of gesture detection. However, the approach described herein was intended for still images (hand scans). Second, the approaches in the literature were mostly intended for detecting the approximate locations of the fingers and hands such that the overall hand shape or gestures could be detected. The goal of the problem domain explored herein was to obtain an accurate measurement of the hand features. Hence, the literature focused on the overall hand shape classification and location, while the presented approach focused on the accurate measurements of hand dimensions. Third, general three-dimensional hand tracking involves also tracking obstructed fingers and fingers inside grasped hands. However, for the hand feature point measurements one can assume that all the fingers are visible, flat and spread out.

5   Conclusions

A spatial method for detecting hand finger points of interest was proposed based on circular Hough transform. The Hough transform over-detect circles in the image and the characteristics of the circles are used to classify a region as simply noise, a fingertip, or finger-hand joints. The method is promising in terms of being robust to background and image noise such as scanning artefacts, lighting interference, etc. However, the method reports both false negatives and false positives. Future work will focus on improving the algorithm further and systematically record its performance of the algorithm.

References

1. Fukumoto, M., Suenaga, Y., Mase, K.: Finger-Pointer: pointing interface by image processing. Comput. Graph. **18**, 633–642 (1994)
2. Coetzee, L., Botha, E.C.: Fingerprint recognition in low quality images. Pattern Recogn. **26**, 1441–1460 (1993)
3. Sandnes, F.E.: Measuring 2D: 4D finger length ratios with Smartphone Cameras. In: Proceedings of IEEE SMC 2014, pp. 1712–1716. IEEE Computer Society Press (2014)
4. Freeman, W.T., Roth, M.: Orientation Histograms for Hand Gesture Recognition. Technical report, Mitsubishi Electric Research Laboratories, Cambridge Research Center, TR-94–03a (1994)
5. Pavlovic, V.I., Sharma, R., Huang, T.S.: Visual interpretation of hand gestures for human-computer interaction: a review. IEEE Trans. Pattern Anal. Mach. Intell. **19**(7), 677–695 (1997)
6. Hou, G., Cui, R., Zhang, C.: A real-time hand pose estimation system with retrieval. In: Proceedings of IEEE SMC 2015, pp. 1738–1744. IEEE Computer Society Press (2015)
7. Ratha, N.K., Chen, S., Jain, A.K.: Adaptive flow orientation-based feature extraction in fingerprint images. Pattern Recogn. **28**, 1657–1672 (1995)
8. Kumar, A., Zhang, D.: Personal recognition using hand shape and texture. IEEE Trans. Image Process. **15**, 2454–2461 (2006)

9. Kong, A., Zhang, D., Kamel, M.: A survey of palmprint recognition. Pattern Recogn. **42**, 1408–1418 (2009)
10. Cappelli, R., Ferrara, M., Maio, D.: A fast and accurate palmprint recognition system based on minutiae. IEEE Trans. Syst. Man Cybern. Part B **42**, 956–962 (2012)
11. Wang, X., Lei, L., Wang, M.: Palmprint verification based on 2D–Gabor wavelet and pulse-coupled neural network. Knowl. Based Syst. **27**, 451–455 (2012)
12. Sandnes, F.E.: An automatic two-hand 2D: 4D finger-ratio measurement algorithm for flatbed scanned images. In: Proceedings of IEEE SMC 2015, pp. 1203–1208. IEEE Computer Society Press (2015)
13. Sandnes, F.E.: A two-stage binarizing algorithm for automatic 2D: 4D finger ratio measurement of hands with non-separated fingers. In: proceedings of 11th International Conference on Innovations in Information Technology (IIT 2015), pp. 178–183. IEEE Computer Society Press (2015)
14. Koch, R., Haßlmeyer, E., Tantinger, D., Rulsch, M., Weigand, C., Struck, M.: Development and implementation of algorithms for automatic and robust measurement of the 2D: 4D digit ratio using image data. Curr. Dir. Biomed. Eng. **1**, 220–223 (2015)
15. Sauvola, J., Pietikäinen, M.: Adaptive document image binarization. Pattern Recogn. **33**, 225–236 (2000)
16. Kakumanu, P., Makrogiannis, S., Bourbakis, N.: A survey of skin-color modeling and detection methods. Pattern Recogn. **40**, 1106–1122 (2007)
17. Sandnes, F.E., Neyse, L., Huang, Y.-P.: Simple and practical skin detection with static RGB-color lookup tables: a visualization-based study. In: Proceedings of IEEE SMC 2016, IEEE Computer Society Press (2016)
18. Davies, E.R.: A modified Hough scheme for general circle location. Pattern Recogn. Lett. **7**, 37–43 (1988)
19. Liang, H., Yuan, J., Thalmann, D.: 3D fingertip and palm tracking in depth image sequences. In: Proceedings of the 20th ACM international conference on Multimedia, pp. 785–788. ACM (2012)
20. Maisto, M., Panella, M., Liparulo, L., Proietti, A.: . IEEE J. Emerg. Sel. Topics Circ. Syst. **3**(2), 272–283 (2013)
21. Alamsyah, D., Fanany, M.I.: Particle filter for 3D fingertips tracking from color and depth images with occlusion handling. In: 2013 International Conference on Advanced Computer Science and Information Systems (ICACSIS), pp. 445–449. IEEE (2013)
22. Lin, Q., Chen, J., Zhang, J., Yao, L.: A reliable hand tracking method using kinect. In: 2019 IEEE 4th International Conference on Image, Vision and Computing (ICIVC), pp. 706–710. IEEE (2019)
23. Silanon, K., Suvonvorn, N.: Fingertips tracking based active contour for general HCI application. In: Herawan, T., Deris, M.M., Abawajy, J. (eds.) Proceedings of the First International Conference on Advanced Data and Information Engineering (DaEng-2013). LNEE, vol. 285, pp. 309–316. Springer, Singapore (2014). https://doi.org/10.1007/978-981-4585-18-7_35
24. Wu, G., Kang, W.: Vision-based fingertip tracking utilizing curvature points clustering and hash model representation. IEEE Trans. Multimedia **19**(8), 1730–1741 (2017)
25. Higuchi, M., Komuro, T.: Robust finger tracking for gesture control of mobile devices using contour and interior information of a finger. ITE Trans. Media Technol. Appl. **1**(3), 226–236 (2013)
26. Li, D., Wen, G., Kuai, Y.: Collaborative convolution operators for real-time coarse-to-fine tracking. IEEE Access **6**, 14357–14366 (2018)
27. Li, D., Wen, G., Kuai, Y., Xiao, J., Porikli, F.: Learning target-aware correlation filters for visual tracking. J. Vis. Commun. Image Represent. **58**, 149–159 (2019)
28. Liu, W., Li, D., Tang, X.: Autocorrelated correlation filter for visual tracking. J. Electron. Imaging **28**(3), 033038 (2019)

29. Grzejszczak, T., Molle, R., Roth, R.: Tracking of dynamic gesture fingertips position in video sequence. Arch. Control Sci. **30** (2020)
30. Wu, G., Kang, W.: Robust fingertip detection in a complex environment. IEEE Trans. Multimedia **18**(6), 978–987 (2016)
31. Baldauf, M., Zambanini, S., Fröhlich, P., Reichl, P.: Markerless visual fingertip detection for natural mobile device interaction. In: Proceedings of the 13th International Conference on Human Computer Interaction with Mobile Devices and Services, pp. 539–544 (2011)
32. Bhuyan, M.K., Neog, D.R., Kar, M.K.: Fingertip detection for hand pose recognition. Int. J. Comput. Sci. Eng. **4**(3), 501 (2012)
33. Do, M., Asfour, T., Dillmann, R.: Particle filter-based fingertip tracking with circular hough transform features. In: Proceedings of International Conference on Machine Vision Applications, Japan (2011)
34. Hasan, M.M., Mishra, P.K.: Real time fingers and palm locating using dynamic circle templates. Int. J. Comput. Appl. **41**(6) (2012)
35. Alam, M.J., Chowdhury, M.: Detection of fingertips based on the combination of color information and circle detection. In: 2013 IEEE 8th International Conference on Industrial and Information Systems, pp. 572–576. IEEE (2013)
36. Biswas, A.: Finger detection for hand gesture recognition using circular hough transform. In: Bera, R., Sarkar, S.K., Chakraborty, S. (eds.) Advances in Communication, Devices and Networking. LNEE, vol. 462, pp. 651–660. Springer, Singapore (2018). https://doi.org/10.1007/978-981-10-7901-6_71

Occupancy Flow Control - Case Study: Elevator Cabin

Dimitra Triantafyllou[1]([✉]), Alexandros Kanlis[1], Stelios Krinidis[1], Georgios Stavropoulos[1], Dimosthenis Ioannidis[1], Iraklis Chatziparasidis[2], and Dimitrios Tzovaras[1]

[1] Information Technologies Institute, Center for Research and Technology - Hellas, Thessaloniki, Greece
{dtriant,alexkanlis,krinidis,stavrop,djoannid,Dimitrios.Tzovaras}@iti.gr
[2] Engineering Research Department, KLEEMANN Lifts, Kilkis, Greece
i.chatziparasidis@kleemannlifts.com

Abstract. In this paper, a method for occupancy analysis for flow control through an automated door is presented. In particular, the use case of an elevator is analysed. The occupancy inside the elevator cabin is detected while information on the number of users expecting to enter the elevator is also extracted. To achieve this, two privacy preserving cameras, i.e. a depth sensor and a thermal camera, are installed inside and outside the elevator, respectively. Moreover, information from the elevator's controller, such as the state of the door (closed/open) and the floor number where the elevator cabin has stopped, is acquired. The results from both cameras and the elevator controller are sent and fused in real time in a web socket server installed in a microcomputer. Experimental results prove that the data fusion provides a leverage to the system leading to robust occupancy analysis. Moreover, the paper discusses the extraction of human features, such as height, weight and top view area, through a presented calibration procedure, highlighting in this way the potential of the proposed system to extract further information that will add extra value to the decision control system.

Keywords: Flow control · Elevator · Sensor fusion

1 Introduction

Nowadays, there is a tendency for "smart", automated buildings and infrastructures for environmental, economic, safety and efficiency reasons. The occupancy of the buildings is one of the main factors determining the decision making in such systems while cameras are widely used in order to detect and analyze it. Special attention is paid on the entrances of the areas of interest so that any transitions are promptly detected.

This work is partially supported by the EU funded SMILE project (H2020-740931).

S. Yildirim Yayilgan et al. (Eds.): INTAP 2020, CCIS 1382, pp. 27–38, 2021.
https://doi.org/10.1007/978-3-030-71711-7_3

Millions of people use elevators in their everyday life. Experience shows that there is plenty of room to ameliorate its function and avoid unnecessary movements or stops if the number of occupants and the persons waiting at different floors to use it are taken into account. The reduction of elevator movements can result in decrease of power consumption producing a meaningful and friendly impact on the environment. Furthermore, taking into account the capacity of the elevator cabin can lead to a more secure and pleasant ride avoiding overcrowding.

In this paper, a system for occupancy detection in elevator cabins is presented. Thermal and depth sensors are installed both inside the elevator cabin and outside it in each floor. In this way, information on the number of the cabin occupants and the people waiting on each floor is acquired. Moreover, data from the elevator controller indicating the floor where the cabin has stopped and the state of the door (i.e. closed or open) is obtained and combined with information from the cameras. The fused result is used to provide leverage to the occupancy detection in the elevator cabin and increase the system's accuracy and robustness.

Despite the fact that the focus of this paper is on the occupancy detection, other useful aspects of the system that show its potential are highlighted as well. Due to the calibration of the depth camera, the extraction of soft biometrics of the occupants such as their height, their top view area or their weight, is considered a straightforward procedure. Such features, that provide the area coverage and the total weight of the elevator users, can further increase the system's efficiency.

The main contribution of the paper is the fusion of the information from the cameras inside and outside the elevator cabin to extract its occupancy and especially the use of data from the elevator controller. In addition, depth and thermal cameras are utilized to explore their capabilities and to ensure privacy rights, nonetheless, useful human traits, that relate to the efficient and secure elevator control, are extracted due to the depth camera calibration.

The remainder of the paper is organized as follows: Sect. 2 comprises related work, Sect. 3 describes the presented methodology while Sect. 4 analyzes the experimental results. Finally, the paper concludes in Sect. 5 with discussion on the proposed approach.

2   Related Work

Nowadays, cameras are used in various applications regarding human detection and tracking, people counting etc. Most of these applications refer to color cameras [1,2] whereas there are cases where privacy preserving sensors such as thermal [3–5] and depth cameras [6–9] are utilized.

To our knowledge, existing work on occupancy detection and flow control applications in confined environments such as an elevator cabin, utilizes color cameras. In [10], a method based on edge detection and calculation of the area defined by the edges provides an approximation of the elevator users. In [11],

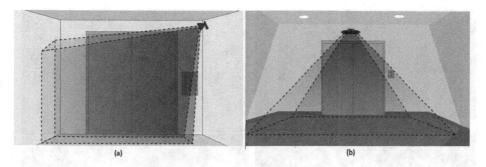

Fig. 1. Installation of cameras inside and outside the elevator car: a) the depth camera is installed at a corner near the door inside the elevator cabin in order to capture the whole cabin floor and all people entering or exiting through the door, b) the thermal sensor is located outside the elevator door monitoring anyone transitioning the door or waiting outside the elevator.

a multiscale approach based on SVM is used for occupancy detection in an elevator cabin. Furthermore, the free space in an elevator is estimated in [12] by combining the use of Horn-Schunck optical flow, that analyzes the state of the door, with a floor segmentation algorithm that extracts the free space in the cabin. Likewise, in [13], one camera is installed outside the elevator to estimate the time the door is fully opened while another camera is located inside the cabin to calculate occupancy from the foreground change.

The last two aforementioned methods [12,13], can be considered the most relevant to the methodology presented in this paper in the sense that they incorporate to their decision system information regarding the state of the door. Nevertheless, in the presented paper this information refers to data acquired from the door's controller, hence it is free from errors that might occur from image processing. Moreover, in this paper, only privacy preserving sensors are utilized in contrast to these methods.

3 Proposed Methodology

In this paper, two privacy preserving cameras, a depth sensor and a thermal camera, are utilized. The depth sensor is installed inside the elevator cabin while the thermal camera is located outside the cabin and above the elevator door (Fig. 1). The input of each sensor is processed independently and their outcomes are fed to a microcomputer that fuses the provided information so as to extract safer and more accurate results. Furthermore, data from the elevator controller is acquired and used during fusion. In particular, the state of the elevator door (closed/opened) and the floor number where the elevator has stopped can be determining for the fusion decision making, as it will be described in the following sections.

Fig. 2. Input from the depth camera installed inside the elevator cabin. The whole elevator floor is visible while a human is standing in different places inside the cabin.

3.1 Occupancy Analysis Inside the Elevator Cabin

In this section, the occupancy analysis inside the elevator cabin is described. In particular, the input from a depth camera (actually, an Asus Xtion was used) installed in the elevator cabin is processed and analyzed (Fig. 2). In order to obtain the desired occupancy information, the applied methodology comprises three steps: 1) camera calibration, 2) human detection and tracking and, 3) extracting occupancy information.

Camera Calibration. For the calibration task, the simple layout but also the limited space of an elevator are taken into account. To avoid the use of calibration tables and to permit camera calibration from distance, an algorithm that takes advantage of the cabin's flat surfaces is developed. Therefore, the flat floor area is detected by applying Ransac algorithm [14]. Since the dimensions of the elevator floor and the location of the camera regarding the elevator door are known, the camera's view can be easily transformed to top view and to be matched to the architectural map of the elevator.

Detection and Tracking. Based on this top view approach, the detection and tracking of humans inside the elevator cabin is implemented as it is described in [7,9]. The detected blobs are transformed through calibration matrices and are monitored from top view (Fig. 3). In this way, the avoidance of false positives, that may occur from reflections in the elevator mirror or the vertical surfaces, is facilitated since they will be located outside the elevator's floor area.

Moreover, due to calibration, information on the detected humans' physical traits can be extracted. In particular, the height, width and top view area of a person are calculated from the corresponding mean values of the detected blob's dimensions as they occur from the top view transformations during the first N frames the tracked blob is entering the elevator. This N-frame window is needed to eliminate big deviations from the real values due to noise from the depth

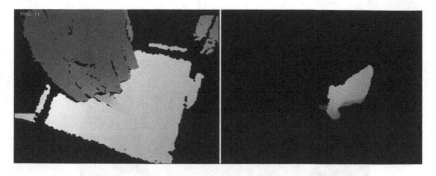

Fig. 3. Example of depth input from the camera inside the elevator cabin and its transition to top view.

sensors. Moreover, utilizing the calculated height, a weight estimation of the detected person's weight can be performed based on [15]. Such biometrics can be utilized for estimating the percentage of the floor area that is covered inside the cabin, an approximation of the total weight of the occupants, the comfort of its users and whether there is available room for extra persons. Despite the fact that these modalities are not further analyzed in this paper, it was considered useful to be mentioned in order to highlight the additional aspects and possibilities that this methodology can offer.

Extraction of Occupancy Information. The occupancy analysis inside the elevator is twofold. In particular, the existence or absence of occupants is investigated while the transitions, i.e. entries or exits, are also calculated. The occupancy detection methodology is straightforward since it is based on the existence of blobs inside the elevator area for more than a predefined amount of time. The time parameter is used to avoid false alarms caused by noise due to reflections that usually have small duration. Furthermore, the transitions detection takes into account the route of the detected and tracked blobs in reference to the door. In particular, the space inside the elevator is separated in three areas: two narrow areas next to the door and a bigger area corresponding to the rest of the cabin (Fig. 4). An occupant has to be detected successively at least to the first and the last of them in order to define an entry or an exit, depending on the route's direction of movement. The middle area is used as a "gray" area to avoid false multiple transitions from people standing at the border of entry and exit area. The first two areas are decided to be narrow since a user that is located in them is not consider to be inside the elevator. Nevertheless, since they are very close to the elevator door, which is an area that people avoid to stand, the case of missing an entrance due to this assumption is minimum. From the difference DT_{depth} between the entries and the exits the total number of persons in the elevator can be extracted.

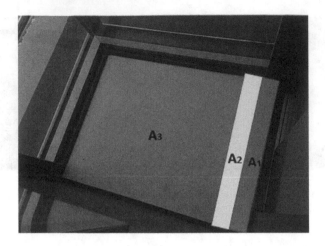

Fig. 4. Top view color image from the depth camera installed inside the elevator depicting the three areas utilized for transitions calculation. Area A_1 is located in front of the elevator door, A_2 is considered "gray" area while A_3 is the area where the elevator's users stand.

Although the calculation of both occupancy existence and transitions detection may seem redundant, it actually provides a leverage to the system. The transitions calculation provide a more accurate number of persons in the elevator, since in occupancy detection there may be occlusions. Furthermore, missed transitions can result to accumulated errors that can be corrected from occupancy detection (e.g. when zero occupants are detected even if the difference between entries and exits is higher it can be reconsidered and corrected to be zero).

In this scope, occupancy detection provides an answer if the elevator cabin is empty or occupied hence it is defined as:

$$Oc_{Depth} = \begin{cases} 0, & \text{if no human is detected} \\ 1, & \text{otherwise.} \end{cases} \tag{1}$$

Moreover, this information is combined with the detected transitions in order to conclude to a final number $N_{insideD}$ of occupants in the elevator. The logic behind the fusion of the modalities is that the occupancy detection provides more accurate information on the occupancy existence/absence while the transitions perform better regarding the number of occupants. Therefore, the final decision on the occupancy is expressed by the following equation:

$$N_{insideD} = max\{1, N_{insideD,prev} + DT_{Depth}\} \cdot Oc_{Depth} \tag{2}$$

where Oc_{Depth} is defined in Eq. (1) and DT_{depth} is the difference between the entries and exits through the door. $N_{insideD}$ is the current elevator occupancy and $N_{insideD,prev}$ is its previous value before the last opening of the elevator door.

Fig. 5. Examples of thermal sensor devices used outside the elevator door. The box made to accommodate them is also displayed.

3.2   Occupancy Analysis Outside the Elevator Door

For the occupancy analysis regarding the area outside the elevator door a thermal sensor (Fig. 5) is installed above the door, as it is displayed in Fig. 1(b). The aim of the camera comprises the extraction of the number of users waiting outside the elevator as well as the transitions from people entering and exiting the elevator at the floor under monitoring.

The first step to achieve the aforementioned goals is the detection and tracking of the monitored people. In this scope, as a preprocessing step, a low pass filter is applied on the thermal sensor input in order to remove any quick transitions of the pixel values since the IR camera sensor produces some noise spikes. Given the very low resolution of the thermal camera, all frames are then upscaled to a 32×32 matrix using linear interpolation. Moreover, once the device is powered, a background frame is captured and is constantly updated as long as there are no intense thermal blobs captured. When intense thermal blobs appear, implying people standing in front of the door, background update is slowed down in order not to introduce these thermal blobs in the background. This background frame plus a constant value is then deducted from each of the captured frames and any negative values are zeroed. In this way, thermal blobs introduced from people appear in the frame as positive non zero values. Another adjustable filter then decides if a blob is intense enough to be considered a person.

For the people counting algorithm, entry, "gray" and exit areas are introduced at the monitoring area (Fig. 6). The entry area is considered to be closest to the elevator door (represented by A_5 in Fig. 6), in particular it covers a part of the elevator floor when the door opens. Blobs appearing in the entry or exit areas are introduced as new people, their position in the 32×32 matrix is saved and their new position is updated in each iteration by matching each new blob to the closest one from the last iteration. From this information the occupancy outside

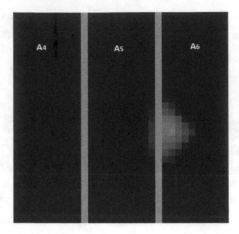

Fig. 6. Top view image from the thermal camera installed outside the elevator depicting the three areas utilized for transitions calculation. Area A_4 is located in front of the elevator door, A_5 is considered "gray" area while A_6 is the area representing people walking away from the elevator area. In the particular shot a person's blob is between A5 and A6 area

the elevator door is straightforward. Furthermore, blobs that appear on the entry area and disappear on the exit area are considered exits from the elevator while blobs that appear on the exit area and disappear on the entry area are considered entries. Since the entries and exits counting algorithm monitors each person individually, their difference $DT_{Thermal}$ equals the total change of the number of occupants inside the elevator. Entry and exit events and the number of people monitored are sent to the decision making server via web sockets.

Thermal sensors located to all floors can be utilized to calculate $N_{insideT}$, i.e. the number of persons inside the elevator cabin. Starting from an initial situation where no one is inside the elevator, then the number of occupants estimated by the thermal sensors is defined as:

$$N_{insideT} = max\{1, N_{insideT,prev} + DT_{Thermal}\} \tag{3}$$

where $N_{insideT,prev}$ is the number of persons inside the elevator calculated before the last opening of the elevator door.

3.3 Data Acquisition from the Elevator Controller

Elevators usually introduce their state by using digital output lines and receiving commands via digital input lines. The current elevator cabin level position, the state of the door and the state of the IR beam sensor that detects activity near the door can be available outputs. Using the inputs, multiple actions can be achieved, such as car calls (calls from withing the elevator), landing calls (calls from the floors) or even keeping the doors open.

Fig. 7. The elevator controller embedded device, its inputs and outputs. The controller can translate the elevator electrical signals into information transmitted via wifi connection while it can receive commands and adjust the elevator status.

In this paper, in order to turn a common elevator into a smart one, an embedded device with integrated wifi connection is introduced. The device (Fig. 7) captures the outputs from the elevator and translates them into states that are transmitted via web sockets to the decision making server. It also listens for calls via a REST capable web interface which then introduces to the elevator as commands. This way the elevator cabin position and the door state is always known by the decision making server which can also send commands to the REST interface in order to control the elevator.

3.4   Data Fusion for Occupancy Analysis Inside the Elevator Cabin

In the previous subsections, each component of the proposed system is described independently and produces each own results. In this section, all the information from these components is combined in order to achieve safer conclusions and obtain better results.

In this scope, a web socket server is installed in a microcomputer. Each component sends data in real time to the server every time the state of the features under monitoring is changed. This time, the information on the elevator door state is provided determining the validity of the cameras' data and the time of the decision making. In addition, the floor where the elevator cabin has stopped is sent as well from the elevator's controller so that the data from the thermal sensors located outside the elevator can be combined with the data from the depth camera inside it. Specifically, transitions are taken into account only when the door is open while the final occupancy of the cabin is determined once the door closes. For the transitions occurring while the door is open the average of the transition differences as they are monitored from inside (depth camera) and outside (thermal camera) the elevator is calculated. In particular, the fused transitions are calculated by the following equation:

$$DT_{fused} = \left\lceil \frac{DT_{Depth} + DT_{Thermal}}{2} \right\rceil \qquad (4)$$

where DT_{depth} and $DT_{Thermal}$ are defined in Subsects. 3.1 and 3.2 respectively.

In the same spirit as in Subsect. 3.1 and by replacing the transitions from the interior of the elevator with the fused transitions as they are defined in Eq. (4), the fused elevator occupancy number is described by the following equation:

$$N_{fused} = max\{1, N_{fused,prev} + DT_{fused}\} \cdot Oc_{Depth} \qquad (5)$$

where N_{fused} is the current fused elevator occupancy and $N_{fused,prev}$ is its previous value before the last opening of the elevator door.

4   Experimental Results

The performance of the proposed system was tested with an elevator located in the CERTH/ITI smarthome [16]. For the needs of the experiments, two thermal cameras were installed at two different floors outside the elevator and about 50 cm higher from the door while a depth camera was installed inside the cabin at the left corner above the door.

For the evaluation of the proposed system 200 decision cases were investigated, i.e. the elevator door opened and closed 200 times during which occupancy changes occurred. One or multiple exits or entries occurred each time the door opened while persons with different heights and weights participated to the experiments.

The results from these experiments are shown at Table 1. It is obvious that the system is very reliable regarding the existence or absence of occupancy since for this case the accuracy and F1-score reach the value of 1. In the case where the occupants' number inside the elevator is calculated from the depth camera, the accuracy is 0.79 and the F1-score 0.88 while for the thermal sensors, they are 0.88 and 0.93 respectively. These numbers prove that the thermal sensor performs better, which is expected, since the monitoring area is more equally separated in entry and exit areas whereas inside the elevator the entry area had to be narrow leading to missed transitions. Furthermore, the accuracy and F1-score of the fused result of the occupancy number are 0.92 and 0.96 respectively proving the leverage provided to the system due to fusion. For the particular experiments both sensors had the same importance for the calculation of the fused results. Nevertheless, as future work the reported weaknesses and advantages of each sensor will be taken into account through machine learning techniques to achieve even better results. Finally, it has to be mentioned that there were no errors regarding the elevator's door state or floor number during the experiments.

Table 1. Occupancy results of the components and fused

	Oc_{Depth}	$N_{insideD}$	$N_{insideT}$	N_{Fused}
Accuracy	1.0	0.79	0.88	0.92
F1-score	1.0	0.88	0.93	0.96

5   Conclusion

In this paper, an occupancy detection system for flow control through an automated door is proposed. In particular, the challenging scenario of an elevator is explored. The extra difficulties in this case is the fact that the area under control is really confined, resulting in small areas in transitions detection from the camera inside the elevator, and movable, therefore extra information on the floor number has to be taken into account. Nevertheless, the proposed system can be applied in other scenarios as well, such as flow control for borders and restricted areas to increase security measures.

To enhance occupancy detection in comparison with a single camera approach, fused information from cameras inside and outside the elevator cabin is proposed. Moreover, the state of the elevator door and the floor where the cabin has stopped is known at real time providing valuable information that facilitates fusion. The leverage of the fused system in comparison to a single camera approach is proved through experiments. Furthermore, experiments showed that the proposed system reaches the value of 1 regarding the precision and F1-score of the occupancy absence/presence detection.

This paper's aim is the description of the fused occupancy detection system. Nevertheless, this is only a part of a "smart" elevator control system and one of the factors planned to affect the elevator's decision making system. The integration of users' physical traits, such as their weight or coverage area, is planned as future work. Moreover, information on the number of persons waiting to use the elevator on each floor will be incorporated to a new decision system. The final goal is to make a smarter and more efficient elevator controller that will handle the elevator calls and stops according to the cabin and the floor occupancy and data relating to the floor area coverage and weight affordance of the cabin.

References

1. Gaon, C., Li, P., Zhang, Y., Liu, J., Wang, L.: People counting based on head detection combining Adaboost and CNN in crowded surveillance environment. Neurocomputing **208**, 108–116 (2016)
2. Luo, J., Wang, J., Xu, H., Lu, H.: Real-time people counting for indoor scenes. Signal Process. **124**, 27–35 (2016)
3. Liu, Q., Lu, X., He, Z., Zhang, C., Chen, W.: Deep convolutional neural networks for thermal infrared object tracking. Knowl. Based Syst. **134**, 189–198 (2017)
4. Qu, D., Yang, B., Gu, N.: Indoor multiple human targets localization and tracking using thermopile sensor. Infrared Phys. Technol. **97**, 349–359 (2019)

5. Younsia, M., Diafa, M., Siarry, P.: Automatic multiple moving humans detection and tracking in image sequences taken from a stationary thermal infrared camera. Expert Syst. Appl. **146**, 113171 (2020)

6. Del Pizzo, L., Foggia, P., Greco, A., Percannella, G., Vento, M.: Counting people by RGB or depth overhead cameras. Pattern Recogn. Lett. **81**, pp. 41–50 (2016)

7. Krinidis, S., Stavropoulos, G., Ioannidis, D., Tzovaras, D.: A robust and real-time multispace occupancy extraction system exploiting privacy-preserving sensors. In: SCCSP (2014)

8. Stavropoulos, G., Moschonas, P., Moustakas, K., Tzovaras, D., Strintzis, M.G.: 3-D model search and retrieval from range images using salient features. IEEE Trans. Multimedia **12**(7), 692–704 (2010)

9. Triantafyllou, D., Krinidis, S., Ioannidis, D., Tzovaras, D.: A real-time, multi-space incident detection system for indoor environments. Int. J. Saf. Secur. **8**(2), 266–275 (2018)

10. Fan, H., Zhu, H., Yuan, D.: People counting in elevator car based on computer vision. In: IOP Conference Series: Earth and Environment Science (2019)

11. Bin, X., Jing, Y., Feng, X., Mangmang, G.: Study of multiscale detection in near distance image for numbers of people in elevator car. In: International Conference on Manufacturing Science and Engineering, pp. 322–328 (2015)

12. Mohamudally, F., Inn, C.S., Yeong, L.S., Chong, C.W.: Estimating free space in an elevator's confined environment. In: TENCON (2015)

13. Zou, J., Zhao, Q.: Occupancy detection in elevator car by fusing analysis of dual videos. In: IEEE Conference on Automation Science and Engineering, pp. 906–911 (2017)

14. Anagnostopoulos, I., Pătrăucean, V., Brilakis, I., Vela, P.: Detection of walls, floors and ceilings in point cloud data. In: Construction Research Congress, pp. 2302–2311 (2016)

15. Kokong, D.D., Pam, I.C., Zoakah, A.I., Danbauch, S.S., Mador, E.S., Mandong, B.M.: Estimation of weight in adults from height: a novel option for a quick bedside technique. Int. J. Emerg. Med. **11**, 1–9 (2018)

16. https://smarthome.iti.gr

Security and IoT

Protecting IoT Devices with Software-Defined Networks

Filip Holik[✉] [iD]

University of Pardubice, Studentska 95, 532 10 Pardubice, Czech Republic
filip.holik@upce.cz

Abstract. The use of IoT devices is becoming more frequent in modern networks, such as Smart Grids, Smart Cities, and Smart Homes. These deployments are experiencing a massive boom, but they often lack proper security mechanisms. This is caused mostly by limited computing capabilities and simplified operating systems of IoT devices. A viable approach of protection of these devices is a communication network. While traditional networks can be used for protection of IoT devices, they are inflexible, costly, vendor-specific, and hard to manage. This paper describes use of software-defined networking - a modern concept of communication networks - for protecting IoT devices. Typical threats of IoT devices are described in addition to possible protection mechanisms of traditional networks. Consequently, protection techniques based on software-defined networks are proposed for the same threats where applicable. These techniques are based on the IEC's five-step protection methodology. Finally, selected protection techniques are verified on a use case application of a typical network connecting IoT devices.

Keywords: IoT devices · Protection methods · Security · Software-defined networks · Threats

1 Introduction

The concept of the Internet of Things (IoT) is merging physical and digital worlds by inter-communicating devices. The technology is growing steadily and it is becoming one of the main traffic generators on the current Internet. In 2018, it generated 33% of all Internet connection and the prediction is, that this number will reach 50% by 2023 [3]. Additional growth of the IoT is expected with deployments of 5G networks [10]. These networks will provide extremely low latencies, which will make IoT devices applicable in new challenging domains such as Tactile Internet [14]. This technology will make remote applications such as training, robot control, patient diagnosis and surgery possible [8]. On the other hand, these scenarios will require high-availability and will increase security demands even more.

An efficient implementation of modern networks interconnecting IoT devices requires innovative networking approaches such as Software-defined Networking

S. Yildirim Yayilgan et al. (Eds.): INTAP 2020, CCIS 1382, pp. 41–52, 2021.
https://doi.org/10.1007/978-3-030-71711-7_4

(SDN), Network Function Virtualization (NFV), or cloud. Unfortunately, from the security perspective, these approaches are still often not fully verified and proven. As papers [6,13] state, many security areas of SDN still need additional research. This includes security-related issues like availability, performance and QoS [11,12].

The main contribution of this paper is to summarize common vulnerabilities of IoT devices and to propose SDN-based techniques to improve their protection. For this reason, the paper is focused only on the protection of end devices (IoT devices or sensors) and ignores the remaining parts of the IoT architecture as described in [7] (communication channels, infrastructure, backend services and intermediary devices).

2   Attacks on IoT Devices

IoT devices are vulnerable not only to common threats known from the IT world, but also to some specific ones. A survey paper [11] analyzed more than 400 publications and defined 16 threats. For the purpose of this paper, these threats were classified into 6 areas, which the communication network can distinguish. This generalization was performed according to the following scheme:

1. Access attacks - include brute force attacks.
2. Availability attacks - include Denial of Service, broadcast tampering and conflict collision.
3. GNSS spoofing attacks - include GPS spoofing and timing attacks.
4. Man-in-the-middle attacks - include replay attacks and eavesdropping.
5. Masquerade attacks - include sybil attacks.
6. Node attacks - include data alteration and modification, malware and node security; and security attacks on devices with limited computational and storage resources.

2.1   Access Attacks

The purpose of these type of attacks is to gain unauthorized access to the IoT device. The successful attack requires use of correct combination of username and password. The most typical type of these attacks is the *brute force* attack. This type tries login combinations "randomly" by consequently trying all possible character combinations. This method is highly ineffective and to guess a password combined from letters, numbers, and special characters can be infeasible in a reasonably short time-frame (if the password length is sufficient). To guess even the most commonly used insecure passwords (name, surname, or typical words like "admin", "user", "root", etc.) takes a significant number of tries and detection of such an attack is therefore relatively easy, as the attack generates a high amount of data traffic.

Several more advanced techniques exist to make the attack more effective. The most common one is a *dictionary attack*, which uses a database of common words, numbers, and their combinations. The attack then tries these combinations instead of random characters. This attack is very efficient if the login credential uses a combination of common or default phrases.

Protection against access attacks is based on restricting the number of unsuccessful login attempts within a defined time period. When the limit is reached, the application should notify the administrator and block additional login attempts for some time in order to slow down the possible attack. A communication network can offer additional protections with firewalls and Intrusion Prevention Systems (IPS).

2.2 Availability Attacks

Attacks on availability of applications, servers, devices and the communication network are also called Denial of Service attacks (DoS). The goal of a DoS attack is to make a service unavailable for legitimate users. IoT devices are especially vulnerable to this type of attack as they have very limited hardware performance. IoT devices are optimized for low-power consumption and long-life operation. To overload these devices is therefore very easy, even with widely available tools such as *iperf* [4] and built-in utilities such as *ping*. A more advanced *distributed* variant of this attack (DDoS) uses multiple devices to perform the attack. These devices can be legitimate workstations of a company which are misused by the attacker without users' knowledge. They are being called *zombies*.

A variant of this attack is *broadcast tampering*, which misuses broadcast messages to transmit false data. In this form, the attacker does not have to know a target's IP address, as he is attacking a range of devices. This attack generates significant amount of traffic and can cause network unavailability. The attack is typically used in network scanning or distribution of malware.

A specific group of availability attacks targets the physical layer. This attack causes signal jamming and it is the most difficult to prevent. In the case of wireless networks, the attack can be especially easy to perform.

Protection against higher-layers availability attacks are IPS and intelligent firewalls, which can detect the attack and automatically block the traffic. An Access Control List (ACL) can also help in mitigation of these attacks. A network monitoring system can help with detection. Such a system can also detect attacks on the physical layer, but there is no simple protection against these attacks.

2.3 GNSS Spoofing Attacks

IoT devices often use signal from Global Navigation Satellite System (GNSS) to determine precise time or location. This system can utilize any combination of services such as GPS, Galileo, GLONASS and BeiDou [5]. An attacker can try to manipulate this information to present fake time or location information. This might be especially dangerous for IoT devices ensuring physical operations such as vehicles. The repercussions of spoofing location data can result in not only financial losses, property damage, and injury, but also the loss of life. Similarly, spoofing timing information might pose a problem in certain safety critical operations such as smart grid networks. Protection messages in these scenarios often have to react to an event within a few milliseconds. Delay, or inappropriate time setting could result in a large-scale blackout and physical damage to the grid equipment.

Partial protection can be achieved with caching of previously received messages. It can detect impossibly high deviations from these values, but it cannot prevent the attack completely. Implementation of Precision Time Protocol (PTP) can also increase the system's security, as it ensures that the time on all devices is consistent.

2.4   Man-in-the-Middle Attacks

These attacks start with interception of communication between two devices. The next step can read, modify, resend, or do any combination with the intercepted messages. Based on the action, these attacks can be classified into:

1. Eavesdropping attacks - in this type of attacks, the message is only captured and read by the attacker. The main danger of this attack is the fact that it can stay undetected for a long time. If the attacker does not modify the traffic flow, nothing suspicious would be detected on the legitimate devices.
2. Integrity attacks - the captured message is modified by the attacker and resend to the destination device. There, it can cause all forms of damage, from insertion of fake data, to malware injection.

Protection against these attacks is traffic encryption via a strong cryptography. In this case, even if the attacker captures the message, the content stays unreadable. The only visible data are the message headers, including information such as MAC addresses, IP addresses, etc. Typical encryption tools include VPN (Virtual Private Network), implementation of PKI (Public Key Infrastructure) and use of encrypted communication protocols (HTTPS, SSH, etc.).

2.5   Masquerade Attacks

Masquerade attacks have several variants, but in all of them, the attacker pretends to be someone else. He can fake his identity by using forged identification certificates, by using expired certificates, or by using someones else's credentials, which were acquired in advance (for example by theft or phishing).

Protection can be achieved with implementation of PKI with a trusted certificate authority, which will issue certificates only to appropriate devices. Another important measure is a proper revocation mechanism, which will eliminate the risk of using certificates after their validity period.

2.6   Node Attacks

These attacks compromise security of an IoT device in order to gain access, collect data, or perform a malicious action. They can include insertion of a malicious code into the IoT device. Such a code can damage the device, steal information, trigger an availability attack, or allow a backdoor access. Detection of this attack can be difficult as the malicious code can perform actions to avoid unnecessary attention. The malware can also be inactive until a defined action is triggered. This can include activation upon defined time, specific sensor value, or remote activation.

Protection include anti-virus programs, firewalls and updated software - especially operating systems. In the last case, it is necessary to ensure that the updates are downloaded from the trusted web site and that they were not modified. This can be ensured by digital signatures.

An active malware can use the communication network and in that case, it can be detected as a network anomaly by specialized networking devices and tools such as IPS and IDS (Intrusion Detection Systems). A problem with these devices is that they are costly, increase the network's complexity, and can limit the network's performance.

3   Software-Defined Network Based Protection Methods

General protection layers of every application according to the IEC 62351 security standard [9] are:

1. Deterrence and delay - avoid or delay the attack in order to allow a more appropriate counter action.
2. Detection of attacks - recognize the attack, including attempts for an attack.
3. Assessment of attacks - determine the nature and severity of the attack.
4. Communication and notification - give the authorities correct information and an option to react accordingly to the attack.
5. Response to attacks - automatic or manual to mitigate the attack and its consequent sub-attacks.

The *deterrence* step in communication networks is common for all types of attacks. It consists of strong and legally appropriate legislative notifications accessible through all communication channels of the company. When an attacker tries to attack the company's assets, he should be notified of possible legal consequences. This measure includes *banner of the day messages* on all access ports (console, virtual terminal lines), warnings before a remote login, messages on the website, etc.

The following part of this section describes the protection steps in detail for concrete attacks from Sect. 2.

3.1 Access Attacks Protection

The most effective protection is to define flow rules in advance (proactive flow rule insertion) for every protected application. These rules should be based on destination ports, IP addresses and MAC addresses. Specified action should be set to a queue, which would perform traffic shaping and drop any traffic exceeding the specified threshold. For monitoring and logging purposes, a selected copy of the traffic should be sent to the controller.

An alternative solution is to send the traffic via the SDN controller. However, this option can cause availability issues if the amount of traffic overwhelms the controller's resources.

1. Deterrence and delay - traffic destined to the protected application has to go via an output queue, or the controller, in order to limit an initial traffic burst.
2. Detection of attacks - attack can be detected if the amount of traffic exceeds the specified value. This threshold is set for every protected application separately.
3. Assessment of attacks - severity of the attack is assessed based on the target, the attacker's source and the amount of generated data. This amount is generally much lower than in an availability attack. For example, more than 3 login attempts within 10 s might already trigger the protection.
4. Communication and notification - the notification should include source and destination of the attack and the amount of traffic generated. An example of attacking traffic should be logged for later analysis. This is useful in determining the nature and the exact type of the attack.
5. Response to attacks - the system should take the action immediately and block the traffic. This action can however be less restrictive than in availability attacks. For example, a dynamic deny rule can be inserted with a defined idle-timeout. If the attack stops for the defined period, the rule will be automatically deleted and traffic allowed again. This will ensure that false positive triggers caused by legitimate users will not block the login procedure completely.

3.2 Availability Attacks Protection

The following protection is effective only against higher-layer availability attacks and not against physical layer attacks.

1. Deterrence and delay - if the attack represents a new data flow, the first packet is sent to the SDN controller (reactive flow rule insertion), while all the consecutive packets are dropped until the controller decides how to handle the flow. The controller can be set to wait a specified amount of time before any allowing rules are created. On the other hand, if the attack is part of an existing flow, it cannot be delayed as these messages are forwarded by networking devices without any interaction with the controller.

The controller must handle the initial burst of traffic. This can be helped by implementation of distributed architecture, where multiple controllers can load-balance the traffic. If the amount of traffic is too high, it can be blocked immediately by the first forwarding device. Alternatively, this flow can be moved to a special output queue. This queue can have QoS policies set to slow down the traffic by limiting the number of packets transmitted over a certain time period.

2. Detection of attacks - is typically based on collected traffic statistics. If these parameters exceed specified values, the attack is detected. The most common statistics are: number of packets, or amount of bytes received from a single source per defined time interval.

3. Assessment of attacks - severity of the attack is based on the collected statistics. Different levels of the attack can be defined for different amounts of traffic. For each level, there can be a different predefined action, which will be applied automatically.

4. Communication and notification - the notification should include source and destination of the attack, the amount of traffic generated, and taken action. The first detected packet can be logged for later analysis, but the following ones should be blocked immediately on the networking device. Sending this traffic to the SDN controller could overload its resources.

5. Response to attacks - the application should automatically take appropriate actions to stop the attack immediately. This can be accomplished by inserting deny rules (set to drop all the traffic from the specified source). Based on the attack severity, these rules can be automatically inserted across all the networking devices. This would save the controller load and speed up the decision process in the case, that the attacker would perform the same attack via a different forwarding device.

It is important to consider appropriate composition of the blocking rule. For example, in some cases, blocking all communication from the attacker might not be the best solution. If the attacker uses a legitimate device which transmits critical data and this device is "only" partially under control of the attacker, only the attack packets should be dropped while critical data should be still allowed (but the operator should be notified about this behavior).

The operator should have an option to override the automatically taken action, but sometimes not in the case of a severe attack. By allowing the attack the system could collapse, so in some cases, it might be safer to deny the override action to the operator.

3.3   GNSS Spoofing Attacks

GNSS signal used for determining position and time information is received directly by IoT devices and does not go over the communication network. SDN can therefore offer no protection against spoofing or jamming attack on this service. SDN can only provide redundant time information, which can be compared on the IoT device and if a difference is detected, the possibility of an attack might be considered.

3.4   Man-in-the-Middle Attacks

The protection against these type of attacks requires use of encryption. SDN can only lower a chance of a possible attack in some specific network topologies. If that is possible, the protected traffic might be sent from the first networking device to the last one straight via the SDN controller. This would reduce the chance of a message capturing by an attacker, but could create significant load on the controller.

Another theoretical SDN protection is to record latency of each flow and to compare it with captured statistics in defined time periods. A significant deviation can indicate the attack and the controller can temporarily start to forward this flow via itself, instead of the normal network. This could stop the current attack, but at the cost of increased controller load.

3.5   Masquerade Attacks

The SDN controller can be set to check the validity of certificates issued within the PKI. In such a case, a defined communication source has to be firstly verified and only if it will be approved, the communication flow rules will be established. It is necessary to establish connectivity between the SDN controller and a certificate authority, which can provide updates about revoked certificates.

1. Deterrence and delay - the first packet from a defined source has to go to the controller first for the certificate validation.
2. Detection of attacks - if the controllers detects that the certificate is invalid, it will be classified as an attack.
3. Assessment of attacks - the severity of the attack depends on status of the certificate validation. The attacker might try to use a revoked certificate or a forged one.
4. Communication and notification - the notification should include source and destination of the attack and the provided certificate. This information can help in identification of the source of the fake certificate. The certificate can be stolen from other devices belonging to the targeted network.
5. Response to attacks - without any further actions, the attacker's communication will not be allowed as no corresponding flow rules will be created on the networking devices.

3.6   Node Attacks

The communication network can potentially stop only attacks done over this network and not locally on the node. The SDN controller can perform application layer inspection, which compares the message payload with a malware database. If a malware is found, it is classified by a severity level from the database and future traffic is handled according to the defined rule. This can include detailed inspection, forwarding to a specified link (a *honeypot* network), or drop.

The controller can also apply ACL and firewall rules to prevent node devices from being accessible to unauthorized sources (it does not prevent against physical access attacks to those devices).

1. Deterrence and delay - all traffic destined to selected IoT devices goes via the SDN controller, which performs the application layer inspection. This slow down is done only on the newly incoming traffic (outgoing traffic from the devices is typically allowed and performed autonomously by networking devices).
2. Detection of attacks - the traffic is compared with a malware database and if a match is found, the attack is detected.
3. Assessment of attacks - classification is based on the severity level included in the malware database.
4. Communication and notification - the notification should include source and destination of the attack, the found threat, probability of the match (some attacks might be detected as false positive) and taken action.
5. Response to attacks - based on the attack classification, the traffic should be automatically blocked, or redirected to a dedicated network segment. This can act as a *honeypot* network to observe the attacker's intention and targets.

4   Evaluation of Protection Methods

Table 1 summarizes the attacks on IoT devices and means of protections in traditional networks and SDN. Protection of traditional networks requires specialized devices, which target only the specific threat. On the other hand, SDN can provide complex security solution for the entire range of threats.

The only necessary solution from traditional networks is encryption, which prevents Man-in-the-Middle type of attacks. It is also important to consider that there is no reliable protection against GNSS spoofing attacks and availability attacks targeting the physical layer.

Table 1. Summary of attacks on IoT devices

Attack	Traditional protection	SDN detection	SDN protection
Access	IPS, FW, login restrictions	Flow statistics	Automatic blocking
Availability	IPS (except physical layer)	Flow statistics	Automatic blocking
GNSS spoofing	Partial (caching, PTP)	Not possible	Redundant time info.
Man-in-the-M.	Encryption	Not possible	Limited
Masquerade	PKI	PKI integration	Deny communication
Node	Antivirus, FW	Flow analytic	Traffic filtering

4.1   Use Case Protection Application

Implementation of the proposed protection methods requires significant work even in the case of SDN. Based on the application purpose, it might not be necessary to implement all protections at once. The advantage of SDN - programability - allows extension of the application in the future, based on newly emerging needs.

To verify the proposed protection methods, a use case application was created. The purpose of this application was to verify SDN-based protection methods against access and availability attacks. The application used the Ryu controller [1] and was tested in an emulated Mininet [2] network topology of a typical network connecting IoT devices. The topology was created as a star network and contained 3 switches. Two switches simulated two IoT domains and they had multiple IoT devices connected (simulating smart traffic and smart mobility sensors). The central switch represented a data center with IoT back-end services. The application collected traffic statistics in one second intervals and compared them to defined security policies. If a limit was reached, it was evaluated as an attack and the protection was triggered as it is depicted in Fig. 1.

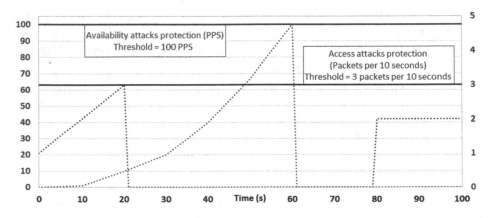

Fig. 1. Evaluation of the use case protection application

4.2   Access Attacks Protection Evaluation

An access attack based on the *brute force* technique was simulated on a server with IP address of 192.168.1.10 and TCP port of 443 (HTTPS). The protection threshold was set to 3 received packets within 10 s. If a traffic flow from a single source to the defined IP address and port reached this threshold, it was classified as an attack. In this case, a deny flow rule was inserted with idle-timeout set to 60 s. This means, that if the attack stopped, the traffic was re-allowed after this period.

4.3   Availability Attacks Protection Evaluation

In this scenario, the protection threshold was set to 100 packets per second with no port specified - all the traffic was counted towards the limit. If the threshold was reached, the application automatically inserted a deny flow rule, so all the consequent packets from the flow were dropped on the first networking device. The rule had both timeouts set to indefinitely (0), so the application did not automatically re-allowed the traffic from the flow.

5 Conclusion

The concept of SDN brings new opportunities to interconnecting IoT devices. The programmability can, at almost no additional costs, add new features on demand. This includes security features, which have specific requirements on adaptability as new threats are quickly emerging and needs of IoT devices are changing. Networks connecting IoT devices will experience a dynamic development and all the required features are not yet known at this moment. The option to update networking features makes the SDN solution more future-proof and competent.

The paper showed the vital nature of SDN in regards to this protection. From the six analyzed attack areas, SDN can enhance detection and protection against four types of them. When combined with encryption from traditional networks, the solution can protect against all threats except the external GNSS attacks. The main advantage of the SDN solution is integration of all protections within a single device - the SDN controller. In this case, it is not required to use multiple separated devices like in traditional networks. This makes the implementation of the SDN protection system for IoT devices a highly effective and elegant solution.

References

1. RYU SDN Framework (2017). https://osrg.github.io/ryu/. Accessed 01 July 2020
2. Mininet (2018). http://mininet.org/. Accessed 01 July 2020
3. Cisco annual internet report (2018–2023). Technical report (2020). https://www.cisco.com/c/en/us/solutions/collateral/executive-perspectives/annual-internet-report/white-paper-c11-741490.pdf. Accessed 01 July 2020
4. iPerf - The ultimate speed test tool for TCP, UDP and SCTP (2020). https://iperf.fr/. Accessed 01 July 2020
5. What is GNSS? (2020). https://www.gsa.europa.eu/european-gnss/what-gnss. Accessed 01 July 2020
6. Aziz, N.A., Mantoro, T., Khairudin, M.A., Murshid, A.F.B.A.: Software defined networking (SDN) and its security issues. In: 2018 International Conference on Computing, Engineering, and Design (ICCED), pp. 40–45 (2018)
7. Bauer, M., et al.: Internet of Things - Architecture IoT-A Deliverable D1.5 - Final architectural reference model for the IoT v3.0 (2013)
8. Bojkovic, Z.S., Bakmaz, B.M., Bakmaz, M.R.: Vision and enabling technologies of tactile internet realization. In: 13th International Conference on Advanced Technologies, Systems and Services in Telecommunications (TELSIKS), pp. 113–118 (2017)
9. Cleveland, F.: IEC TC57 WG15: IEC 62351 Security Standards for the Power System Information Infrastructure (2012)
10. Condoluci, M., Araniti, G., Mahmoodi, T., Dohler, M.: Enabling the IoT machine age with 5G: machine-type multicast services for innovative real-time applications. IEEE Access **4**, 1 (2016)
11. Gharaibeh, A., et al.: Smart cities: a survey on data management, security and enabling technologies. IEEE Commun. Surv. Tutor. **19**, 2456–2501 (2017)

12. Liguori, A., Winandy, M.: The diamond approach for SDN security. In: IEEE Softwarization (2018)
13. Liu, Y., Zhao, B., Zhao, P., Fan, P., Liu, H.: A survey: typical security issues of software-defined networking. China Commun. **16**(7), 13–31 (2019)
14. Varsha, H.S., Shashikala, K.P.: The tactile internet. In: 2017 International Conference on Innovative Mechanisms for Industry Applications (ICIMIA), pp. 419–422 (2017)

Digital Forensic Readiness in IoT - A Risk Assessment Model

Alexander D. Forfot$^{(\boxtimes)}$ ⓘ and Grethe Østby ⓘ

NTNU, Teknologiveien 22, 2815 Gjøvik, Norway
alexadf@stud.ntnu.no, grethe.ostby@ntnu.no

Abstract. With the increased adoption of IoT devices they have become an important source of digital evidence, and could be a vital part of investigations both for companies and law enforcement agencies. There are however some present challenges such as identification of devices, what data could be evidence (if the device stores any), and privacy. Because of this, digital forensics readiness is essential in these ecosystems. It is an important part of both risk assessment and preparation for contingencies. The devices, their potential, and procedures in case of an incident or attack, needs to be predetermined. In this paper we suggest a risk assessment model to prepare for forensic analysis in IoT, which we have called Forensics Readiness in IoT Implementation (FRIoTI), to meet the mentioned challenges.

Keywords: IoT · Forensics readiness · IoT forensics · IoT forensics readiness · Risk assessment · IoT implementation

1 Introduction

Internet of Things, abbreviated IoT, is a very fast growing field within IT. Statista estimates that there will be 35.82 billion connected IoT devices installed worldwide by 2021. This is a 34.36% increase compared to 2019, which had an estimated 26.66 billion devices [18].

The purpose of IoT devices is to create convenience for the end user through use of technology and data. Extending to already existing products such as cars, water heaters, fridges, traffic lights etc., aiming to modernize them and increase their user friendliness. A modernization process which introduces a vast amount of devices to internet connectivity. This is a source of new information security vulnerabilities, which leads to unknown incidents that will require new Digital Forensics procedures [2]. Thereby it is essential for these IoT-devices to be Digital Forensics Ready. Important information related to crimes or incidents can be tracked on these devices, and methods to extract relevant data should be predetermined. The ability to achieve this is currently a problem, due to the lack of solutions and standardization. These are vulnerability aspects that are present within the potential digital forensic processes related to them. There are generally very few or no solutions in place that could be used independent of

© Springer Nature Switzerland AG 2021
S. Yildirim Yayilgan et al. (Eds.): INTAP 2020, CCIS 1382, pp. 53–64, 2021.
https://doi.org/10.1007/978-3-030-71711-7_5

device manufacturers, due to new technology which are present in all IoT devices who pops up. Independent solutions are usually tailored towards products from the same provider, with no real standardization [13]. This makes it harder to develop universal tools that could make these devices Digital Forensics Ready. In this paper we present a model we have called Forensics Readiness in IoT Implementation (FRIoTI) as a solution to these issues.

After this introduction, in Sect. 2 we present the background, before relevant literature is discussed in Sect. 3. In Sect. 4 we present our research approach before our discussion with our model is presented in Sect. 5. In Sect. 6 we present our conclusion and suggestions for future research.

2   Background

Internet of Things is in simple terms an environment of interconnected devices. It utilizes the internet to share data and nearly any device one may think of can connect to it [9]. Similarities within IoT products are that they in some way gather and/or track data for a specific purpose, further they can be used to display information to the end user or in a broader experiment to gather test data.

[4,9] have presented timelines which show the development of IoT from 1999 up to 2019. They present a gradual introduction of devices, leading up to the release of the first iPhone. From 2007 and onwards the growth is exponential within IoT, and as presented in the introduction, this growth has continued, and will continue into the future [3,18]. These timelines create a basic understanding of the progression of IoT.

2.1   Digital Forensic Potential with IoT

Estimated growth in number of devices in the coming years [18] will in parallel increase the sources that can provide evidence from incidents or malicious attacks. Equally relevant for both law enforcement investigations and internal investigations within an organization. New use cases for such devices may however leave them vulnerable to potential attackers. Security flaws within the devices are a risk and one of the main reasons enterprise customers are not buying IoT devices [1].

IoT devices provide another layer of abstraction within the boundaries of an organization. It adds another type of device that could be used to gather data. Many organizations use IoT devices in a variety of scales. Ranging from simple RFID smart-cards for physical access to smaller sensors in a larger network within a factory. All of these devices can, in case an incident or an attack occurs, provide valuable forensic evidence. The type of incident or attack may also dictate what IoT devices could provide evidence. Data from RFID smart-cards could be of interest if there are suspicions towards a specific employee. Variations in temperature readings before a factory breakdown could also be an important part of an investigation. The analysis of data from IoT devices may lead to quicker clarification during internal investigations.

Moreover, this is relevant for law enforcement agencies. Evidence collected by IoT devices could help back up alibis and speed up forensic investigations, given that investigators know what they are looking for (an issue highlighted in Sect. 2.2). Law enforcement can however legally collect data from other entities, if it is a part of the investigation and justified [2]. This may suggest that they do not always know the systems they are collecting data from, which present a need for Digital Forensics Readiness within organizations. IoT devices may be a part of an investigation, and law enforcement may require data from them. Introduction of readiness could improve the investigative process for both the company and law enforcement agency [2].

2.2 Evidence Identification, Collection and Preservation

Identification, collection and preservation of evidence is an integral part to any digital forensic process [2]. Without proper tools or knowledge one will not be able to complete these steps in a forensically sound manner. In some cases it may even be hard to identify the IoT device itself, and to attempt to understand how to collect data from it is difficult. Lack of standards within software makes it hard to know whether data is relevant and how one can collect it. Preservation of the collected data from IoT devices is not challenging. Traditional techniques such as hashing are viable. The challenge lies in the preservation of the scene where the location of the crime or incident occurred. IoT devices generally communicate in real-time with other devices. This makes it difficult to determine the scale of a compromise and the boundaries of a scene [6].

2.3 Evidence Analysis and Correlation

Large amounts of IoT devices do not store metadata, a result of the constrained environments that they operate within [6]. This creates a new challenge for investigators, or incident response teams, when trying to acquire historical data from such devices. No metadata means that there will be no information such as created, modified, or last accessed times available for investigation. Correlations often rely on metadata for verification. Within analysis and correlation there is an emphasis on privacy [12]. Privacy within digital investigations is a huge concern [7]. Ideally digital investigators should only analyze data that could be relevant to the investigation, and not all available data [2]. This is a problem for IoT devices, since the devices can collect sensitive information. Running in a multi-tenancy environment will also make it hard to distinguish the different users, potentially revealing personal information related to someone outside the scope of the investigation [17].

2.4 Attack or Deficit Attribution

Forensic investigations aim to find a perpetrator, someone responsible, for an attack or "accidental" infiltration. Finding the perpetrator is one of the steps of bringing them to justice and it could additionally be a way to discover other vulnerabilities. Developments within the car industry show that autonomy is becoming an area of research for many manufacturers and service providers which is presented by [9] and [4]. Growth within this industry also brings liability issues - about who is actually responsible for an incident. The ability to cover liability issues is difficult without proper methods and forensically sound tools for collection and analysis of the relevant data [6]. Issues related to multi-tenancy also appear within IoT environments. A single user can be tracked down without proper authentication within IoT devices. Finding the perpetrator might therefore be relatively difficult. In addition, to be able to attribute malicious activity detected within an IoT environment becomes very difficult when there is no reliable standard that ensures forensically sound logging and monitoring of systems [6].

3   Relevant Literature

With a lack of existing tools and frameworks there is a range of frameworks that are being proposed by researchers as potential solutions [13]. The proposed frameworks are generally theoretical and not based on widespread use within the market. Consequently there is little knowledge on how courts will view the gathered evidence and whether it will be admissible or not [13]. However, it will be seen as positive if methods to obtain evidence are based on a standardized framework, especially within a field which currently does not have this [13].

3.1   Generic Digital Forensic Framework for IoT

The main issue is the absence of a framework that is accepted to aid in Digital Forensic Investigations within IoT-environments. Digital Forensic Investigation Framework for IoT (DFIF-IoT), aims to tackle this issue [13]. The framework proposes methods to gather, examine and analyse potential evidence from IoT environments. In the description of the framework it is split into three main steps that are looked at separately and an additional fourth, which is a concurrent process that is done for each step [13]. The proactive process handles forensic readiness (DFR) and the reactive process is targeting the forensic investigation (DFI).

An advantage with this framework compared to the others is that it is compliant with ISO/IEC 27043:2015 [13], an international standard that handles information technology, security techniques, and incident investigation principles and processes [11]. There is however one large disadvantage that becomes apparent with this framework. The authors of the DFIF-IoT framework do not critically look at the framework and present disadvantages. The framework provides a topological outline of how different processes should be approached, but it does not look at specific methods to accomplish this, a disadvantage that is caused by the goal of being as generic as possible. Moreover, there is no way to estimate how impactful this framework can be - without thorough testing. This is somewhat acknowledged by the authors in their conclusion, where they determine that their claims can only be verified by using a working prototype [13].

3.2   Forensic State Acquisition from IoT

FSAIoT is a generalized framework that aims to monitor state changes for various IoT devices [15]. IoT devices do generally not have the capability to store or record data related to their state, due to minimal hardware and lack of protocol implementations. This makes it hard to acquire forensically sound data from the devices. Growth within the "always-connected" principle creates potential for data to be collected. FSAIoT aims to gather data that present state changes for the device in question e.g. temperature changes, if a car was parked, when a door was open/locked etc. [15]. The Forensic State Acquisition from Internet of Things (FSAIoT) framework builds on a generalized controller called the Forensic State Acquisition Controller (FSAC) [15]. This controller functions as a regular IoT controller, but with forensics in mind. This includes considerations towards forensic soundness, accurate timing data from state changes, and the ability to store collected data securely with the possibility to verify its integrity.

However, evidence collection in a forensically sound manner has not been covered by the authors in regards to the IoT controller, but mentioned as a part of the future work [15]. At the current stage their focus was directed towards providing a functional proof-of-concept. A consequence of this is that not all current challenges have a proposed solution. It requires further work to be able to actually operationalize forensics readiness. Important to any investigation is also the ability to access historical and deleted data, a functionality the framework is currently lacking. Additionally, the type of communication technology used by different IoT devices introduce their own challenges - certain technologies would require the addition of further hardware support within the IoT controller. Areas that have been highlighted by the authors as current limitations and potential for further work [15].

3.3   Forensic Investigation Framework for IoT Using a Public Digital Ledger

The Forensic Investigation Framework for IoT using a Public Digital Ledger (FIF-IoT) has a unique approach compared to the other frameworks. The aim is to collect interactions from IoT-based systems, storing the information in a public digital ledger [8]. This is an alternative approach to more common applications of blockchains, which highlights other capabilities within the emerging technology. The interactions can be separated into three categories 1) Things to Users[1], 2) Things to Cloud[2], and 3) Things to Things[3].

---

[1] IoT devices that can be accessed by users directly or through a cloud service.
[2] IoT devices that can publish data to a cloud service.
[3] IoT devices communicating with other IoT devices.

To use a public ledger creates a new layer of complexity in the handling phase. The interactions need to be organized and published to the blockchain. FIF-IoT does this by creating transactions based on the gathered information, these transactions are further sent to the public ledger network. Miners receive the transactions and combine them to create an interaction block. These blocks are what gets published on the blockchain. By doing this one also ensures that chronological order of the data is maintained. A lot more details surrounding the process is given by Hossain et al. [8]. While the authors provide a great framework to gather evidence from devices based on their interactions, and additionally covering the challenges imposed by the public ledger, there are some challenges that are introduced. The complexity is the main concern. Implementation of this framework requires significant knowledge by the developer, requiring larger investments to be appropriately implemented. The presentation of evidence could also become an inconvenience due to the complexity, as it is harder to explain and justify how evidence has been gathered without the recipients already have a fundamental understanding of the technologies that are used. Additionally, the necessary encryption introduces a larger energy consumption for the hardware constrained IoT devices [8].

3.4 Forensics Edge Management System

The Forensics Edge Management System (FEMS) is a system that focuses on IoT devices that are found within a smart home environment, aiming to provide autonomous security and digital forensics services [16]. FEMS looks at environments that are user-manageable solutions, a type of solution that is not impacted by vendors further than providing the hardware and software, which smart homes could be categorized as [16]. The FEMS framework introduces a new outlook of the digital forensic process, where the three stages 1) configuration of the forensics system, 2) automated forensics, and 3) user, are introduced before involving a forensics investigator [16].

Oriwoh and Sant have conducted a thorough coverage of the challenges with the FEMS framework, which can be found in Sect. 5 of their paper [16]. The need to perform further testing under various conditions has been presented, as well as further configuration being needed to effectively introduce it to a live smart-home environment. Moreover, another challenge that is present is the intended use of the framework - directly targeting smart-home environments. This in turn reduces the ability to introduce the framework in more widespread use.

3.5 Digital Forensic Approaches for Amazon Alexa Ecosystem

This framework is an example of a more contained approach to IoT devices, when the devices target the Amazon Alexa ecosystem [5]. The Alexa ecosystem is based on devices that build on Alexa: A cloud based intelligent virtual assistant (IVA) developed by Amazon. Many will recognize the Amazon Echo, a smart speaker within the ecosystem. This speaker is the main source of all voice commands submitted to Alexa. By targeting a specific ecosystem it is possible to develop a tailored solution that could further aid in the development of more generic frameworks in the future. Chung, Park & Lee's proposed framework may be tailored towards Alexa, but it highlights a new and efficient approach when combining cloud-native and client-side forensics [5].

Similar to FEMS, this framework also targets one specific environment: the Amazon Alexa ecosystem. However, the authors have created a toolkit referred to as CIFT (Cloud-based IoT Forensic Toolkit) which is used to gather native artifacts from Alexa. Chung, Park and Lee briefly mentioned in future work that they aim to further develop this toolkit to cover other cloud-based IoT environments as well. The framework does however struggle to cover challenges presented in Sect. 2.3 and Sect. 2.4. Firstly, the ability to exactly pinpoint who interacts with the Alexa device is not present, which makes attribution difficult. Secondly, it collects all data that is produced by the device. We raise the concern that it gathers data that is not relevant to an investigation and this could include sensitive information that should not be gathered without consent or investigative intentions.

4 Research Approach

The main goal of the research is to develop a model that can be used by organizations to confidently implement a digital forensics readiness approach to their existing- or planned IoT systems. The model will be simple to follow and provide information about important aspects that need to be considered.

The authors approach the goal by what can be referred to as sophisticated falsificationism approach. The sophisticated falsificationism approach starts by looking at existing research to try to find the most optimal framework that could be implemented before validating it in the real world [14].

In this paper information has been gathered from various publications, articles, books, and other resources. The information acts as a foundation for further discussion into digital forensic readiness in IoT, and its' importance on a managerial level for risk decision purposes on digital forensics readiness. In this paper we have highlighted frameworks that could be used for digital forensic readiness within IoT. In this paper we suggest a model that aims to mitigate the challenges that have been previously presented. We present a topological model that expands on some of the concepts presented in the existing frameworks, and add to them by providing solutions to existing flaws.

5 A Risk Assessment Model for Forensic Analysis in IoT

A part of risk management is to identify all information assets within a company [19]. This is meant to create an overview over the organizations assets, and potentially highlight which ones create a risk. Surveillance of all IoT devices will also be a part of this. Another managerial task [19] is that the company should be prepared for incidents and attacks that could occur. To enable appropriate risk management for IoT device implementations and incident handling, digital forensics readiness is necessary.

An IoT environment that is digital forensics ready is however not very straight forward. It currently has a lot of challenges (Sect. 2), but with the implementation of some of the frameworks listed in Sect. 3 it will become more viable.

By implementing our model the time spent reaching a conclusion when investigating incidents and attacks would be shortened due to readiness. The organization would ideally know which devices to collect evidence from, and which evidence would be useful. That is: Pre-determined within the incident response planning.

Some of the frameworks presented in Sect. 3 require much work to implement and might potentially make it harder for management to justify the investment in digital forensics readiness. The FEMS (Sect. 3.4) and Digital Forensic approaches for Amazon Alexa ecosystem (Sect. 3.5) are frameworks that could be the most difficult to implement. This is because they are based on research done into specific IoT segments. The first one looks at the smart home environment, while the latter looks further into the Alexa ecosystem.

A middle ground in regards to the frameworks are FSAIoT (Sect. 3.2) and FIF-IoT (Sect. 3.3). Both of them provide possibilities for digital forensic readiness within generic IoT environments. FSAIoT introduces controllers that enable state acquisition from IoT devices. FIF-IoT builds on the use of a public digital ledger to store and manage data related to IoT devices. The reason we regard these frameworks as the middle ground is that they do not currently comply with any information security standard. Managers ability to present compliance with a widely accepted standard could be the difference between receiving funds for implementation, or being ignored. This is where DFIF-IoT (Sect. 3.1) comes in: The framework presents three main factors: (1) It has a generic approach from the beginning, (2) Is not aimed at a specific IoT environment, and (3) It complies with an information security standard. From a managerial perspective it is also the easiest to adapt out of the discussed frameworks, as it complies with ISO/IEC 27043:2015. Compliance with a recognized information security standard makes it easier to receive company resources during budgeting. Additionally, it might be easier to justify an investment into a new area of IT-security if the proposed framework complies with already recognized standards.

With the proposition of a framework, challenges like those presented in Sect. 2 would need to be handled. Something that the DFIF-IoT framework does. At its base, the framework builds on good proactive work where evidence identification and collection is very important. Building an understanding of the IoT environment and data which can be collected. In cases where an identified device does not already collect relevant data, it gives the company the ability to introduce solutions that enable this. Preservation of the data is also handled, by using guidelines found in ISO/IEC 27037:2012 and ISO/IEC 10118-2:2010 - highlights the use of hash functions [10]. The framework does highlight the importance to only gather relevant data and to stay within the scope of the investigation. Privacy related to individuals is however not directly discussed. Concerns related to privacy would be at the discretion of the company and investigative team. Policies in regards to privacy should be implemented as an addition to the framework. To protect the privacy, concerns must be handled appropriately.

Attack or deficit attribution relies on how the evidence from IoT environments are used and to what extent. If such evidence is the only evidence gathered and is the baseline for an investigation these challenges could occur. Evidence gathered from IoT environments should be supportive. It should be able to back up hypotheses in a supportive manner, e.g. the use of a workers access card late at night, shortly before malicious activity was discovered on a workstation. Such information could be used to try and create a timeline of what happened. There may not necessarily be a correlation, but it would be something the investigative team would have to look further into - a potential lead. It could be discovered that the worker has had his access card stolen or duplicated.

Based on our findings we have created a model that considers all the issues that have been discussed. We have called the model a risk assessment model for forensic analysis in IoT, which is presented in Fig. 1.

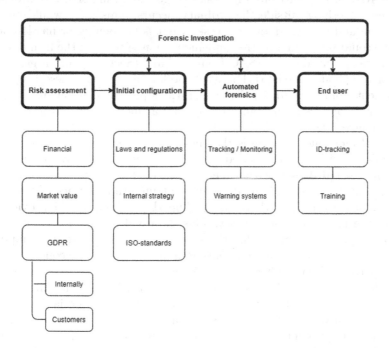

Fig. 1. A risk assessment model for forensic analysis in IoT

The figure is based on a few key principles, introduced by the FEMS, but further expands on these to cover multiple challenges. A basic outline is the different stages (1) Risk assessment, (2) Initial configuration, (3) Automated forensics, and (4) End user - with (5) Forensics investigation being a process that needs to be taken into account during all stages. The risk assessment is what needs to be done initially within the organization. This includes both financial, market and GDPR risk assessment. The next step is the initial configuration. This includes system setups, laws and regulations, internal strategy (based on step 1), and ISO-standards.

Compliance would act as an assurance for upper management, as well as a marketing tool for the business. Automated Forensics is the technology (or system) that enables the monitoring and logging of the IoT system. Based on our research this implementation would be largely different depending on the type of environment it is to be implemented within, as presented in Sects. 3.2 and 3.5. The creation of a fully generic system currently seems impossible, seeing as there is no standardization between different types of IoT devices and how they handle data. If the initial configuration is conducted properly, one should not have issues related to the data itself within this stage. Considerations towards the laws and regulations have already been taken. The most important aspect then becomes the level of automation that is present. The minimum level of functionality that needs to be present is tracking. Very much like an intrusion detection system, the automated forensics stage should in some way provide an alert when something outside the ordinary occurs. This alert would enable a user to go in and analyze data logs to see what is happening or has happened. This stage could be covered by the implementation of some of the frameworks in Sect. 3, more specifically the FSAC from FSAIoT (Sect. 3.2) and a generalized version of the Cloud-based IoT Forensic Toolkit (Sect. 3.5). These frameworks would benefit from the additional considerations presented in our model and it would further enhance their ability to be used as methods for data acquisition for forensic investigations.

The final independent stage is the end-user. The end-user is a person that would interact with the automated system in place, and have the ability to look at the related data when an alert has been raised. It is important that appropriate authentication is used, to prevent unauthorized access, as well as give the ability to analyze ID-tracking. The ID-tracking would provide data related to the user and their activity. This data will be an important method to detect compromised data within the system. Additionally, it is an important aspect of the forensic investigation. During an investigation the concept of 5WH is very important, (Who, Where, What, When, Why, and How) [2], which would require information about the user and their actions. Maintaining integrity and the ability to provide a robust timeline of actions within a potential investigation would depend on which information is available both from the system and the user. With the implementation of our model we believe that these points should be taken into consideration. The authentication and data related to the user are important aspects, but to mitigate errors generated by an unknowing user - sufficient training is essential. The user needs a fundamental understanding of the IoT system, how the data is generated, and what to actually look for. Providing this would have a positive outcome on the effectiveness on the system as a whole, while also ensuring that data is handled in a forensically sound manner.

While all these stages describe the process of initialization and the intentions of the system, it is important to highlight the forensic investigation as a concurrent process that needs to be involved within all stages. The aim of the model is to be able to use gathered data to contribute within a forensic investigation. If this is not done, the entire process would be considered a waste.

To conduct a reliable investigation there are some principles that have to be covered, these include: Forensic soundness[4], Evidence integrity[5], and the Chain of custody[6] [2]. How these principles are covered need to be considered at all stages. If some of these principles are not covered, actions need to be taken to ensure their implementation throughout the process. This is an instrumental part of being able to conduct a thorough investigation that could be used as a part of a court case.

6   Conclusion and Future Work

As previously highlighted IoT is a very fast growing field. Digital forensics has however been neglected during the introduction of these kinds of devices. Challenges related to digital forensics, such as: Evidence collection, storage, privacy, liability etc., will only continue to grow with the widespread use of IoT devices. Unless certain measures are taken. The introduction of digital forensics readiness (DFR) will aim to tackle some of these challenges. However, it is the responsibility of management to introduce measures to improve digital forensics readiness within a company.

There are various ways to accomplish this, but in our paper we suggest four steps (1) Risk assessment, (2) Initial configuration (3), Automated forensics, and (4) End user - with (5) Forensics investigation being a process that needs to be taken into account during all stages.

We would like to iterate that while our model is suggested based on falsification, it still has to be tested in actual situations. We suggest a collaboration with an IoT-company to test the model when implementing new features. It is difficult to assume how the model may work in real scenarios outside the scope of the proof-of-concepts provided. To be able to determine possible issues one would need to implement the frameworks in smaller scale and track impact and discover their potential. With further success, large scale implementation should be a goal.

References

1. Ali, S., Bosche, A., Ford, F.: Cybersecurity is the key to unlocking demand in the internet of things (2018). https://www.bain.com/insights/cybersecurity-is-the-key-to-unlocking-demand-in-the-internet-of-things. Accessed 30 Oct 2019

---

[4] An investigation is considered forensically sound if evidence has not been tampered with or destroyed on accident or on purpose.

[5] The degree to which evidence has been preserved; unchanged.

[6] Documentation on how evidence has been handled and by whom.

2. Årnes, A.: Digital Forensics. Wiley, New York (2017)
3. Bosche, A., Crawford, D., Jackson, D., Schallehn, M., Schorling, C.: Unlocking opportunities in the internet of things (2018). https://www.bain.com/insights/unlocking-opportunities-in-the-internet-of-things. Accessed 29 Oct 2019
4. Braun, A.: History of IoT: a timeline of development (2019). https://www.iottechtrends.com/history-of-iot. Accessed 18 Oct 2019
5. Chung, H., Park, J., Lee, S.: Digital forensic approaches for amazon Alexa ecosystem. Digital Invest. **22**, S15–S25 (2017)
6. Conti, M., Dehghantanha, A., Franke, K., Watson, S.: Internet of things security and forensics: challenges and opportunities (2018)
7. Dehghantanha, A., Franke, K.: Privacy-respecting digital investigation. In: 2014 Twelfth Annual International Conference on Privacy, Security and Trust, pp. 129–138. IEEE (2014)
8. Hossain, M., Karim, Y., Hasan, R.: FIF-IoT: a forensic investigation framework for iot using a public digital ledger. In: 2018 IEEE International Congress on Internet of Things (ICIOT), pp. 33–40. IEEE (2018)
9. HQSoftware: The history of IoT: a comprehensive timeline of major events, infographic (2018). https://hqsoftwarelab.com/about-us/blog/the-history-of-iot-a-comprehensive-timeline-of-major-events-infographic. Accessed 18 Oct 2019
10. ISO: ISO/IEC 10118–2:2010 information technology - security techniques - hash-functions - part 2: Hash-functions using an n-bit block cipher (2010). https://www.iso.org/standard/44737.html. Accessed 06 Nov 2019
11. ISO: ISO/IEC 27043:2015 information technology - security techniques - incident investigation principles and processes (2015). https://www.iso.org/standard/44407.html. Accessed 09 Oct 2019
12. Jordaan, J.: The GDPR and DFIR (2017). https://www.sans.org/cyber-security-summit/archives/file/summit-archive-1513005472.pdf. Accessed 05 Apr 2020
13. Kebande, V.R., Ray, I.: A generic digital forensic investigation framework for internet of things (IoT). In: 2016 IEEE 4th International Conference on Future Internet of Things and Cloud (FiCloud), pp. 356–362. IEEE (2016)
14. Kowalski, S.: It Insecurity: a multi-disciplinary inquiry (1996)
15. Meffert, C., Clark, D., Baggili, I., Breitinger, F.: Forensic state acquisition from internet of things (FSAIoT): a general framework and practical approach for IoT forensics through IoT device state acquisition. In: Proceedings of the 12th International Conference on Availability, Reliability and Security, p. 56. ACM (2017)
16. Oriwoh, E., Sant, P.: The forensics edge management system: a concept and design. In: IEEE 10th International Conference on Ubiquitous Intelligence and Computing and IEEE 10th International Conference on Autonomic and Trusted Computing, pp. 544–550. IEEE (2013)
17. Ruan, K., Carthy, J., Kechadi, T., Crosbie, M.: Cloud forensics. In: Peterson, G., Shenoi, S. (eds.) DigitalForensics 2011. IAICT, vol. 361, pp. 35–46. Springer, Heidelberg (2011). https://doi.org/10.1007/978-3-642-24212-0_3
18. Statista: Internet of things - number of connected devices worldwide 2015–2025 (2019). https://www.statista.com/statistics/471264/iot-number-of-connected-devices-worldwide. Accessed 30 Oct 2019
19. Whitman, M.E., Mattord, H.J.: Management of Information Security. Nelson Education, Toronto (2018)

System Requirements of Software-Defined IoT Networks for Critical Infrastructure

Filip Holik[✉][iD]

University of Pardubice, Studentska 95, 532 10 Pardubice, Czech Republic
filip.holik@upce.cz

Abstract. Critical infrastructure is becoming dependent on Internet of Things (IoT) sensors. These sensors measure various physical values and send them via a communication network in the form of electronic data. Data is then used by a management center for detailed analysis and system control. This technology can be used in various scenarios, from smart grid networks to autonomous vehicles. All these scenarios require innovative technologies in order to stay productive, efficient and resource friendly. These technologies include software-defined networks, which support network programmability. This allows rapid deployment of innovative applications, which can be dynamically adjusted as needs of the network change. The adjustment requires only a software modification which provides scalability of the solution. The key part of such a solution is quality of the control software application and the system configuration.

Currently, there is no unified methodology which would summarize the best practices for developing such a system. This paper provides a list of system requirements for software-defined IoT networks for critical infrastructure. This list is one of the key phases in every system development process. Use of the list can help with development of high quality, scalable, efficient, and secure SDN systems, which can be deployed in critical infrastructure scenarios.

Keywords: Critical infrastructure networks · IoT networks · Software-defined networks development · System requirements

1 Introduction

Critical infrastructure includes processes essential for proper functionality of a nation. It consist of assets, facilities, networks, services and technologies from the various sectors such as agriculture, commercial, communication, critical manufacturing, defense, chemical, energy, financial, government, health-care, information technology, transportation and water processing. To become more efficient, critical infrastructure has started to utilize IoT devices and internet connectivity. Although this approach offers many benefits, it also negatively influences security as is apparent from recent cyber attacks.

According to [14], the number of incidents on critical infrastructure increased from 39 in 2010 to 290 in 2016. Moreover, these attacks are becoming more

© Springer Nature Switzerland AG 2021
S. Yildirim Yayilgan et al. (Eds.): INTAP 2020, CCIS 1382, pp. 65–77, 2021.
https://doi.org/10.1007/978-3-030-71711-7_6

sophisticated and may have widespread consequences as was shown in recent attacks on electricity distribution in Ukraine. The first such attack caused a blackout affecting 225 000 customers in 2015 [18]. It started with attackers connecting remotely to the SCADA (Supervisory Control and Data Acquisition) management system and disconnecting several substations. Use of the *Industroyer* malware - a tool specifically developed to attack electrical grids - caused another significant power outage in 2016, disconnecting 20% of Kiev for one hour [5].

It is clear that use of modern technologies in critical networks must be carefully planned, monitored and controlled. One of the most effective approaches is software-defined networking (SDN), which can provide efficient central monitoring and network control. It also enables programmability, allowing for dynamic modification of network functions on demand. This includes security protection which has to be frequently updated.

Currently, the research in the area of SDN and critical infrastructure is very limited. Several general IoT architectures were proposed [12,16,20], but in critical infrastructure there is only one work: replacing traditional Intrusion Detection Systems by SDN to provide more simple network monitoring [15]. More research in the area is clearly needed and this paper aims to deliver the first relevant contribution.

1.1   Used Terminology

Software-defined Internet of Things Networks (SDIoTN) for critical infrastructure have to meet stringent requirements on safety and security. The critical element of every SDN system is its control application and correct configuration of the SDN core subsystem, which is composed from the SDN controller and the SDN-enabled networking devices. This terminology is depicted in the left part of Fig. 1.

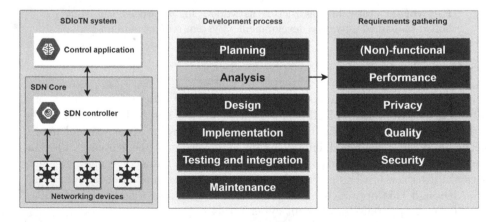

Fig. 1. Used terminology and the paper scope

1.2 Development Process of SDIoTN

A control application of SDIoTN for critical infrastructure must meet specific criteria, which can be verified during a certification process such as the ISO/IEC 27001 [2]. It is therefore important to follow the best practices set for a software system development. Several divergent methodologies exist for this development. The most general one is composed of the following phases:

1. Planning - identifies the project risks, costs and goals.
2. Analysis - requirements gathering.
3. Design - defines methods for achieving goals set in the analysis phase.
4. Implementation - programming of the application.
5. Testing and integration - deployment on a real infrastructure, performance monitoring and debugging.
6. Maintenance - evaluation and updates.

This paper is focused on the analysis phase - the requirements gathering as shown in Fig. 1. The requirements specify what the application does, what its inputs and outputs are, and how it will operate. In every development process, these requirements have to be gathered from various sources including interviews with system users and operators. Due to this fact, this phase is usually very time consuming and requires several iterations. By providing the list of requirements (in Sect. 2) this phase can be significantly sped up. Section 3 then summarizes SDN features, which can be used to accomplish requirements associated with the SDN core subsystem setting.

2 SDIoTN System Requirements

Requirements in this section are based on an extensive analysis of general IoT application requirements. This analysis used various sources [1,3,6–9,13,17,19] and found 48 applicable requirements. These requirements were then filtered and only ones applicable to SDN were taken into the account. The analysis was furthermore extended by additional requirements based on specifics of critical infrastructure networks. Identified requirements were merged into 29 requirement areas and classified into 5 sections described below.

It is important to mention that these requirements are applicable for a wide scope of general critical infrastructure applications and not all of them have to be used in each critical infrastructure sector. During the analysis phase, it is necessary to select and implement only the relevant ones. Implementation of unrelated ones would bring no advantages, but slow down the development and increase the solution cost.

2.1 Functional and Non-functional Requirements

These requirements specify what the application should do and how this behavior should be achieved [6].

Data caching - most of the IoT devices rely on battery power with a limited power. In this case, data collection and transmission is kept to minimum in order to ensure long-life operation without a need to replace a battery. The communication network has to be aware of specific transmission intervals and possible one-way communication. The SDN controller has to maintain information about allowed time intervals for communication with specific devices and support message caching for delivering these messages.

Data filtering - large-scale networks connect various IoT devices from different vendors. These devices can use incompatible data formats, which have to be converted, cleaned, de-duplicated and aggregated. This places high demands on data processing done by the back end system. The SDN controller can lower this load by intelligent filtering of duplicated messages before they are delivered to the back end system. If this filtering is performed on access layer networking devices, the solution can also reduce bandwidth utilization of core links.

Interoperability - the system should use open and standard application interfaces (APIs) for all necessary domains. This includes southbound APIs for communication with networking devices, northbound APIs for communication with external applications, westbound APIs for communication with other SDN controllers in the distributed architecture, and eastbound APIs for communication with legacy network protocols.

The most widely used protocols are OpenFlow for southbound communication and REST with JSON for northbound communication. It is also important to consider a suitable version of each protocol. For example, the OpenFlow protocol is available in 6 major versions and even when the newest one is 1.5.1, the 1.3 version is still the most widely supported [4].

Usability - user interface (UI) of the control application should use the common and responsive layout adapted to various types of devices (PC, laptops, smartphones, tablets). This can be achieved by relative positioning of control elements, adaptive page widths and dynamic navigation menus.

Maintainability - the application should use the modular architecture with minimal cohesion. This simplifies future development, speeds-up bug fixing and limits number of potential errors. Modules should use either internal APIs for maximum performance, or external APIs according to the interoperability principle.

Recoverability - the system should support creation of configuration and data backups and recovery from created files. This process might be manual, automatic or a combination of both.

2.2   Performance Requirements

Performance requirements should be defined as explicitly as possible, but only the essential ones should be used.

Bandwidth - defines the amount of data transferred between two devices over a certain time period. Each flow can have different bandwidth requirements. If a single physical link is shared between several flows, QoS might be used to comply with minimal bandwidth requirements. IoT networks are typically not too bandwidth demanding as they transmit relatively small amounts of data with low frequency. The challenge is only aggregated traffic on core links. These links have to be projected for the required bandwidth while taking anomaly situations into consideration, which can generate a lot of burst traffic.

Keepalive timeout - networking devices and the SDN controller are periodically exchanging Hello messages. If no such message is received within a specified keepalive interval (typically 3× - 4× longer than the Hello messages interval), the connection between the device and the controller is lost. The device then transitions into one of the fail-back modes: *fail-standalone* or *fail-secure*.

The settings of the Hello messages interval and the keepalive timeout should correspond to the application needs and infrastructure capabilities. Lower intervals can detect a failure quicker, but cause additional network load. A typical default setting is 10 s for Hello messages interval and 30 s for the keepalive timeout [11], but the specific setting is vendor dependent. More responsive applications require much lower values.

OpenFlow rules performance - includes multiple performance characteristics associated with the OpenFlow protocol. Not all of these characteristics must be defined - their specification depends on the application purpose. These characteristics include: maximum flow table capacity, maximum latency of a flow rule modification, maximum number of flow rule modifications per second, forwarding latency of software and hardware flow tables, and forwarding performance based on the flow table utilization.

Packet latency - is one-way packet delay on the entire path from the source to the destination. There are two types in SDN: latency of the first packet and the typical latency.

The first packet latency is associated only with establishment of a new data flow and it is much higher than the typical latency. A similar behavior is also present in traditional networks, if Address Resolution Protocol (ARP) has to firstly determine the target's MAC address, or if Domain Name System (DNS) has to resolve the IP address. SDN add another layer of complexity in a case that the flow rule is not present on the networking device. In this case, the device has to firstly contact the controller for further processing instructions. The controller must determine how to forward the packet and insert corresponding flow rules into all networking devices in the path (otherwise, each device will have to ask the controller for instructions).

The first packet latency is in average about 4 ms higher than typical latency of the following packets [10]. This time depends on the network conditions, load, topology and the SDN controller. The controller can use the proactive flow rule insertion method to insert rules in advance to eliminate this latency.

Typical latency - this type of latency represents most of the time in a communication between two devices and it is therefore the most accurate measurement for typical network operations. It is measured after flow rules are created (and inserted into all networking devices), end devices know MAC and IP addresses of other devices (no further ARP or DNS queries are required) and networking devices have mapping entries in port-to-mac structures.

Depending on the network size, load and used networking devices, the typical one-way latency in LAN environments can be under 0.1 ms [10].

Scalability - critical infrastructure must dynamically react on various unexpected situations such as disasters, outages and accidents. During these situations, the amount of generated data by IoT devices might significantly increase. The network must have sufficient resource reserves to handle these bursts. The network must be also prepared for future expansions and upgrades based on the topology growth.

Seamless connectivity - some of the IoT devices can be mobile and they might require continuous connectivity (autonomous vehicles, parts tracking, unmanned aerial vehicles). This requires seamless transitions between different communication gateways and in some cases network types. The SDN controller must monitor these data flows and modify forwarding accordingly.

Statistics polling frequency - the OpenFlow protocol uses the request/reply concept for collection of statistics. Request messages are sent from the controller in defined time intervals and networking devices reply with their statistics. The interval length depends on the application needs, but typically it is in a range of 1–60 s. A shorter interval provides more accurate insight into the network operation, while a longer interval reduces associated network overhead.

Throughput - is similar to bandwidth, but measures only the amount of usable data transferred between two devices over a certain time period. It is therefore always lower than bandwidth, which measures all data. The overhead of unusable data depends on used protocols and technologies. Each ISO/OSI layer adds its own header with additional control data.

Moreover, some protocols have features, which also affect throughput. An example is Transmission Control Protocol (TCP) and its receive window size. It specifies the maximum number of data, which can be sent before an acknowledgment from the receiving side is required. A higher value can achieve higher throughput. Encryption techniques (such as VPN) add even more overhead. A proper specification of the target throughput therefore requires knowledge of all used protocols and technologies.

2.3 Privacy Requirements

Privacy requirements significantly affect the system architecture and any future changes can lead to large scale modifications and increased cost. They can be classified into the following areas [7–9].

Aggregation - data processed within the system should be as general as possible, so identity of a specific user cannot be revealed. This includes OpenFlow rules created on the controller and inserted into networking devices. These rules can identify specific users via flow communication, determined by information such as source, destination and traffic type. Rules aggregation not only lowers chance of a privacy leak, but also saves the flow table capacity.

Anonymization and minimization - modern IT systems collect and log a large amount of data. The system should use metadata and fingerprinting to minimize this amount as much as possible. If applicable, data should be anonymized, so the users' privacy will not be violated in case of a security breach.

Encryption - sensitive data should be encrypted to prevent a misuse. Depending on the system scope, this might include data present in the application code, in the SDN controller, in networking devices and also data transferred during communication.

Enforcement and demonstration - system operators should comply with a privacy policy document, which clearly specifies rules for the system operation and sanctions for each breach of these rules. Supporting techniques such as privacy management, logging and auditing should be used for effective detection and handling of possible violations.

Transparency - all entities using and accessing the system have to be informed about what type of data is collected, how is it processed, and there has to be an option to control it. An example of this principle are cookie banners, which have been required in the EU since 2012.

Virtualization - certain data traffic flows can have higher potential for malicious content than others. An example is traffic from mobile devices, which cannot be managed by the organization's security staff. These flows should be virtually or physically separated from other traffic types in order to increase privacy protection.

2.4 Quality Requirements

Quality requirements describe mainly usage specifics of both the application and the system [13]. They are highly dependent on the system purpose and predicted life cycle.

Compatibility - the application must not negatively influence any part of the controller's architecture. It should use only built-in northbound APIs, or documented internal APIs of the controller. The application can optionally provide APIs to allow external access to its data.

Effectivity, efficiency and satisfaction - the application and the system should utilize only necessary hardware and software resources. The UI of the application should use standard design layouts and principles to provide intuitive control.

Maintainability and portability - the application should use the modular architecture and open APIs to support future modifications (potentially even a change of the SDN controller).

Reliability - is defined as availability over a longer time period. It can be specified for certain conditions such as during the typical operation, during a specific failure, etc. Based on the required level of reliability, advanced techniques for ensuring availability might be required (more in the availability section).

Safety - includes minimization of a potential loss of life, injury and equipment damage. This point is essential for safety-critical infrastructure such as smart grid networks and might require passing an official certification process.

2.5 Security Requirements

Security requirements significantly complicate the system development and their need should be carefully analyzed. These requirements have to be implemented into the system from the beginning as their later implementation can introduce vulnerabilities into the system architecture.

Authentication and authorization - user verification and role assignment should be required for access to private data. Each login attempt should be logged. It provides not only protection, but it is often required for legislative purposes.

Availability - includes the distributed controller architecture, redundant network devices and links, and an intelligent control application with protections against (D)DoS attacks. This might utilize techniques such as traffic limiting, use of access control lists and firewall rules.

Confidentiality and integrity - protection against unauthorized access and modifications can be achieved with data encryption. It should be implemented within the whole system - the application, the controller, and on all related communication links and network devices. Based on the system goals, encryption might be required only for sensitive information as it significantly increases complexity of the application development and future modifications.

Non-repudiation - all important actions performed by users and the system should be logged. This mechanism will ensure that every action is accounted and cannot be renounced. The information should include date, time, user (MAC and IP addresses, web browser, OS) or system event (corresponding code handler - function and class) and details of the action.

If the action is performed by the controller in reaction to an OpenFlow message, it should include details of this message such as type, code and associated networking device's ID.

3   SDN Features for Requirements Implementation

Requirements listed in Sect. 2 might require implementation within the control application, configuration of the SDN core, or the synergy of the entire SDIoTN system. This section describes SDN features for implementation of requirements, which need cooperation of the SDN core subsystem and cannot be implemented only within the control application. Features and the targeted requirements are summarized in the Table 1.

Backup communication paths - to achieve high availability, an instant transition between multiple links might be required. OpenFlow 1.1 introduced a concept of *group tables*, which allows multiple ports to be specified for various data forwarding. The *fast failover* group is ideal for implementation of backup communication paths, as data is forwarded to the first active port. Other groups can be used for flooding, multicasting and other specific forwarding.

Table 1. SDN features for requirements implementation

SDN feature	Main requirement targets
Backup communication paths	Availability
Distributed controllers architecture	Reliability, safety
Failover mechanism	Availability, reliability, safety
Hybrid SDN	Effectivity, keepalive timeout, portability
Load-balancing	Availability, bandwidth, effectivity, throughput
Proactive rule insertion	Latency, OpenFlow rules performance
Quality of Service	Bandwidth, latency, safety, throughput

Distributed controllers architecture - reliability can be ensured by redundancy on all system levels, including the SDN controller. The distributed controller architecture was introduced in OpenFlow protocol version 1.2 [4], and all advanced controllers (ONOS, OpenDaylight) support it.

Failover mechanism - compliance with safety might require specification of behavior for connection loss between networking devices and controllers. The failover mechanism specifies two modes: fail-standalone and fail-secure.

Fail-standalone - when a connectivity loss is detected, all the flow rules are removed from the flow tables and the networking device will transit into the legacy mode. In this case, it is important to configure the device for the legacy forwarding, so that it will behave desirably when the fault happens.

Fail-secure - in this mode, flow rules are kept in flow tables, unless their timers expire. The only flow rule, which will be removed immediately is the default one (forward to the controller). This approach allows preservation of the SDN functionality as it was in the moment of the failure. On the other hand, until the connectivity is restored, no new flow rules can be learned. This mode does not need any configuration of the legacy forwarding.

The choice of which mode to use, is a trade-off between availability and security. The fail-standalone mode can be easily configured to preserve basic connectivity, although no traffic filtering, QoS, or any other advanced features, implemented in SDN, will be present in the network. The fail-secure mode, on the other hand, can preserve these features, but there is a risk that some less active flows can lose connectivity (if their flow rules expire) and new flows will be automatically dropped (as there will be no associated flow rule).

Hybrid SDN - functionality of the legacy forwarding and SDN can be combined in various ways. The typical one is with support of networking devices. In this case, some networking functions might be left to the traditional mode of the device, and therefore do not have to be implemented in SDN. This can significantly simplify and speed up the application deployment process. Implementation of this principle uses the action called *normal* - all the flows corresponding to the rule with this action are forwarded to the traditional layer.

Load-balancing - redundant topology links can be used simultaneously for increased performance and availability. This mechanism also uses the *group tables* feature of the OpenFlow protocol with the type *select*. Algorithms for link selections are vendor specific, with the most common ones being hash and round-robin [4].

Proactive rule insertion - if the first packet latency in all cases must stay as low as possible, the proactive rule insertion method must be used. This will ensure sub-ms latency by creating and inserting flow rules before they are used. This technique requires intelligent decisions about rules composition and knowledge of the flow table utilization. Its use therefore significantly increases the application complexity.

Quality of Service - traffic classification and use of queues allow for the virtual separation of different traffic flows and ensure that they meet set performance criteria. Virtual separation can achieve similar results as use of multiple dedicated physical links, while making the solution much more efficient. The OpenFlow protocol supports different types of queues: guaranteed minimum rates (since version 1.0), guaranteed minimum and maximum rates (since version 1.2), and metered queues (since version 1.3).

4   Conclusion

Communication networks for critical infrastructure must utilize state of the art technologies to achieve strict safety, security and functionality requirements. SDN and IoT can deliver innovative functions and provide a platform for efficient network monitoring and control. In every system deployment it is however important to consider SDN benefits. Sometimes, the effort required to implement a feature in SDN does not pay off if compared to a similar solution in traditional networks. Examples of these cases are specific security and encryption technologies such as identity and access management, key management systems, VPNs and reputation and trust systems. In these scenarios, it is more efficient to utilize hybrid SDN to integrate features into the system, instead of programming them within SDN.

In all cases, quality of the SDIoTN system depends on appropriate system configuration and most importantly on quality of the control application. Only a properly designed and implemented code which utilizes recommended principles can be effectively used. Such a code can share its data and libraries with other applications, can be extended, and is easy to troubleshoot for any potential problems. The presented list of requirements and SDN features for their implementation can help to develop such software.

References

1. ISO/IEC 25010:2011. https://www.iso.org/standard/35733.html. Accessed 30 June 2020
2. ISO/IEC 27001 Information Security Management. https://www.iso.org/isoiec-27001-information-security.html. Accessed 23 June 2020
3. ISO/IEC 29100:2011. https://www.iso.org/standard/45123.html. Accessed 30 June 2020
4. Openflow switch specification, version 1.5.1 (protocol version 0x06). https://www.opennetworking.org/wp-content/uploads/2014/10/openflow-switch-v1.5.1.pdf. Accessed 30 June 2020
5. Industroyer: Biggest malware threat to critical infrastructure since Stuxnet (2017). https://www.eset.com/int/industroyer/. Accessed 01 July 2020
6. Bauer, M., et al.: Internet of Things - architecture IoT-a deliverable D1.5 - final architectural reference model for the IoT v3.0 (2013)
7. Eckhoff, D., Wagner, I.: Privacy in the smart city-applications, technologies, challenges, and solutions. IEEE Commun. Surv. Tutor. **20**(1), 489–516 (2018)
8. Finn, R.L., Wright, D., Friedewald, M.: Seven types of privacy. In: Gutwirth, S., Leenes, R., de Hert, P., Poullet, Y. (eds.) European Data Protection: Coming of Age, pp. 3–32. Springer, Dordrecht (2013). https://doi.org/10.1007/978-94-007-5170-5_1
9. Hoepman, J.-H.: Privacy design strategies. In: Cuppens-Boulahia, N., Cuppens, F., Jajodia, S., Abou El Kalam, A., Sans, T. (eds.) SEC 2014. IAICT, vol. 428, pp. 446–459. Springer, Heidelberg (2014). https://doi.org/10.1007/978-3-642-55415-5_38
10. Holik, F.: Meeting smart city latency demands with SDN. In: Huk, M., Maleszka, M., Szczerbicki, E. (eds.) ACIIDS 2019. SCI, vol. 830, pp. 43–54. Springer, Cham (2020). https://doi.org/10.1007/978-3-030-14132-5_4
11. Holik, F., Broadbent, M., Findrik, M., Smith, P., Race, N.: Safe and secure software-defined networks for smart electricity substations. In: Sitek, P., Pietranik, M., Krótkiewicz, M., Srinilta, C. (eds.) ACIIDS 2020. CCIS, vol. 1178, pp. 179–191. Springer, Singapore (2020). https://doi.org/10.1007/978-981-15-3380-8_16
12. Jararweh, Y., et al.: SDIoT: a software defined based Internet of Things framework. J. Ambient Intell. Humaniz. Comput. **6**(4), 453–461 (2015)
13. Kakarontzas, G., Anthopoulos, L., Chatzakou, D., Vakali, A.: A conceptual enterprise architecture framework for smart cities: a survey based approach. In: 2014 11th International Conference on e-Business (ICE-B), pp. 47–54 (2014)
14. Noguchi, M., Ueda, H.: An analysis of the actual status of recent cyberattacks on critical infrastructures. NEC Tech. J. **12**, 19–24 (2018)
15. Lallo, R., et al.: Leveraging SDN to monitor critical infrastructure networks in a smarter way. In: 2017 IFIP/IEEE Symposium on Integrated Network and Service Management, pp. 608–611 (2017)
16. Vilalta, R., et al.: Improving security in Internet of Things with software defined networking. In: 2016 IEEE Global Communications Conference (GLOBECOM), pp. 1–6 (2016)

17. Rathore, M.M., Ahmad, A., Paul, A., Rho, S.: Urban planning and building smart cities based on the Internet of Things using big data analytics. Comput. Netw. **101**, 63–80 (2016)
18. Lee, R.M., Assante, M.J., Conway, T.: Analysis of the cyber attack on the Ukrainian power grid. Technical report (2016). https://ics.sans.org/media/E-ISAC_SANS_Ukraine_DUC_5.pdf. Accessed 01 July 2020
19. Schlegel, R., Obermeier, S., Schneider, J.: A security evaluation of IEC 62351. J. Inf. Secur. Appl. **34**, 197–204 (2016)
20. Varadharajan, V., Tupakula, U.: Software defined networks based security architecture for IoT infrastructures. Technical report, The University of Newcastle (2019). https://isif.asia/software-defined-networks-based-security-architecture-for-iot-infrastructures/. Accessed 02 July 2020

An Optimized IoT-Based Waste Collection and Transportation Solution: A Case Study of a Norwegian Municipality

Wajeeha Nasar[✉], Anniken Th. Karlsen, Ibrahim A. Hameed, and Saumitra Dwivedi

Norwegian University of Science and Technology, Trondheim, Norway
{wajeehan,saumitrd}@stud.ntnu.no, {anniken.t.karlsen,ibib}@ntnu.no

Abstract. Smart and sustainable solid waste management systems (SWMS) are of major interest in the development of smart sustainable cities (SSC). Selective waste collection and transportation are known to be major expenditures of city waste management systems. In this paper, we investigate a waste management system for domestic waste in a Norwegian municipality as a case study. Different scenarios for route planning are considered to improve cost and time usage. The study provides an auxiliary management system for multi-objective TSP using Google Maps and operation research (OR) tools for optimal domestic waste collection. Additionally, a prediction model for scheduling future waste collection trips is provided, whereby challenges such as road conditions, road traffic, CO_2 and other gases emissions, and fuel consumption are considered. The proposed prediction model considers the hazards associated with food waste bins that need to be emptied more frequently than bins containing other waste types such as plastic and paper. Both proposed models signify consistency and correctness.

Keywords: Cost and time effective · Domestic waste · IoT technologies · Multi-objective optimization · Route length · Smart and sustainable solutions · Smart waste bins · Solid waste management · Smart sustainable city · Traveling salesman problem

1 Introduction

The smart city paradigm encompasses important factors that can affect the society in terms of smart economy, smart traffic, smart health, smart energy, a smart municipality and so on. These factors are interlinked with ICT technologies and the use of Internet of things' (IoTs) applications for the development of a smart city. A smart sustainable city (SSC) can be defined as [11]:

"An innovative city that uses information and communication technologies (ICTs) and other means to improve quality of life, efficiency of urban

© Springer Nature Switzerland AG 2021
S. Yildirim Yayilgan et al. (Eds.): INTAP 2020, CCIS 1382, pp. 78–90, 2021.
https://doi.org/10.1007/978-3-030-71711-7_7

operation and services, and competitiveness, while ensuring that it meets the needs of present and future generations with respect to the economic, social, environmental, as well as cultural aspects."

Pertaining to urbanization and climate change, waste management is an important focus of many cities and municipalities [1]. There are ongoing initiatives taken by governments and public authorities around the world to manage waste collection and its disposal. With the growth of ICT technologies and infrastructure facilities in economically developing countries, the implementation of smart and sustainable solid waste management system (SWMS) has become a key objective. Internet of Things (IoT) technologies enable new services and reshapes existing technologies in SSC. IoT represents an internet evolution known as the next generation of the internet (i.e., the Fourth Industrial Revolution) [2]. Equipping waste bins with IoT-based sensors provides a smarter future for waste management.

Generally, solid waste refers to the solid material in a flow pattern that is discarded as useless or unwanted by society. It includes organic and inorganic waste materials which have lost their value to the first user in categories of domestic waste, industrial waste, commercial and institutional waste. In turn, solid waste management (SWM) involves waste sorting, collection, recycling, and transportation.

There are different key indicators proposed for SSC and the SWM key performance indicators (KPIs) organized in the environmental category by the United for Smart Sustainable Cities (U4SSC) EU report [11]. In our research, a set of cores and supporting SWM KPIs was used to find the optimal way for waste collection from the waste bins. The intelligent way of waste collection links with complex tasks such as route planning and planning for transportation networks.

In this paper we focus on the optimal transportation problem where the solution for domestic waste collection relates to achieving minimal route length along with reduced fuel consumption, and minimal associated costs and work time [12]. Correspondingly, smart waste management also reduces the emissions of CO_2 and other gases in the environment due to the reduction in unnecessary trips to waste bins.

The paper is structured as follows: Sect. 2 presents a literature review in the area of smart sustainable solid waste management systems for smart cities. The current practices and main features of the case study are described in Sect. 3. The multi-objective TSP and prediction model used to implement the developed smart, cost, and time effective, sustainable waste management system are described in Sect. 4. Section 5 concludes the paper and Sect. 6 provides future recommendations.

2   Literature Review

A solid waste management system (SWMS) includes waste collection, sorting, recycling, and transportation. The area of route planning and optimizing logistics purposes has contributed to the development of hundreds of intelligent transportation systems. Even so, there are still many projects going on, all around the world, to provide effective and efficient systems for waste collection and management. The waste collection and transportation problems are also considered as combinatorial optimization problem [8,12,13]. Different techniques in literature are used to solve this problem. For instance, a dynamic decision model (DSS) which is integrated in a GIS- based decision support system is proposed by Anghinolfi et al. [6]. In [7] five routes in different areas of Ipoh city of Malaysia are optimized to reduce the length of the routes collectively in terms of time required to complete the tasks. GIS tools and a combinatorial optimization technique are used to minimize collection time, operational and transportation costs whilst enhancing the current solid waste collection practices [8].

In [9] the optimization of vehicle routes and the planning for municipal solid waste collection in Eastern Finland is described. The solutions are generated by a developed guided variable neighborhood thresholding meta-heuristic that is adapted to solve real-life waste collection problems. In [10] a dynamic routing algorithm is proposed for a situation whereby a truck is overloaded or damaged and needs a replacement. The solution also incorporates a system model which assumes two types of trucks for waste collection, a low capacity truck and a high capacity truck. By incorporating high capacity trucks, the researchers in [10] achieved a reduction in waste collection operational costs because of a reduced need for trips to waste bins.

In [5] an advanced DSS for efficient waste collection in smart cities is proposed. The proposed system integrates a model for real-time data sharing among truck drivers for waste collection and adaptive route optimization. Furthermore, the proposed system can handle inadequate waste collection in problematic areas and provide evidence to the authorities.

[12] proposes an optimal transportation solution of classified garbage that improves the sustainability of the present practices and considers a city of China as a case study. In [13] an optimization model for municipal solid waste (MSW) collection and transportation through heuristic solutions is proposed. The proposed heuristic solutions minimize the route length which efficiently reduces waste collection and transportation cost.

The mentioned publications have inspired and directed our research development of a visualization tool providing insight into optimal route lengths and plans for waste collection trips. An optimization model is embedded into the tool to achieve the shortest possible route for collecting waste in minimum time and cost.

3   Current Practices and Main Features - A Case Study

Generally, system architecture for waste management has two main targets [12]. The first target is to provide software as a service (SaaS) for service provider companies. These companies own their own waste trucks, hire the truck drivers, give contracts to other companies for performing different tasks and pass waste for recycling or recovering other profitable values from waste [12]. The second target is to develop a system focusing on cooperative communication among all the stakeholders involved in the chain of development of a smart sustainable city.

The current solid waste management practices and infrastructure for domestic waste have three different types of waste bins for selective waste collection as shown in Fig. 2. The sensor-based waste collection bins notify the volume of waste in bins, if it is filled or empty to schedule the trip for waste collection truck drivers as shown in Fig. 6. However, the lack of optimal transportation is a major concern in current practices. This technical gap makes the current solutions time and cost inefficient which effects the listed stakeholders of the investigated municipality. A list of possible stakeholders and their roles in SWM is presented below:

1. *City administration* must understand the broad picture of waste management such as generating reports and ensuring overprice control etc.
2. *District administrations* are interested in controlling the waste collection process and checking the quality of services (QoS) to resolve disputes and problems effectively.
3. *Waste management companies* need a system for organizing and optimizing their business processes without the need for large investments in developing, deploying, and supporting such a system.
4. *Waste truck drivers* need optimal solutions for smart navigation to fulfill their tasks. Some major needs are automatic insight into route lengths, road traffic, and the ability to report problems to operators in the office, instead of wasting time in thinking how to solve the problem themselves.
5. *Managers of disposal sites and recycling plants* can publish their needs or possibilities for obtaining certain amounts of waste for recycling.
6. *Traffic police* can get reports on unpleasant incidents that have caused hazards in waste collection processes.
7. *Citizens* are interested in and can experience better services at lower costs through an improved waste collection system.

All these stakeholders are generally interdependent in smart and sustainable municipality using IoT technologies and it is possible to develop plenty of system usage scenarios to fulfill each stakeholder's need. In what follows, we present our insight into the development of a time and cost effective optimal SWM system addressing current practices and infrastructure for reduction in route length, fuel consumption, CO_2 and other gases emissions. A prediction model is embedded into the system to enable the planning of trips for waste trucks drivers based on prediction of the level of waste volume in bins. With this prediction model in place, future trips for selective waste collection can be planned in an improved manner compared to current practices.

3.1 Challenges and Risks

Waste collection and transportation are well-known challenges in many cities or municipalities. In the case we studied, the challenges and risks for the municipality to deploy a smart and sustainable SWMS were subject for investigation. The following challenges were collected and taken into consideration when developing the prediction model:

1. *Narrow and steep roads* in the city center make the task of collecting waste sometimes impossible for waste collection trucks.
2. *Busy roads* are one of the major concerns in the current infrastructure. At present, there is no optimal template for truck drivers to pursue whilst planning trips for waste collection. Present practices are cost and time inefficient.
3. *Non-environment friendly* and non-optimal ways of waste collection cause delays which can create an uncomfortable and unsanitary environment in the neighborhood.
4. *Location of Waste bins* in the municipality is also an issue. Many bins are allocated relatively far away from the road. It is quite challenging and time-consuming for truck drivers to collect waste from such locations as shown in Fig. 1-a.
5. *Open Bins* is a problem becoming rare with the growth of urbanization, but still present in some areas thereby causing unpleasant odor and sight for inhabitants as shown in Fig. 1-b.

At the initial stage of our research, the proposed solution for addressing challenges in current practices and infrastructure focused on the city center where there are narrow and steep roads with normal size waste bins. Various types of waste bins for selective waste collection are scattered around the city as shown in Fig. 2. Due to extreme weather and road conditions in present practices are time-consuming and cost inefficient for trucks with waste collection done in a non-optimal manner. The service providers need to spend a lot of money on feasible trucks able to function in such challenging locations. The smart and sustainable SWMS we propose, considers current practices and infrastructure of the municipality where waste truck drivers among others report on their inability to collect waste in rush hours. Evidently traffic and conjugation on roads increase fuel consumption and CO_2 emissions in the environment and is both cost and time consuming.

4   Waste Collection Models

In a case like this, smart decisions depend on details of the surroundings and require geographical information to help distinguish one place from another and to make appropriate decisions for that location [14]. Recent developments in ICT have opened-up vast potentials in communication and in, spatial and temporal data analysis. It is possible to store and process data representing the real world for later presentation in simplified form for suitable needs. In the waste generation model, geographical information of the city is viewed through Google Maps. The Google Maps app has its own Geo-analytical tools and can perform network analysis. It enables traffic and driving queries [15]. Google Maps provides rich, multi-layered maps that are proved easy to combine with our data and third-party data. It also provides various features such as maps, street view, routes, directions, distance matrix, roads, time zone, places details and so on [15], making it a relevant tool in systems development.

Fig. 1. Challenges and risks in the city (a) Waste bins located aside from the roads, (b) Open Waste bins

Fig. 2. Types of waste bins (top-Standard underground waste bins, left bottom-Sensor-based underground bins, right bottom-normal bins)

4.1 Optimization Model

Fig. 3. Optimized shortest route length with estimated cost, distance, and time via multi-objective TSP

For the development of the waste generation model, data collected from standard underground and sensor-based underground waste bins was analyzed. In general, an optimized waste collection and transportation scheme effectively reduces the cost for waste collection and transportation and tends to minimize the route length of each trip for transportation. Studies related to these problems are generally divided into three categories with respect to the number of disposal sites [14].

Table 1. Traveling time and distance covered by vehicle

Traveling time	2.58 h
Traveling distance	136.4 km
Route for vehicle	$0->3->1->9->5->2->4->7->6->8->0$

- Single disposal site, single route
- Single disposal site, multiple routes
- Multiple disposal sites, multiple routes

The following are important aspects of waste collection associated with our case:

- Number of trucks: There is one vehicle available at a time for selective waste collection and its optimized route is shown in Table 1.
- *Starting and Stopping points*: The starting and ending points along with the number of stopping points are known to the drivers. A starting point indicates the truck's starting location and the ending point is normally the recycling site or the landfills site.
- *Selective Waste type*: In the investigated case, different types of sorted selective waste collection bins are placed at each residential area. For each selective waste collection, there are dedicated trucks in this Norwegian municipality shown in Fig. 2. Usually two disposal sites are used to dispose waste collected from selective waste bins. One disposal site for recycling of waste such as paper, cardboard, plastic, glass and metal and another disposal site for residual and food waste.

The waste collection and transportation problem can be solved by the traveling salesman problem (TSP) [14]. Generally, TSP is known as a NP-hard problem and there is no polynomial time algorithm for obtaining its exact solution [14]. TSP can be defined as:

A list of cities N and the distances between each pair of cities is given. The traveling salesman must find the shortest possible route to visit each city and return to the origin city.

TSP can be classified as single-objective optimization problem (SOP) such as calculating optimal routes with minimal length, and as multi-objective optimization problem (MOO) such as calculating optimal routes with minimum cost, time, distance and so on [16]. The problem can be represented graphically as [16]:

$$G = (V, E) \tag{1}$$

where $V = v_1, v_2...., v_N$ is a set of N nodes and E is a set of edges. While the distance d_{ij} and time t_{ij} are associated with each edge $(v_i, v_j) \in E$ respectively as in Fig. 5. In the investigated case, we are classifying TSP as MOO which can be represented as [18]:

$$TSP_{MOO} = \left\{ min \ F(x) = (f_1(x), f_2(x), ..., f_m(x)) \quad \text{s.t.} \quad x \in S \right. \tag{2}$$

where $F(x)$ is the objective vector; $m \geq 2$ is the number of objective functions; $x = (x_1, x_2, ..., x_n)$ is the decision variable vector where n is the of cities/waste bins; x is a permutation of $1, 2, ..., n$ that minimizes $F(x)$. S is feasible solution space. The set $O = F(S)$ corresponds to the feasible solution in the objective space, and $y = (y_1, y_2, y_3, .., y_m)$, where $y_i = f_i(x)$ is a solution. For the TSP under consideration, m = 2 where $f_1(x) = traveling \ distance$ and $f_2(x) = traveling \ time$ [16].

An OR-tool solves the optimization problems by computing the cost of transportation by distance matrix between two nodes (x_i, y_i), (x_j, y_j) is calculated using Manhattan distance which sum up the absolute distance of $x \ and \ y$ coordinates respectively in Table 1 and Fig. 3. This can be mathematically obtained as [20]:

$$C = |x_i - x_j| + |y_i - y_j| \quad where \quad i \neq j \tag{3}$$

The mathematical representation of the stated problem is as follows:

$$min \begin{cases} f_1 = \sum_{i,j=1,i\neq j}^{N} d_{ij}c_{ij} \\ f_2 = \sum_{i,j=1,i\neq j}^{N} t_{ij}c_{ij} \end{cases} \tag{4}$$

where

$$\begin{cases} c_{i,j,i\neq j} = 1, & if \ bi, j \geq \gamma \\ c_{i,j,i\neq j} = 0, & elsewhere \end{cases} \tag{5}$$

In here, d_{ij} is the distance between nodes $i \ and \ j$, c_{ij} is the collection decision. If $c_{ij} = 0$, then the nodes do not belong to the optimal route, the truck does not visit the between the i_{th} bin and j_{th} bin. The optimization model shows the optimal shortest route for waste collection with minimum driving time, driving distance, driving cost in Fig. 3 and 4. The locations of waste bins are pinned in a map to visualize the route for selective waste collection. The route is established according to a threshold of waste volume. The threshold γ is set according to current practices, i.e., if the waste volume reaches or exceeds the set threshold. The γ is calculated by the waste volume in the bin over the total number of opening of lid. The truck driver schedules a trip for waste collection accordingly. The optimization model achieves the following aimed solid waste key performance indicators (KPIs) [11]:

1. Reduction in fuel combustion.
2. Reduction of the CO_2 emissions in environment.
3. Reduction in unnecessary road traffic.
4. Improved cost and time effectiveness.
5. Minimization of route length.
6. Reduction in the trips for drivers due to optimal planning solutions.

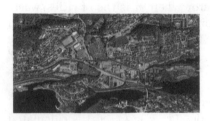

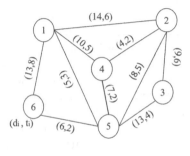

Fig. 4. Satellite view with optimal routes by TSP

Fig. 5. MOO-TSP representation with edges- traveling distance and time, and nodes b_N

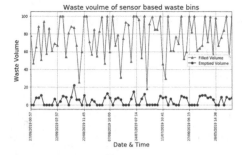

Fig. 6. Waste volume gather through sensors

High Threshold Fillup Date

#	Garbage Bin ID	Next Fill up Date
0	7001	2020-01-25
1	7003	2020-01-26
2	7010	2020-01-26
3	7013	2020-01-25
4	7018	2020-01-25
5	7020	2020-01-29
6	7023	2020-01-25
7	7026	2020-01-26
8	7031	2020-01-28
9	7034	2020-01-25
10	7038	2020-01-28
11	7044	2020-01-29
12	7045	2020-01-28
13	7046	2020-01-28
14	7050	2020-01-27

Fig. 7. Prediction model for trips scheduling

4.2 Prediction Model

According to the current practices of the investigated municipality, the total volume of waste collected in 2019 from domestic sensor-based bins is 930.40 m^3. The sensors tracked waste volume of each bin to update the database. One of the major problems in current practices is that trips scheduled for waste collection are often overlooked or delayed. This causes an unsanitary environment. The proposed optimal SWMS solves the delaying problem by using a prediction model. In our case, the prediction model is scheduling trips for waste collection truck drivers as illustrated in Fig. 4. The prediction coefficient (γ) predicts waste volume for each bin. In the prediction model dummy variables are used to predict time *(t)* for the next trip and driving cost of each trip as shown in Fig. 7 and 6.

$$\gamma = waste\ volume_{threshold}$$

$$\nabla\ volume = \gamma * t$$

Table 2. Time and cost comparison between current practices and the developed data-driven solution

Route	Waste type	Waste bins b_N	Current practices		Developed practices		Cost Saving %
			Time (hours)	Cost (NOK)	Time (hours)	Cost (NOK)	
1	Paper	b_1, b_2	1.50	1207.0	0.57	459.0	62.0
2	Residual	b_1, b_2, b_3	2.06	1661.0	1.09	877.0	47.0
3	Paper	b_1, b_2, b_3, b_4	2.50	2013.0	1.55	1248.0	38.0
4	Paper	b_1, b_2, b_3, b_4, b_5	3.00	2348.0	2.42	1984.0	17.0
5	Residual	b_1, b_2, b_3, b_4, b_5	3.00	2348.0	2.42	1984.0	17.0
6	Plastic	b_1, b_3, b_5, b_6	3.20	2576.0	2.00	1610.0	37.5
Total			15.27	12153.0	10.05	8090.0	33.4

5 Discussion and Conclusion

Smart and sustainable solid waste management systems are main concerns for smart sustainable municipality development initiatives. This paper present findings from the investigation of current infrastructure and practices of waste collection from waste bins and its transportation in a municipality, and provides a solution to achieve smarter ways for waste collection. The objective of achieving solid waste KPIs is fulfilled to some extent and optimized multi-objective TSP algorithm used to find the shortest route length in minimal time for each trip. The route planning is based on the prediction model. In the developed data driven solution, the historic data is used for implementing an optimization model and a prediction model. The solution can easily integrate real-time data to predict and plan trips for truck drivers with minimal cost, distance and time. The time (in hours) and cost (in Norwegian kroner) comparison between current and a data-driven practice is shown in Table 2 and in Fig. 8. The bar graphs based on Table 2 clearly show that the smart and sustainable SWMS is cost and time effective. In the table, six different routes are used to calculate the driving time, driving cost and driving distance between current practices and the developed data-driven system. The 33.4% saving cost shows that the data-driven system is more profitable than the existing one. In these routes, the truck drivers are subject to selective waste collection from different bins $b_1, b_2, ..., b_N$ and the routes are calculated by MOO-TSP. The developed system is data-driven as it is based on analysis of the data retrieved from current practices and infrastructure which is practical and helpful for future developments.

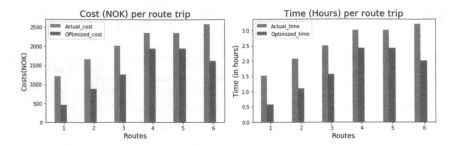

Fig. 8. Comparison between Proposed system and current system

6   Future Recommendations

In this research, the focus is to contribute insights into building an optimal solution for the sensors and for the standard underground waste bins scattered around a Norwegian municipality. A next step towards smart and sustainable SWMS development process can be to integrate the developed optimized solution into a generic waste management system. This can then easily integrate future developments such as multiple disposal sites and multiple routes such as MOO-mTSP.

The tasks regarding developing a waste management system usually include waste collection, sorting, recycling and transportation. This paper focuses on MOO waste collection and transportation by finding the shortest path with minimal cost and time usage. It can be extended for smart sorting and recycling with the help of IoT technologies such as cameras, actuators and wireless networks. For instance, the sensors can be modified for smart sorting to sense and classify the waste material. The waste management system can also be modified by studying and taking into account the behavior of inhabitants as regards how their age and general living conditions for example influence the waste production, sorting and management.

The multi-objective can also be used in many other applications where the developers need to solve such a problem with achieving multi-objectives such as printing scheduling, mission planning and so on.

Acknowledgment. This work is supported by the project Smart Circular City. We thank Espen L. Mikkelborg for his extraordinary support in this research process.

A   Current Technologies

Senor-based waste bins transmit data in real-time through wireless networks to the BioEnable waste management system. 2G and 3G telecommunication modules available through WCDMZ and GSM networks for data transfer. One of the main problems in current SWM practices is lack of optimal solutions which affects the SSC goals for SWMS.

References

1. https://www.environment.no/Topics/Waste (2016)
2. Pardini, K., Rodrigues, J.J.P.C., Kozlov, S.A., Kumar, N., Furtado, V.: IoT-based solid waste management solutions a survey. J. Sens. Actuator Network **8**(5), 5 (2019)
3. Weber, M., Lucic, D., Lovrek, I.: Internet of Things context of the smart city. In: IEEE Conference Publications, pp. 187–193 (2017)
4. Navghane, S.S., Killedar, M.S., Rohokale, V.M.: IoT based smart garbage and waste collection bin. Int. J. Adv. Res. Electron. Commun. Eng. (IJARECE) **5**(5), 1576 (2016)
5. Medvedev, A., Fedchenkov, P., Zaslavsky, A., Anagnostopoulos, T., Khoruzhnikov, S.: Waste management as an IoT-enabled service in smart cities. In: Balandin, S., Andreev, S., Koucheryavy, Y. (eds.) ruSMART 2015. LNCS, vol. 9247, pp. 104–115. Springer, Cham (2015). https://doi.org/10.1007/978-3-319-23126-6_10
6. Anghinolfi, D., Paolucci, M., Robba, M., Taramasso, A.: A dynamic optimization model for solid waste recycling. Waste Manag. **33**(2), 287–296 (2013)
7. Malakahmad, A., Md Bakri, P., Radin Md Mokhtar, M., Khalil, N.: Solid waste collection routes optimization via GIS techniques in Ipoh city, Malaysia. Procedia Eng. **77**, 20 (2013)
8. Arribas, C.A., Blazquez, C.A., Lamas, A.: Urban solid waste collection system using mathematical modelling and tools of geographic information systems. Waste Manag. Res. **28**(4), 355–363 (2010)
9. Nuortio, T., Kytöjoki, J., Niska, H., Bräysy, O.I.: Improved route planning and scheduling of waste collection and transport. Expert Syst. Appl. **30**(2), 223–232 (2006)
10. Anagnostopoulos, T., Zaslavsky, A., Medvedev, A.: Robust waste collection exploiting cost efficiency of IoT potentiality in smart cities. In: International Conference on Recent Advances in Internet of Things (RIoT), Singapore, pp. 1–6 (2015)
11. Recommendation ITU-T Y.4900/L.1600: Overview of key performance indicators in smart sustainable cities, International Telecoms Union (2016). https://ec.europa.eu/futurium/en/urban-agenda
12. Xiaocui Lou, C., Shuai, J., Luo, L., Li, H.: Optimal transportation planning of classified domestic garbage based on map distance. J. Environ. Manag. **254**, 109781 (2020)
13. Das, S.W., Bhattacharyya, B.K.R.: Optimization of municipal solid waste collection and transportation routes. Waste Manag. **43**, 9–18 (2015)
14. Del Borghi, A., Gallo, M., Del Borghi, M.: A survey of life cycle approaches in waste management. Int. J. Life Cycle Assess. **14**, 597–610 (2009)
15. https://developers.google.com/optimization
16. Hameed, I.A.: Multi-objective solution of traveling salesman problem with time. In: Hassanien, A.E., Azar, A.T., Gaber, T., Bhatnagar, R., F. Tolba, M. (eds.) AMLTA 2019. AISC, vol. 921, pp. 121–132. Springer, Cham (2020). https://doi.org/10.1007/978-3-030-14118-9_13
17. Nasar, W., Karlsen, A.T.H., Hameed, I.A.: A Conceptual Model of an IoT-based Smart and Sustainable Solid Waste Management System for a Norwegian Municipality. Accepted in Communications of the ECMS, vol. 34, no. 1 (2020)
18. Jozefowiez, N., Glover, F., Laguna, M.: Multi-objective Meta-heuristics for the traveling salesman problem with profits. J. Math. Model. Algorithms **7**, 177–195 (2008)

19. Weisstein, E.W.: Traveling salesman problem. Mathworld-a wolfram web resources (2010). http://mathworld.wolfram.com/TravelingSalemanProblem.html
20. Ibrahim, A., Rabiat, A., Jeremiah, I.: Capacitated vehicle routing problem. Int. J. Res. Granthaalayah **7**, 310–327 (2019)

Health and AI

Machine Learning Based Methodology for Depressive Sentiment Analysis

Emaduddin Shah[1], Muhammad Kamran Ahsan[2], and Ibtesam Mazahir[3]($\boxtimes$)

[1] College of Computing and Information Sciences, Karachi Institute of Economics and Technology, Karachi, Pakistan
[2] Department of Computer Science, Federal Urdu University for Arts, Science and Technology, Karachi, Pakistan
[3] Department of Media Science, Bahria University Karachi Campus, Karachi, Pakistan
ibtesam.bukc@bahria.edu.pk

Abstract. Depression is one of the most common and growing mental disorder advancing at a very fast pace. Despite of the availability of medication and cure, a number of people yet to receive such treatment due to the lack of information regarding the symptoms and occurrence of the depression. Here we propose a text based information systems for the diagnosis of symptoms of depression based on machine learning algorithms. This systems works on textual data collected from different social media sources or search engine queries like FaceBook, Twitter, Google Search and YouTube etc. and analyze them against a system trained with depressive sentiments with different machine learning based algorithms. The systems classify the queries with stress and without stress. A comparative analysis is conducted to evaluate the performance of different ML algorithms in the domain of subject.

Keywords: Depression detection · Text classification · Sentiment analysis · Assistive technology

1 Introduction

Depression is classified as one of the major growing cognitive illnesses occurs due to occurrence of negative emotions and behavior. It is sadness, loss of interest, low self-esteems, and lack of concentration impairing ability to work properly in routine life [1]. It is reported that almost 65% of the population have episodes of depression in their lifetime [2–4]. It can even lead into suicidal attempt. There could be a number of reasons for depression. These includes difficulty in partnership, occupational stress, isolation, unemployment, negative social influences, frustration, early childhood trauma, physical, sexual or emotional abuse, consistent personal conflicts, financial loss, death of a beloved one, failure in job or exam. Family history of depression sometimes also contributes to the risk of depression [5, 6]. There is no particular age group that is more sensitive to depression but the frequencies are higher in people aging from 24–44 [7]. Although medication for curing depression is available still more than 50% don't receive such treatment [7] due to social pressure in some societies (Fig. 1).

© Springer Nature Switzerland AG 2021
S. Yildirim Yayilgan et al. (Eds.): INTAP 2020, CCIS 1382, pp. 93–99, 2021.
https://doi.org/10.1007/978-3-030-71711-7_8

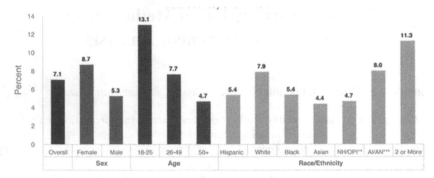

Fig. 1. Depression statistics take from [8]

On the other hand, enhancement in ICT and use of digital and social media applications has increased dramatically in past few years [9, 10]. Information collected from different social media application like FaceBook, Twitter, Instagram, YouTube could be very useful in exploiting personality trait of the person and physiological analysis of different diseases particularly stress and depression. In this paper, we have proposed a novel mechanism for the identification of stress and depression based on text classification. In this non clinical method, we have exploited the information contained by textual data in order to find the occurrence on depression at a very preliminary level.

We propose a mobile application based on machine learning algorithms which works on sentiment analysis and text classification technique. We believe that this application will work in similar fashion in the diagnosis of stress and depression as other gadgets do in the monitoring of glucose and blood pressure.

2 Materials and Methods

There are several techniques for finding personality traits, occurrence of stress and depression. These method includes emojis [11], voice pitch [12], body language [13], eye gaze [14]. Speech-based and text-based methods are also available [15, 16] and widely used to support clinicians in order to diagnose depressions in the patients.

Authors in paper [17] claims that textual depression detection methods could have similar performance as multi model methods do. They proposed a multi task model for the presence of depression along with severity. The model uses pre trained word embedding. However the practicing psychologist often debate that at the serve stage of depression the patient often refrain oneself from the society and social media. Therefore, in this study, we not only detect and classify depression using five different machine learning algorithms including Naïve Bayes, Decision Tree, Support Vector Machine, Stochastic Gradient Descent and Random Forest but also urge the importance of balanced class in our proposed methodology (Fig. 2).

Stress and depression recognition from sentence delegated positive or negative utilizing lexical investigation is one of the classical approaches being utilized for sentiment analysis [18]. We utilized a comparable methodology proposed by [19]. We utilize these assessment vocabularies to recognize the event stress and depression in an individual.

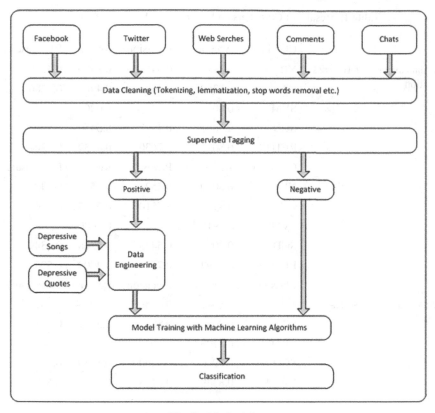

Fig. 2. Methodology

For this reason, we utilize the sentiments of information marked as depression positive or depression negative.

For this purpose we need a data set of communication i.e. chats, comments and posts. We created this data set by crawling Twitter, a social media application for sharing micro blogs. People often use Twitter for sharing their feeling and views about a particular event or subject. Crawling was done using Twitters API available as open source. We initially collected more than 250,000 tweets. These tweets contains a lot of textual noise in the form of names, symbols, improper use of language or grammatical rules, tweets in other languages and unwanted links. These tweets also contains re-tweets or duplicated tweets.

The dataset was then cleaned from such noises and duplicated. A random sample of 2400 tweets was selected for further processing. Three independent practicing psychologist were hired to label these tweets as depression position or negative. The data set was exploited with the inclusion of several other data including depressive songs and quotes in several combination. The data set was divided into two parts for the purpose of training and testing. State of the art machine learning algorithm i.e. naïve bayes, decision trees, support vector machine, stochastic gradient decent and random forest tree are used to obtained the results available in Table 1 below.

Table 1. Results of Classifiers on Different combination of data

Data set	Classifier	Accuracy	Precision	Recall	F1 measure
-Our data average of 10 cross validation	NB	0.8180	0.5418	0.3496	0.4250
	DT	0.8289	0.5623	0.4987	0.5286
	SVM	0.8076	–	0.0000	–
	SGD	0.8066	0.4977	0.5450	0.5202
	RFT(100)	0.8625	0.7630	0.4139	0.5367
	Classifier	Accuracy	Precision	Recall	F1 measure
Tweets + quotes + shuffle	NB	0.8060	0.5523	0.3566	0.4334
	DT	0.8113	0.5510	0.5035	0.5262
	SVM	0.7919		0.0000	
	SGD	0.8094	0.5433	0.5268	0.5349
	RFT(100)	0.8492	0.7611	0.4009	0.5252
	Classifier	Accuracy	Precision	Recall	F1 measure
Tweets + quotes + songs + shuffle	NB	0.8042	0.6146	0.3963	0.4819
	DT	0.8038	0.5805	0.5257	0.5517
	SVM	0.7703		0.0000	
	SGD	0.7910	0.5460	0.5359	0.5409
	RFT(100)	0.8349	0.7708	0.4004	0.5270

3   Results

We validated our original dataset of labelled tweets on state of the art classifiers. These classifies includes Naïve Bayes, Random Forest Tree with Tree size equal to 100, Decision Tree, Support Vector Machine, Stochastic Gradient Descent t. Later the data was engineered with the addition of depressive songs and depressive quotes in different combinations. We run above mention algorithms on the different set of data using 10-cross validation. Results are interpreted using different graphs and tables mentioned below (Figs. 3, 4 and 5).

We have four evaluating metrics i.e. Accuracy (A), Recall (R), Precision (P), and F1-measure (FM). These metrics are calculated using the counts of True Positives (TP) and True Negatives (TN) which mean documents having positive and negative labels respectively given by both (humans and machine classifier), False Positives (FP) i.e. the documents actually having negative labels but falsely classified as positive, and similarly False Negatives (FN) which mean documents actually having positives labels but falsely classified as negatives. Hence the formulae for metrics are:

```
1. A  = TP + TN / (TP +FP +TN +FN),
2. P = TP / (TP + FP),
3. R = TP / (TP + FN) ,
4. FM = 2.P.R / (P + R)
```

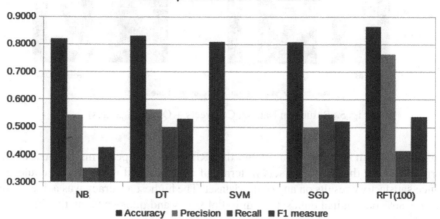

Fig. 3. Result on data set A (Tweets only)

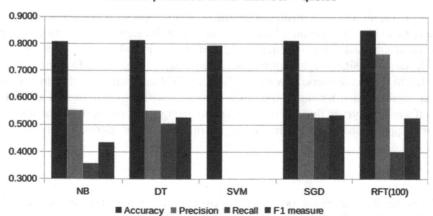

Fig. 4. Results on Data set B (Tweets + Quotes)

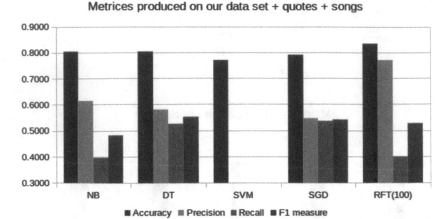

Fig. 5. Results on Data set C (Tweets + Quotes + Songs)

It is clear from the graphs and table that RFT(100) out performs the rest of the algorithms for all the used data sets in terms of accuracy and recall. SVM could not produce satisfactory results on any of the dataset. The highest accuracy was achieved by RFT was 86% on original data set. Addition of songs and quotes affects the efficiency of the algorithm negatively.

4 Conclusion

The rise in the use of social media and internet technologies has opened new paradigm for healthy living. Data produced by social media in the form of posts, tweets, captions, comments and communication reveal sufficient personality traits. This data can provide various insights regarding the user's feelings and emotions. This information provided to their caregivers, psychologist and medical companies so that they could take noticeable action for curing them. This approach will help in design of an intelligent information system that can provide healthy living to people of different age with different applications by controlling the degree of happiness or sadness among them.

References

1. World Health Organization: Depression and other common mental disorders: global health estimates. No. WHO/MSD/MER/2017.2. World Health Organization (2017)
2. Eaton, W.W., et al.: Population-based study of first onset and chronicity in major depressive disorder. Arch. Gen. Psychiatry **65**(5), 513–520 (2008)
3. Monroe, S.M., Harkness, K.L.: Recurrence in major depression: a conceptual analysis. Psychol. Rev. **118**(4), 655 (2011)
4. Yiend, J., et al.: Long term outcome of primary care depression. J. Affect. Disord. **118**(1), 79–86 (2009)
5. Lauber, C., et al.: Lay beliefs about causes of depression. Acta Psychiatr. Scand. **108**, 96–99 (2003)

6. Pulcu, E., Browning, M.: Using computational psychiatry to rule out the hidden causes of depression. JAMA Psychiatry **74**(8), 777–778 (2017)
7. LiveScience: Middle-age women have highest rate of depression (2018). Retrieved 22 March 2018. Accessed 3 May 2018
8. https://www.psycom.net/depression.central.html
9. Song, Q., et al.: Impact of the usage of social media in the workplace on team and employee performance. Inf. Manage. **56**(8), 103160 (2019)
10. Kim, B., Kim, Y.: College students' social media use and communication network heterogeneity: implications for social capital and subjective well-being. Comput. Hum. Behav. **73**, 620–628 (2017)
11. Marengo, D., Giannotta, F., Settanni, M.: Assessing personality using emoji: an exploratory study. Pers. Individ. Differ. **112**, 74–78 (2017)
12. Dibeklioğlu, H., Hammal, Z., Cohn, J.F.: Dynamic multimodal measurement of depression severity using deep autoencoding. IEEE J. Biomed. Health Inform. **22**(2), 525–536 (2017)
13. Yang, L., et al.: Decision tree based depression classification from audio video and language information. In: Proceedings of the 6th International Workshop on Audio/Visual Emotion Challenge (2016)
14. Alghowinem, S., et al.: Multimodal depression detection: fusion analysis of paralinguistic, head pose and eye gaze behaviors. IEEE Trans. Affect. Comput. **9**(4), 478–490 (2016)
15. Morales, M., Scherer, S., Levitan, R.: A cross-modal review of indicators for depression detection systems. In: Proceedings of the Fourth Workshop on Computational Linguistics and Clinical Psychology—From Linguistic Signal to Clinical Reality (2017)
16. Sahu, S., Espy-Wilson, C.Y.: Speech features for depression detection. In: INTERSPEECH (2016)
17. Dinkel, H., Wu, M., Yu, K.: Text-based depression detection: what triggers an alert. arXiv preprint arXiv:1904.05154 (2019)
18. Barnaghi, P., Ghaari, P., Breslin, J.G.: Opinion mining and sentiment polarity on twitter and correlation between events and sentiment. In: 2016 IEEE Second International Conference on Big Data Computing Service and Applications (BigDataService), pp. 52–57. IEEE (2016)
19. Khan, M.Y., Emaduddin, S.M., Junejo, K.N.: Harnessing english sentiment lexicons for polarity detection in urdu tweets: a baseline approach. In: 2017 IEEE 11th International Conference on Semantic Computing (ICSC), pp. 242–249. IEEE (2017)

Simultaneous Artefact-Lesion Extraction for Skin Cancer Diagnosis

Michael Osadebey[1(✉)], Marius Pedersen[1], and Dag Waaler[2]

[1] Department of Computer Science, Norwegian University of Science and Technology, Teknologivegen 22, 2815 Gjøvik, Norway
{michael.osadebey,marius.pedersen}@ntnu.no
[2] Department of Health Sciences, Norwegian University of Science and Technology, Teknologivegen 22, 2815 Gjøvik, Norway
dag.waaler@ntnu.no

Abstract. Presence of clutters, occlusions and dark corner artifacts in dermatoscopy images causes unsupervised and intensity-based image analysis systems to erroneously segment lesion boundaries required for accurate and reliable skin cancer diagnosis. Preprocessing algorithms designed to address these challenges increase resources, computational cost and introduce extraneous features, thereby reducing the efficacy of the diagnostic system. We propose a new approach to accurately segment skin lesions without the need for preprocessing steps to eliminate these confounding factors. The proposed method begins by thresholding with a correction factor in a color channel image with optimal discrimination between the target object and background. Next, the output of the preliminary segmentation undergoes angular displacement. Finally, we iterate, a number of times, the set difference between the binarized image and its rotated version, to simultaneously detect lesion borders and eliminate occlusions and clutters. The proposed method outperform selected state-of-the-art segmentation algorithms on 600 images with different types of confounding factors.

Keywords: Skin lesion · Segmentation · Set theory

1 Introduction

Common artifacts in dermatoscopy images are skin hairs which occlude the lesion boundary and clutter the background. Other artefact include clutters such as ruler markings, colour charts, gel bubbles, date stamps and ink markers. Cluttering and occluding objects present high gradients which mimic skin lesion boundaries. Consequently, it becomes challenging for unsupervised and intensity-based image analysis systems to accurately detect the lesion boundary and extract color and texture information required for classification of skin

Michael Osadebey: Supported by The European Research Consortium on Informatics and Mathematics (ERCIM).

S. Yildirim Yayilgan et al. (Eds.): INTAP 2020, CCIS 1382, pp. 100–112, 2021.
https://doi.org/10.1007/978-3-030-71711-7_9

cancer [1]. To address these challenges, a pre-processing algorithm or a robust segmentation algorithm which considers each of these confounding factors, is incorporated into a computerized skin cancer diagnosis system [2].

The contribution by [3] combine shadow attenuation with median filtering to attenuate artifacts before modified Otsu thresholding is applied to an intensity image. Another robust segmentation algorithm proposed by [4] detects confounding factors such as shading and specular reflections followed by an inpainting operation and preliminary segmentation which eliminate skin hairs and create a initial binary mask. A morphological post-processing operation refines the binary mask and extracts the lesion region. Region-based techniques have been applied to produce several robust segmentation algorithms. An example of region-based techniques is the Mumford-Shah method [5] which divides an image into several regions and subsequently merge the region with close pixel intensities based on an energy functional. Active contour without edges proposed by [6] is based on the Mumford-Shah method. Other robust segmentation algorithms have been based on the expectation maximization (EM) technique proposed by [7]. The EM algorithm is an iterative procedure to determine the model parameters that most likely describe the observed data. Each iteration of the EM algorithm alternates between the expectation and the maximization steps. The expectation step estimate the missing data given the observed data and current estimate of the model parameters. In the maximization step, the estimate of the missing data in the E-step are used in lieu of the actual missing data followed by maximization of the likelihood function. The likelihood increases at every iteration. The algorithm terminates when there is no significant change between the values at the E-step and the M-step. Techniques based on artificial intelligence have also produced robust skin lesion segmentation. The contribution by [8] is based on feature learning and the use of dictionaries. The first step applies Non-Negative Matrix Factorization (NMF) to construct an initial sparse representation of the image and initial feature dictionary. The feature dictionary is then optimized in the second stage to segment the image.

Most current robust segmentation techniques require hair removal preprocessing step because they perform poorly in the presence of cluttering and occluding objects [9,10]. Preprocessing algorithms designed to address these challenges increase resources, computational cost and introduce extraneous features, thereby reducing the efficacy of a computerized system for skin cancer detection. Pre-processing algorithms for hair elimination and restoration are based on morphological operation and diffusion-based techniques which have the tendency to introduce blurring into the image. Texture restoration within lesion region is an invasive and delicate operation with high risk of distorting the original texture which drastically reduce the quality of the segmented image. When the texture is disturbed it will be difficult to utilize the segmented image for automatic lesion change detection and for inclusion in an efficient and effective computerized tool for skin cancer diagnosis [11]. Inspired by our previous work [12] on plant leaves segmentation in cluttered and occluded images, this paper proposes a method that can remove artefact and segment lesion in dermatoscopy images without the need for a separate pre-processing step for artefact removal.

2   Materials and Methods

2.1   Sources and Description of Data

This study utilize 464 images from the International Skin Imaging Collaboration (ISIC) archive https://isic-archive.com/ and 136 images from the Dermatology Service of Hospital Pedro Hispano, Matosinhos, Portugal http://www.fc.up.pt/addi/. This gives a total of 600 test images from the two databases. The range of the row M dimensions for the images are $\{765 \leq M \leq 6668\}$. Corresponding column N dimensions are $\{572 \leq N \leq 4439\}$. Each image has ground truths provided by certified dermatologists. The test images can be further categorized into 233 normal, 84 dark corners, 93 hair occlusion, 57 clutter and 133 multiple artifacts images. For each image in a given category, six visual attributes were identified and quantitatively evaluated based on the image ground truth. The first visual attribute is perceptual quality D_1. It was evaluated using BRISQUE, a no-reference image quality assessment method proposed by [13]. The range of values for BRISQUE was rescaled to lie between 0 and 1. Metrics for quantifying the remaining visual attributes are defined in Eq. 1–5. The second attribute (see Eq. 1) is the area D_2 of the lesion, scaled as percentage of image area, where A_g is the number of pixels within the lesion region in the ground truth image. The third attribute (see Eq. 2) is the spatial extent D_3, scaled as percentage of image area, where A_s is the total number of pixels that describe the region occupied by the lesion, cluttering and occluding objects in a test image. The fourth attribute (see Eq. 3) is the lesion position D_4 relative to the image centroid, where (x_s, y_s) and (X_g, Y_g) are the pixel location of the lesion and image centroids, respectively. It is scaled to lie from 0, for lesion located at the center of the image and 1, for lesion located at the image corners and the perimeter. The fifth attribute (see Eq. 4) is the eccentricity of lesion D_5, where a, b are the semi-major and semi-minor axes lengths of the lesion. The sixth attribute (see Eq. 5) is the level D_6 of cluttering and occlusion, scaled as percentage of image area, where A_{gs} is the total number of pixels that do not belong to either lesion nor healthy skin in the test image.

$$D_2 = 100 \left(\frac{A_g}{MN} \right) \qquad (1) \qquad\qquad D_3 = 100 \left(\frac{A_s}{MN} \right) \qquad (2)$$

$$D_4 = \left(\frac{\sqrt{(x_s - X_g)^2 + (y_s - Y_g)^2}}{\sqrt{X_g^2 + Y_g^2}} \right) \qquad (3)$$

$$D_5 = \left(\sqrt{1 - \frac{b^2}{a^2}} \right) \qquad (4) \qquad\qquad D_6 = 100 \left(\frac{A_{gs}}{MN} \right) \qquad (5)$$

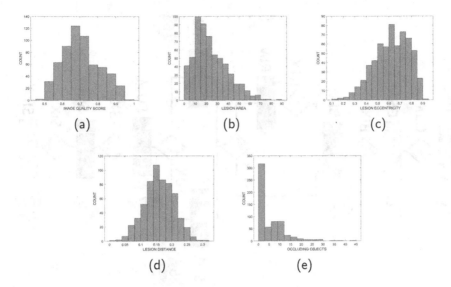

Fig. 1. Histogram distribution of five attributes of the 600 test images. (a) Perceptual quality. (b) Area (c) Eccentricity. (d) Lesion distance. (e) Level of cluttering and occlusion.

Histogram distribution of the five attributes of the test images are displayed in Fig. 1. Figure 1a shows that the range and mean perceptual quality scores of the test images are $\{0.47 \leq D_1 \leq 0.96\}$ and 0.70, respectively. They can be considered as having acceptable image quality. The average area and eccentricity of the lesions, as shown in Fig. 1b and Fig. 1c, are 24 and 0.62, respectively, a quarter of each image area belongs to the lesion region and the lesion region can generally be approximated by an ellipse. Figure 1d shows that the mean and range of the lesions distance from the image center are 0.16 and $\{0.01 \leq D_5 \leq 0.30\}$, respectively, which suggest that most of the lesions are located closer to the center of the image. The histogram plot in Fig. 1e shows that about half of the test images contain different types and levels of cluttering and occluding objects.

2.2 Methodology

The proposed method was implemented in the MATLAB computing environment. Figures 2–3 explains the nine successive steps to implement the proposed method using an hair-occluded test image **TIM** with identification number ISIC_0000138 from the ISIC challenge 2018.

1. Read Original Image
   The RGB test image **TIM** shown in Fig. 3a is read by the algorithm.
2. Colour Space Transformation
   The **TIM** is transformed **GSX** to a suitable color space. In this example,

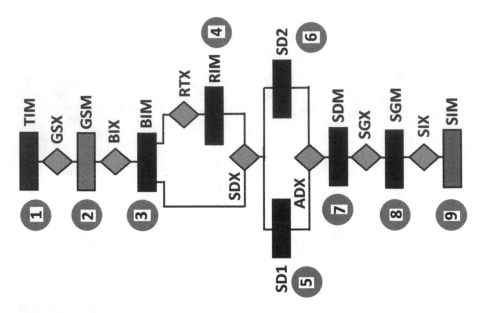

Fig. 2. Flow chart for implementation of the proposed skin lesion segmentation in a dermatoscopy image.

the color space is the HSV colour space, followed by the extraction of the saturation channel image **GSM** shown in Fig. 3b that gives the optimal discrimination between target object and the background.

3. Threshold-based Binarization

The operation of the algorithm requires that the core of the lesion and the lesion borders as well as the cluttering and occluding objects in the binary image are dominated by dark pixels. The reasoning behind this requirement will be evident in the subsequent steps. To satisfy this requirement, we compute the complement of the **GSM** image. Thereafter, we apply threshold-based technique. In this example, the global threshold set at the mean of image pixels, convert **BIX** the complement image to a binary image shown in Fig. 3c. The computation of the image complement is not required, for example, binary images generated from grayscale and the luminance channel of the CIELAB colour space because they satisfy the operation requirement of the algorithm. We consider that, cluttering and occluding objects, in the absence of other confounding factors, contribute to the relative contrast as well as the ratio of class sizes in the image. To compensate for this shortcomings we determine, for each image, a correction factor α defined as

$$\alpha = 1 + \left(\frac{1}{D_3}\right) \tag{6}$$

The correction factor is multiplied with the average pixel intensity level of the test image. The reasoning behind the correction factor is that images

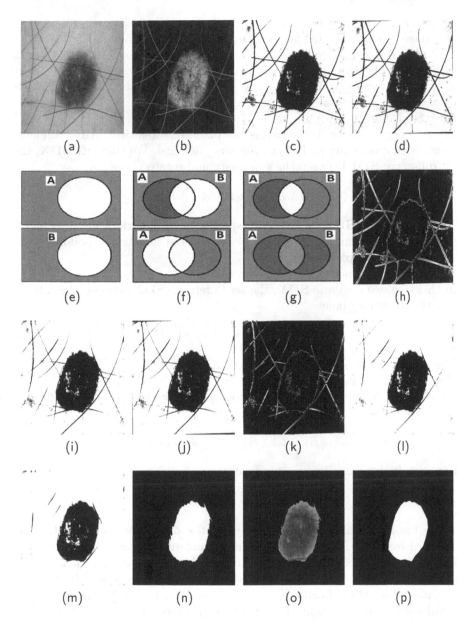

Fig. 3. The implementation of proposed method. Detailed explanation is in Setp 3 of Sect. 2.2 (Color figure online)

with increasing spatial extent tend to be homogeneously dominated by large lesion, so the corrected threshold $\mu_c \approx \mu$. Conversely, images with lower spatial extent tends to be heterogeneous composed of relatively small lesion and skin hairs, so the corrected threshold $\mu_c > \mu$.

4. Rotation Transformation

We make a copy of **BIM** and rotate **RTX** the duplicate image clockwise around its center by a small angle $\theta = 1°$. The rotated image **RTM** is shown in Fig. 3d. The stationary binary image A and its rotated version B are regarded as two separate sets $A \subset U, B \subset U$, respectively, of logical pixels belonging to a universal set U (see Fig. 3e).

5. First Set Difference

Prior to displacement, both images are pixel-wise identical. After displacement, both images are no longer pixel-wise identical. We compute **SDX**, the set difference **SD1** between the stationary and rotated image:

$$(A \setminus B) = \{x | x \in A \wedge \notin B\} \tag{7}$$

The set difference **SD1** are pixels in a specific location in the stationary image (red coloured region in Fig. 3f) but are not in the same corresponding pixel location in the displaced image.

6. Second Set Difference

In this step, we compute **SDX**, the set difference **SD2** between the rotated and the stationary image:

$$(B \setminus A) = \{x | x \in B \wedge x \notin A\} \tag{8}$$

The set difference is the purple coloured region in Fig. 3f.

7. Symmetric Difference

Figure 3g (top figure) shows that the union of A and B is the equivalent of three disjoint sets:

$$(A \cup B) = (A \setminus B) \cup (B \setminus A) \cup (A \cap B) \tag{9}$$

Equation 9 above can be expressed as:

$$(A \cup B) = (A \oplus B) \cup (A \cap B) \tag{10}$$

where the first term, $A \oplus B$ is the symmetric difference of A and B (blue coloured region in Fig. 3g). The symmetric difference image **SDM** shown in Fig. 3h is the set of elements which are in either of the sets and not in their intersection. The bright pixels in the symmetric difference image (in Fig. 3h) provides information on all the pixels that are disturbed and weakened by the small angular displacement. The disturbed (shifted) pixels are the boundary pixels of the lesion region. The weakened pixels are the cluttering and occluding objects such as the skin hairs which are severely weakened because their spatial extent and circularity are very low in comparison to lesions. The second term $(A \cap B)$ on the right hand side of Eq. 10 (brown coloured region in Fig. 3g) account for pixels which are preserved under rotation transformation. The preserved pixels shown in Fig. 3h are the dark pixels that dominate the healthy skin and the core of the skin lesion regions.

8. Segmentation mask

Now we will show why the algorithm requires a binary image which the lesion and occluding objects are dominated by dark pixels. The bright pixels in the **SDM** image shown in Fig. 3h (occluding hair and skin lesion borders) are used to replace (erase) corresponding locations (dark pixels) in the stationary image shown in Fig. 3c. This pixel replacement action simultaneously reduces hair occlusion and detects the lesion border producing the image shown in Fig. 3i. Borrowing knowledge from [15], a single operation of computing the symmetric difference image may not be sufficient to detect all the hairs and skin lesion boundary pixels. For this reason, the computation of the **SDM** is iterated β number of times:

$$\beta = \lfloor \log_2 D_3 \rfloor \tag{11}$$

The attribute D_3 is logarithmically transformed to scale down its relatively large range of values. In the second iteration, the output from the first iteration (Fig. 3i) is rotated $\phi = 1°$ clockwise around the image centroid to produce the image shown in Fig. 3j. Figure 3k is the **SDM** between Fig. 3i and Fig. 3j. Figure 3l is the output of the second iteration obtained by using the bright pixels in Fig. 3k to replace the dark pixels in Fig. 3i. Figure 3m is the binary image obtained after 5 iterations. The segmentation mask shown in Fig. 3n was derived after area thresholding to remove small structures and hole filling operation.

9. Segmented RGB Image

The segmented image **SIM** shown in Fig. 3o is a RGB image. The three colour channels are derived **SIX** by pixel-wise multiplication of each colour channel of the original dermatoscopy image with the segmentation mask followed by vector summation of the three channels. The ground truth image is shown in Fig. 3p.

3   Results

In Table 1 we display the mean and standard deviation (in bracket) Dice scores of the proposed method using five threshold-based techniques and thirteen channels from four colour spaces. The colour channels are denoted RGB (r,g,b,G), where G denote the gray scale, HSV (h,s,v), CIELAB (L,A,B) and CIEXYZ (x,y,z). The preliminary segmentation for each colour space experiment was implemented using five different threshold-based techniques. Notations for the threshold techniques are ISODATA [16], MEAN [14], MINERROR [17], MOMENT [18] and OTSU [19]. Letter F in the table indicates Dice score less than 0.65. Red colored bold text indicate Dice score recorded after the thresholding with correction factor.

Examples of segmentation results for the saturation channel of the HSV colour space are displayed in Fig. 4. The first, second, third and last column of

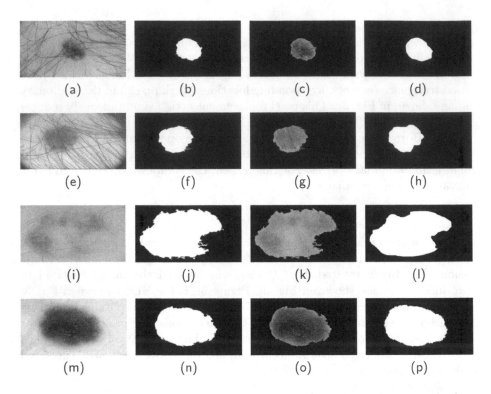

Fig. 4. Segmentation results before the application of correction factor to the binarization techniques. The first, second, third and fourth columns are the test image, segmented mask, segmented RGB image and the ground truth image, respectively.

Table 1. Mean and standard deviation (in bracket) Dice scores recorded by the proposed method using five threshold-based techniques and thirteen channels from four colour spaces. Letter F denotes Dice score less than 0.65. Red-coloured numbers are Dice scores recorded after the application of threshold correction factor.

Threshold methods	Colour space channel												
	r	g	b	G	h	s	v	L	A	B	x	y	z
ISODATA ([16])	F	0.66 (0.31)	F	F	F	0.83 (0.2)	F	F	F	F		F	F	0.68 (0.39)
MEAN ([14])	F	F	F	F	F	0.82 (0.26), 0.91 (0.20)	F	F	0.66 (0.32)	0.72 (0.32)	F	F	F
MINERROR ([17])	F	F	0.74 (0.32)	F	F	0.82 (0.24), 0.85 (0.18)	F	F	F	0.69 (0.33)	F	F	0.70 (0.30)
MOMENT ([18])	F	F	0.68 (0.39)	F	F	0.81 (0.12)	F	F	F	F		F	F	0.65 (0.40)
OTSU ([19])	F	0.67 (0.31)	F	0.65 (0.31)	F	0.83 (0.15)	F	F	F	F		F	F	0.71 (0.36)

Fig. 4 are the test image, segmented mask, segmented RGB image and ground truth image, respectively. First row of Fig. 4 are the results for hair-occluded test image, ISIC_0000095 using MINERROR thresholding technique with parameters

($\beta = 5, \phi = 1$). Second row show the result for another hair-occluded test image IMD003 using OTSU technique with parameters ($\beta = 6, \theta = 1$). Third and fourth rows are the results for normal test images, IMD014 and ISIC_0015130 using ISODATA and MOMENT techniques, respectively. The corresponding operating parameters are ($\beta = 2, \theta = 1$) and ($\beta = 4, \theta = 1$), respectively.

The relationship between the Dice score-based performance of the proposed method and the five attributes of the datasets was quantified using the Spearman rank correlation coefficient ρ [20]:

$$\rho = 1 - \frac{6\sum_{i=1}^{L} t_i^2}{L(L^2 - 1)} \tag{12}$$

where t_i is the difference between the two ranks of each observation and $L = 600$ is the number of observations. Table 2 shows the correlation coefficient between the performance of the proposed method, implemented in the saturation channel with five binarization techniques, and five dataset attributes.

Table 2. Correlation coefficient between performance of proposed method (implemented in the saturation channel with five binarization techniques) and five dataset attributes.

Dataset attributes	Threshold methods				
	ISODATA [16]	MEAN [14]	MINERROR [17]	MOMENT [18]	OTSU [19]
D1	0.24	0.01	−0.02	0.20	0.26
D2	0.07	0.34	0.10	−0.21	0.02
D3	−0.12	−0.18	−0.10	−0.07	−0.14
D4	0.01	0.03	−0.04	0.01	−0.04
D5	0.05	−0.17	−0.29	0.10	0.10

Table 3 shows the results of evaluating the proposed method alongside five selected state-of-the-art skin lesion segmentation algorithms based on the mean and standard deviation of five performance metrics; Jaccard, Dice, accuracy, sensitivity and specificity. The denotations and the references of the algorithms are SDI [4], ESEG [7], CVESE [6], MSHA [5] and DICT [8]. The proposed method is denoted Proposed.

Table 3. Comparative performance evaluation of proposed method with 5 state-of-the-art methods on 600 test images based on mean and standard deviation of 5 performance metrics. Red colored texts indicate best performance recorded for each metric.

Methods	P_1 JACC		P_2 DICE		P_3 ACCU		P_4 SENS		P_5 SPEC	
	μ	σ	μ	σ	μ	σ	μ	σ	μ	σ
Proposed	0.83	0.09	0.91	0.06	0.96	0.043	0.94	0.09	0.95	0.08
SDI Ref 4	0.79	0.19	0.87	0.17	0.94	0.12	0.92	0.15	0.96	0.06
EM Ref 7	0.60	0.26	0.71	0.23	0.88	0.10	0.71	0.25	0.93	0.10
Chan Vese Ref 6	0.57	0.23	0.70	0.22	0.88	0.10	0.75	0.27	0.91	0.09
Mumford Ref 5	0.57	0.23	0.70	0.22	0.88	0.10	0.75	0.27	0.91	0.09
Dictionary Ref 8	0.66	0.34	0.72	0.36	0.87	0.20	0.73	0.37	0.92	0.15

4   Discussion

The results from Table 1 suggests that segmentation accuracy varies with the choice of colour space and binarization technique. Furthermore, the saturation channel of the HSV colour space can be considered the optimal colour channel for skin lesion segmentation. Image thresholding with correction factor improve the segmentation accuracy (red colour in Table 1) from 0.82 to 0.91 for the MEAN technique and from 0.82 to 0.85 for the MINERROR technique. Table 2 suggest the followings: (1) the MEAN and MINERROR binarization techniques are more robust to variations in perceptual quality. (2) Lesion size can influence the MEAN and MOMENT binarization techniques. (3) Lesion position and eccentricity does not significantly influence segmentation accuracy. (4) The level of cluttering and occluding objects have significant influence on the performance of the proposed method implemented with MEAN and MINERROR techniques and correction factor can enhance the performance of the MEAN and MINERROR techniques. Table 3 shows that the proposed method implemented with MEAN technique, with mean Dice score of 0.91 demonstrate best performance, closely followed by SDI [4] which incorporates separate hair removal pre-processing step. The other methods, despite the strong theoretical formulation behind their design, are trailing behind our proposed method and the SDI algorithm because they do not incorporate hair removal pre-processing step.

5   Conclusions and Future Work

We hereby propose a new method to segment skin lesion in dermatoscopy images without the need for a separate hair removal preprocessing step. The proposed method demonstrate better performance than selected current state-of-the art methods. It is potentially efficient and robust to images with different attributes. Parameters which define the algorithm operation can be either manually or automatically adjusted to optimize segmentation accuracy. Future work will utilize larger volume of dataset, explore alternative correction factor techniques and the influence of the algorithm parameters on segmentation accuracy. The MATLAB implementation code is available on request from www.colourlab.no/software.

References

1. Lequan, Yu., Chen, H., Dou, Q., Qin, J., Heng, P.-A.: Automated melanoma recognition in dermoscopy images via very deep residual networks. IEEE Trans. Med. Imaging **36**(4), 994–1004 (2017)
2. Mishra, N.K., Celebi, M.E.: An overview of melanoma detection in dermoscopy images using image processing and machine learning. arXiv preprint arXiv:1601.07843 (2016)
3. Zortea, M., Flores, E., Scharcanski, J.: A simple weighted thresholding method for the segmentation of pigmented skin lesions in macroscopic images. Pattern Recogn. **64**, 92–104 (2017)
4. Guarracino, M.R., Maddalena, L.: SDI+: a novel algorithm for segmenting dermoscopic images. IEEE J. Biomed. Health Inform. **23**(2), 481–488 (2019)
5. Mumford, D., Shah, J.: Optimal approximations by piecewise smooth functions and associated variational problems. Commun. Pure Appl. Math. **42**(5), 577–685 (1989)
6. Chan, T.F., Vese, L.A.: Active contours without edges. IEEE Trans. Image Process. **10**(2), 266–277 (2001)
7. Dempster, A.P., Laird, N.M., Rubin, D.B.: Maximum likelihood from incomplete data via the EM algorithm. J. R. Stat. Soc. Ser. B (Methodol.) **39**, 1–38 (1977)
8. Flores, E., Scharcanski, J.: Segmentation of melanocytic skin lesions using feature learning and dictionaries. Expert Syst. Appl. **56**, 300–309 (2016)
9. Le, T.H.N., Savvides, M.: A novel shape constrained feature-based active contour model for lips/mouth segmentation in the wild. Pattern Recogn. **54**, 23–33 (2016)
10. Majtner, T., Lidayova, K., Yildirim-Yayilgan, S., Hardeberg, J.Y.: Improving skin lesion segmentation in dermoscopic images by thin artefacts removal methods. In: 2016 6th European Workshop on Visual Information Processing (EUVIP), pp. 1–6. IEEE (2016)
11. Abbas, Q., Celebi, M.E., García, I.F.: Hair removal methods: a comparative study for dermoscopy images. Biomed. Sig. Process. Control **6**(4), 395–404 (2011)
12. Osadebey, M., Pedersen, M., Waaler, D.: Plant leaves region segmentation in cluttered and occluded images using perceptual color space and k-means-derived threshold with set theory. In: 2019 IEEE 17th International Conference on Industrial Informatics (INDIN), vol. 1, pp. 1211–1216, July 2019
13. Mittal, A., Moorthy, A.K., Bovik, A.C.: No-reference image quality assessment in the spatial domain. IEEE Trans. Image Process. **21**(12), 4695–4708 (2012)
14. Glasbey, C.A.: An analysis of histogram-based thresholding algorithms. CVGIP: Graph. Models Image Process. **55**(6), 532–537 (1993)
15. Wong, A., Scharcanski, J., Fieguth, P.: Automatic skin lesion segmentation via iterative stochastic region merging. IEEE Trans. Inf. Technol. Biomed. **15**(6), 929–936 (2011)

16. Ridler, T.W., Calvard, S., et al.: Picture thresholding using an iterative selection method. IEEE Trans. Syst. Man Cybern. **8**(8), 630–632 (1978)
17. Kittler, J., Illingworth, J.: Minimum error thresholding. Pattern Recogn. **19**(1), 41–47 (1986)
18. Tsai, W.-H.: Moment-preserving thresolding: a new approach. Comput. Vis. Graph. Image Process. **29**(3), 377–393 (1985)
19. Otsu, N.: A threshold selection method from gray-level histograms. IEEE Trans. Syst. Man Cybern. **9**(1), 62–66 (1979)
20. Fieller, E.C., Hartley, H.O., Pearson, E.S.: Tests for rank correlation coefficients. i. Biometrika 44(3/4), 470–481 (1957)

A Statistical Study to Analyze the Impact of External Weather Change on Chronic Pulmonary Infection in South Norway with Machine Learning Algorithms

Ayan Chatterjee[1]([⊠]), Martin W. Gerdes[1], Andreas Prinz[1], and Santiago Martinez[2]

[1] Department of Information and Communication Technology, Centre for e-Health, University of Agder, Kristiansand, Norway
{ayan.chatterjee,martin.gerdes,andreas.prinz}@uia.no
[2] Department of Health and Sports, Centre for e-Health, University of Agder, Kristiansand, Norway
santiago.martinez@uia.no

Abstract. In this paper, we analyzed the holistic impact of external weather on chronic pulmonary infection in the Agder region with traditional machine learning algorithms. Millions of people are diagnosed with Chronic Obstructive Pulmonary Disease (COPD). Our study is dedicated in the Agder region, the Southern part of Norway. Norway has four seasons – winter (December-February), late winter/spring (March-May), Summer (June-August), and Autumn (September-November) in a year with average annual temperature approx. 7.5 °C | 45.5 °F and an annual rainfall of 1260 mm or 49.6 in. in Kristiansand. As predicted by the World Health Organization (WHO), in 2016, Norway suffered from 8% mortality due to c(1)hronic respiratory diseases. The disease is strongly afflicted by meteorological and environmental factors in distinct regions worldwide. This article explores correlation and dependency between COPD and temperature, barometric pressure, and humidity in the Agder region. We relate multiple prognostic models for patient evaluation based on patient condition and weather information. The COPD data were accumulated from 94 patients that reside in the Agder region as part of a major EU-funded project called "United for Health". Outcomes showed that there is a dependence between air temperature and the patient's condition. However, there is no significant dependency between air pressure and humidity, and the patient assessment results in that region. The results help to predict the condition of COPD patients in south Norway based on the weather forecast.

Keywords: eHealth · General health · Intervention · COPD · SPO2 · Recommendation · Agder · Assessment · Logistic regression · Decision tree · Random forest · Gradient boosted trees

1 Introduction

COPD is a term used to describe progressive lung diseases and is characterized by increasing breathlessness. Generally, it develops slowly, and the symptoms exacerbate

S. Yildirim Yayilgan et al. (Eds.): INTAP 2020, CCIS 1382, pp. 113–124, 2021.
https://doi.org/10.1007/978-3-030-71711-7_10

over time. The disease is projected by the WHO to become one of the four leading causes of death worldwide by 2030 [1]. There are around 16 million people diagnosed with COPD, and many more might have the disease but are unaware of it [2]. COPD is related to meteorological factors and environmental conditions, such as weather phases [3]. Extreme temperatures can have adverse effects on COPD patients. For example, the risk of hospitalization for COPD patients increased by 7.6% for every 1 °C increase above a threshold temperature of 29 °C in New York City [4]. Other studies showed that the elderly with COPD suffer from an increased risk for adverse health effects from heat exposure [5]. Colder temperatures can also increase mortality and morbidity among COPD patients. For instance, a study in Michigan, USA, showed that people with COPD had a 19% increased risk of dying on cold days [6]. Another study in London linked cold temperatures with decreases in lung function in COPD patients [7]. The humidity of air is another essential factor for COPD patients. Humid air has a high-water content that makes it dense. This density can increase airway resistance in the body that makes it hard to inhale. Deficient humidity levels can also worsen COPD symptoms, as dry air can cause the airways to narrow [8]. According to [9], the effect of humidity did not have a statistically significant effect on the COPD symptoms. The study, however, indicated that there was a negative effect on patients from certain temperature-humidity combinations. A study in Germany showed that the impact of humidity was significant only in the north, but not in south Bavaria [10]. Another study found out that low humidity would increase COPD exacerbation in Taiwan [11]. The impact of humidity is, therefore, dependent on location and can vary based on region. Another meteorological factor that can affect COPD patients is barometric pressure. A drop in the pressure decreases the oxygen-carrying capacity of the air. Even though the drop might be small, it may make COPD patients feel like they cannot catch their breath [12]. A study found a positive correlation between barometric pressure and blood oxygen saturation for the elderly [13]. It implies that changes in the pressure may cause physiologic changes so that barometric pressure might be a relevant weather parameter for morbidity and mortality in population in general, and in COPD patients specifically. When barometric pressure is higher than the pressure in the lungs (usually at lower elevations), oxygen molecules can diffuse more quickly into the bloodstream, making it easier to breathe. Based on the introduction, COPD can be affected by meteorological factors. It is sometimes a combination of weather parameters that could impact COPD patients. Location is also important as different regions in the world have different weather conditions. In this paper, we present a study investigating correlation and dependency between COPD and temperature, barometric pressure, and humidity in the Agder region, South Norway. The aim is to build a predictive model for patient assessment in the Agder region based on the patient's condition and the weather information.

The remainder of this article is organized as follows. Section 2 discusses related work in this field. Section 3 describes the method used for the data collection process. Section 4 presents a statistical analysis of the data. Section 5 discusses the models and lists the results. Finally, Sect. 6 concludes the paper and presents future work.

2 Related Work

Many studies have been conducted to analyze the influence of meteorological factors on COPD. COPD depends on geographical location, such as altitude, distance from the river, meteorological factors, such as temperature, dew point, relative humidity, rainfall, barometric pressure, and wind speed [14]. Different studies demonstrated that spontaneous pneumothorax (SP), primary SP, bronchial asthma, and dyspnea are main COPD, accountable for leading mortality and morbidity [3, 15–17].

Bulajich et al. [3] did a retrospective study in Belgrade, Serbia over five years on 659 patients with primary SP and SP associated with COPD, to conclude a correlation with weather phases (2ts: the anticyclonic situation with warm & dry weather and 5hv: passing of the cold front). The result showed that the highest occurrence of SP is between October to March, but it peaks between November and February. Fall in environmental temperature is closely associated with COPD and leads to cold-related morbidity with admission to the hospitals [18]. Researchers found a correlation between the number of asthma patients admitted to the hospitals and meteorological factors like temperature, rain, and humidity [15]. The frequency of asthma exacerbations is high on misty, hazy, or foggy nights rather than clear nights [17, 19]. Dyspnea is another problematic symptom for patients with COPD. Ayham Daher et al. [17] investigated on 230 patients in Germany to conclude the importance of change in weather conditions and environmental factors in dyspnea. The proposed method included a comparative study between different air and weather conditions (rising/falling air pressure, sunny, foggy, rainy, windy, snowy, hazy, high ozone levels, and airborne pollen) and environmental circumstances (cooking, grilling, perfumes, cigarette smoke, gasoline odor, and flower scents). The result showed a connection between foggy weather, exposure to perfumes, and dyspnea. Some studies showed that the transition from warm and humid weather to cold and dry weather conditions increases seasonal hospitalization count for the patients suffering from respiratory diseases. Robert E. Davis et al. [20] conducted a research based on the data of daily respiratory admissions to the University of Virginia over 19 years to conclude that the warm to cold transition during autumn had higher mortality than the comparable cold to warm transition period during spring. G.C. Donaldson et al. [7] studied east London on 76 COPD patients for one year to conclude that an inevitable fall in temperature (both indoor and outdoor) has a potential risk of increased morbidity for patients with COPD. The collaboration of abridged lung function and exacerbation during cold weather can lead to high cold-related morbidity and mortality in COPD patients who are previously suffering from chronic respiratory infirmity and increased vulnerability to respiratory catastrophe. Shao Lin et al. [4] exposed the association of high temperature and respiratory diseases. They studied the effect of temperature, humidity on COPD patients, and hospitalization count with different meteorological conditions in summer throughout 1991–2004 in New York City. Result demonstrates that at high temperature (29 °C–36 °C), the hospitalization rates go high (2.7% to 3.1%) for COPD patients and the rates are more for the Hispanic persons (6.1%/°C) and the elderly (4.7%/°C). Uta Ferrari et al. [10] studied north and south part of Bavaria, Germany and found one percent increase of daily consultations (around 103 visits) with a change of 0.72 K temperature, 209.55 of log surface pressure in Pascal, and a decrease of one percent of daily consultations with 1,453,763 Ws m2 of solar radiation. Data were collected with a period of 6 h daily (large scale precipitation (m), convective precipitation (m), solar radiation at the surface (Ws/m2), a zonal component of surface stress (Ns/m), and a meridional component of surface stress (Ns/m)) from both south and north Bavaria and followed by a comparative study conducted on following parameters - 2 m temperature (K), log surface pressure (Pa), zonal wind component (m/s), meridional wind component (m/s), combined variable wind speed (m/s), specific humidity (g/m3), boundary layer height (m), and cloud cover. The result showed that solar radiation, temperature, and pressure has a significant impact on COPD patients. C. Arden Pope III et al. [13] investigated 90 older adults in Utah Valley, USA, during the winter of 1995–1996 to establish a connection between barometric pressure and respiratory problem. The result illustrated a connection of oxygen saturation and pulse rate with a change in barometric pressure. If the pressure low at high altitude, it generates hypoxia (low oxygen saturation) and affects the human respiratory system. Alfésio L. F. Braga et al. [5] directed research to estimate the effect and influence of weather (temperature, pressure) on respiratory death in 12 different US cities. Observation found that temperature was related to augmented daily cause-specific deaths in both cold and hot cities. In hot cities, neither hot nor cold temperatures had a more significant effect on COPD deaths, but in cold cities, both heat and cold contributed to daily cause-specific deaths. Hence, the analysis of climatic change with regional weather differences is essential. The authors also found no visible impact of humidity alone on COPD patients. Another study was conducted by Zhe Mu et al. [9] on 106 COPD patients in Shanghai, China, to find the effect of both humidity and low temperature on COPD patients' symptoms. The result shows a remarkable collaborative effect between low temperature and humidity on COPD patients with $p < 0.0001$. Low temperature with high humidity enhances the risk of COPD. The research reveals that maintaining the indoor temperature at least 18.2 °C and the humidity under 70% are positive approaches to mitigating COPD symptoms. Physical inactivity associated with temperature, sunshine, rainfall also influences COPD. During cold and wet weather, physical activity drops drastically. Ayedh D. Alahmari et al. [21] examined pedometric data collected over 16,478 days, an average of 267 days per patient in London to conclude that colder weather below 22.5 °C, reduced daily step count by 43.3 steps day per °C ($p = 0.039$) and activity was lower on rainy days than dry days ($p = 0.002$) and on overcast compared to sunny days. In contrast to the related work articles, we focus on the effect of meteorological factors on COPD in the Agder region, South of Norway. We investigate how weather conditions can affect COPD patients in this specific region, to give indications to healthcare professionals about COPD patients status based on weather data.

3   Data Collection

The COPD data were collected from 94 patients that live in Kristiansand municipality, the Agder region, the southern part of Norway, as part of a major EU-funded project called "United for Health" [22]. The project goal was to find universal solutions in telemedicine deployment for European healthcare and establish telemedical monitoring for patients discharged from hospitals. The COPD patients were recruited to use a telemedicine monitoring solution 30 days after discharge from hospital treatment for acute exacerbations. They were instructed for the first two weeks to report daily measurements of pulse and transdermal peripheral capillary oxygen saturation (SpO2) and a symptom-specific questionnaire. Based on reported data, the telemedicine system determined a color-coded health status level that represents the status of the patient: Green: The patient is in a stable or improved clinical condition with unchanged medication, Yellow: The patient is in a condition that needs special attention, and Red: The patient is in critical condition. The historical weather data for Kristiansand area covering five years were purchased from the "Open Weather API" website [23]. The weather data was recorded every hour for five years, and it includes information about temperature, barometric pressure, humidity, wind speed, precipitation volume of rain, and snow volume.

4   Data Processing

In this study, we explored the impact of weather features on the conditions of COPD patients in southern Norway. The patient status assessment described in Sect. 3 was taken as an estimation of the patient's condition. In this section, we build multiple predictive models for patient assessment results and evaluate if adding weather factors can improve patient assessment prediction results. We constructed the models for all four considered assessments: pulse rate assessment, SpO2 rate assessment, assessment using the questionnaire, and final manual assessment, which was completed by a professional and should consider all other features. The output variable was a color-coded health status (green, red, yellow), as described in Sect. 3. The output was treated as an absolute value. We considered the following variables as potential predictors for the assessment results: a. Historical information: A history of the corresponding assessment over several previous days can be viewed as a summary of the patient's condition. History over the previous 1–6 days was considered. The only history of a specific assessment type was included for each assessment model. For instance, only manual assessment history over the last several days was included for the manual assessment model, and the values of pulse, SpO2, and questionnaire-based assessments were excluded, and b. Weather information: The features like temperature (Kelvin degrees), pressure (mBars), and humidity (percentage) usually correspond to the average over the last several hours relative to the assessment time. The averaging intervals of 4–12 h (with a step of 4 h) were considered. We also considered the most recent (without any averaging) available weather information as a potential predictor. To evaluate the weather data's significance, we started with building logistic regression models [24] of the assessment results based on weather features alone. Green assessment result is taken as a default class (Table 2 will show later that this class is dominating). Since the patient information is not considered yet, the high variance is expected, but the evaluation of significance is possible. The models are separate for each combination of the weather averaging (average 4 h of weather data, 8 h, 12 h, or use current weather) and the assessment type (pulse, questionnaire based, SpO2, and manual). We evaluated the p-values of those coefficients being not equal to zero. As a null hypothesis, we took the hypothesis that there is no linear dependency, and the regression coefficient has a non-zero value only due to random fluctuations. If this hypothesis can be rejected, it means that there is enough evidence of dependency between the weather feature and the assessment results. The p-value for this null hypothesis corresponds to the probability of getting this regression coefficient (or more significant in absolute value) by pure chance in the absence of any real linear dependency. If the p-value is below a certain threshold, it is taken as evidence that linear dependency is present [26]. We chose the standard significance level of 0.05 as a p-value boundary [27]. To account for multiple comparisons, we used Bonferroni correction [28] - the most cautious estimate of statistical significance, aimed to reduce the number of false positives. Here we have 16 models: each combination of 4 assessment types and four averaging duration for the weather. We have six relevant coefficients for each model: there are three weather-related coefficients for Zyellow and 3 for Zred. Although the intercept is in the model, we are not interested in its p-value in this study. There are therefore 16 * 6 = 96 comparisons, and the boundary for p-value is 0.05/96 ≈ 0.0006.

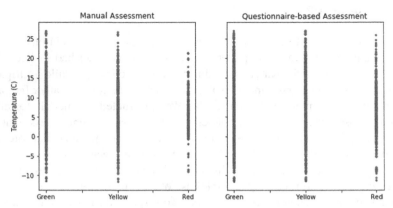

Fig. 1. Correspondence between assessment results and air temperature at the time of assessment.

Table 1. Mcfadden r-square values for logistuic regression models.

Assessment	Weather			
	Current	Average 4 h	Average 8 h	Average 12 h
Questionnaire	0.0022	0.0015	0.0016	0.0018
Pulse	0.0030	0.0031	0.0023	0.0019
SpO2	0.0017	0.0014	0.0018	0.0026
Manual	0.0075	0.0078	0.0081	0.0083

Figure 1 and Table 1 show the dependency between temperature and questionnaire-based assessment and manual assessment. Table 1 shows that McFadden R-square [29] values are very low. Even the largest one never exceeds 1%. It is further confirmed by Fig. 1 - due to high variance, the dependency between temperature and assessment results is barely visible. Therefore, the temperature is proven to be statistically significant for those assessments, but it cannot be used alone for prediction purposes. Since the temperature has a statistically significant dependency on the assessment results, it means it potentially can improve the assessment prediction models [24]. To further evaluate the weather's effect, we need to augment our analysis with a comparison of multiple predictive models that consider both weather features and patient conditions. We included all the weather features into the model, even the ones that did not show statistical significance for the linear regression coefficient. Those features can still be valuable in the case of intersection and non-linear dependencies. Before constructing the model, we split the data in 90:10 (training: testing) typical for machine learning tasks [30] We considered the following predictive models with grid search evaluation – logistic regression, decision tree, stratified random guess predictor, random forest, and gradient boosted trees [24].

Table 2. Prevalence of assessment results in the training set.

Assessment	Green	Yellow	Red
Pulse	71.60%	11.12%	17.28%
SpO2	90.87%	4.68%	4.45%
Question	56.85%	35.10%	8.05%
Manual	53.38%	35.94%	10.68%

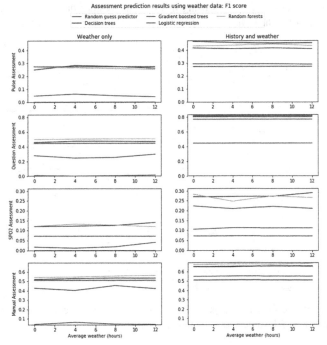

Fig. 2. Predicting various assessments using history and weather data [history length (1–6 days]. (Color figure online)

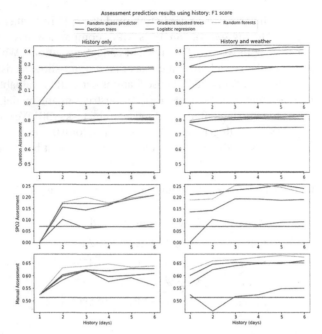

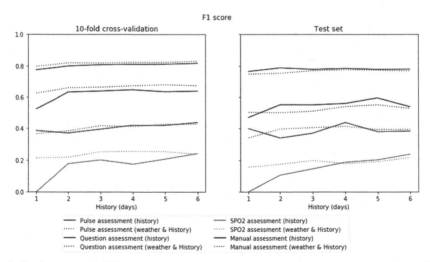

Fig. 3. Predicting various assessments using history and weather data [averaging the weather data: averaging over 4 h, 8 h, 12 h, or taking the current weather only] (Color figure online)

Fig. 4. Performance of different models. For each model type and for each number of considered history days the largest F1 value was selected (averaged over 10-fold cross validation over the training set)

We used K-fold (K = 10) cross-validation technique. The average performance over the K iterations was used for comparison and for model selection [31, 33]. The performance of the models is summarized in Figs. 2–4.

Table 3. Best performing models depending on the variables considered.

Assessment	Weather	History					
		1	2	3	4	5	6
Questionnaire	No	LR	DT	RF	RF	GBT	RF
	Yes	RF/4 h	RF/12 h	RF/8 h	RF/8 h	RF/8 h	RF/cur.
Pulse	No	DT	RF	RF	RF	RF	RF
	Yes	DT/12 h	DT/cur.	DT/4 h	DT/12 h	DT/8 h	DT/8 h
SpO2	No	DT	RF	RF	RF	DT	DT
	Yes	DT/12 h	DT/cur.	RF/cur.	RF/cur.	DT/12 h	DT/4 h
Manual	No	DT	RF	RF	RF	RF	RF
	Yes	RF/12 h	RF/8 h	RF/12 h	RF/8 h	RF/4 h	RF/4 h

5 Discussion and Results

Figure 2 shows that the predictability of different assessments varies greatly: for example, the F1 score exceeds 0.8 and significantly exceeds the stratified predictor baseline for questionnaire-based assessment, while for SpO2 assessment, we can barely improve the F1 score over 0.25. The left column of Fig. 2 shows that the weather information alone is not enough to predict the assessment results - most models perform barely better than a majority guess. Those results are understandable from a commonsense point of view: it is implausible to predict the patient's state if no information about the patient or the disease stage is considered. This problem is partially remediated by adding assessment history as model features. Right columns of Fig. 2 show visible prediction improvement when assessment history is considered. Figure 2 also shows that there is no significant difference in the case of weather-aware and weather-ignorant models. It is further reinforced by Figs. 3 and 4, which show that for all the model types, weather-aware models barely (if at all) outperform weather-ignorant models. Combined with significance analysis, it shows that even though the effects of the weather on the patient's condition are statistically significant, the corresponding variance is just too high for the weather to be a useful predictor variable. Figure 4 compares performance on the training set and on the test set to show the signs of some overfit for manual assessment prediction models and no sign of overfitting for other assessment predictions. Table 3 reveals that the best performing models are decision trees and random forests (only for several configurations outperformed by logistic regression and gradient boosted trees). No weather averaging strategy outperforms others. Note that some models perform worse than a random guess according to the F1 criterion. The reason is related to the fact that the classes are skewed:

for example, for SpO2 assessment, a simple majority predictor can achieve 90.87% training set accuracy by always predicting "green" (see Table 1). However, such predictions will result in zero F1 score - there will be no positive prediction and, therefore, no true positive (or false positive) values. If the model cannot learn the structure of the data and if high accuracy results in the low loss function, then the model can degenerate into a majority predictor. For example, if the data classes are linearly inseparable, then the logistic regression model can devolve into a de-facto majority predictor when all the data end up on one side of a separating hyperplane. It happens in some cases in this study - some weather-only models predict barely any positive ("yellow" and "red") values and hence result in high accuracy but low F1 score, which is reflected in Figs. 2 and 3. The results of this study can be summarized as follows: (a.) according to the COPD and weather datasets collected in southern Norway, there is a statistically significant dependency between air temperature and patient condition. Questionnaire-based assessment results and manual assessment results tend to get slightly worse when the air temperature is lower. However, it should be specially noted that we cannot claim that air temperature is a sole influence on the patient's condition: for example, air temperature can be a proxy variable for the season or any other temperature-correlated aspect, (b.) no statistically significant dependency was detected between air pressure and humidity and patient assessment results, and (c.) history-based assessment prediction methods show some promise in predicting the patient's future state based on several previous days of the patient's assessment.

Including weather features into history-based models does not significantly improve the history-based models for predicting the patient assessment. However, the fact of statistically significant dependency between air temperature and patients' health status gives hope that it can be used in other models: either assessment prediction models that rely on other features or adjacent models (e.g., how many patients will request help the next day, according to the history and weather forecast).

6 Conclusion

This paper presented an investigation of the correlation and dependency between COPD and temperature, barometric pressure, and humidity in the Agder region, the Southern part of Norway. We built predictive models for patient assessment in that region based on the patient's condition and the weather information. We used various models, including logistic regression, decision trees, random forests, and gradient boosted trees. Moreover, we detected statistically significant dependency between manual assessment results and current air temperature. The achieved results can help predict COPD patients' conditions in south Norway based on the weather forecast. Our future research goal is to deliver automatic, evidence-based, context-specific, personalized recommendations to achieve personal wellness goals, addressing obesity as a study case. This paper's research outcome will help us create useful context-based activity recommendations for our future eCoach [32] system.

References

1. Mathers, C.D., Loncar, D.: Updated projections of global mortality and burden of disease, World Health Organization (2005)
2. Guiqin, F., Xiakun, Z., Huayue, L.: Study on the correlation between temperature and chronic obstructive pulmonary disease in Shijiazhuang, China—retrospective cohort. J. Geosci. Environ. Prot. **5**, 25–31 (2017)
3. Bulajich, B., Subotich, D., Mandarich, D., Kljajich, R.V., Gajich, M.: Influence of atmospheric pressure, outdoor temperature, and weather phases on the onset of spontaneous pneumothorax. Ann. Epidemiol. **15**(3), 185–190 (2005)
4. Lin, S., Luo, M., Walker, R., Liu, X., Hwang, S., Chinery, R.: Extreme high temperatures and hospital admissions for respiratory and cardiovascular diseases. Epidemiology **20**(5), 738–746 (2009)
5. Braga, A., Zanobetti, A., Schwartz, J.: The effect of weather on respiratory and cardiovascular deaths in 12 U.S. cities. Environ. Health Perspect. 2002 **110**, 859–863 (2002)
6. Schwartz, J.: Who is sensitive to extremes of temperature? A case-only analysis. Epidemiology **16**(1), 67–72 (2005)
7. Donaldson, G., Seemungal, T., Jeffries, D., Wedzicha, J.: Effect of temperature on lung function and symptoms in chronic obstructive pulmonary disease. Eur. Respir. J. **13**(4), 844–849 (1999)
8. Medical News Today. By MaryAnn de Pietro, Reviewed by J. Keith Fisher, M.D. https://www.medicalnewstoday.com/articles/323657.php
9. Mu, Z., et al.: Synergistic effects of temperature and humidity on the symptoms of COPD patients. Int. J. Biometeorol. **61**, 1919–1925 (2017)
10. Ferrari, U., et al.: Influence of air pressure, humidity, solar radiation, temperature, and wind speed on ambulatory visits due to chronic obstructive pulmonary disease in Bavaria. Germany. Int. J. Biometeorol. **56**, 137–143 (2012)
11. Tseng, C.M., et al.: The effect of cold temperature on increased exacerbation of chronic obstructive pulmonary disease: a nationwide study. PLoS ONE **8**(3), e57066 (2013)
12. Health Central. By John Bottrell, reviewed by Eli Hendel, M.D. https://www.healthcentral.com/article/7-ways-weather-affects-copd
13. Pope, C.A., Dockery, D.W., Kanner, R.E., Villegas, G.M., Schwartz, J.: Oxygen saturation, pulse rate, and particulate air pollution: a daily time-series panel study. Am. J. Respir. Crit. Care Med. **159**(2), 365–372 (1999)
14. Price, G.: Effects of Weather, Air Quality and Geographical Location on Asthma and COPD Exacerbations in the Localities of Worcester and Dudley, Coventry University in collaboration with the University of Worcester and … (2007)
15. Chan, C.-L., et al.: A survey of ambulatory-treated asthma and correlation with weather and air pollution conditions within Taiwan during 2001–2010. J. od Asthma, 1–9 (2018)
16. Ping, J.: Influence of hazy weather on patient presentation with respiratory diseases in Beijing, China. Asian Pac. J. Cancer Prev. **16**(2), 607–611 (2015)
17. Daher, A., et al.: Characterization and triggers of dyspnea in patients with chronic obstructive pulmonary disease or chronic heart failure: effects of weather and environment. Lung **197**(1), 21–28 (2019)
18. Bakerly, N.D., Roberts, J.A., Thomson, A.R., Dyer, M.: The effect of COPD health forecasting on hospitalisation and health care utilisation in patients with mild-to-moderate COPD. Chronic Respir. Dis. **8**(1), 5–9 (2011)
19. Ren, J., Li, B., Yu, D., Liu, J., Ma, Z.: Approaches to prevent the patients with chronic airway diseases from exacerbation in the haze weather. J. Thorac. Dis. **8**(1), E1 (2016)

20. Davis, R.E., Enfield, K.B.: Respiratory hospital admissions and weather changes: a retrospective study in Charlottesville Virginia, USA. Int. J. Biometeorol. **62**(6), 1015–1025 (2018)
21. Alahmari, A.D., et al.: Influence of weather and atmospheric pollution on physical activity in patients with COPD. Respir. Res. **16**(1), 71 (2015)
22. United4Health, FP7 EU project United4Health. http://www.united4health.no/. Accessed 12 June 2019
23. OpenWeather data. https://openweather.co.uk/. Accessed 12 June 2019. https://openweathermap.org/api
24. Alpaydin, E.: Introduction to Machine Learning. MIT Press, 4 December 2009
25. Nunavath, V., Goodwin, M., Fidje, J.T., Moe, C.E.: Deep neural networks for prediction of exacerbations of patients with chronic obstructive pulmonary disease. In: Pimenidis, E., Jayne, C. (eds.) EANN 2018. CCIS, vol. 893, pp. 217–228. Springer, Cham (2018). https://doi.org/10.1007/978-3-319-98204-5_18
26. Nix, T.W., Barnette, J.J.: The data analysis dilemma: ban or abandon. A review of null hypothesis significance testing. Res. Schools **5**(2), 3–14 (1998)
27. Decramer, M., Gosselink, R., Troosters, T., Verschueren, M., Evers, G.: Muscle weakness is related to utilization of health care resources in COPD patients. Eur. Respir. J. **10**(2), 417–423 (1997)
28. Spring 2008 - Stat C141/ Bioeng C141 - Statistics for Bioinformatics: https://www.stat.berkeley.edu/~mgoldman/Section0402.pdf
29. McFadden, D.: Conditional logit analysis of qualitative choice behavior. In: Zarembka, P. (ed.) Frontiers in Econometrics. Academic Press, pp. 105–142 (1974)
30. Mitchell, T., Buchanan, B., DeJong, G., Dietterich, T., Rosenbloom, P., Waibel, A.: Machine learning. Ann. Rev. Comput. Sci. **4**(1), 417–433 (1990)
31. Hosmer Jr, D.W., Lemeshow, S., Sturdivant, R.X.: Applied Logistic Regression, vol. 398. John Wiley & Sons, Hoboken (2013)
32. Chatterjee, A., Gerdes, M.W., Martinez, S.: eHealth initiatives for the promotion of healthy lifestyle and allied implementation difficulties. In: 2019 International Conference on Wireless and Mobile Computing, Networking and Communications (WiMob), pp 1–8. IEEE, October 2019
33. Chatterjee, A., Gerdes, M.W., Martinez, S.G.: Identification of risk factors associated with obesity and overweight—a machine learning overview. Sensors **20**(9), 2734 (2020)
34. WHO COPD page. Webpage: https://www.who.int/news-room/fact-sheets/detail/chronic-obstructive-pulmonary-disease-(copd). Accessed 20 May 2020

Deep Learning

Interpretable Option Discovery Using Deep Q-Learning and Variational Autoencoders

Per-Arne Andersen[✉], Morten Goodwin, and Ole-Christoffer Granmo

Department of ICT, University of Agder, Grimstad, Norway
{per.andersen,morten.goodwin,ole.granmo}@uia.no

Abstract. Deep Reinforcement Learning (RL) is unquestionably a robust framework to train autonomous agents in a wide variety of disciplines. However, traditional deep and shallow model-free RL algorithms suffer from low sample efficiency and inadequate generalization for sparse state spaces. The options framework with temporal abstractions [18] is perhaps the most promising method to solve these problems, but it still has noticeable shortcomings. It only guarantees local convergence, and it is challenging to automate initiation and termination conditions, which in practice are commonly hand-crafted.

Our proposal, the Deep Variational Q-Network (DVQN), combines deep generative- and reinforcement learning. The algorithm finds good policies from a Gaussian distributed latent-space, which is especially useful for defining options. The DVQN algorithm uses MSE with KL-divergence as regularization, combined with traditional Q-Learning updates. The algorithm learns a latent-space that represents good policies with state clusters for options. We show that the DVQN algorithm is a promising approach for identifying initiation and termination conditions for option-based reinforcement learning. Experiments show that the DVQN algorithm, with automatic initiation and termination, has comparable performance to Rainbow and can maintain stability when trained for extended periods after convergence.

Keywords: Deep reinforcement learning · Clustering · Options · Hierarchical reinforcement learning · Latent-space representation

1 Introduction

The interest in deep Reinforcement Learning (RL) is rapidly growing due to significant progress in several RL problems [2]. Deep RL has shown excellent abilities in a wide variety of domains, such as video games, robotics and, natural language progressing [13,14,16]. Current trends in applied RL has been to treat neural networks as black-boxes without regard for the latent-space structure. While unorganized latent-vectors are acceptable for model-free RL, it is disadvantageous for schemes such as options-based RL. In an option-based RL, the

© Springer Nature Switzerland AG 2021
S. Yildirim Yayilgan et al. (Eds.): INTAP 2020, CCIS 1382, pp. 127–138, 2021.
https://doi.org/10.1007/978-3-030-71711-7_11

policy splits into sub-policies that perform individual behaviors based on the current state of the agent. A sub-policy, or option, is selected with initialization criteria and ended with a termination signal. The current state-of-the-art in option-based RL primarily uses hand-crafted options. Option-based RL algorithms work well for simple environments but have poor performance in more complicated tasks. There is, to the best of our knowledge, no literature that addresses good option selection for difficult control tasks. There are efforts for making automatic options selection [17], but no method achieves notable performance across various environments.

This paper proposes a novel deep learning architecture for Q-learning using variational autoencoders that learn to organize similar states in a vast latent-space. The algorithm derives good policies from a latent-space that feature interpretability and the ability to classify sub-spaces for automatic option generation. Furthermore, we can produce human-interpretable visual representations from latent-space that directly reflects the state-space structure. We call this architecture DVQN for deep Variational Q-Networks and study the learned latent-space on classic RL problems from the Open AI gym [4].

The paper is organized as follows. Section 3 introduces preliminary literature for the proposed algorithm. Section 4 presents the proposed algorithm architecture. Section 5 outlines the experiment setup and presents empirical evidence of the algorithm performance. Section 2 briefly surveys work that is similar to our contribution. Finally, Sect. 6 summarises the work of this paper and outlines a roadmap for future work.

2   Related Work

There are numerous attempts in the literature to improve interpretability with deep learning algorithms, but primarily in the supervised cases. [22] provides an in-depth survey of interpretability with Convolutional Neural Networks (CNNs). Our approach is similar to the work of [20], where the authors propose an architecture for visual perception of the DQN algorithm. The difference, however, is primarily our focus on the interpretability of the latent-space distribution via methods commonly found in variational autoencoders. There are similar efforts to combine Q-Learning with Variational Autoencoders, such as [11,19], and shows promising results theoretically but with limited focus on interpretability. [1] did notable work on interpretability among using a distance KL-distance for optimization but did not find convincing evidence for a deeper understanding of the model. The focus of our contribution deviates here and finds significant value in a shallow and organized latent-space.

Options. The learned latent-space is valuable for the selection of options in hierarchical reinforcement learning (HRL). There is increasing engagement in HRL research because of several appealing benefits such as sample efficiency and model simplicity [3]. Despite its growing attention, there are few advancements within this field compared to model-free RL. The options framework [18] is perhaps the most promising approach for HRL in terms of intuitive and convergence guarantees. Specifically, the options framework defines semi-Markov decision processes (SMDP), which is an extension of the traditional MDP framework [21]. SMDP features temporal abstractions where multiple discrete time steps are generalized to a single step. These abstract steps are what defines an option, where the option is a subset of the state-space. In the proposed algorithm, the structure of the latent-space forms such temporal abstractions for options to form.

3 Background

The algorithm is formalized under conventional Markov decision processes tuples $<S, A, P, R, \gamma>$ where S is a (finite) set of all possible states, A is a (finite) set of all possible actions, P defines the probabilistic transition function $P(S_{t+1} = s'|s, a)$ where s is the previous state, and s' is the transition state. R is the reward function $R(r_{t+1}|s, a)$. Finally, the γ is a discount factor between $\gamma \in [0 \ldots 1]$ that determines the importance of future states. Lower γ values decrease future state importance while higher values increase.

4 Deep Variational Q-Networks

Our contribution is a deep Q-learning algorithm that finds good policies in an organized latent space from variational autoencoders.[1] Empirically, the algorithm shows comparable performance to traditional model-free deep Q-Networks variants. We name our method the **D**eep **V**ariational **Q**-**N**etwork (DVQN) that combines two emerging algorithms, the variational autoencoder (VAE) [12] and deep Q-Networks (DQN) [14].

In traditional deep Q-Networks, the (latent-space) hidden layers are treated as a black-box. On the contrary, the objective of the variational autoencoder is to reconstruct the input and **organize** the latent-vector so that similar (data) states are adjacently modeled as a Gaussian distribution.

In DQN, the latent-space is sparse and is hard to interpret for humans and even option-based machines. By introducing a VAE mechanism into the algorithm, we expect far better interpretability for creating options in RL, which is the primary motivation for this contribution. Variational autoencoders are, in contrast to deep RL, involved with the organization of the latent-space representation, and commonly used to generate clusters of similar data with t-SNE or PCA [23]. The DVQN algorithm introduces three significant properties. First, the algorithm fits the data as a Gaussian distribution. This reduces the policy-space, which in practice reduces the probability of the policy drifting away from global minima. Second, the algorithm is generative and does not require exploration schemes such as ϵ-greedy because it is done in re-parametrization during training. Third, the algorithm can learn the transition function and, if desirable, generate training data directly from the latent-space parameters, similar to the work of [8].

---

[1] The code will be published upon publication.

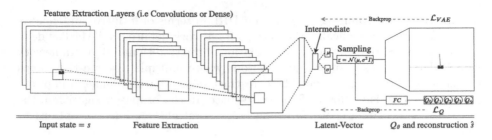

Fig. 1. The deep variational Q-Networks architecture.

Figure 1 illustrates the architecture of the algorithm. The architecture follows general trends in similar RL literature but has notable contributions. First, features are extracted from the state-input, typically by using convolutions for raw images and fully-connected for vectorized input. The extracted features are forwarded to a fully connected intermediate layer of a user-specified size commonly between 50 to 512 neurons. The intermediate layer splits into two streams that represent the variance μ and standard deviation σ and is used to sample the latent-vector using a Gaussian distribution through the re-parameterization. The latent-vector is forwarded to the decoder for state reconstruction and the Q-Learning stream for action-value (Q-value) optimization. The decoder and Q-Learning streams have the following loss functions:

$$\mathcal{L}_{VAE} = MSE(s, \hat{s}) + D_{KL}[q_\psi(z|s) \| p_\theta(z|s)] \tag{1}$$

$$\mathcal{L}_{DQN} = (r + \gamma Q(s', \arg\max_{a'} Q(s', a'; \theta_i); \theta_i) - Q(s, a; \theta_i))^2 \tag{2}$$

$$\mathcal{L}_{DVQN} = c_1 \mathbb{E}_{\sim q_\psi(z|s)}[\mathcal{L}_{VAE}] + c_2 \mathbb{E}_{s,a,s',D \sim r}[\mathcal{L}_{DQN}]. \tag{3}$$

The global loss function $\mathcal{L}_{DVQN}$ is composed of two local objectives: $\mathcal{L}_{DQN}$ and $\mathcal{L}_{VAE}$. In the VAE loss, the first term is the mean squared error between the input s and its reconstruction $\hat{s}$. The second term is regularization using KL-distance to minimize the distance between the latent distribution and a Gaussian distribution. The DQN loss is a traditional deep Q-Learning update, as described in [14].

Algorithm 1. DVQN: Minimal Implementation

1: Initialise Ω
2: Initialise DVQN model π
3: Initialise replay-buffer D_π
4: **for** N episodes **do**
5:     $D_\pi \leftarrow$ Collect samples from Ω under the untrained policy π via the generative policy sampling.
6:     Train model π on a mini-batch from D_π with objective from Eq. 3

Algorithm 1 shows a general overview of the algorithm. First, the environment is initialized. Second, the DVQN model from Fig. 1 is initialized with the desired hyperparameters, and third, the replay-buffer is created. For a specified number of episodes, the algorithm samples actions from the generative policy for exploration and stores these as MDP tuples in the experience replay. After each episode, the algorithm samples mini-batches from the experience replay and performs parameter updates using stochastic gradient descent. The (loss function) optimization objective is described in Eq. 3. The process repeats until the algorithm converges.

5   Experiments and Results

In this section, we conduct experiments against four traditional environments to demonstrate the effectiveness of the DVQN algorithm. We show that the algorithm can organize the latent-space by state similarity while maintaining comparable performance to model-free deep Q-learning algorithms.

5.1   Experiment Test-Bed

We evaluate the DVQN in the following environments; CartPole-v0, Acrobot-v1, CrossingS9N3-v0, and FourRooms-v0, shown in Fig. 2. These environments are trivial to solve using model-free reinforcement learning and hence, excellent for visualizing the learned latent-space. The FourRooms-v0 environment is especially suited for option-based RL and can solve the problem in a fraction of time steps compared to model-free RL. Although the DVQN algorithm **does not quantify options for analysis** (see Sect. 6), the primary goal is to organize the latent-space so that it is possible to extract meaningful and interpretable options automatically. The aim is to have **comparable performance** to vanilla deep Q-Network variants found in the literature [5,10,14]. DVQN benchmarks against vanilla DQN, Double DQN, and Rainbow.

FourRooms-v0 and CrossingS9N3-v0 are a grid-world environment where the objective is to reach the terminal-state cell (In the lower right of the image in both environments). In FourRooms-v0, the agent has to enter several doors and only complete a part of the goal for each door it enters. FourRooms-v0 is an ideal environment for option-based reinforcement-learning because each door is considered a sub-goal. While the environment is solvable by many deep reinforcement learning algorithms, option-based RL is more efficient. The agent receives small negative rewards for moving and positive rewards for entering the goal-state (global) or the doors (local). The Crossing is a simpler environment where the agent has to learn the shortest path to the goal state. In both grid-environments, the agent can move in any direction, one cell per time step.

To further show that the algorithm works in simple control tasks, we perform experiments in CartPole-v0 and Acrobot-v1. The objective in CartPole-v0 is to balance a pole on a cart. Each step generates a positive reward signal while receiving negative rewards if the pole falls below an angle threshold. The agent

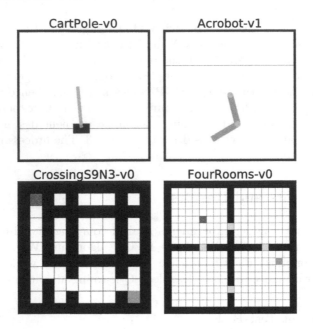

Fig. 2. The experiment test-bed contains the following environments; CartPole-v0, Acrobot-v1, CrossingS9N3-v0, and FourRooms-v0

can control the direction of the cart at every time step. The Acrobot-v1 has a similar aim to control the arm to hit the ceiling in a minimal number of time steps. The agent receives negative rewards until it reaches the ceiling. The CartPole-v0 and Acrobot-v1 environments origins from [4] while CrossingS9N3-v0 and the FourRooms-v0 origins from [6].[2]

5.2   Hyperparameters

During the experiments, we found DVQN to be challenging to tune. Initially, the algorithm used ReLU as activation but was discarded due to vanishing gradients resulting in divergence for both policy and reconstruction objectives. By using ELU, we found the algorithm to be significantly more stable during the experiments, and it additionally did not diverge if training continued after convergence. We will explore the underlying cause of our future work. Table 1 shows the hyperparameters used in our experiments where most of the parameters are adopted from prior work. Recognize that the DVQN algorithm does not use ϵ-greedy methods for exploration. The reason for this is that random sampling is done during training in the variational autoencoder part of the architecture. In general, the algorithm tuning works well across all of the tested domains, and better results can likely be achieved with extended hyperparameter searches.

---

[2] A community-based scoreboard can be found at https://github.com/openai/gym/wiki/Leaderboard.

Table 1. Algorithm and hyperparameters used in the experiments. For the Rainbow algorithm, we used the same hyperparameters described in [10]. The DDQN had target weight updates every 32k frames.

Algorithm	DQN	DDQN	Rainbow	DVQN (ours)
Optimiser		Adam		RMSProp
Learning Rate		0.003		0.000025
Activation		ReLU		ELU
Batch Size		32		128
Replay Memory		1m		
Epsilon Start		1.0		N/A
Epsilon End		0.01		N/A
Epsilon Decay		0.001 (Linear)		N/A
Gamma		0.95		
Q-Loss		Huber		MSE

For DVQN, we consider such tuning for our continued work on DVQN using options, see Sect. 6.

5.3   Latent-Space Evaluation

An attractive property of our model is that the latent-space is a Gaussian distribution. As seen in Fig. 3, the DVQN algorithm can produce clustered latent-spaces for all tested environments. For example, in the CartPole-v0 environment, there are three clusters where two of them represent possible terminal states and one that represents states that give a reward. To fully utilize the capabilities of DVQN, the latent-space can be used to generate options for each cluster to promote different behavior for every region of the state-space.

Figure 4 illustrates the visualization of the latent-space representation in CartPole-v0. We find that each cluster represents a specific position and angle of the pole. The latent-space interpolates between these state variations, which explains its shape. Although the clusters are not perfect, it is trivial to construct separate classification for each cluster with high precision, and this way automatically construct initiation and termination signals for options.

5.4   Performance Evaluation

Figure 5 illustrates a comparison of performance between state-of-the-art Q-Learning algorithms and the proposed DVQN algorithm. The performance measurement is the mean of 100 trials over 1500 episodes for CartPole-v0, CrossingS9N3-v0, FourRooms-v0, and 3000 episodes for Acrobot-v1. The performance is measured in accumulated rewards and is therefore negative for environments where each time step yields a negative reward.

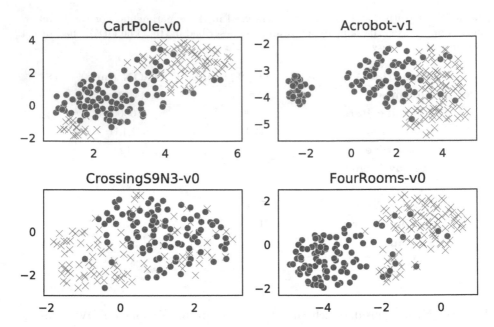

Fig. 3. The learned latent space for all of the tested environments. DVQN successfully trivialise the selection of options as seen in the well-separated state clusters. The circular points illustrate states with positive reward while cross illustrates negative rewards.

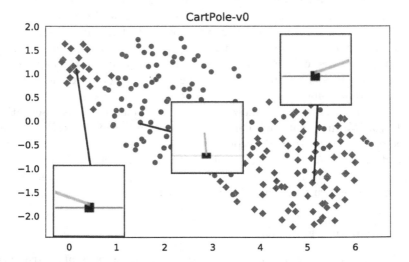

Fig. 4. The relationship between states and the latent-space for the CartPole-v0 environment. DVQN can separate each angle, left, middle and right into separable clusters, which are especially useful in option-based reinforcement learning. Additionally, the visualization of the latent space that the Q-head uses to sample actions is trivial to interpret.

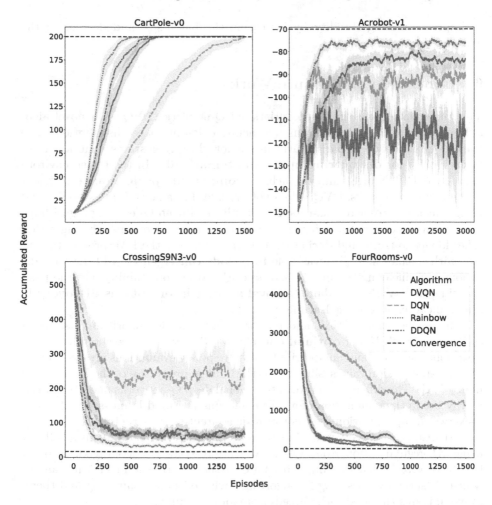

Fig. 5. The accumulative sum of rewards of the DVQN compared to other Q-Learning based methods in the experimental environments. Our algorithm performs better than DQN from [14], and shows comparable results to DDQN from [9] and Rainbow from [10]. We define an episode threshold for each of the environments (x-axis) and accumulate the agent rewards as the performance metric for CartPole-v0 and Acrobot-v1. The scoring metric in CrossingS9N3-v0 and the FourRooms-v0 is based on how many steps the agent used to reach the goal state.

The DVQN algorithm performs better than DQN and shows comparable performance to DDQN and Rainbow. DVQN is not able to find a good policy in the Acrobot-v1 environment but successfully learns a good visual representation of the latent space. In general, the DVQN algorithm is significantly harder to train because it requires the algorithm to find a good policy within a Gaussian distribution. We found this to work well in most cases, but it required fine-tuning of hyperparameters. The algorithm is also slower to converge, but we were able to improve training stability by increasing the batch-size and decreasing the learning-rate.

6   Conclusion and Future Work

This paper introduces the deep variational Q-network (DVQN), a novel algorithm for learning policies from a generative latent-space distribution. The learned latent-space is particularly useful for clustering states that are close to each other for **discovering options automatically**. In the tested environments, the DVQN algorithm can achieve **comparable performance** to traditional deep Q-networks. DVQN does not provide the same training stability and is significantly harder to fine-tune than traditional deep Q-learning algorithms. For instance, network capacity is increased. As a result of this, the algorithm takes longer to train, and during the experiments, only the RMSprop optimizer [15] with a small step size was able to provide convergence. Additionally, the exponential linear units from [7] had a positive effect on stability. On the positive side, the DVQN contributes a **novel approach for options discovery** in hierarchical reinforcement learning algorithms.

The combination of VAE and reinforcement learning algorithms has interesting properties. Under **optimal conditions**, the latent-space should, in most cases follow a true Gaussian distribution where policy evaluations always provide optimal state-action values, since this is the built-in properties of the latent space in any VAE. The difference between traditional deep Q-networks and DVQN primarily lies in the elimination of a sparse and unstructured latent-space. In deep Q-Networks, optimization does not provide a latent-space structure that reflects a short distance between states but rather a distance between Q-values [14]. By using KL-regularization from VAE, low state-to-state is encouraged. Another benefit of VAE is that we sample from a Gaussian distribution to learn μ and σ, which is especially satisfying for algorithms with off-policy sampling and therefore eliminates the need for (ϵ-greedy) random sampling.

In the continued work, we wish to do a thorough analysis of the algorithm to justify its behavior and properties better. A better understanding of the Gaussian distributed latent-space is particularly appealing because it would enable better labeling schemes for clustering, or perhaps fully automated labeling. Finally, we plan to extend the algorithm from model-free behavior to hierarchical RL with options. The work of this contribution shows that it is feasible to produce organized latent-spaces that could provide meaningful options, and the hope is that this will result in state-of-the-art performance in a variety of tasks in RL.

References

1. Annasamy, R.M., Sycara, K.: Towards better interpretability in deep Q-networks. In: Proceedings, The Thirty-Third AAAI Conference on Artificial Intelligence, September 2018. http://arxiv.org/abs/1809.05630

2. Arulkumaran, K., Deisenroth, M.P., Brundage, M., Bharath, A.A.: Deep reinforcement learning: a brief survey. IEEE Sig. Process. Mag. **34**(6), 26–38 (2017). https://doi.org/10.1109/MSP.2017.2743240

3. Barto, A., Mahadevan, S., Lazaric, A.: Recent Advances in Hierarchical Reinforcement Learning. Technical Report, PIGML Seminar-AirLab (2003)

4. Brockman, G., et al.: OpenAI Gym. arxiv preprint arXiv:1606.01540, June 2016

5. Chen, W., Zhang, M., Zhang, Y., Duan, X.: Exploiting meta features for dependency parsing and part-of-speech tagging. Artif. Intell. **230**, 173–191, September 2016. https://doi.org/10.1016/j.artint.2015.09.002, http://arxiv.org/abs/1509.06461

6. Chevalier-Boisvert, M., Willems, L., Pal, S.: Minimalistic Gridworld Environment for OpenAI Gym. https://github.com/maximecb/gym-minigrid (2018)

7. Clevert, D.A., Unterthiner, T., Hochreiter, S.: Fast and accurate deep network learning by exponential linear units (ELUs). In: The International Conference on Learning Representations, vol. 16, November 2015. http://arxiv.org/abs/1511.07289

8. Ha, D., Schmidhuber, J.: Recurrent world models facilitate policy evolution. In: Bengio, S., Wallach, H., Larochelle, H., Grauman, K., Cesa-Bianchi, N., Garnett, R. (eds.) Advances in Neural Information Processing Systems, vol. 31, pp. 2450–2462. Curran Associates Inc., Montréal, CA, September 2018. http://papers.nips.cc/paper/7512-recurrent-world-models-facilitate-policy-evolution.pdf

9. van Hasselt, H., Guez, A., Silver, D.: Deep reinforcement learning with double Q-learning. In: Proceedings, The Thirtieth AAAI Conference on Artificial Intelligence, p. 13, September 2015. http://arxiv.org/abs/1509.06461

10. Hessel, M., et al.: Rainbow: combining improvements in deep reinforcement learning. In: Proceedings 32nd Conference on Artificial Intelligence, AAAI 2018, pp. 3215–3222. AAAI Press, New Orleans, Louisiana USA, October 2018. https://www.aaai.org/ocs/index.php/AAAI/AAAI18/paper/download/17204/16680

11. Huang, S., Su, H., Zhu, J., Chen, T.: SVQN: sequential variational soft Q-learning networks. In: International Conference on Learning Representations (2020). https://openreview.net/forum?id=r1xPh2VtPB

12. Kingma, D.P., Welling, M.: Auto-encoding variational bayes. In: Proceedings of the 2nd International Conference on Learning Representations, December 2013. https://doi.org/10.1051/0004-6361/201527329, http://arxiv.org/abs/1312.6114

13. Levine, S., Finn, C., Darrell, T., Abbeel, P.: End-to-end training of deep visuomotor policies. J. Mach. Learn. Res. **17**(1), 1334–1373 (2016). http://www.jmlr.org/papers/volume17/15-522/15-522.pdf

14. Mnih, V., et al.: Human-level control through deep reinforcement learning, December 2015. https://doi.org/10.1038/nature14236, http://arxiv.org/abs/1312.5602

15. Nair, V., Hinton, G.E.: Rectified linear units improve restricted boltzmann machines. In: Proceedings of the 27th International Conference on Machine Learning, p. 8 (2010)

16. Silver, D., et al.: Mastering the game of Go without human knowledge. Nature (2017). https://doi.org/10.1038/nature24270

17. Stolle, M.: Automated Discovery of Options in Reinforcement Learning. Ph.D. thesis, McGill University (2004)

18. Sutton, R.S., Precup, D., Singh, S.: Between MDPs and semi-MDPs: a framework for temporal abstraction in reinforcement learning. Artif. Intell. **112**(1–2), 181–211 (1999)

19. Tang, Y., Kucukelbir, A.: Variational deep Q network. In: Advances in Neural Information Processing Systems, vol. 30. Long Beach, CA, USA, November 2017. http://arxiv.org/abs/1711.11225
20. Wang, J., Gou, L., Shen, H.W., Yang, H.: DQNViz: a visual analytics approach to understand deep Q-networks. IEEE Trans. Visualization Comput. Graph. **25**(1), 288–298 (2019). https://doi.org/10.1109/TVCG.2018.2864504
21. Younes, H.L.S., Simmons, R.G.: Solving generalized semi-markov decision processes using continuous phase-type distributions. In: Proceedings, The Ninth AAAI Conference on Artificial Intelligence (2004). www.aaai.org
22. Zhang, C., Patras, P., Haddadi, H.: Deep learning in mobile and wireless networking: a survey. IEEE Commun. Surv. Tutorials (2018). http://arxiv.org/abs/1803.04311
23. Zheng, Y., et al.: Variational deep embedding: a generative approach to clustering. In: International Joint Conference on Artificial Intelligence, vol. 17, p. 8 (2017). http://arxiv.org/abs/1611.05148

Evaluating Predictive Deep Learning Models

Patrick Ribu Gorton$^{(\boxtimes)}$ ⓘ and Kai Olav Ellefsen ⓘ

Department of Informatics, University of Oslo, Oslo, Norway
patrick.ribu@gmail.com , kaiolae@ifi.uio.no

Abstract. Predicting the future using deep learning models is a research field of increasing interest. However, there is a lack of established evaluation methods for assessing their predictive abilities. Images and videos are targeted towards human observers, and since humans have individual perceptions of the world, evaluation of videos should take subjectivity into account. In this paper, we present a framework for evaluating predictive models using subjective data. The methodology is based on a mixed methods research design, and is applied in an experiment to measure the realism and accuracy of predictions of a visual traffic environment. Our method is shown to be uncorrelated with the predominant approach for evaluating predictive models, which is a frame-wise comparison between predictions and ground truth. These findings emphasise the importance of using subjective data in the assessment of predictive abilities of models and open up a new direction for evaluating predictive deep learning models.

Keywords: Video prediction · Model evaluation · Deep learning

1 Introduction

Humans constantly use information from experience to perform predictive processing, which in turn can improve future behaviour. This bridging over different temporal points with past considerations is suggested to be the core capabilities which makes our cognitive brain so versatile and efficient [2]. Recent advances in artificial intelligence have allowed computers to learn internal models of physical environments, and predict images of how the environments will evolve in the future. Equipping an intelligent agent with the ability to predict future states and results of potential actions may improve its performance and robustness in environments comprised of complex physical systems [7]. Also, research has shown that the type of image used to represent an environment may influence the model's ability to predict future states [14].

Because the future is rich with uncertainty, predicting future events is a challenging task, and so suitable ways of evaluating predictive models are needed

---

Supported by the University of Oslo.

S. Yildirim Yayilgan et al. (Eds.): INTAP 2020, CCIS 1382, pp. 139–150, 2021.
https://doi.org/10.1007/978-3-030-71711-7_12

to properly assess their predictive abilities. Predictive deep learning models are usually evaluated with methods for frame-wise comparison, which quantifies the level of numerical resemblance between predicted and true states, like videos. Such objective similarity metrics face challenges in that they are sensitive to pixel intensity and slight mismatch between predicted and true states, in either space or time. They are also often specific to the type of image in use, thus comparing predictive models that process different image types with this type of method may not be applicable.

But the ultimate receivers of images and videos are human observers, and not all differences between images are equally significant to humans [15]. With the interpretation of images and video being highly subjective, why is model evaluation mainly performed using objective, numerical methods? Video prediction using deep learning is in demand for alternative methods for evaluating models. The contribution of this paper is a framework for evaluating predictive models using subjective data, which addresses some of the challenges related to model evaluation by frame-wise comparison.

Outline. The remaining parts of this paper are as follows: Sect. 2 includes an overview of related work. Section 3 describes the research problem. Section 4 introduces our research methods and the experimental setting. Section 5 presents the results based on the experiment and the proposed evaluation framework, which is the main contribution of this paper. Section 6 concludes the paper and discusses future work.

2   Related Work

There is currently a growing interest in the field of predicting the future using deep learning with an increasing number of contributions. The focus in most of the literature is related to designing models that are superior to the current state of the art, and there is insufficient focus on scientific evaluation of these models. Researchers evaluate and report results of their model, and the predominant approach of doing this is to perform a numerical frame-wise comparison between ground truth and predicted states or sequences, e.g. with MSE, PSNR and SSIM [11,13,14,20]. These metrics are not necessarily indicative of prediction quality and realism, in which structural ambiguities and geometric deformations are a dominant factor [11].

[15] emphasises the importance of assessing image and video quality with methods that take into account how humans perceive visual stimuli, and perhaps the work most related to our approach are those that integrate human judgement as a part of their model evaluation. For example, [12] predict whether a tower of blocks will fall, and compare the outcome to human expectation. [20] and [11] employ crowd-sourced human preference evaluation to determine an object's colour and shape throughout a prediction, and to assess the realism of video predictions. Common for these evaluation approaches are their small scales and lack of standardisation to follow. [3] has made a similar remark about the

shortcomings related to evaluating predictive deep learning models, and states that 'there is in general a lack of common test ground for this kind of models'.

3   Problem Description

In this paper, we attempt to develop a suitable method for evaluating predictive models using subjective data. This leads to the following relevant questions:

1. How can subjective data be used to evaluate predictive deep learning models?
2. Which model properties should be assessed in the evaluation?

3.1   Evaluating Video Predictions

Evaluating video predictions is a field that has not been investigated in-depth, and there is a lack of well-established standards for measuring the quality and plausibility of such predictions [3]. Generally speaking, evaluating unsupervised models is challenging because vague properties such as *meaningfulness* is difficult to measure analytically [22]. Whether a piece of information is considered meaningful depends entirely on what that piece of information is meant to represent, in other words; meaningful information is contextual [4]. A frame-wise comparison does not take into account contextual information specific to the environment but rather relates objectively to the evaluation task, which may lead to some challenges.

A prediction may be identical to a true scenario, categorically speaking, even though objects are not completely overlapping in space or time. Take, for instance, a scenario from a traffic environment wherein the ground truth there are four vehicles passing in the left lane, but in the prediction, there are only two. Although the prediction failed to foresee all the vehicles, it is still very accurate in relation to the context. A frame-wise comparison might, on the other hand, consider this a poor prediction because of the dissimilarity in the image regions where the vehicles are missing. We argue that since a frame-wise comparison does not consider the required context, it might be an unreliable way of evaluating the predictive model.

3.2   A Mixed Methods Research Design

The considerations above lead to the idea of conducting surveys to help evaluate the content of video predictions. Sometimes the most appropriate way to answer a research question requires the use of two or more research methods [21, p. 28]. Combining qualitative and quantitative methods within the same study is referred to as a *mixed methods research design* (MMRD), a methodology for conducting research that involves collecting, analysing and integrating quantitative and qualitative research to expand and strengthen a study's conclusions [18]. Mixed methods research may be used when the integration of these research types provides a better understanding of the research problem than either of each alone.

Describing the contents of video clips, or more specifically video predictions, is a subjective matter which should not be left to a single person or machine to do, to preserve a shared opinion. This indicates that using a quantitative method alone might not suffice. [22] argues that crowdworkers' opinions may be well suited to indicate coherency between categorical data. We suggest first conducting a qualitative survey to learn more about aspects of the environment that are considered essential to humans, followed by a quantitative survey designed based on these results to collect a more considerable amount of data for further analysis. Finally, by using numerical and statistical measures on the collected data, we may learn how good a predictive deep learning model is at predicting the future of an environment.

4   Research Methods

4.1   Model and Implementation

To verify our proposed method for evaluating video predictions, we extend a recent impactful method for generating visual predictions of the future; the World Models architecture [7], which builds upon the idea that intelligent agents benefit from running an internal model of the world it operates within.

Discrete representations are a natural fit for complex reasoning, planning and predictive learning [16], and so the predictive model used in this experiment is inspired by World Models, though comprised of a vector-quantised variational autoencoder [16] and an LSTM network [9]. We here summarise the model architecture briefly but devote attention to the *model evaluation*. Thus, we encourage readers eager for more detail to familiarise themselves with the original work by [7] (Fig. 1).

To address the challenge of evaluating video predictions of distinct image types, such as RGB and semantic segmentation, we create two models with

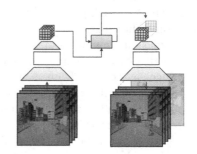

Fig. 1. The VQ-VAE compresses a sequence of images into a corresponding sequence of latent representations, used by the LSTM to predict an arbitrary number of future states.

this setup; one receives RGB images of size $128 \times 128 \times 3$, and the other semantically segmented images with 13 classes of size $128 \times 128 \times 13$. In both cases, the VQ-VAE encoders output discrete 5-bit latent variables of size 8×8, meaning each element in the latent space contains an integer in the range [0, 31].

The models are implemented in PyTorch 1.1.0 and trained using the Adam optimisation method [10] with learning rates $3e-4$. The embeddings of the VQ-VAEs are trained using exponential moving averages, according to [17].

The models are trained within the CARLA traffic simulator [6] with RGB and semantic segmentation sequences at 5 FPS.

4.2 Evaluation Method and Experimental Setting

This paper's contribution (Sect. 5.5) is a framework for evaluating predictive models using subjective data, and to form its basis we propose a MMRD consisting of two surveys; a qualitative survey S_1 and a quantitative survey S_2. Conducting S_1 establishes which aspects of the environment that are considered important to human observers. This information is used within S_2 to collect a large amount of data related to the predictive abilities of the proposed models. The S_2 submissions are then analysed using numerical and statistical methods that assess model performance.

Both surveys are web-based, in which participants observe short video clips from the environment and perform specific tasks related to these videos. All videos have a frame rate of 5 FPS and a length of 50 frames, which equals a 10-second duration in the environment. However, for visual purposes, the videos' playback speed is increased by a factor of two. The VQ-VAEs process all videos such that ground truth and predicted videos appear visually similar so as not to create a bias in the MMRD.

The Qualitative Survey. In the qualitative survey, S_1, participants obtained by convenience sampling [1] observed and created descriptions for 52 ground truth video clips from the specified traffic environment. These ground truth videos were sampled from the CARLA validation sequences.

Among the 52 videos, 26 were of image type RGB and the other 26 of semantic segmentation, presented in random order. All sequences were processed by the VQ-VAEs, and were thus subject to some quality change. For convenience, the descriptions created by the participants could consist of up to four words, suggesting a video's main event. New participants were recruited until theoretical saturation [21, p. 71] among the descriptions was achieved, which for this experiment was achieved with seven participants. The submitted video descriptions usually portrayed one or two main events per video, and the most recurring descriptions among these were accepted to be used as categories for the quantitative survey, S_2.

Table 1. The most recurring descriptions from S_1, selected as categories for S_2.

Recurring descriptions selected as categories			
c_1	Driving straight	c_5	Breaking for traffic
c_2	Left turn	c_6	Approaching vehicle
c_3	Right turn	c_7	Oncoming vehicle(s)
c_4	Standing still	c_8	Following vehicle

The Quantitative Survey. In the quantitative survey, S_2, the categories obtained from S_1 were used by new participants to describe new videos. In addition to the categories in Table 1, another category, 'undefined', is added to be used in cases where the participants of S_2 consider none of the other categories to be appropriate. The videos of S_2 are 52 randomly selected, unique sets of CARLA validation sequences. This means that for both image types, RGB and semantic segmentation, there are 52 ground truth videos and 52 corresponding video predictions, representing the same sequences across image types. In total there are $2 \times 2 \times 52 = 208$ videos.

Owing to this large number of videos, S_2 is divided into four subsets with 52 videos each, so as not to tire the participants. However, they may complete as many of the subsets as they wish, though only the same subset once. The order of all videos is randomised across the four subsets to reduce a potential ordering effect [19]. Two inquiries follow every video; the category of choice recorded on a nine-level nominal scale, and the degree of perceived realism recorded on a five-level ordinal scale, as shown in Fig. 2.

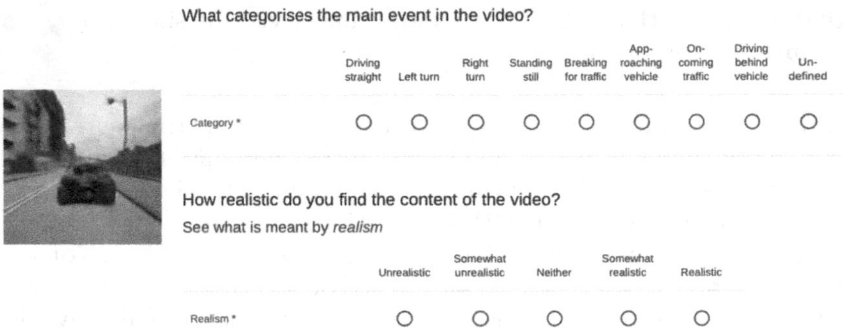

Fig. 2. A snippet from the quantitative survey. A video is followed by two inquiries; its event category and the participants' degree of perceived realism.

S_2 received 453 submissions (not all were from unique participants), of which approximately 95% were from users of the Amazon Mechanical Turk service [5], while the remaining proportion of submissions were from participants obtained by convenience sampling. 24 submissions were discarded by outlier detection based on median absolute deviation.

5   Results

The following results are obtained by evaluating the 52 sets of videos used in S_2 (in total $2 \times 2 \times 52 = 208$ videos). Both model evaluation with frame-wise comparison and with our MMRD are presented.

5.1   A Visual Interpretation of Samples

First, we inspect a couple of samples to help fully understand the results in this experiment. A *sample* consists of the condition used to generate a video prediction, the video prediction itself and its corresponding ground truth, as shown in Fig. 3. The condition is comprised of ten input frames, which the model uses as context to predict a future trajectory.

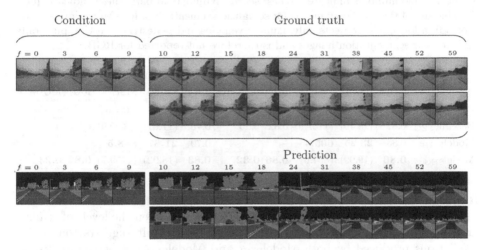

Fig. 3. Examples of an RGB *sample* (top) and a semantic segmentation *sample* (bottom). The top row contains a sequence of ground truth images, where the first ten frames are the condition used by the model to predict future states. The bottom row contains the corresponding predicted sequence generated by the model. The frame number in a sample is denoted by f.

Figure 3 shows two samples, commented from top to bottom:

1. (RGB) The model succeeds in predicting some of the oncoming traffic in the left lane, in addition to the right turn towards the end of the sequence.
2. (SEG) The model predicts a right turn followed by traffic clog, while the ground truth shows a left turn followed by traffic clog.

5.2   The Frame-Wise Comparison

A frame-wise comparison reveals the following similarity scores at two scopes; short-term prediction (5 frames) and long-term prediction (50 frames). In addition to reporting results for the predictive models ($\text{Model}_{\text{RGB}}$ and $\text{Model}_{\text{SEG}}$), a naive baseline model is included. This baseline model is a repeated copy of the last conditional input frame and gives a basis for comparison of the similarity scores. With MSE and PSNR being of questionable use on $\text{Model}_{\text{SEG}}$'s predictions, SSIM is the only measure applicable to both models. The SSIM metric suggests that $\text{Model}_{\text{SEG}}$ is somewhat superior to $\text{Model}_{\text{RGB}}$. However, both models are superior to their baselines, which indicates that they both have learnt some dynamics of the environment.

5.3   The MMRD

Using the proposed MMRD, we now assess two properties of the predictive models, namely prediction realism and prediction accuracy. Prediction accuracy is divided into two evaluation objectives; video classification and a pairwise comparison of categorical distributions (Table 2).

Table 2. Bold numbers indicate the best scores. Numbers in parenthesis indicate questionable use of the similarity metric for semantic segmentation. IoU-MO is intersection over union for moving objects only, namely vehicles and pedestrians. IoU applies only for semantic segmentation images and is therefore not reported for RGB.

Method	Short-term (5 frames)					Long-term (50 frames)				
	SSIM	PSNR	MSE	IoU	IoU-MO	SSIM	PSNR	MSE	IoU	IoU-MO
Baseline$_{RGB}$	0.79	21.56	797.4	–	–	0.75	19.95	1187.8	–	–
Baseline$_{SEG}$	0.82	(18.49)	(1157.9)	0.82	0.25	0.78	(17.67)	(1499.9)	0.76	0.20
Model$_{RGB}$	0.83	**23.25**	**605.4**	–	–	0.79	**21.87**	**888.5**	–	–
Model$_{SEG}$	**0.86**	(19.99)	(854.6)	**0.86**	**0.32**	**0.83**	(18.92)	(1159.7)	**0.82**	**0.23**

Realism. Wilcoxon-Mann-Whitney tests with significance levels of 0.05 reveal that for both image types, no significant difference between the levels of realism in ground truth and predictions is identified. This result suggests that video predictions produced by both Model$_{RGB}$ and Model$_{SEG}$ are perceived just as realistic as the ground truth videos.

Video Classification. The classification scores by Model$_{RGB}$ Model$_{SEG}$ are compared using a two-sided z-test of equality for two proportions. Using a single label, Model$_{SEG}$ is significantly better classifying videos with a p-value of $1.401e-4$ at significance level $\alpha = 0.05$. When using multiple labels (2–3 labels), no significance difference between the models can be identified with a p-value of 0.1995. The classification scores are summarised in Table 3.

Table 3. Classification scores for Model$_{RGB}$ and Model$_{SEG}$ with the single-label and multi-label classification tasks, reported accuracy in terms of average, median and standard deviation.

Video classification						
Model	Accuracy: single-label			Accuracy: multi-label		
	Average	Median	Std.	Average	Median	Std.
Model$_{RGB}$	32.8%	32.1%	20.2%	48.0%	53.8%	20.60%
Model$_{SEG}$	35.8%	34.8%	21.2%	47.6%	54.1%	19.9%

Inter-rater Agreement. The Krippendorff's alpha test [8] reveals that the general agreement between raters in S_2 is poor ($\alpha_{Krip} < 0.667$). The poor agreement explains the somewhat low classification scores, and we should treat the evaluation objective differently.

Pairwise Comparison Between Categorical Distributions. The similarity between categorical distributions is measured using cosine similarity. $\cos \theta = 0$ equals complete dissimilarity, and $\cos \theta = 1$ equals complete similarity. A Wilcoxon-Mann-Whitney test gives a p-value of 0.8561, which at significance level $\alpha = 0.05$ reveals that there is no significant difference in prediction accuracy between the two models. In essence, comparing categorical distributions with cosine similarity arrives at the same conclusion as the multi-label video classification does: Representing the visual environment with either RGB images or semantic segmentation makes no significant difference in terms of how accurate the generated video predictions are (Table 4).

Table 4. Cosine similarity measures resemblance between categorical distributions for all video pairs. We report the average, median and standard deviation of similarity between distributions.

$\cos \theta$ between categorical distributions			
Model	Average	Median	Std.
Model$_{\text{RGB}}$	0.7988	0.8649	0.1969
Model$_{\text{SEG}}$	0.7992	0.8660	0.2023

5.4   Comparing the MMRD to the Frame-Wise Comparison

Measuring the correlation between the frame-wise comparison and the proposed evaluation method reveals to what extent the two approaches measure similar properties of the predictive models. Figure 4 shows scatter plots of single-label classification (SLC), multi-label classification (MLC) and cosine similarity ($\cos \theta$).

$$\{\text{SLC vs. SSIM}\}_{\text{RGB}} : r(50) = -.06, p = .672 \rightarrow \text{not significant}$$
$$\{\text{MLC vs. SSIM}\}_{\text{RGB}} : r(50) = .16, p = .257 \rightarrow \text{not significant}$$
$$\{\cos \theta \text{ vs. SSIM}\}_{\text{RGB}} : r(50) = .03, p = .833 \rightarrow \text{not significant}$$
$$\{\text{SLC vs. SSIM}\}_{\text{SEG}} : r(50) = .07, p = .621 \rightarrow \text{not significant}$$
$$\{\text{MLC vs. SSIM}\}_{\text{SEG}} : r(50) = .06, p = .672 \rightarrow \text{not significant}$$
$$\{\cos \theta \text{ vs. SSIM}\}_{\text{SEG}} : r(50) = .19, p = .177 \rightarrow \text{not significant}$$

The two evaluation approaches are *uncorrelated*, which in practice means that the frame-wise comparison evaluates video predictions differently to how humans perceive them. This finding emphasises the shortcomings related to using a frame-wise comparison for model evaluation.

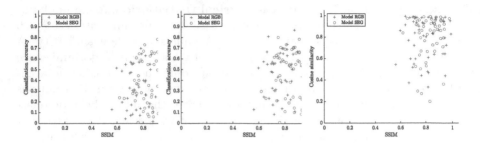

Fig. 4. Scatter plots of the single-label classification (left), multi-label classification (middle) and cosine similarity (right) versus SSIM for video predictions with 50 frames.

5.5   Model Evaluation Framework

The results in this experiment lead to the development of an improved version of our evaluation method. We present the main contribution of this paper; a framework for evaluating predictive models using subjective data, shown in Fig. 5. The term *predictive models* refers mainly to deep learning models that predict future visual states of environments. We do believe that the framework is applicable to other and similar models and prediction tasks. The steps of the framework are as follows:

1. Determine assessment of quality, select video sample size and populations of human evaluators.
2. Conduct the qualitative survey until theoretical saturation of descriptions and the number of suggested possible events is achieved.

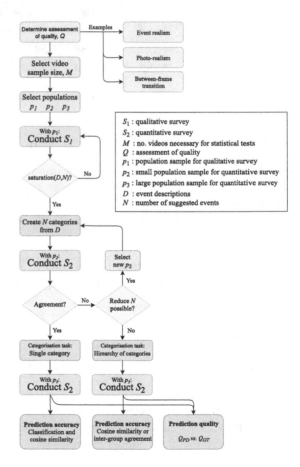

Fig. 5. The proposed framework for evaluating predictive models using subjective data.

3. Conduct the quantitative survey with a limited population of participants. Reduce the number of categories if the inter-rater agreement is poor. If not possible, enable a hierarchy of categorical events.
4. Conduct the quantitative survey with a large population of participants and evaluate model performance according to the evaluation objectives.

6   Conclusions and Future Work

The work in this paper presents a new method for evaluating predictive models using subjective data, which measures mainly two properties of predictive models; the realism and the accuracy of the predictions they produce. The evaluation method is based on a mixed methods research design, which involves conducting surveys to gather subjective data about videos generated by predictive models, with minimal prior information about the environment. The data collection is followed by statistical analyses that reveal the quality and prediction accuracy of the models.

The proposed evaluation method was compared to the currently acknowledged evaluation method in the field of video prediction with deep learning, which is a frame-wise comparison between ground truth and video predictions. Analyses reveal that the two evaluation methods are uncorrelated, and thus measure different properties of a video. Furthermore, this confirms that the acknowledged evaluation method, i.e. the frame-wise comparison, evaluates video predictions differently to how humans perceive them, a discovery consistent with the findings of [15]. This implies that future contributions to the research field in the form of model architectures most certainly should evaluate the model's performance using subjective data, if not only as a part of the evaluation. This paper contributes to the research field with a framework for performing exactly this type of model evaluation. We, therefore, encourage others to either use it in their research as is or as a source of inspiration.

Future work should investigate the evaluation framework's scalability in terms of evaluating more models simultaneously, and its application to other domains.

References

1. Battaglia, M.: Encyclopedia of Survey Research Methods (2008). https://doi.org/10.4135/9781412963947. http://sk.sagepub.com/reference/survey
2. Bubic, A., von Cramon, D.Y., Schubotz, R.I.: Prediction, cognition and the brain (2010). https://doi.org/10.3389/fnhum.2010.00025
3. Castelló, J.S.: A comprehensive survey on deep future frame video prediction (2018)
4. Cox, S.: What is Meaningful Information? - Voice - Two Twelve (2014). http://www.twotwelve.com/voice/what-is-meaningful-information.html
5. Crowston, K.: Amazon mechanical turk: a research tool for organizations and information systems scholars. In: Bhattacherjee, A., Fitzgerald, B. (eds.) IS&O 2012. IAICT, vol. 389, pp. 210–221. Springer, Heidelberg (2012). https://doi.org/10.1007/978-3-642-35142-6_14

6. Dosovitskiy, A., Ros, G., Codevilla, F., López, A., Koltun, V.: CARLA: an open urban driving simulator. Technical report (2017)
7. Ha, D., Schmidhuber, J.: World models (2018). https://doi.org/10.5281/zenodo.1207631
8. Hayes, A.F., Krippendorff, K.: Answering the call for a standard reliability measure for coding data. Commun. Methods Measures **1**(1), 77–89 (2007). https://doi.org/10.1080/19312450709336664
9. Hochreiter, S., Schmidhuber, J.: Long short-term memory. Technical report 8 (1997). http://www7.informatik.tu-muenchen.de/~hochreitwww.idsia.ch/~juergen
10. Kingma, D.P., Ba, J.L.: Adam: a method for stochastic optimization. In: 3rd International Conference on Learning Representations, ICLR 2015 - Conference Track Proceedings (2015)
11. Lee, A.X., Zhang, R., Ebert, F., Abbeel, P., Finn, C., Levine, S.: Stochastic adversarial video prediction (2018). https://doi.org/10.1080/08870440802530798
12. Lerer, A., Gross, S., Fergus, R.: Learning physical intuition of block towers by example (2016). https://doi.org/10.1016/j.neucom.2015.11.100
13. Lotter, W., Kreiman, G., Cox, D.: Deep predictive coding networks for video prediction and unsupervised learning, pp. 1–18 (2016). https://doi.org/10.1063/1.1727962. http://arxiv.org/abs/1605.08104
14. Luc, P., Neverova, N., Couprie, C., Verbeek, J., Lecun, Y.: Predicting deeper into the future of semantic segmentation. In: Proceedings of the IEEE International Conference on Computer Vision (2017), https://doi.org/10.1109/ICCV.2017.77
15. Moorthy, A.K., Wang, Z., Bovik, A.C.: Visual perception and quality assessment. In: Optical and Digital Image Processing: Fundamentals and Applications, pp. 419–439 (2011). https://doi.org/10.1002/9783527635245.ch19
16. van den Oord, A., Vinyals, O., Kavukcuoglu, K.: Neural discrete representation learning. In: Advances in Neural Information Processing Systems. vol. 2017-Decem, pp. 6307–6316 (2017)
17. Razavi, A., van den Oord, A., Vinyals, O.: Generating diverse high-fidelity images with VQ-VAE-2. In: Wallach, H., Larochelle, H., Beygelzimer, A., d Alché-Buc, F., Fox, E., Garnett, R. (eds.) Advances in Neural Information Processing Systems, vol. 32, pp. 14866–14876. Curran Associates, Inc. (2019). http://papers.nips.cc/paper/9625-generating-diverse-high-fidelity-images-with-vq-vae-2.pdf
18. Schoonenboom, J., Johnson, R.B.: How to construct a mixed methods research design. KZfSS Kölner Zeitschrift für Soziologie und Sozialpsychologie **69**, 107–131 (2017). https://doi.org/10.1007/s11577-017-0454-1
19. Strack, F.: "Order effects" in survey research: activation and information functions of preceding questions. In: Schwarz, N., Sudman, S. (eds.) Context Effects in Social and Psychological Research, pp. 23–34. Springer, New York (1992). https://doi.org/10.1007/978-1-4612-2848-6_3
20. Wichers, N., Villegas, R., Erhan, D., Lee, H.: Hierarchical long-term video prediction without supervision, June 2018. http://arxiv.org/abs/1806.04768
21. Willig, C.: Introducing Qualitative Research in Psychology, 3rd edn (2013)
22. Vaughan, J.W.: Making better use of the crowd: how crowdsourcing can advance machine learning research. Technical report (2018). http://jmlr.org/papers/v18/17-234.html

Pre-trained CNN Based Deep Features with Hand-Crafted Features and Patient Data for Skin Lesion Classification

Sule Yildirim-Yayilgan[1]($\boxtimes$), Blend Arifaj[2], Masoomeh Rahimpour[3],
Jon Yngve Hardeberg[1], and Lule Ahmedi[2]

[1] Faculty of Information Technology and Electrical Engineering, NTNU – Norwegian University of Science and Technology, Gjøvik, Norway
sule.yildirim@ntnu.no

[2] Faculty of Electrical and Computer Engineering, University of Prishtina, Prishtina, Republic of Kosovo

[3] Catholic University of Leuven, Leuven, Belgium

Abstract. Skin cancer is a major public health problem, with millions newly diagnosed cases each year. Melanoma is the deadliest form of skin cancer, responsible for the most over 6500 deaths each year in the US, and the rates have been rising rapidly over years. Because of this, a lot of research is being done in automated image-based systems for skin lesion classification. In our paper we propose an automated melanoma and seborrheic keratosis recognition system, which is based on pre-trained deep network combined with structural features. We compare using different pre-trained deep networks, analyze the impact of using patient data in our approach, and evaluate our system performance with different datasets. Our results shown us that patient data has impact on characteristic curve metric value with around 2–6% and different algorithm in final classification layer has impact with around 1–4%.

Keywords: Deep networks · CNN · Handcrafted features · Skin lesion classification and segmentation · Image processing

1 Introduction

Malignant melanoma are among the most rapidly increasing types of cancer in the world with a considerable mortality rate. The American Cancer Society predicted more than 100.350 melanoma cases in 2020, of which more than 6.850 persons are expected to lose their lives [1]. However, early detection of melanoma leads to a cure rate of over 90% in low risk melanoma patients, and the use of dermoscopy images [6] plays an important role in this process. Dermoscopy images are mainly used to evaluate pigmented skin lesions in order to distinguish malignant skin lesions from benign ones such as melanocytic nevus and seborrhoeic keratosis. However, due to the visual similarity of different skin lesions, melanoma diagnosis using human vision alone can be subjective and

© Springer Nature Switzerland AG 2021
S. Yildirim Yayilgan et al. (Eds.): INTAP 2020, CCIS 1382, pp. 151–162, 2021.
https://doi.org/10.1007/978-3-030-71711-7_13

inaccurate even among experienced dermatologists. Lesions' varying size, shape and fuzzy boundaries, different skin colors, presence of different artifacts including hair and bubbles are some of the reasons that make the detection process more challenging.

In this paper, we propose two architectures using two different categories of features extracted from images of skin lesions, namely handcrafted and deep features. We compare the performance of these two kinds of features separately and also consider a combined use of these features to provide a single classification decision for melanoma diagnosis.

The remaining paper is organized as follows. In Sect. 2 a survey of state-of-the-art on melanoma classification is presented. Section 3 describes the theory behind the proposed method including deep networks and dermoscopic features. The experimental results of the proposed method on melanoma classification and a comparative study are presented in Sect. 4. Finally, the discussion and conclusion remarks are given in Sect. 5.

2   Related Works

The success of melanoma detection task highly depends on the features extracted from the lesion. There are different clinical approaches that are commonly used to extract diagnostic features from dermoscopy images such as ABCD(E) rule, pattern analysis, seven-point checklist and Menzies method [36]. The ABCD(E) rule is based on asymmetry, border, colour, diameter, and evolution (or elevation) features [34]. The pattern analysis approach facilitates melanoma diagnosis by determining the presence of specific patterns visible in dermoscopic images. The features employed in pattern analysis approach refer both to the chromatic characteristics and to the shape and/or texture of the lesion. These include Atypical Pigment Network, Blue-whitish Veil, Atypical Vascular Pattern, Irregular Streaks, Irregular Pigmentation, Irregular Dots/Globules, and Regression Structures [19]. The seven-point checklist provides a simplification of the standard pattern analysis and compared to ABCD(E), allows less experienced observers to achieve higher diagnostic accuracy values. The Menzies approach facilitates to identify the colour patterns and asymmetry within the lesion. Computational methods based on the Menzies' criteria have been proposed to analyze the presence of six basic colour classes (white, red, light brown, dark brown, blue–grey, and black) for dermoscopic images [33].

The features used in automated dermoscopy image analysis mostly have been inspired by the clinical methods which have been mentioned above. Table 1 shows a distribution of feature categories known as hand-crafted features commonly employed in the literature. We categorize these features in four main classes including structural (shape), geometrical (spatial), chromatic (colour) and texture features. The interested reader is referred to [33] for detailed classification.

Recently, Convolutional Neural Networks (CNNs) have shown an impressive performance in image classification tasks. Different features detected at the different convolutional layers enable the network to handle large variations in the

Table 1. Hand-crafted categorizes in automated melanoma classification

Feature	Structural	Geometric	Chromatic	Textural
Sadeghi et al. [35]	√	√	√	√
Møllersen et al. [31]			Divergence-based	
Ballerini et al. [7]			RGB, HSV, CIE	GCM
Tomas et al. [25,26]				LBP and RSurf
Codella et al. [14]	Edge Histogram		Color Histogram	MSLBP
Ma et al. [24]	√		√	√
Barata et al. [10]			√	√
Garnavi et al. [19]	√			√
Zhou et al. [44]	Fourier transformation			
Damian et al. [16]	Fourier transform amplitude	Asymmetry, circularity	Color distribution	

dataset which may result in higher diagnostic accuracy and sensitivity in classification. In comparison with fully connected networks, CNNs have much fewer
connections and parameters and hence they are easier to train. They build the
property of translation invariance of image statistics by replicating the same
neurons. They model the low-level features of images locally by enabling the
local connectivities, and make the high-level features of image coarser as they
are in nature [40] using repeated pooling/sub-sampling layers.

In 2014, Simonyan et al. [37] investigated the effect of depth component in
CNNs by introducing VGG network which achieved 7.3% error rate in ILSVRC
(ImageNet Large Scale Visual Recognition) competition. This network is characterized by its simplicity which has increased the depth of network by adding
more convolutional layers. In comparison to the previous networks, VGG (with
16 or 19 layers) models more non-linearity and has less parameters by employing
small convolutional filters (3 * 3) in each layer. Szegedy et al. [40] presented two
different concepts in CNNs including a new level of organization in the form of
the "Inception module" and increased network depth. They proposed a deeper
network (22-layer) with computational efficiency in the case of the GoogLeNet.

However, there was another challenge by increasing the depth of network; it
has been depicted that adding extra layers beyond the certain layers does not
help obtain promising results and may results in higher training and validation
errors. In 2015, He et al. [20] presented a new architecture called Deep Residual
Network (ResNet) which won ILSVRC 2015 with an incredible error rate of
3.57%. ResNet consists of a number of residual blocks with each block comprising
of several convolution layers, batch normalization layers and ReLU layers. The
residual block enables to bypass a few convolution layers at a time [41].

Most of these architectures (VGGNet, GoogLeNet, ResNet) are available as
the pre-trained models initially trained on approximately one million natural
images from the ImageNet dataset [17]. Such networks are widely employed for

melanoma detection. Codella et al. [13] used a pre-trained CNNs named Caffe to extract the features for skin image classification and proved that deep features outperform traditional hand-crafted features. Majtner et al. [27] used AlexNet as pre-trained deep network for features extraction and proved that deep feature has potential on image classification. Devassy et al. [29] replaced the complex handcrafted features with standard and deep feature, extracted from ResNet. This combination outperformed state of the art results. Zhao et al. [43] showed that CNN has a great ability for localizing the objects. They proposed a technique called Class Activation Mapping (CAM) by using global average pooling (GAP) in CNNs. A class activation map for a particular category indicates the discriminative image regions used by the CNN to identify the category.

Despite all these algorithms, there is still room for automated algorithm that shows reasonable results. This motivate us to develop a new approach that combines pre-trained deep networks and structural features to detect skin lesions.

3   Methodology

We proposed a structure that combines state-of-the-art developments of deep neural networks and machine learning techniques to automated analysis of melanoma images. The main pipeline of our proposed framework for melanoma classification is depicted in Fig. 1. Similar to most common approaches employed in computational systems for skin lesion diagnosis, it includes six main steps 1) Preprocessing, 2) Data Augmentation 3) Segmentation 4) Feature Extraction 5) Feature Selection and 6) Classification. In the following, more details for each step are presented.

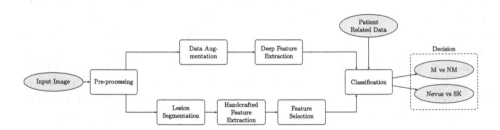

Fig. 1. Pipeline of automated melanoma image classification

3.1   Preprocessing

Dermoscopy images are often obtained with different imaging devices under varying acquisition conditions. Changes in the illumination of image acquisition devices adversely affect the color of images and reduce the performance of diagnostic systems. Hence, it is a crucial task to normalize the color and illuminance balance of images by applying color constancy methods. Different research groups have proposed color normalization strategies to deal with dermoscopy images. Gray_world, Max_RGB, Shades of Gray and General Gray World methods are among these methods that are fast, easy to implement and require the tuning of few parameters [8]. In this study, we applied the Shades of Gray method. Interested readers is referred to [12] for a detailed description of different methods.

3.2 Segmentation

First, automatic border detection is performed to separate the lesion from the background skin. To do this job we applied deep Residual U-Net [42]. The main benefits from this model are: residual units ease training of deep networks and this model allow us to design a deep network with fewer parameters however and better performance [42]. To train this network we applied 2000 pairs of lesion-mask and for validation we applied 200 pairs lesion-mask. Those pairs lesion-mask are provided from ISIC 2017 challenge [15].

3.3 Data Augmentation

It is well known that data augmentation notably improves the performance of deep neural networks. Particularly if the amount of training data is limited, augmentation would improve the robustness of the model [23]. There are different kinds of geometrical transformations that can be applied on the images before providing them as input to the CNN to generate new versions of the images such as applying random transformations: cropping, flipping, etc. In the following, the process of data augmentation employed in this study has been described:

1. Considering four rotation angles (45, 90, 135 and 180), we generate four rotated images per original image.
2. Finding the largest inner rectangle, we crop each image to ensure that all pixels belong to the original image.
3. Finally, we perform square crops to resize each image of 224 * 224, since the CNN network requires square input images.

Considering the orientation changes and crops preformed, we generate eight versions of each image which, then will be provided to the trained network [18].

3.4 Feature Extraction

The performance of automated approaches for skin lesion detection greatly depends on the choice of meaningful descriptive features derived from the dermoscopic images. In this study, we have considered three types of features which are useful in automated skin lesion detection for improving the overall classification performance.

Deep Features. As our first attempt for feature extraction, we employed a model based on the VGG network. According to the CNN models and based on our observations in the experiments using VGG and VGG-Deep, we employed

ResNet as the next learning architecture to extract the deep features. Our CNNs were fine-tuned with the training samples from the initially pre-trained model to perform classification on the ILSVRC 2015 data [20]. In the last layer of ResNet, there are 2048 features related to high-level concepts of the input image which are ready to be fed to the classification layer.

Handcrafted Features. Feature extraction aims to represent a set of descriptors to separate each image into different classes by feeding them to the classifier. As mentioned is previous section, in order to extract the deep features, all the images need to be resized to a fixed size of 224 × 224 pixels. As a result, some important features related to the size and shape of object might be eliminated. To address this problem, some valuable features called handcrafted features have been extracted and added to previous deep features to strengthen our feature set. Once the image has been segmented into the object and background as stated in Sect. 3.2, the important handcrafted features must be extracted from the object. Three main categories of handcrafted features have been employed in this study including shape features, color features, and texture features.

Shape Features: Shape features provide important information about the lesion that can be deterministic for lesion's classification [39]. To shape feature we used lesion's mask, provided as output from lesion segmentation step in Fig. 1.

Color Features: Color feature descriptors delineate the colour distribution of images. In order to quantify the color features, statistics features over the channels of different color spaces were calculated where the color spaces consist of RGB, HSV, and L*a*b*. The most used descriptors are mean, standard deviation, skewness, kurtosis, and median. *Texture features*: Texture features provide important information about the spatial disposition of the grey levels and the relationship with their neighbourhoods. For texture feature we have applied the following methods: SURF [11], SIFT [22], ORB [3], and LBP [32].

Patient Related Data. Dermatologists do not base their diagnosis solely on the analysis of the skin lesion. Patient-related context is also of relevance in making a diagnosis. There are a lot of factors that may affect the final decision such as age, gender, skin type, personal disease history and part of body [4].

3.5   Feature Selection

Feature selection is an important preprocessing step in many machine-learning tasks. The purpose is to reduce the dimensionality of the feature space by eliminating redundant, irrelevant or noisy features. From the classification perspective, there are numerous potential benefits associated with feature selection: (i) reduced feature extraction time and storage requirements, (ii) reduced classifier complexity, (iii) increased prediction accuracy, (iv) reduced training and testing times, and (v) enhanced data understanding and visualization. To do this step we have employed PCA [5], as feature selector, and select 250 features.

3.6 Classification

This block aims to perform classification among three types of skin lesions. This includes two independent binary classifications. The first classifier is used for the categorization of dermoscopic data into (a) melanoma and (b) nevus and seborrheic keratosis. The second classifier uses the extracted features for categorizing the dermoscopic images into (a) seborrheic keratosis and (b) nevus and melanoma. We have exploited different kinds of classifiers including SVM, Linear SVM (LSVM), RUSBoost Classifier.

4 Experimental Results

Dataset and Evaluation Metrics: The proposed structure is trained on the dermoscopic image sets provided from the International Skin Imaging Collaboration (ISIC) 2017 Challenge "Skin Lesion Analysis towards Melanoma Detection" – Part 3: Lesion Classification and the Seven-Point Checklist dataset [21]. The created model is evaluated on two datasets: ISIC 2017 Test Dataset [15] and on PH-2 Dataset [30] (patient data are not provided on this dataset).

Results: The first part of the model consisted of the VGG 16 layers up to the last convolutional layer, but without the last max pooling layer and the fully-connected layers. We initialized our network with the weights of a VGG 16 model pretrained on the ImageNet dataset. Also, we did the same for ResNet model. During training, the inputs are pre-processed by zero mean unit standard deviation normalization. We evaluate the proposed structure as follows:

1. Compare the VGG-16 network to the deeper ResNet-101.
2. Compare the performance of proposed appoaches.
3. Compare the performance of different classifier as a final decision layer.
4. Attempt to use the patient data (age and sex) on classification.

The classification results are evaluated under metrics:

- Characteristic curve (ROC) - measure of how well a parameter can distinguish between two diagnostic groups.
- Sensitivity (SE) - the fraction of true positives that are correctly identified
- Specificity (SP) - the fraction of true negatives that are correctly identified
- Accuracy (ACC) - the number of correct predictions divided by the total number of predictions

Experiments are made on ISIC 2017 Test Dataset, that provide us 600 images (117 melanomas, 90 seborrhoeic-keratoses and 393 nevus) and to strengthen our conclusions we test our approach on PH2 dataset, that provided us 200 images (140 nevus and 60 melanomas).

To make comparison between deep networks, ResNet and VGGNet, we run experiments on three classifiers with every possible combination between deep features, handcrafted features (HF) and patient data (PD). Results are summarized in Table 2, in columns we have features that are used with ResNet respectively VGGNet. We can observe that the results with ResNet, as deep feature extractor, outperforms the results with VGGNet, as feature extractor, in every possible combination. In classifier A, ResNet as deep feature extractor, outperform the VGGNet in every combination. Best results achieved in classifier A from ResNet features is 67.45% and for VGGNet features is only 58.12%. In classifier B, also, ResNet features outperform VGGNet features in every combination. The best result archieven from ResNet features, in classifier B, is 75.65% and from VGGNet features is 71.05%. In PH2-dataset results are more closer. The difference between ResNet feature and VGGNet feature is approx 2%. Also, in this dataset ResNet achieved better result than VGGNet. The best result achieved from ResNet features is 86.25% and from VGGNet features is 84.38%. Another thing that we can observe in Table 2, is that it is clear that patient data increase ROC value from 1% to 2% in classifier A and from 4% to 6% in classifier B. Also, with patient data we receive an highest Specificity in classifier A with 64.10% and in classifier B with 84.44%. Also, from Table 2 we can clearly observe that, In classifier A if we use only handcrafted feature the best results that we can achieve, based on ROC metric, is 58.10%. If we use deep features, result is improve to 64.00% and when we combine those features we improve result to 67.45%. For classifier B when we use only handcrafted and deep feature separately we achieve results 62.94% respectively 71.99%, but result is improve, when we combine those features to 75.65%. In PH2 dataset we can figure out that combination of deep and handcrafted feature increase result to 86.25%, in comparison when we use those feature separately, 69.94% respectively 71.81%.

Table 2. Comparing ResNet vs VGGNet

Challenge	Metric	ResNet				VGGNet			
		–	PD	HF	HF+PD	–	PD	HF	HF+PD
ISIC 2017 classification A	ROC	63.84%	64.00%	65.15%	**67.45%**	55.12%	58.08%	57.37%	58.12%
	SE	76.39%	93.78%	67.90%	70.80%	93.99%	69.15%	93.37%	59.83%
	SP	51.28%	34.20%	62.39%	64.10%	16.24%	47.00%	21.37%	56.41%
	ACC	71.50%	82.17%	66.83%	69.50%	78.83%	64.83%	79.33%	59.17%
ISIC 2017 classification B	ROC	68.10%	71.99%	69.93%	**75.65%**	65.16%	68.79%	66.37%	71.05%
	SE	91.76%	91.76%	70.98%	65.68%	92.55%	63.13%	92.74%	57.64%
	SP	44.44%	52.22%	68.89%	84.44%	37.78%	74.44%	40.00%	84.44%
	ACC	84.67%	85.83%	70.67%	68.50%	84.33%	64.83%	84.83%	61.67%
PH2 dataset	ROC	71.81%	–	**86.25%**	–	69.38%	–	84.38%	–
	SE	90.63%	–	92.50%	–	88.75%	–	93.75%	–
	SP	53.00%	–	80.00%	–	50.00%	–	75.00%	–
	ACC	83.00%	–	90.00%	–	81.00%	–	90.00%	–

To find out which algorithm perform better results in our approach, we have run experiments with three different algorithms: SVM, Linear SVM (LSVM) and RUSBoosting. In Table 3 we have summarized the best results for each algorithm. From results we observe that RUSBoost perform better results in all three classifier under ROC metric. In classifier A the ROC value is 4.46% higher than SVM and 2.26% higher than LSVM. In classifier B the ROC value is 4.25% higher than SVM and 3.50% higher than LSVM. In PH2 dataset the ROC value is 2% higher than SVM and 5 % higher than LSVM. In Table 4, we have summarized the best results from our approaches and the other results, include state of the art, to the best of our knowledge those are the only one who did the validation on PH2 dataset. From those results, we observe that our approach performs better than others under accuracy metric (90.00 %), and under ROC metric (86.50%) we are the just behind state of the art (89.50 %). Also, our approach achieve sensitivity 92.50% that outperform state of the art with 4.50%, but our specificity is for about 3% lower than state of the art.

Table 3. Compare the performance of different classifiers as a final decision layer

Challenge	Algorithm	ROC	SE	SP	ACC
ISIC 2017 classification A	SVM	65.04%	95.03%	35.04%	83.33%
	LSVM	67.24%	90.89%	43.59%	81.67%
	RUSBoost	67.45%	70.80%	64.10%	69.50%
ISIC 2017 classification B	SVM	71.40%	93.92%	48.89%	87.17%
	LSVM	72.15%	90.98%	53.33%	85.33%
	RUSBoost	75.65%	65.68%	84.44%	68.50%
PH2 dataset	SVM	84.38%	93.75%	75.00%	90.00%
	LSVM	81.56%	90.63%	72.50%	87.00%
	RUSBoost	86.25%	92.50%	80.00%	90.00%

Table 4. Comparing our approach best results with others in PH2 dataset

Paper	ROC	SE	SP	ACC
Abbas [2]	**89.50%**	88.00%	**91.00%**	89.00%
Proposed	86.25%	92.50%	80.00%	**90.00%**
Barata [9]	86.00%	85.00%	87.00%	87.00%
Marques [28]	85.00%	**94.00%**	77.00%	79.00%
Situ [38]	85.00%	86.00%	85.00%	85.00%

5   Conclusions

In this study, we did not aim to develop a new deep network, but we tried to use the deep features extracted from available architectures. Considering the restrictions in ISIC 2017 dataset including the limited size and the problem of unbalanced data, we feed these features to a RUSboost classifier and we apply data augmentation. From the results discussed above, we can come to some conclusions. First conclusion is that: combination of deep with hand-crafted features approach improve the results in comparison to approach with only deep or handcrafted features. Second conclusion from the results is that: feature extracted from ResNet are more representative than those extracted from

VGGNet. The results showed us that features from ResNet when they are combined with handcrafted feature and patient data, if they are provided, achieve the best results in compare to other combinations or any combination of features from VGGNet with handcrafted feature and patient data. Also, this combination of features from ResNet with those handcrafted outperform state of the art, on PH-2 dataset, in accuracy and sensitivity. Next conclusion is relevance of patient data. From the results is shown that when patient data are used results are improved for 1 to 6 %. Also, RusBoost as a final classifier performs better results in comparison to SVM or Linear SVM. The difference between these classifiers varies from 1 to 4%.

Acknowledgement. This research was supported in part by the grants from the IQ-MED (Image Quality enhancement in MEDical diagnosis, monitoring and treatment) project, funded by the Research Council of Norway; and ERASMUS+ funding.

References

1. Key statistics for melanoma skin cancer. https://www.cancer.org/cancer/melanoma-skin-cancer/about/key-statistics.html. Accessed 05 Jan 2020
2. Abbas, Q., Emre Celebi, M., Garcia, I.F., Ahmad, W.: Melanoma recognition framework based on expert definition of ABCD for dermoscopic images. Skin Res. Technol. 19(1), e93–e102 (2013)
3. Abdulmajeed, M., Seyfi, L.: Object recognition system based on oriented fast and rotated brief, December 2018
4. Alcón, J.F., et al.: Automatic imaging system with decision support for inspection of pigmented skin lesions and melanoma diagnosis. IEEE J. Sel. Top. Signal Process. 3(1), 14–25 (2009)
5. Garate-Escamila, A.K., El Hassani, A.H., Andrés, E.: Classification models for heart disease prediction using feature selection and PCA. In: Informatics in Medicine Unlocked. Elsevier (2020)
6. Argenziano, G., et al.: Dermoscopy: A Tutorial. EDRA, Medical Publishing & New Media, p. 16 (2002)
7. Ballerini, L., Fisher, R.B., Aldridge, B., Rees, J.: A color and texture based hierarchical K-NN approach to the classification of non-melanoma skin lesions. In: Celebi, M., Schaefer, G. (eds.) Color Medical Image Analysis, pp. 63–86. Springer, Dordrecht (2013). https://doi.org/10.1007/978-94-007-5389-1_4
8. Barata, C., Celebi, M.E., Marques, J.S.: Improving dermoscopy image classification using color constancy. IEEE J. Biomed. Health Inform. 19(3), 1146–1152 (2015)
9. Barata, C., Marques, J.S., Rozeira, J.: Evaluation of color based keypoints and features for the classification of melanomas using the bag-of-features model. In: Bebis, G., et al. (eds.) ISVC 2013. LNCS, vol. 8033, pp. 40–49. Springer, Heidelberg (2013). https://doi.org/10.1007/978-3-642-41914-0_5
10. Barata, C., Ruela, M., Francisco, M., Mendonça, T., Marques, J.S.: Two systems for the detection of melanomas in dermoscopy images using texture and color features. IEEE Syst. J. 8(3), 965–979 (2014)
11. Bay, H., Ess, A., Tuytelaars, T., Van Gool, L.: Speeded-up robust features (SURF). Comput. Vis. Image Underst. 110, 346–359 (2008)

12. Cherepkova, O., Hardeberg, J.Y.: Enhancing dermoscopy images to improve melanoma detection. In: 2018 Colour and Visual Computing Symposium (CVCS), pp. 1–6 (2018)
13. Codella, N., Cai, J., Abedini, M., Garnavi, R., Halpern, A., Smith, J.R.: Deep learning, sparse coding, and SVM for melanoma recognition in dermoscopy images. In: Zhou, L., Wang, L., Wang, Q., Shi, Y. (eds.) MLMI 2015. LNCS, vol. 9352, pp. 118–126. Springer, Cham (2015). https://doi.org/10.1007/978-3-319-24888-2_15
14. Codella, N., Nguyen, Q.B., Pankanti, S., et al.: Deep learning ensembles for melanoma recognition in dermoscopy images. arXiv preprint arXiv:1610.04662 (2016)
15. Codella, N.C., Gutman, D., Celebi, M.E., Helba, B., et al.: Skin lesion analysis toward melanoma detection: a challenge at the 2017 international symposium on biomedical imaging (ISBI), hosted by the international skin imaging collaboration (ISIC). arXiv preprint arXiv:1710.05006 (2017)
16. Damian, F., Moldovanu, S., Dey, N., Ashour, A.S., Moraru, L.: Feature selection of non-dermoscopic skin lesion images for nevus and melanoma classification, April 2020. https://doi.org/10.3390/computation8020041
17. Deng, J., Dong, W., Socher, R., Li, L.J., Li, K., Fei-Fei, L.: ImageNet: a large-scale hierarchical image database, pp. 248–255 (2009)
18. Díaz, I.G.: Incorporating the knowledge of dermatologists to convolutional neural networks for the diagnosis of skin lesions. arXiv preprint arXiv:1703.01976 (2017)
19. Garnavi, R., Aldeen, M., Bailey, J.: Computer-aided diagnosis of melanoma using border-and wavelet-based texture analysis. IEEE Trans. Inf. Technol. Biomed. 16(6), 1239–1252 (2012)
20. He, K., Zhang, X., Ren, S., Sun, J.: Deep residual learning for image recognition. In: Proceedings of the IEEE Conference on Computer Vision and Pattern Recognition, pp. 770–778 (2016)
21. Kawahara, J., Daneshvar, S., Argenziano, G., Hamarneh, G.: Seven-point checklist and skin lesion classification using multitask multimodal neural nets. IEEE J. Biomed. Health Inform. 23(2), 538–546 (2019)
22. Ke, Y., Sukthankar, R.: PCA-SIFT: a more distinctive representation for local image descriptors, vol. 2, pp. II-506, May 2004
23. Kumar, A., Kim, J., Lyndon, D., Fulham, M., Feng, D.: An ensemble of fine-tuned convolutional neural networks for medical image classification. IEEE J. Biomed. Health Inform. 21(1), 31–40 (2017)
24. Ma, L., Staunton, R.C.: Analysis of the contour structural irregularity of skin lesions using wavelet decomposition. Pattern Recogn. 46(1), 98–106 (2013)
25. Majtner, T., Yildirim-Yayilgan, S., Hardeberg, J.Y.: Combining deep learning and hand-crafted features for skin lesion classification. In: 2016 6th International Conference on Image Processing Theory Tools and Applications, pp. 1–6. IEEE (2016)
26. Majtner, T., Yildirim-Yayilgan, S., Hardeberg, J.Y.: Efficient melanoma detection using texture-based RSurf features. In: Campilho, A., Karray, F. (eds.) ICIAR 2016. LNCS, vol. 9730, pp. 30–37. Springer, Cham (2016). https://doi.org/10.1007/978-3-319-41501-7_4
27. Majtner, T., Yildirim-Yayilgan, S., Hardeberg, J.Y.: Optimised deep learning features for improved melanoma detection. Multimed. Tools Appl. 78(9), 11883–11903 (2018). https://doi.org/10.1007/s11042-018-6734-6
28. Marques, J.S., Barata, C., Mendonça, T.: On the role of texture and color in the classification of dermoscopy images. In: 2012 Annual International Conference of the IEEE Engineering in Medicine and Biology Society, pp. 4402–4405 (2012)

29. Melit Devassy, B., Yildirim Yayilgan, S., Hardeberg, J.Y.: The impact of replacing complex hand-crafted features with standard features for melanoma classification using both hand-crafted and deep features. Adv. Intell. Syst. Comput. (2018)
30. Mendonça, T., Ferreira, P.M., Marques, J.S., Marcal, A.R.S., Rozeira, J.: PH2 - a dermoscopic image database for research and benchmarking. In: 2013 35th Annual International Conference of the IEEE Engineering in Medicine and Biology Society (EMBC), pp. 5437–5440 (2013)
31. Møllersen, K., Hardeberg, J.Y., Godtliebsen, F.: Divergence-based colour features for melanoma detection. In: Colour and Visual Computing Symposium (CVCS), 2015, pp. 1–6. IEEE (2015)
32. Ojala, T., et al.: Performance evaluation of texture measures with classification based on Kullback discrimination of distributions. In: Proceedings of 12th International Conference on Pattern Recognition, vol. 1, pp. 582–585 (1994)
33. Oliveira, R.B., Mercedes Filho, E., Ma, Z., Papa, J.P., et al.: Computational methods for the image segmentation of pigmented skin lesions: a review. Comput. Methods Programs Biomed. **131**, 127–141 (2016)
34. Oliveira, R.B., Papa, J.P., Pereira, A.S., Tavares, J.M.R.: Computational methods for pigmented skin lesion classification in images: review and future trends. Neural Comput. Appl. **29**(3), 613–636 (2018)
35. Sadeghi, M., et al.: Detection and analysis of irregular streaks in dermoscopic images of skin lesions. IEEE Trans. Med. Imaging **5**, 849–861 (2013)
36. Sáez, A., Acha, B., Serrano, C.: Pattern analysis in dermoscopic images. In: Computer Vision Techniques for the Diagnosis of Skin Cancer, pp. 23–48 (2014)
37. Simonyan, K., Zisserman, A.: Very deep convolutional networks for large-scale image recognition. arXiv preprint arXiv:1409.1556 (2014)
38. Situ, N., Wadhawan, T., Hu, R., Lancaster, K., Yuan, X., Zouridakis, G.: Evaluating sampling strategies of dermoscopic interest points. In: 2011 IEEE International Symposium on Biomedical Imaging: From Nano to Macro, pp. 109–112 (2011)
39. Somwanshi, D., Chaturvedi, A., Mudgal, P.: ABCD features extraction-based melanoma detection and classification. In: Mathur, G., Sharma, H., Bundele, M., Dey, N., Paprzycki, M. (eds.) International Conference on Artificial Intelligence: Advances and Applications 2019. AIS, pp. 327–335. Springer, Singapore (2020). https://doi.org/10.1007/978-981-15-1059-5_37
40. Szegedy, C., et al.: Going deeper with convolutions. In: Proceedings of the IEEE Conference on Computer Vision and Pattern Recognition, pp. 1–9 (2015)
41. Veit, A., et al.: Residual networks behave like ensembles of relatively shallow networks. In: Advances in Neural Information Processing Systems (2016)
42. Zhang, Z., Liu, Q., Wang, Y.: Road extraction by deep residual U-Net. IEEE Geosci. Remote Sens. Lett. **15**(5), 749–753 (2018)
43. Zhou, B., Khosla, A., Lapedriza, A., Oliva, A., Torralba, A.: Learning deep features for discriminative localization, pp. 2921–2929 (2016)
44. Zhou, Y., Smith, M., Smith, L., Warr, R.: A new method describing border irregularity of pigmented lesions. Skin Res. Technol. **16**(1), 66–76 (2010)

Data-Driven Machine Learning Approach for Human Action Recognition Using Skeleton and Optical Flow

Yen-Ting Lee$^{(\boxtimes)}$, Thitinun Pengying$^{(\boxtimes)}$, Sule Yildirim Yayilgan$^{(\boxtimes)}$, and Ogerta Elezaj$^{(\boxtimes)}$

Norwegian University of Science and Technology, Teknologivegen, 22, 2815 Gjøvik, Norway
leeyt1377@gmail.com, thitinup4@gmail.com, {sule.yildirim, ogerta.elezaj}@ntnu.no

Abstract. Human action recognition is a very challenging problem due to numerous variations in each body part. In this paper, we propose a method for extracting optical flow information from skeleton data to address the problem of body part movement variation in human action recognition. The additional arm part information was also analyzed how valuable it was. Then, different machine learning methods are applied such as k-Nearest Neighbors (KNNs) and deep learning to recognize human actions on the UTKinect-Action 3D dataset. We then design and train different KNNs models and Deep Convolutional Neural Networks (D-CNNs) on the obtained image and classify them into classes. Different numbers of features from histogram data collection are used to recognize 10 categories of human actions. The best accuracy we obtained is about 88%. The proposed method had improved accuracy to almost 97% with only 5 classes. These features are representative to describe the human action and recognition which does not rely on plenty of training data. Results of experiments show that using deep learning can lead to better classification accuracy.

Keywords: Human action recognition · Skeleton · Optical flow · KNNs · Deep learning

1 Introduction

Action classification is one of the challenging problems because different persons perform the same action differently which leads to variation in body part movement and variation from frame to frame in videos. However, this problem caught attention from various application areas e.g. video surveillance, healthcare system and robotics.

With the development of depth map, researchers began to apply it to human action recognition since it provides 3D data instead of 2D. In particular, depth data based human skeleton tracking technology achieves outstanding precision and stimulates the research on human action recognition to use skeleton data [1]. So far, skeleton-based action recognition has been widely studied where input data is 3D skeleton data (RGB images and depth map) in general.

© Springer Nature Switzerland AG 2021
S. Yildirim Yayilgan et al. (Eds.): INTAP 2020, CCIS 1382, pp. 163–175, 2021.
https://doi.org/10.1007/978-3-030-71711-7_14

Moreover, different approaches have been utilized for higher efficiency. Histograms of 3D joint locations (HOJ3D) extracted from Kinect 3D skeletal joint locations by using Linear Discriminant Analysis (LDA) projection to represent poses and then modelling by discrete hidden Markov models (HMMs) gives more than 90% accuracy [2]. Using skeleton data extracted via RGBD sensors has shown promising classification results on five different datasets where clustering and Support Vector Machine (SVM) classification has been used [3]. Converting dissimilarity space with 3D skeleton joints to torso-PCA- frame (TPCAF) coordinate system have shown equivalent performance with other methods on available datasets [4]. However, skeleton-based methods have two major obstacles: inaccurate skeleton estimation and intra-class variation in human actions. Nowadays, there are many open source skeleton extraction algorithms available. OpenPose is one of the well-known algorithms that has been proposed to detect 2D pose of multiple people in images or videos with great performance [5]. DRPose3D is another algorithm that used depth information together with 2D human joint locations and Convolutional Neural Networks (CNNs). It exceeded state-of-the-art method (KNNs) on Human3.6 M dataset [6].

As deep learning gains more attention recently, there are many poses estimation-based research on it. Some solved the action classification problem by using CNNs on the MPII Human Pose dataset. Both [7] and [8] achieve state-of-the-art accuracy by using multiple stacked hourglass modules and combining heatmaps and regression respectively. Even some researchers have introduced unsupervised learning for human action recognition and use generative adversarial networks which has discriminator for this purpose to improve accuracy and let the generator learn more conceivable features for pose estimation. The first network improvised two discriminators and a multi-task pose generator which is robust to occlusions and human body distortion while the second network possesses identical discriminator and generator with the aid of heatmaps that help improve the prediction accuracy [9, 10].

Skeleton-based action recognition can also be solved by using the deep learning approach. Inputting 3D skeleton data to CNNs with Long Short Term Memory (LSTM) regularization improves the accuracy from the-state-of-the-art method [11]. Separating the skeleton data into five parts before entering it into each subnet and hierarchically merging body parts back to the output layer of the recurrent neural network (RNN) accomplished both good performance and low computation time [12]. Besides the skeleton-based approach, videos can also be used as input data for training. Video representations learned by CNNs with long-term temporal convolutions (LTC) with flow help improve the performance over RGB and results in accurate optical flow estimation with a superior performance than state-of-the-art [13].

Optical flow is a major feature used in motion estimation alone or together with other aids. Spatial and temporal CNNs architecture trained on optical flow achieved good performance on the UCF-101 dataset [14]. Training only Farneback optical flow from RGB visualizations with CNNs on the KTH dataset showed assuring results. That is, the accuracy is good but still does not reach state of the art from using only a single feature [15]. In addition, applying neural networks enhance the performance of the flow. Fine tuning the different flow algorithms showed that action recognition accuracy correlates with flow near the boundary and small movements [16]. Using spatial gradients of feature maps and temporal gradients obtained from different frames as a feature to train the network have achieved very high accuracy on UCF-101 dataset [17].

Using optical flow as a feature with KNNs and Principal Component Analysis (PCA) achieved 100% accuracy on the KTH dataset [18]. On the other hand, KNNs have shown slight improvement of the accuracy with SVM than SVM alone on Wizeman dataset [19]. Based on the review provided so far, it is clear that optical flow helps obtain better results than state of the art and hence in this paper, we propose to train KNNs and deep learning with optical flow data extracted from skeleton data to classify human actions in videos with human activities.

This paper is organized as follows. Section 2 describes our methodology. Section 3 introduces the dataset and discusses the experimental results. Section 4 concludes the paper and also presents the future works.

2   Methodology

Figure 1 illustrates the overall process of our method. In this section, we will provide an explanation of the processes in our method.

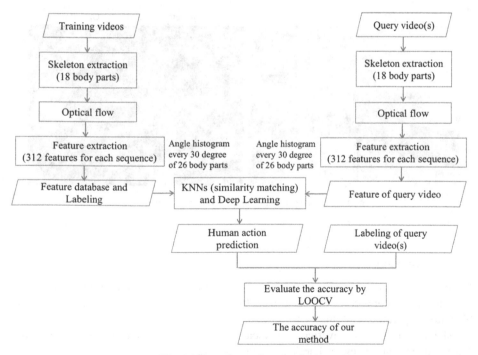

Fig. 1. Flowchart of our method.

2.1 Skeleton

In this project, OpenPose [5, 20, 21] is used to extract skeleton data from the frames. OpenPose is one of the open sources available (https://github.com/CMU-Perceptual-Computing-Lab/openpose) and it is the first real-time multi-person system to jointly detect human body, hand, facial, and foot keypoints (in total 135 keypoints) on single image. It efficiently detects the 2D pose of multiple people in an image by using a non-parametric representation, referred to as Part Affinity Fields (PAFs) to learn to associate body parts with individuals in the image [5].

In our experiments, OpenPose represents a person by 25 body parts with 18 different colors. These 18 colors are regarded as the key body parts for human action recognition. Figure 2 shows the *sit down* example and its skeleton result, the key body parts contain 18 different colors where the lower leg and foot are illustrated by the same color. In this paper, the input data of OpenPose is RGB images and it renders the skeletons on a black background as the output data to eliminate the undesired influence from the background. The user can modify the setting of OpenPose to have a different combination of key points in the output results. For example, different output format and keypoint ordering, body skeleton output, face keypoint output, hand keypoint output, and so on.

(A) Original RGB image   (B) Skeleton extraction by OpenPose

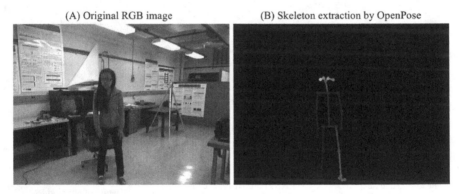

Fig. 2. The result of skeleton by OpenPose.

2.2 Optical Flow

The extracted skeleton images are combined back to the .avi video by ImageJ [22] with 7 frames/second and converted to a .mov file which is compatible with Matlab in the Macintosh operating system.

Then, each frame is converted to grayscale before estimating the optical flow from the consecutive frames using the Farneback method. The result of the optical flow extraction process is shown in Fig. 3 where the left one displays the skeleton data obtained from OpenPose in the video of *carry* category and the right represents the optical flow of the video by the blue arrows. The larger the arrow is, the greater the movement of that part.

After that all flows are collected from all videos, but this optical flow combines four properties: Vx, Vy, Orientation and Magnitude where the first two are the X and

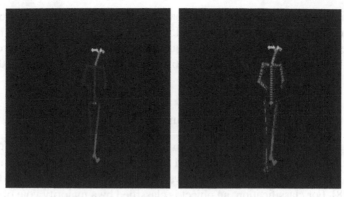

Fig. 3. Optical flow procedure: Left - original skeleton data and Right - optical flow.

Y components of velocity respectively and the last two are the phase angles in radians and the magnitude of optical flow in 480 × 640 pixels. If all the flow information is exploited, the features' size will be larger and further extend the complexity of training. Also Orientation and Magnitude are more meaningful so they are chosen to use as the features.

Every frame of the video is extracted into different parts by using 18 color pixels but the size of the body in the image varied, therefore, the centroid of each part is found to represent the overall. The centroids of all 18 different parts can be seen in green compared to the whole skeleton in purple in Fig. 4. Then, the mean values of orientation and magnitude of each part of the continuous frames in each video are calculated as the features. Each video is composed of 18 orientation points and followed by another 18 magnitude points as features. As arm movements are very essential to distinguish between actions like *wave hands and clap hands*, two left and right points to the centroid of 4 arm parts are collected in order to get both orientation and magnitude for additional information. The comparison of 18 and 26 body parts will be demonstrated.

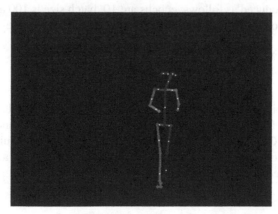

Fig. 4. Centroids of all parts are shown in green color where the skeleton is shown in pink. (Color figure online)

After that, angle histogram is plotted from each video and every 10, 30, 60 and 90° data are collected to be the features. In total, there are 26 parts (18 from all body parts and 8 from enhanced arm parts) so each sequence has $26 \times 36 = 936$ features for 10°, $26 \times 12 = 312$ features for 30°, $26 \times 6 = 156$ features for 60° and $26 \times 4 = 104$ features for 90°.

2.3 KNNs for Human Action Recognition

k-Nearest Neighbors (KNNs) algorithm is a non-parametric method used for classification and regression [23]. It is mostly used for action recognition because it does not require any learning processes and it is invariant to view-point, spatial and temporal variations [18]. For classification, an object is classified by a majority vote of its k nearest neighbors. For example, to find out which human action a query belongs to, we use correlation distance to decide the k closest neighbors and $k = 3$ to 10 are used to generate the classification models. Then, a query will be assigned to a class which is the most common among those k neighbors.

2.4 Deep Learning

Deep learning, as a part of machine learning methods, based on artificial neural networks, has become a hotspot of big data and artificial intelligence. Deep learning is self-learning by building a multilayer model and training and evaluating the model using big amounts of data. When the data are complex and large, usually this method improves the accuracy of the classification, leading to better prediction [24]. The network architecture used is a simple network with one dense hidden layer, having 216 output units using the ReLU activation function, followed by an output layer with the softmax activation function, using a multi-class cross-entropy loss function (MCXENT) as optimization objective. To avoid the overfitting problem, we set up l2 regularization that "penalizes" the network for too large weights and prevents overfitting. The proposed solution is implemented using Waikato Environment for Knowledge Analysis (WEKA 3.8) [25]. The training parameters are introduced as follows, epochs are 10, batch size is 100 and learning rate is 0.001. 10-fold cross validation is implanted to partition the sequences into training set and testing set.

2.5 Evaluation

The UTKinect-Action 3D dataset is used in this paper and the detailed information is given in Sect. 3.1. [1–4, 26, 27] had been tested with the same dataset and leave-one-out-cross-validation (LOOCV) was chosen to evaluate the recognition results. Therefore, to compare our method with the previous works, LOOCV is applied and the model is trained on all the sequences except the testing one.

3   Results and Discussion

3.1   Dataset

The UTKinect-Action 3D dataset [2] is composed of 10 different subjects (9 males and 1 female) performing 10 actions twice, which are *walk, sit down, stand up, pick up, carry, throw, push, pull, wave hands, and clap hands*. The dataset contains 4 parts, which are RGB images (480 × 640 pixels), depth images (320 × 240 pixels), skeleton joint locations and labels of action sequences.

A number of 199 sequences are available because one sequence (action: *carry*) is not labeled. This dataset is challenging because the length of sample actions ranges from 5 to 120 frames, occlusions of objects on the human or invisibility of body parts also have been demonstrated and the sequences are captured from different views. Since the link for downloading the description of the skeleton joint locations does not work, we cannot understand the meaning of the data in the skeleton file. Hence, OpenPose is employed to extract skeleton information. OpenPose can achieve desirable accuracy but our results with it had shown a false negative of the body in few images. This might also affect the result of our method.

3.2   Features Extraction

After getting the skeleton image from OpenPose, the optical flow of each image in the video and the centroids of each part are found and compared to collect only the orientation and magnitude information. The additional arm parts are also treated similarly for supportive differentiation in the arm area. Then, the features are collected every 10, 30, 60 and 90° from the angle histogram of each video. Therefore, there are features from 18 and 26 body parts with 4 different angle histograms to compare.

3.3   Recognition Results

This section presents the principal findings of the experiment. The results obtained from analyzing the performance of KNNs and correlation distance classifiers are summarized in Table 1 and Table 2. LOOCV is applied to evaluate our method. The 198 sequences are randomly selected as training data and the one remainder is used for testing. Table 1 and Table 2 present the recognition accuracy using different k values for KNNs classifier and different collecting frequency from histogram. What stands out in Table 1 is that the highest accuracy in the dataset with 18 body parts is 77.32% ($k = 6$ and 30°), whereas, 26 body parts we obtain the highest accuracy 87.98% with k = 4 and 30°. This can be explained by the fact that 26 body parts provided more information in the arm areas that can distinguish the actions using hands like pushing and pulling better. The overall accuracy is depending on the frequency of collecting data as features. Applying 90° during feature extraction, less features are extracted and for this reason the accuracy is degraded in both 18 and 26 body parts. What stands out from the comparison between all feature selection methods, is the significant improvement in accuracy for the dataset with higher number of features, except the 10°, where irrelevant features are presented reducing the overall accuracy of classifiers.

Table 1. The accuracy (%) of features of 18 body parts with different angle histograms.

k-nearest neighbors	Per 10	Per 30	Per 60	Per 90
$k = 3$	65.71	75.79	71.76	63.66
$k = 4$	68.79	76.84	74.82	62.21
$k = 5$	69.74	74.23	73.26	65.13
$k = 6$	70.24	**77.32**	73.29	**65.63**
$k = 7$	70.74	74.76	73.24	62.58
$k = 8$	71.71	75.26	**76.29**	62.08
$k = 9$	72.71	75.24	73.26	61.58
$k = 10$	**74.21**	77.23	75.79	61.61

Table 2. The accuracy (%) of features of 26 body parts with different angle histograms.

k-nearest neighbors	Per 10	Per 30	Per 60	Per 90
$k = 3$	82.32	85.37	83.32	75.68
$k = 4$	**83.37**	**87.98**	83.32	77.76
$k = 5$	80.76	84.84	**83.84**	75.16
$k = 6$	80.34	83.37	82.29	**78.16**
$k = 7$	79.79	84.34	82.82	76.11
$k = 8$	81.32	84.42	79.76	74.61
$k = 9$	80.29	85.32	81.29	74.13
$k = 10$	81.23	82.32	81.29	74.13

In order to analyze the accuracy for each class of the dataset, the confusion matrix of the best accuracy of each scheme is calculated and illustrated in Fig. 5. With only 18 body parts, the accuracy of *throw* class is the lowest. *Push* and *pull* classes also show misclassification between classes. This also happened with classification of *carry* class that confused with *walk* class. On the other hand, including additional arm parts in the feature using 26 body parts has improved the overall accuracy but not the accuracy of *throw* class.

Table 3. The accuracy (%) of classifying 5 human actions with features of 26 body parts every 30°.

k-nearest neighbors	Accuracy (%)
$k = 3$	93.79
$k = 4$	**96.95**
$k = 5$	93.74
$k = 6$	94.89
$k = 7$	94.84
$k = 8$	92.84
$k = 9$	91.68
$k = 10$	90.74

The results from our experiments are compared with previous works where the same dataset is used. Authors in [3] had chosen only 5 classes (*walk, sit down, stand up, pick up and carry*) to train with only AAL (Active and Assisted Living) related activities and achieved 96.7% accuracy, while we reached slightly better accuracy at 96.97% (almost 97%), as Table 3 lists, with 26 body parts, 30° histogram collection and KNN with k = 4, meaning that our method is comparable and even better. Meanwhile, the accuracy is enhanced significantly from 10 classes to 5 classes, as Table 4 lists. This improvement happens from less confusion between classes and obvious differentiation between these 5 actions.

These features had been used to build the model based on deep learning in order to compare the results from the proposed method as well. The results are presented in Table 4. Only 5 actions have significantly higher accuracy in both 18 and 26 body parts because the selected classes are less confused between them. With 18 body parts, deep learning performs better on 10 actions while the proposed method provides higher accuracy with 5 classes and reaches largest accuracy at 93.79%. On the other hand, 26 body parts, which include the additional information in the arm areas, performs better in all classes. The accuracy is approximately 88% even for the dataset with 10 classes, whereas KNNs performs slightly better on 5 actions dataset.

Table 5 summarizes the results of our method and the proposed algorithms for UTKinect Action 3D dataset and LOOCV. The accuracy of all proposed algorithms are above 90%. However, our algorithm obtained 87.98% accuracy with KNNs for the dataset with 10 classes. [3] obtained the best accuracy 96.7% for 5 classes and it introduced 3D skeleton data and SVM to classify human actions. Since only 2D skeleton data is included in our algorithm, the less information is provided for training the model. Also, SVM is supervised learning for classification and regression. On the other hand, using a deep learning method for 5 classes we obtained 95.96% accuracy. The accuracy and performance of a classifier is depending on the method used for feature extraction and number of features. To accurately develop an efficient human action recognition system, different ML methods should be considered for finding the method that better fits the needs, as these systems are much related to the data set characteristics.

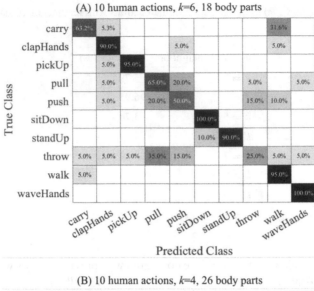

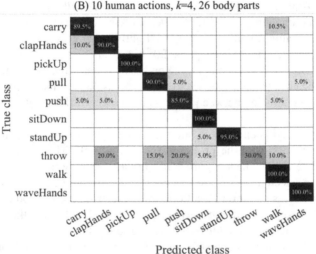

Fig. 5. The confusion matrix on the UTKinect-Action 3D dataset with the best accuracy for (A) 10 actions and 18 body parts, (B) 10 actions and 26 body parts.

Table 4. Comparison of proposed methods based on KNNs and deep learning.

Accuracy		KNNs	Deep learning
18 body parts	5 classes	**93.79**	89.90
	10 classes	77.32	85.93
26 body parts	5 classes	**96.95**	**95.96**
	10 classes	87.98	88.44

Table 5. Comparison of the proposed method with other ML techniques.

Algorithm	Nr. of classes	Methods	Accuracy
Our method	10	KNNs	**87.98**
Our method	5	KNNs	**96.95**
Our method	5	Deep Learning	**95.96**
Xia et al. [2]	5	Hidden Markov Models	90.9
Theodorakopoulos et al. [4]	5	Dissimilarity Space	90.95
Ding et al. [26]	10	Support Vector Machine	91.5
Jiang et al. [1]	10	Random Forests	91.9
Liu et al. [27]	10	Coupled hidden conditional random fields	92.0
Cippitelli et al. [3]	5	Support Vector Machine	96.7
Cippitelli et al. [3]	10	Support Vector Machine	95.1

4 Conclusions and Future Work

Human action recognition is a very challenging problem. The aim of this study is to introduce a solution by collecting histogram information from the optical flow of extracted skeleton data. Then, applying KNNs and deep learning methods with LOOCV on the UTKinect-Action 3D dataset. Skeleton extraction provides some false data which can lead to wrong optical flow, so we extract only from the centroid to avoid this problem and also decrease the data size. The supplementary features from arm parts have improved the accuracy remarkably. The additional data from histogram helps improve the accuracy where every $30°$ presented the best performance. Using KNNs classifier, the best accuracy obtained is 88% with $k = 4$. However, only 5 classes display much better accuracy at about 97% with the same k value for KNN. The results are also compared with deep learning with 26 body parts. The proposed method is simpler and more efficient since those features in a sequence are characteristics to define the action, so it is not a necessity of inputting numbers of training data. The experimental results showed that by selecting the most significant features, can lead to better classification accuracy.

To improve our algorithm and classification accuracy, in the future, we will try to define the indicative position in a body part for each human action instead of taking optical flow of the centroid body part. Also, in this paper, all the features are given the same weight, we think the ideal way should be giving different weights to the features according to which body parts can exhibit the specific human action better. Finally, the SVM method will be considered for recognition.

References

1. Jiang, M., Kong, J., Bebis, G., Huo, H.: Informative joints based human action recognition using skeleton contexts. Sig. Process. Image Commun. **33**, 29–40 (2015)
2. Xia, L., Chen, C.-C., Aggarwal, J.K.: View invariant human action recognition using histograms of 3D joints. In: Proceedings of the IEEE Computer Society Conference on Computer Vision and Pattern Recognition Workshops (CVPRW 2012), Providence, RI, pp. 20–27 (2012)
3. Cippitelli, E., Gasparrini, S., Gambi, E., Spinsante, S.: A human activity recognition system using skeleton data from RGBD sensor. Comput. Intell. Neurosci. **2016**, 1–14 (2016)
4. Theodorakopoulos, I., Kastaniotis, D., Economou, G., Fotopoulos, S.: Pose-based human action recognition via sparse representation in dissimilarity space. J. Vis. Commun. Image Represent. **25**(1), 12–23 (2014)
5. Cao, Z., Simon, T., Wei, S.-E., Sheikh, Y.: Realtime multi-person 2D pose estimation using part affinity fields. In: CVPR (2017)
6. Wang, M., Chen, X., Liu, W., Qian, C., Lin, L., Ma, L.: DRPose3D: depth ranking in 3D human pose estimation. In: Proceedings of the Twenty-Seventh International Joint Conference on Artificial Intelligence, pp. 978–984 (2018)
7. Newell, A., Yang, K., Deng, J.: Stacked hourglass networks for human pose estimation. In: Leibe, B., Matas, J., Sebe, N., Welling, M. (eds.) Computer Vision – ECCV 2016. ECCV 2016. LNCS, vol. 9912, pp. 483–499. Springer, Cham (2016). https://doi.org/10.1007/978-3-319-46484-8_29
8. Bulat, A., Tzimiropoulos, G.: Human pose estimation via Convolutional Part Heatmap Regression. In: Leibe, B., Matas, J., Sebe, N., Welling, M. (eds.) Computer Vision – ECCV 2016. ECCV 2016. LNCS, vol. 9911, pp. 717–732. Springer, Cham (2016). https://doi.org/10.1007/978-3-319-46478-7_44
9. Chen, Y., Shen, C., Wei, X., Liu, L., Yang, J.: Adversarial PoseNet: a structure-aware convolutional network for human pose estimation. In: IEEE International Conference on Computer Vision (2017)
10. Chou, C.J., Chien, J.T., Chen, H.T.: Self adversarial training for human pose estimation. In: APSIPA Annual Summit and Conference (2018)
11. Mahasseni, B., Todorovic, S.: Regularizing long short term memory with 3D human-skeleton sequences for action recognition. In CVPR (2016)
12. Du, Y., Wang, W., Wang, L.: Hierarchical recurrent neural network for skeleton based action recognition. In: CVPR, pp. 1110–1118 (2015)
13. Varol, G., Laptev, I., Schmid, C.: Long-term temporal convolutions for action recognition. CoRR, abs/1604.04494 (2016)
14. Simonyan, K., Zisserman, A.: Two-stream convolutional networks for action recognition in videos. In: NIPS, pp. 568–576 (2014)
15. Gupta, A., Balan, M.S.: Action recognition from optical flow visualizations. In: Chaudhuri B., Kankanhalli M., Raman B. (eds.) Proceedings of 2nd International Conference on Computer Vision & Image Processing. AISC, vol. 703, pp 397–408. Springer, Singapore (2018). https://doi.org/10.1007/978-981-10-7895-8_31

16. Sevilla-Lara, L., Liao, Y., Guney, F., Jampani, V., Geiger, A., Black, M.J.: On the integration of optical flow and action recognition. CoRR, abs/1712.08416 (2017)
17. Sun, S., Kuang, Z., Ouyang, W., Sheng, L., Zhang, W.: Optical flow guided feature: a fast and robust motion representation for video action recognition. In: IEEE Conference on Computer Vision and Pattern Recognition (CVPR 2018), Salt Lake City (2018)
18. Biswas, S.A., Bhonge, V.N.: Motion based action recognition using k-nearest neighbor. Int. J. Res. Eng. Tech. 3(1), 587–590 (2014)
19. Kaur, J., Kaur, E.M.: Human action recognition using SVM and KNN classifiers. Int. J. Innov. Advance. Comput. Sci. 5, 13–18 (2016)
20. Simon, T., Joo, H., Mattews, I., Sheikh, Y.: Hand keypoint detection in single images using multiview bootstrapping. In: CVPR (2017)
21. Wei, S.E., Ramakrishna, V., Kanade, T., Sheikh, Y.: Convolutional pose machines. In: CVPR (2016)
22. ImageJ. https://imagej.net/Introduction#What_is_Fiji.3F. Accessed 16 Nov 2018
23. Altman, N.S.: An introduction to kernel and nearest-neighbor nonparametric regression. Am. Stat. 43(3), 175–185 (1992)
24. Yu, K., Jia, L., Chen, Y.Q., Xu, W.: Deep learning: yesterday today and tomorrow. J. Comput. Res. Dev. 50, 1799–1804(2013)
25. Hall, M., Frank, E., Holmes, G., Pfahringer, B., Reutemann, P., Witten, I.H.: The WEKA data mining software. ACM SIGKDD Explor. Newsl. 11(1), 10 (2009)
26. Ding, W., Liu, K., Cheng, F., Zhang, J.: STFC: spatio-temporal feature chain for skeleton-based human action recognition. J. Vis. Commun. Image Represent. 26, 329–337 (2015)
27. Liu, A.-A., Nie, W.-Z., Su, Y.-T., Ma, L., Hao, T., Yang, Z.-X.: Coupled hidden conditional random fields for RGB-D human action recognition. Sig. Process. 112, 74–82 (2015)

Biometrics

Multilingual Voice Impersonation Dataset and Evaluation

Hareesh Mandalapu$^{(\boxtimes)}$, Raghavendra Ramachandra$^{(\boxtimes)}$,
and Christoph Busch$^{(\boxtimes)}$

Norwegian University of Science and Technology, 2815 Gjøvik, Norway
{hareesh.mandalapu,raghavendra.ramachandra,christoph.busch}@ntnu.no

Abstract. Well-known vulnerabilities of voice-based biometrics are impersonation, replay attacks, artificial signals/speech synthesis, and voice conversion. Among these, voice impersonation is the obvious and simplest way of attack that can be performed. Though voice impersonation by amateurs is considered not a severe threat to ASV systems, studies show that professional impersonators can successfully influence the performance of the voice-based biometrics system. In this work, we have created a novel voice impersonation attack dataset and studied the impact of voice impersonation on automatic speaker verification systems. The dataset consisting of celebrity speeches from 3 different languages, and their impersonations are acquired from YouTube. The vulnerability of speaker verification is observed among all three languages on both the classical i-vector based method and the deep neural network-based x-vector method.

Keywords: Biometrics · Speaker recognition · Voice impersonation · Presentation attack

1 Introduction

Biometric authentication for providing access to information, devices, and networks have been used in security applications for many years. Speaker recognition is one of the modalities that has been prominently used as biometrics for the last few decades. Though computational intelligence has advanced, biometric systems are still vulnerable in the authentication of individuals. In voice-based person verification, there are emerging new ways of attacks every day. The popular speaker verification vulnerabilities are voice impersonation, audio replay attack, speech synthesis, and voice conversion. Though speech synthesis and voice conversion can cause severe impact, these attacks can only be performed with certain access to the biometric system. The conventional physical access attacks can only be performed by voice impersonation or replay attacks.

Voice impersonation is discussed to be having minimal impact on speaker recognition systems when compared to other kinds of attacks [17]. However, studies have shown that a professional impersonator having enough training on

© Springer Nature Switzerland AG 2021
S. Yildirim Yayilgan et al. (Eds.): INTAP 2020, CCIS 1382, pp. 179–188, 2021.
https://doi.org/10.1007/978-3-030-71711-7_15

the target's speech can perform a successful attack [2,3]. It is also a simple way of attacking a voice-based biometric system. By adjusting the vocal cords, an impersonator can mimic a target speaker's voice. Though it has been observed that it is difficult to impersonate untrained target's voices, well-known impersonators after multiple attempts can successfully attack a speaker recognition system. Automatic speaker verification and the vulnerability evaluation have multiple dependencies like text, language, and channel effects [6]. After considering the issues mentioned above, there is a requirement of research work in fully understanding the effect of impersonation with all the dependencies.

In this work, two popular speaker recognition systems are evaluated over the effect of impersonation. We have included three different languages with no text-dependency and various channel data to accommodate the previously mentioned dependencies of automatic speaker verification. Further, this work is organized as follows. A literature review on the previous studies on voice impersonation is presented in Sect. 2. In Sect. 3, the impersonation dataset captured is mentioned with details. The Automatic speaker Verification methods chosen for our experiments and trained dataset used are discussed in Sect. 4. Section 5 explains the experiments performed and results obtained in impersonation vulnerability evaluation. The conclusion of this work and future directions are presented in Sect. 6.

2   Related Work

In the initial works, amateur impersonators were used in performing attacks. Lau et al. [8] have performed experiments on the YOHO dataset, which contains 138 speakers. Two subjects acted as impersonators, and the vulnerability of the speaker recognition system towards such mimicry attack was verified. Upon performing multiple attempts, it was observed that an impostor could perform an attack if the impostor has the knowledge about enrolled speakers in the database [9]. In [10], Mariéthoz et al. assessed the vulnerability of state-of-the-art text-independent speaker verification system based on Gaussian mixture models (GMMs) to attacks conducted by a professional imitator. It was observed that the GMM based systems are robust to mimicry attacks.

Farrús et al. [2] performed experiments on prosodic features extracted from voices of professional impersonators to perform mimicry attacks on speaker identification systems. The increase in acceptance rates was observed when imitated voices are used for testing. Panjwani et al. [12] proposed a generic method and used crowd-sourcing for identifying impersonators. The GMM-UBM based method displays an increase in impostor attack presentation match rate (IAPMR) when using professional impersonators. Hautamäki et al. [3] used three modern speaker identification systems to test the case of voice mimicry. It has been observed that the EER values for GMM-UBM based method are decreased but increased for two other i-vector based methods.

The ASVspoof (Automatic Speaker Verification spoof) challenges are a series of evaluations focus on improving countermeasures to attacks on speaker verification systems. Voice conversion and speech synthesis attacks are the primary focus in the first ASVspoof challenge [17]. The Second ASVspoof challenge is evaluated for countermeasures to different kinds of replay attacks [7]. The recent challenge in this series includes both physical (replay attacks) and logical access (voice conversion, speech synthesis) attacks [16]. Impersonation attacks are not considered in any series of these competitions, mentioning that impersonation's relative severity is uncertain. However, the attacks discussed in these series assumed to have access to the biometric system. For example, the audio sample's digital copy is necessary to perform replay attacks, and logical access attacks need access into the system where the digitally manufactured copy of utterance is presented. Impersonation is a physical access attack on voice-based biometrics that does not require any access to the biometric system, which makes it an interesting research topic for this study.

It was observed in most of these methods that voice impersonation has a considerable impact on speaker verification systems, but all these methods possess certain challenges, which are observed as follows.

- There is no publicly available impersonation attack dataset similar to other attacks like replay, voice conversion, and speech synthesis. Also, there is a requirement of professional impersonators to compose a dataset.
- State-of-the-art speaker verification systems are not employed in the evaluation.
- The text-dependent methods are used to perform an attack, which is not a generalized scenario.
- The impact of language and channels are not discussed in the previous evaluations.
- Standard protocols were not used to evaluate the impact of impersonation.

The following contributions are made in this paper to address the challenges mentioned above.

- A dataset of bona fide and impersonator samples is created from YouTube videos for three different languages, which will be made publicly available (similar to VoxCeleb dataset).
- Three different languages, text-independent speeches, and multiple channel data are captured in the dataset.
- Extensive experiments are carried out on one classical and one state-of-the-art speaker verification systems in three different languages.
- Results are presented following ISO/IEC standards for biometric system performance evaluation and presentation attack detection.

3   Voice Impersonation Dataset

The dataset of bona fide speeches and corresponding impersonated speeches are acquired in a process similar to that of the VoxCeleb database. The easiest way to obtain this type of attack dataset is by looking for popular people and their impersonators' speeches that are uploaded to YouTube. In this work, three languages are chosen as per the authors' knowledge: English and two Indian languages: Hindi and Telugu. Multi-lingual data samples also help us to understand the impact of language used in training data on ASV systems. The bona fide speakers and their well-known impersonators are carefully selected from different subjects in each language. The speakers include political figures and actors.

The bona fide speeches are taken from the interview videos of the target speakers. The impersonation speeches are obtained from YouTube videos of television shows and performances by mimicry artists ranging from amateurs to professionals. The speeches are manually annotated and segmented to individual speakers without any loss in the quality of audio. The speech samples with dominating background noise like applause and music are ignored. The number of speakers and utterances for each language in this dataset is presented in Table 1.

Table 1. Details of impersonation attack dataset.

Language	No. of speakers	Bona fide utterances	Impersonation utterances
English	15	506	411
Hindi	15	768	449
Telugu	15	677	549

4   Vulnerability of ASV Systems to Voice Impersonation

The impact of voice impersonation on automatic speaker verification (ASV) systems are verified by performing a presentation attack on the ASV methods using impersonation samples. The initial step in this process is to acquire voice impersonation samples for a set of speakers. Due to the lack of professional impersonators for several speakers, and based on the authors' knowledge of target speakers, we have chosen an obvious way of obtaining impersonation samples from YouTube and included three different languages.

4.1   Training Dataset

In our work, we have used the pre-trained models[1] from Kaldi toolkit [13]. The models are trained on verification split of the VoxCeleb1 and entire VoxCeleb2 dataset [11]. The training dataset is a part of the VoxCeleb dataset, which is an audio-visual dataset consisting of short clips of human speech, extracted from interview videos uploaded to YouTube. The main reasons for choosing VoxCeleb trained model are a huge variety of speakers and samples in the dataset (more

---

[1] VoxCeleb Models: http://kaldi-asr.org/models/m7.

than 1 million samples and over 7200 speakers) and also the similarity to our dataset of mimicry samples from YouTube. The training dataset contains speech from speakers of a wide variety of cultures, accents, professions, and ages. The details of dataset is presented in Table 2 and 3.

Table 2. Details of the verification split of VoxCeleb1 dataset

VoxCeleb1	Dev set	Test set
No. of speakers	1211	40
No. of videos	21,819	677
No. of utterances	148,642	4,874

Table 3. Details of VoxCeleb2 dataset

VoxCeleb2	Dev set	Test set
No. of speakers	5994	118
No. of videos	145,569	4911
No. of utterances	1,092,009	36,237

4.2   Automatic Speaker Verification (ASV) Systems

The next step is to obtain ASV systems to examine vulnerability due to voice impersonation. We chose two different methods for this purpose 1. a classical i-Vector based system and 2. a state-of-the-art deep neural network-based x-vector method.

I-vector Method. The I-vector based automatic speaker verification method is the state-of-the-art approach proposed in [1]. I-vectors are the low dimensional representation of a speaker sample that is estimated using Joint Factor Analysis (JFA), which models not only the channel effects but also information about speakers. With the help of i-vector extraction, a given speech utterance can be represented by a vector, which includes total factors. The channel compensation in i-vectors is carried out in a low-dimensional total variability space. In this method, we have employed probabilistic linear discriminant analysis (PLDA) [14] to train the speaker models. The trained PLDA models are then used to compute the log-likelihood scores of the target samples to verify the speaker.

X-vector Method. The deep learning and end-to-end speaker verification approaches are the recent popular methods replacing handcrafted methods. The x-vector based speaker verification is one of the latest approaches using deep neural network (DNN) embeddings [15]. This approach uses trained DNN to differentiate speakers by mapping their variable-length utterances to a fixed-dimensional embedding called as x-vectors. A large amount of training data is one of the biggest challenges in this approach. Therefore, data augmentation with added noise and reverberation is used to increase the size of training data.

In the implementation of ASV methods, we have used the pre-trained Universal Background Models, i-vector extractor, x-vector extractor, and speaker recognition codes from Kaldi[2].

5   Experimental Results and Discussion

The test set of the VoxCeleb1 dataset is used to verify the performance of obtained ASV methods using pre-trained models. The results of ASV methods on the VoxCeleb1 test set are in Table 4. The thresholds used for attack samples matching bona fide samples are from this test set evaluation.

Table 4. Performance of ASV methods on VoxCeleb1 test set

ASV method	EER (%)
I-vector method	5.3
X-vector method	3.1

The performance of the speaker recognition systems is evaluated using the standardised metrics from ISO/IEC on biometric performance [4]. In addition the Equal Error Rate is reported. The Equal Error Rate (EER) is the rate at which false match rate (FMR) and false non-match rate (FNMR) are equal. The detection error trade-off (DET) curve is used to plot the relationship between the false match rate (FMR) and the false non-match rate (FNMR) for zero-effort impostors and impersonation attacks. Further, the impostor attack presentation match rate (IAPMR) is calculated for each language in two ASV methods. Impostor attack presentation match rate (IAPMR) is the proportion of impostor attack presentations using the same PAI species in which the target reference is matched [5]. In this case, it is the percentage of impersonation attack samples when matched with target speakers above the threshold, which is set by the test set for each ASV system.

---

[2] Kaldi GitHub:https://github.com/kaldi-asr/kaldi.

5.1 Equal Error Rate (EER) Comparison

Table 5. Equal Error Rate (EER%) values of zero-effort impostors and impersonation attacks for the ASV methods on each language

Language	Scenario	I-vector method	X-vector method
English	Zero-effort impostors	5.99	3.83
	Impersonation attacks	12.94	11.10
Hindi	Zero-effort impostors	7.88	5.72
	Impersonation attacks	11.17	12.22
Telugu	Zero-effort impostors	4.84	3.86
	Impersonation attacks	5.57	4.77

The EERs (%) are presented in Table 5 for both zero-effort impostors and impersonation presentation attacks in order to compare the vulnerability caused by voice impersonation on ASV methods. The zero-effort impostors' evaluation is performed with no targeting attacks, whereas the presentation attacks are evaluated by presenting attack samples targeting corresponding speakers. It is important to remember that the zero-effort impostor scores are computed by targeting one speaker on other speakers only in the same language. However, the impersonation samples of one speaker are intended only to target that particular speaker. The IAPMR values that are presented show how many attack samples are matched with target speakers' bona fide samples.

The results show that the increase in the EER (%) values when impersonation attacks are performed. The vulnerability due to the voice impersonation can be seen in both ASV methods. Although the x-vector method has better performance without any attacks (in zero-effort impostors), it can be seen that the vulnerability due to impersonation is similar to i-vector based method. This raises the point that impersonation attacks have an impact even on an advanced deep neural network-based approach similar to the classical method. The comparison of the impact of impersonation attack among different languages deduces some important points. It is interesting to see that the impact is high in the English language when compared to other languages. The reason for this could be that the language in the training dataset is English. This makes ASV methods to recognize the English impersonators more efficiently than other languages.

5.2 FMR vs FNMR Comparison

The False match rates versus false non-match rate comparisons show the performance of a biometric system by examining the rate of mismatches in both bona fide and impostor samples. We have fixed the false match rate at 0.001 for each case of zero-effort impostors and attacks, then obtained thresholds to compute the false non-match rate. This shows the number of bona fide samples that are

Table 6. False non-match rate (FNMR %) of zero-effort impostors and impersonation attacks when False match rate is at 0.001 (i.e. FMR = 0.1%) on each language.

Language	Scenario	I-vector method	X-vector method
English	Zero-effort impostors	18.23	16.36
	Impersonation attacks	51.93	66.22
Hindi	Zero-effort impostors	27.43	22.63
	Impersonation attacks	37.29	44.74
Telugu	Zero-effort impostors	15.34	12.04
	Impersonation attacks	18.31	14.55

not allowed into the system with a fixed allowance of impostors into the system (Table 6).

The increase in the amount of bona fide samples that result in false match is observed in all languages when attacks are performed. The highest number of mismatches can be seen in the English language in x-vector based method, where more than 66% of FNMR is observed. Further, the DET curves in Fig. 1 shows the FMR versus FNMR of two methods in different languages with and without attacks. The increase in error rates can be seen among all systems when the impersonation attack is carried out among all three languages.

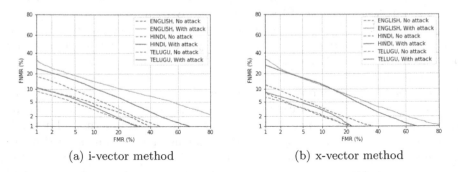

(a) i-vector method   (b) x-vector method

Fig. 1. Detection Error Tradeoff (DET) curves of the ASV methods with and without impersonation attacks.

5.3   IAPMR Evaluation

The IAPMR values in Table 7 show the percentage of impersonation attack samples that are matched with bona fide samples in each language. The classical i-vector based method has 62.87% of attacks matched in English, which is a considerable amount showing the reasonable impact of voice impersonation on

Table 7. IAPMR (%) values of the impersonation attacks.

Language	I-vector method	X-vector method
English	62.87	58.14
Hindi	46.97	53.87
Telugu	33.43	41.90

the ASV method. The state-of-the-art x-vector method accepts 58.14% of the samples. This displays a high vulnerability of the ASV method towards impersonation even on the state-of-the-art methods. For other languages Hindi and Telugu, IAPMR values are lower, which shows the language dependency of the speaker recognition. It is interesting to see that the x-vector method has a higher impact than i-vector method in Hindi and Telugu, unlike English. This impact can also be due to the dependency on the language used in training, which is English.

6   Conclusion

Impersonation attack have been considered as an obvious way of attacking an automatic speaker verification system. In this work, we have studied previous works on voice impersonation evaluation, and a novel dataset of voice impersonation is created. The dataset is captured in a similar way of the VoxCeleb data capturing mechanism in three different languages. The vulnerability of voice impersonation as an attack is examined on a classical and another state-of-the-art speaker recognition systems. The state-of-the-art speaker recognition method is based on a deep neural network-based method that resembles the current technology. Experiments are performed, and evaluations are carried out using ISO/IEC standards with EER, FMR/FNMR, and IAPMR metrics. The results show that the voice impersonations make the ASV methods vulnerable, with many attacks being accepted by the system. It is also interesting to see the vulnerability variation among different languages. The future works on this topic will examine the specific characteristics of the impersonator that are useful in making a successful attack on ASV methods. Also, choosing a training dataset with different languages to examine the language dependency of ASV methods and working on speaker-specific features, like residual phase, to avoid the vulnerability caused by impersonation.

References

1. Dehak, N., Kenny, P.J., Dehak, R., Dumouchel, P., Ouellet, P.: Front-end factor analysis for speaker verification. IEEE Trans. Audio Speech Lang. Process. **19**(4), 788–798 (2011). https://doi.org/10.1109/TASL.2010.2064307

2. Farrús Cabeceran, M., Wagner, M., Erro Eslava, D., Hernando Pericás, F.J.: Automatic speaker recognition as a measurement of voice imitation and conversion. Int. J. Speech Lang. Law **1**(17), 119–142 (2010)
3. Hautamäki, R.G., Kinnunen, T., Hautamäki, V., Laukkanen, A.M.: Automatic versus human speaker verification: the case of voice mimicry. Speech Commun. **72**, 13–31 (2015)
4. ISO/IEC JTC1 SC37 Biometrics: ISO/IEC 19795–1:2006. Information Technology - Biometric Performance Testing and Reporting - Part 1: Principles and Framework. International Organization for Standardization and International Electrotechnical Committee, March 2006
5. ISO/IEC JTC1 SC37 Biometrics: ISO/IEC FDIS 30107–3. Information Technology - Biometric presentation attack detection - Part 3: Testing and Reporting. International Organization for Standardization (2017)
6. Kinnunen, T., Li, H.: An overview of text-independent speaker recognition: from features to supervectors. Speech Commun. **52**(1), 12–40 (2010)
7. Kinnunen, T., et al.: The ASVspoof 2017 challenge: assessing the limits of replay spoofing attack detection (2017)
8. Lau, Y.W., Tran, D., Wagner, M.: Testing voice mimicry with the YOHO speaker verification corpus. In: Khosla, R., Howlett, R.J., Jain, L.C. (eds.) KES 2005. LNCS (LNAI), vol. 3684, pp. 15–21. Springer, Heidelberg (2005). https://doi.org/10.1007/11554028_3
9. Lau, Y.W., Wagner, M., Tran, D.: Vulnerability of speaker verification to voice mimicking. In: Proceedings of 2004 International Symposium on Intelligent Multimedia, Video and Speech Processing, 2004, pp. 145–148, October 2004. https://doi.org/10.1109/ISIMP.2004.1434021
10. Mariéthoz, J., Bengio, S.: Can a professional imitator fool a GMM-based speaker verification system? Technical report, IDIAP (2005)
11. Nagrani, A., Chung, J.S., Zisserman, A.: VoxCeleb: a large-scale speaker identification dataset. In: Lacerda, F. (ed.) Interspeech 2017, 18th Annual Conference of the International Speech Communication Association, Stockholm, Sweden, 20–24 August 2017, pp. 2616–2620. ISCA (2017). https://doi.org/10.21437/Interspeech. http://www.isca-speech.org/archive/Interspeech_2017/abstracts/0950.html
12. Panjwani, S., Prakash, A.: Crowdsourcing attacks on biometric systems. In: Symposium On Usable Privacy and Security (SOUPS 2014), pp. 257–269 (2014)
13. Povey, D., et al.: The Kaldi speech recognition toolkit. In: IEEE 2011 Workshop on Automatic Speech Recognition and Understanding. No. CONF, IEEE Signal Processing Society (2011)
14. Prince, S., Li, P., Fu, Y., Mohammed, U., Elder, J.: Probabilistic models for inference about identity. IEEE Trans. Pattern Anal. Mach. Intell. **34**(1), 144–157 (2012)
15. Snyder, D., Garcia-Romero, D., Sell, G., Povey, D., Khudanpur, S.: X-vectors: robust dnn embeddings for speaker recognition. In: 2018 IEEE International Conference on Acoustics, Speech and Signal Processing (ICASSP), pp. 5329–5333, April 2018. https://doi.org/10.1109/ICASSP.2018.8461375
16. Todisco, M., et al.: ASVspoof 2019: future horizons in spoofed and fake audio detection. arXiv preprint arXiv:1904.05441 (2019)
17. Wu, Z., Evans, N., Kinnunen, T., Yamagishi, J., Alegre, F., Li, H.: Spoofing and countermeasures for speaker verification: a survey. Speech Commun. **66**, 130–153 (2015)

A Survey on Unknown Presentation Attack Detection for Fingerprint

Jag Mohan Singh[(✉)], Ahmed Madhun, Guoqiang Li,
and Raghavendra Ramachandra

Norwegian Biometrics Laboratory, Norwegian University of Science and Technology
(NTNU), Trondheim, Norway
{jag.m.singh,ahmed.madhun,guoqiang.li,raghavendra.ramachandra}@ntnu.no

Abstract. Fingerprint recognition systems are widely deployed in various real-life applications as they have achieved high accuracy. The widely used applications include border control, automated teller machine (ATM), and attendance monitoring systems. However, these critical systems are prone to spoofing attacks (a.k.a presentation attacks (PA)). PA for fingerprint can be performed by presenting gummy fingers made from different materials such as silicone, gelatine, play-doh, ecoflex, 2D printed paper, 3D printed material, or latex. Biometrics Researchers have developed Presentation Attack Detection (PAD) methods as a countermeasure to PA. PAD is usually done by training a machine learning classifier for known attacks for a given dataset, and they achieve high accuracy in this task. However, generalizing to unknown attacks is an essential problem from applicability to real-world systems, mainly because attacks cannot be exhaustively listed in advance. In this survey paper, we present a comprehensive survey on existing PAD algorithms for fingerprint recognition systems, specifically from detecting unknown PAD. We categorize PAD algorithms, point out their advantages/disadvantages, and future directions for this area.

Keywords: Presentation attack detection · Anomaly detection · Biometrics · Information security · Anti-spoofing · Fingerprint · Spoofing material

1 Introduction

Biometrics based authentication systems provide more security than traditional information security-based systems based on passwords/Personal Identification Number (PINs), and keys/cards [10]. The primary limitations with traditional information security methods are that they lack good user experience, using the same security measure with multiple applications, and forgetting/losing the password/PINs [6]. Especially for keys/cards, they can be duplicated apart from the previously mentioned limitations. Since biometric systems are based on human characteristics such as the face, fingerprint, or iris, which are unique

© Springer Nature Switzerland AG 2021
S. Yildirim Yayilgan et al. (Eds.): INTAP 2020, CCIS 1382, pp. 189–202, 2021.
https://doi.org/10.1007/978-3-030-71711-7_16

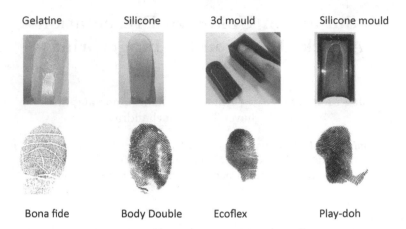

Fig. 1. Different attacks on the fingerprint recognition systems shown as photographs that are taken from [21] and as fingerprints that are taken from [29]).

for every individual, they have a definite advantage over information security-based systems. Due to these advantages, biometric systems are widely deployed in smartphones, border control (both in automated, and attended scenarios), and national identity cards. However, biometric systems are vulnerable to Presentation Attacks (PA) [26], due to which some crimes have been reported in the media, where the biometric systems were spoofed [30,46,50]. An attacker can perform the attack on the biometric system by presenting a biometric artefact or a Presentation Attack Instruments (PAIs) [35]. PA can be performed in different biometric modalities, including the face, fingerprint, and iris. Since fingerprint recognition systems are widely deployed in critical security systems, it is essential to develop fingerprint PAD (Fig. 1).

PAIs for fingerprint can either be an artificial object such as a gummy finger (made from play-doh, silicone, or gelatine) or a 2D/3D printed photo. In terms of implementation, PAD systems can be either a hardware-based or a software-based, whose main task is to distinguish between a real (bona fide) user or a malicious (imposter) attacker [1]. A summary of existing fingerprint PAD methods can be found in Marcel et al. [25], Marasco et al. [23], Galbally et al. [13], and Sousedik et al. [41]. In the current scenario, most of the existing PAD methods consist of training a classifier to model the characteristics of the PAI accurately. However, such an approach suffers from the problem of generalization to detect unknown attacks [25]. Thus, developing a reliable PAD technique for unknown attacks is a significant problem that can also be posed as anomaly (outlier) detection. Fingerprint recognition systems have been widely deployed, as mentioned earlier, and are prone to PA. Since the attacks cannot be listed in advance, detecting unknown attacks for the fingerprint is critical. Our survey on fingerprint Presentation Attack Detection (FPAD) presents the following:

- Comprehensive survey of existing methods for FPAD for unknown attacks.
- Categorization of existing methods for the FPAD of unknown attacks.
- Discussion on advantages/disadvantages of existing methods for FPAD, especially for unknown attacks.
- Concluding remarks with future directions for the area of FPAD.

In the rest of the paper, a comparison between traditional PAD done in a supervised manner, and anomaly detection based FPAD in Sect. 2, which is followed by Sect. 3 summarizing related work in FPAD which includes their categorization, advantages, and disadvantages in terms of generalization, and finally we present conclusions & future directions for FPAD in Sect. 4.

2 Traditional PAD and Anomaly Detection Based PAD

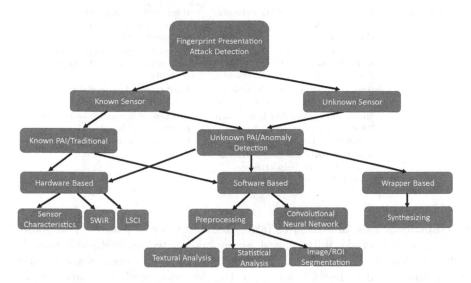

Fig. 2. Illustration of taxonomy for fingerprint presentation attack detection where SWIR indicates Short Wave Infrared and LSCI indicates Laser Speckle Imaging.

In this section, we present a comparison between traditional PAD (a form of supervised classification) and anomaly detection (supervised/unsupervised classification) based PAD, as shown in Fig. 2. Since we are interested in unknown attack detection for fingerprint, this can be achieved by Anomaly detection [3]. We now briefly review Anomaly detection in the following subsection:

2.1 Anomaly Detection

Anomaly Detection refers to the determination of irregularity in a dataset. The dataset contains a set of records (aka., instances, objects, or entities), where each

Table 1. Characteristics, advantages and disadvantages of Anomaly detection based PAD as compared to Traditional PAD for biometrics.

	Traditional PAD	Anomaly detection based PAD
Characteristics	– Information about PAI is gathered and known in advance	– Establish profiles of normality features which are extracted from regular data
	– Look for PAIs' features each time a presentation occurs	– Compares the normality features of each new presentation against the established profiles
	– Alerts for PA if any PAI is found to be in the new presentation	– Alerts for PA if a deviation from normality is detected in the new presentation based on threshold
Advantages	– Possibility to detect known PAs	– Possibility to detect known and unknown PAs
	– There is a possibility of using existing knowledge to recognize new forms of old PAs	– Does not care about the used PAI during the attack
Drawbacks	– For each novel PA, PAD methods should be updated and tested with the new PAI	– Hard to define a profile of normality features for each bona fide presentation
	– As the number of PAs increases, and correspondingly PAIs increase, the complexity of PAD increases	– Higher false-positive for PAs depending on accessibility or usability
	– Hard to detect previously unseen PAs	– Hard to set the optimal threshold value for PAD
	– Simple changes to PAI in a known PA can be enough to miss the detection of the PA	– The size of normality feature can be considerable, which leads to a high false-positive rate
	– A leak of PAIs' list that a system maintains could help attackers bypass the system's PAD method	

record includes a set of attributes (aka., characteristics or features), as pointed out by Chandola et al. [3]. In general, an anomaly detection method is provided with a record/set of records as an input, where no information about either anomalies or regular classes is known to the detection method in advance [27]. The three modes of anomaly detection methods, according to Chandola et al. [3] are as follows:

- **Supervised anomaly detection**:
  Anomaly methods based on a predictive model are trained by a labeled dataset of two classes (i.e., normal and anomaly records). Any unseen record is then compared against the model to determine whether it is a normal or an anomaly record. This can be achieved by using publicly labeled fingerprint datasets for training. This form of anomaly detection is used in traditional PAD and in unknown attack detection where the sensor is known in advance for FPAD.
- **Semi-supervised anomaly detection**:
  Anomaly methods are based on a single classifier trained using only normal behavior records from a dataset, as only those are labeled. This form of

anomaly detection is used for unknown attack detection for the known sensor, & unknown sensor for FPAD.

- **Unsupervised anomaly detection:**
  Anomaly methods do not require training data, but no records are labeled in the dataset if training is applied. This method is based on the assumption that regular records are far more frequent than anomalies in training and testing datasets, and can lead to high false reject rate if this assumption is violated. This form of anomaly detection is used for unknown attack detection for the known sensor, and the unknown sensor for FPAD.

Table 1 shows a description of traditional and anomaly detection based PAD. Theoretically, the main advantage of anomaly-based PAD methods over traditional methods is capturing both the known and the unknown PAs. In contrast, the traditional PAD methods can detect known PAs, and maybe new forms of these attacks. For instance, if a traditional PAD method is trained only to detect gummy fingers of play-doh, it may not detect gummy fingers of other materials like silicone or gelatine. This requires the traditional PAD methods to make a long list of PAIs gathered from known PAs, and the methods should be updated and re-trained each time a new unknown PA is revealed. Consequently, the list of PAIs and known PAs can become long and hard to maintain. Moreover, if an attacker gets access to the list of PAIs used to train a biometric system, the attacker will be able to conduct a PA using a novel PAI that is not known to the systems.

Even if anomaly PAD methods solve several drawbacks in traditional PAD methods, they come with high risks, implementation difficulties, and critical disadvantages. In general, it is difficult to define and extract all features of bona fide presentations (i.e., normality features), because these features can have a broad scope and thus become hard to use for an implementation of a PAD method. Moreover, the threshold used to distinguish between PAs and bona fide presentations is affected by accessibility or usability issues between the subject, and the capture device, making it hard to define. Thus, the size of the normality features will be large, and it may require prioritizing some features over others during the feature selection. Nevertheless, size reduction methods can be used to reduce the number of features normality. However, this will lead to more false-positive alarms as the normality features are not precise enough to distinguish between all the cases of PAs and bona fide presentations.

3   Known and Unknown Presentation Attack Detection for Fingerprints

We now review the related work for FPAD in general, and specifically for unknown attack detection of fingerprints. Many software and hardware PAD methods are presented in the literature to detect PAs against fingerprint recognition systems. PAs can be conducted using PAIs in two fingerprint forms (e.g., overlays), and additionally using 3d printed fingers [41]. Software approaches use

Table 2. Overview of Fingerprint PAD using anomaly detection for unknown PAs. (where the abbreviations used are Anomaly Detection (A. D.), Software/Hardware/ Wrapper (S/H/W), Supervised (S), Semi-Supervised (SS), and Unsupervised (U))

Ref.	S/H/W	Dataset	Pre-processing	Post-processing	# unknown PAs	A. D. methods	A. D. mode
[24]	S	LivDet 2009	–	–	1	–	S
[37]	S	LivDet 2011	GLCM, HOG, BSIF LPQ, LBP, BGP	–	2	SVM,Rule-based	S
[38]	S	LivDet 2011	LBP	Score fusion	4	SVM	S
[36]	S	LivDet 2011	BSIF, LBP, LPQ	–	3	SVM	S
[34]	S	LivDet 2011, LivDet 2013, LivDet 2015	Image segmentation (part of CNN)	–	4	CNN	S
[49]	S & H	Own dataset	ROI segmentation	–	6	Pre-trained CNN	S
[15]	S & H	Own dataset	ROI segmentation	Score fusion	3	SVM	S
[14]	S & H	Own dataset	ROI segmentation	Score fusion	5	SVM,CNN,Pre-trained CNN	S
[48]	S & H	Own dataset, LivDet 2017	ROI segmentation, RGB image creation	Score fusion	5	SVM, CNN, Pre-trained CNNs	S
[4]	S	MSU-FPAD, PBSKD	Minutiae detection, Patches creation, Patches alignment	Score fusion	6	Pre-trained CNN	S
[40]	S	LivDet 2011, LivDet 2013, LivDet 2015, LivDet 2019	Dense-SIFT	Score fusion	$8\leq$	SVM, K-means, PCA	S, U
[5, 12]	W	MSU-FPAD v2, LivDet 2015, LiveDet 2017	Patches extraction	Score fusion	3	Pre-trained CNN	S

features extracted by standard sensing technologies, which can further be divided into static (e.g., sweat pores and texture of ridges and valleys) and dynamic features (e.g., skin color change over time due to pressure). Software approaches are usually cheaper to implement (as no extra hardware is needed), and less intrusive to the user [13]. Hardware approaches introduce a new device to the sensing technology to capture more details than standard sensors (e.g., fingerprint sweat, blood pressure, or odor). Keeping in mind that hardware solutions are only used to capture data, and they usually have associated software solutions with them that distinguish between bona fide and PAs, which can either be inbuilt in the sensor or as stand-alone software. So, in theory, if two different hardware approaches as in [14] and [19] use Short Wave Infrared (SWIR) and Laser Speckle Contrast Imaging (LSCI) techniques respectively, they can still process each other datasets using the same software in their approaches. According to Galbally et al. [13] hardware-based approach introduces a higher fake detection rate than a software-based approach. This survey paper considers the type of approach (i.e., hardware and software) as a comparison factor, as shown in Table 2.

3.1 Pre-processing Techniques (Software-Based)

We now briefly review the pre-processing techniques in the literature attached to the PAD methods presented in Table 2. These can be texture-based descriptors such as Local Binary Pattern (LBP) [32], Grey Level Co-occurrence Matrix (GLCM) [17], Histogram of Oriented Gradients (HOG) [7], Binary Statistical Image Features (BSIF) [37], Local Phase Quantization [33], Binary Gabor Patterns (BGP) [51], Dense-SIFT [40] or techniques such as Image Segmentation, Region of Interest (ROI) Segmentation or Finger-print Minutae detection.

3.2 Convolutional Neural Network (Software-Based)

We now briefly review the deep learning-based approaches; Park et al. [34] presented a supervised software-based approach using a convolution neural network (CNN), which did not use the PAD of unknown PAs. However, they tested the approach on the LivDet 2015 data sets that contains four unknown PAs [29]. The CNN network devised by them takes the full image of a fingerprint. It outputs a three-dimensional tensor used to determine the probability of the image being a bona fide or an attack presentation. The liveness probability is compared to an optimal threshold obtained from the training phase, where they achieved an average classification error of 1.5% for the unknown PAs. The usage of deep learning approaches has become a trend in the last decade, which is mainly due to the freely available pre-trained networks such as VGG [39], GoogleNet [42], and ResNet [18]. Tolosana et al. [48] published a new experiment, where a PAD method relies on the use of SWIR and RGB images. Deep features from RGB images are extracted via two pre-trained CNNs, namely VGG19 and MobileNet, and a ResNet network trained from scratch. The features output by the CNNs is feed to an SVM. Additionally, handcrafted features as spectral signatures were extracted from SWIR images. For the final evaluation, a score fusion applied, and the reported D-EER for this experiment was 1.36%.

3.3 Known Sensor and Known Attacks

Marasco et al. [23] provided an overview of PAD methods in the literature for fingerprint recognition systems, and they specifically point out that commercial fingerprint recognition systems can be spoofed. Most of these approaches test their performance on a test dataset with the same PAs as used during the training. Thus, these PAs are considered known to the PAD-method, which is a less realistic scenario than a real-world environment setup where additional PAIs may be used to conduct PAs (i.e., unknown attacks).

3.4   Known Sensor and Unknown Attacks

To the best of our knowledge, Tan et al. [44] were the first to point to the effect of environmental conditions and new PAI materials on PAD methods for fingerprints. They showed that new PAI to increases the error rate by at least 14% and up to 55,6 % on different fingerprint scanners as Identix, Crossmatch, and Digital Persona. Moreover, their experiment showed that the error rate drops back into an acceptable range once new PAIs are used in the training phase. This was later confirmed by Marasco et al. in [24], in which they experimented the increase of spoof detection error rates of five fingerprint liveness detection methods (given by Marasco et al. [22], Moon et al. [28], Shankar et al. [31], Abhyankar et al. [2], and Tan et al. [45]) when tested on the new PAIs that were not used during training. Marasco et al. [24] used the leave-one-out approach in their experiment, where only one PAI out of gelatine, play-doh, and silicone is used for testing, and the other two are used for training as they train the PAD methods using both PAs and bona fide presentations and can be classified as supervised anomaly detection approach.

To solve unknown PAIs, Rattani et al. [37] proposed a scheme for automatic detection and adoption of the liveness detector to new PAIs. Their liveness detection is a combination of a multiclass-SVM and rule-based approaches that form an AdaBoost-based classifiers [11]. The Adaboost classifiers are used to detect novel PAs, and new PAIs used in each attack, followed by a binary classification SVM that corresponds to live and spoof classes, where the thresholds are maintained by multi-class SVM. In a case where a novel PA is presented to the detector, two rules apply to determine whether the PA is novel or already known. The first rule computes the maximum posterior probabilities for each known PA and bona fide. So, PA is considered novel if it overcomes a defined threshold else it is regarded as a known PAs and belongs to the corresponding class value. The second rule estimates the standard deviation of the posterior probabilities computed in the first rule. A low standard deviation value indicates doubt in classifying the PA as a known.

Additionally, they state the possibility of their PAD method to update the maintained binary classification SVM automatically. Thus, it is always considered learned to known PA materials. This method is considered supervised because two out of four materials in the LiveDet 2011 dataset were used for training (i.e., two known PAIs and two unknown PAIs). The published results mentioned up to 46% improvements in detecting unknown PAIs. Rattani et al. [38] published a study where they tried to reduce the material-specific noise and apply a software-based method that learns the general artifacts in images from PAIs that correspond to different materials. This is done using two SVMs that combine linear filtering and non-linear denoising using wavelet decomposition of PAIs on an LBP-based textural-analysis liveness detector. Their experimental results gained up to 44% improvements in detecting unknown PAs on LiveDet 2011 dataset. The training phase during the experiment is done using one material out of five. Thus, the method is tested on four unknown attacks. Rattani et al. [37] used Weibull-calibrated SVM (W-SVM) can be used both for the detection of liveness and spoofs, and discovery of new novel PAs and PAIs. Also, they claim W-SVM that supports interoperability between individual detectors. The results show 44% improvements in detecting novel materials on Livedet 2011 dataset. Tolosona et al. [49] used a VGG pre-trained network as a PAD method in the finger recognition system. They use ShortWave Infrared Imaging (SWIR) images since the skin reflection within the SWIR spectrum of 900–1700 nm is independent of the skin tone as analyzed by the National Institute of Standards Technology (NIST). Thus, they used a hardware sensor approach to capture SWIR images of bona fide and PAs (i.e., own dataset), and a software-based approach for PAD. A total number of six unknown PAIs were detected by their PAD method, giving high convenience and secure, supervised PAD method. The same hardware developed by [49] is capable of capturing finger vein images (i.e., Visible Light Images, VIS) and speckle contrast images (LSCI) in addition to SWIR images.

Gomez-Barrero et al. [15] proposed a multi-modal finger PAD method where they use different ad-hoc approaches in parallel for each image type, and several SVM classifications are set to output a score of each ad-hoc approach where the final score is given by the weighted sum of all individual scores obtained. The evaluation in this approach is applied to known and unknown PAIs (in total 35, three are unknown), resulting in a Detection Equal Error Rate (D-EER) of 2.7%. Gomez-Barrero et al. proposed another multi-modal approach [14], in which the proposed PAD method relies on a weighted sum of two CNN networks based on SWIR images and textural and gradient information from averaged LSCI images. They applied a pre-trained VGG19 network and a ResNet network that was trained from scratch for the CNNs. The textural and gradient information extracted from averaged LSCI images is passed into three SVMs for classification. They used the dataset from [15], increasing the number of unknown attacks to five PAIs, and reporting a decrease in the D-EER from 2.7% to 0.5%. Chugh et al. [4] proposed a software-based FPAD method with a generalization against PAIs not seen during training. They studied the characteristics of twelve different PAIs and bona fide presentations using deep features extracted by a pre-trained CNN, namely, MobileNetv1. Further, they applied an agglomerative clustering based on the shared characteristics of PAIs. Thus, they concluded that a subset of PAIs, namely silicone, 2D paper, play-doh, gelatine, latex body paint, and monster liquid latex, are essential PAIs to include during the training to achieve a robust PAD. An android smartphone application is presented without a significant drop in performance from the original PAD method. They achieved a True Detection Rate (TDR) of 95.7% and False Detection Rate (FDR) of 0.2% when the generalization set is used for training (i.e., the six PAIs). Recently, Tolosana et al. [47] collected a new dataset of fingerprints using a custom SWIR device, which was followed by extracting features from the training of deep-learning architectures either from scratch or using pre-trained networks. This was followed by using multiple SVMs as classifiers. The evaluation protocol followed the unknown attack scenario for which they achieved a D-EER of 1.35% outperforming few handcrafted features for which D-EER was 12%.

3.5 UnKnown Sensor and Unknown Attacks

Rattani et al. [36] declared the need for fingerprint PAs detection to be considered an open set recognition problem. Thus, incomplete knowledge about neither PAs nor PAIs is known to the PAD method during training. Therefore, they adopted W-SVM, which uses recent advances in extreme value theory statistics for machine learning to directly address the risk of the anomalies in an open set recognition problem. Ding et al. [8] proposed using an ensemble of One-Class Support Vector Machines (OC-SVM) using bona fide samples to generate a hypersphere boundary which is refined by a small number of spoof samples, for classification of unknown PAIs. Jain et al. [9] developed a one-class classifier based on training on learning of bona fide samples using multiple GANs (Generative-Adversarial Networks) which can reject any PAI. González-Soler et al. [40] proposed a software-based PAD method and achieved an overall accuracy by 96.17% on the LivDet2019 competition. This method relied on three image representation approaches, which combine both local and global information of the fingerprint, namely Bag-of-words (BoW) [16], Fisher Vector (FV) [43], and Vector Locally Aggregated Descriptors (VLAD) [20]. They computed Dense-SIFT descriptors at different scales, and the features are then encoded using a previously learned visual vocabulary using the previously mentioned image representation approaches.

A linear SVM classifier is applied to classify the fingerprint descriptor in each method. A weighted sum computes the final decision score. BoW approach uses K-means clustering local features and presents it as a pyramid of spatial histograms. FV approach is based on statistical and spectral-based techniques, where the Gaussian Mixture Model (GMM) locates local features that lie under the same distribution. Then, these features are presented in a lower dimension via Principal Component Analysis (PCA).

On the other hand, the VLAD approach relied on non-probabilistic techniques and is used to reduce the high-dimension image representation in BoW and FV. They experimented with both scenarios of their PAD method, namely supervised (i.e., known PAs) and unsupervised (i.e., unknown PAs) situations. Chugh et al. [5] and Gajawada et al. [12] present a wrapper that can be adopted by any fingerprint PAD method to improve the generalization performance of the PAD method against unknown PAIs. These approaches are based on synthesizing fingerprint images that correspond to unknown PAs and bona fide images as well. The goal is to transfer the characteristics into a deep feature space so that a more precise presentation helps the PAD method increase its generalization performance. The method is based on multiple pre-trained VGG19 CNNs that encode and decode the content and style loss of the synthesized images, as they can be further used to train the PAD method. They use the same PAD software method as done by Chugh et al. [4] to experiment with the wrapper. Moreover, this approach is a supervised method in which they use the leave-one-out technique on each PAI for MSU-FPADv2, where the other PAIs are known in training. On the other hand, in LivDet 2017 dataset, three PAIs were considered unknown.

4 Conclusions and Future Directions

This survey paper presented unknown attack detection for fingerprints, including a survey of existing methods summarized & categorized in Table 2, additionally a taxonomy of FPAD is presented in Fig. 2. Currently, most unknown attack detection methods for fingerprints are solving the problem of known sensors and unknown PAIs, and there are only a few methods which are unknown sensor, and unknown PAI, including cross-dataset.

Unknown attack detection with unknown sensors is a relatively new area of research for FPAD and should be the focus area in near-future. The first approach to solving it is synthesis, as done by Jain et al. [9]. The second approach is to arrive at a common deep-feature representation, such as the one used by González-Soler et al. [40]. The challenge in the synthesis-based approach is to do high-quality synthesis of the bona fide samples. The difficulty in arriving at a common deep-feature representation is the degree of invariance it can provide to sensor type and PAI.

References

1. Information technology - biometric presentation attack detection - part 1: Framework. Standard, International Organization for Standardization, Geneva, CH, iSO 30107–1:2016(E), January 2016
2. Abhyankar, A., Schuckers, S.: Integrating a wavelet based perspiration liveness check with fingerprint recognition. Pattern Recogn. 42(3), 452–464 (2009). https://doi.org/10.1016/j.patcog.2008.06.012. http://www.sciencedirect.com/science/article/pii/S0031320308002458
3. Chandola, V., Banerjee, A., Kumar, V.: Anomaly detection: a survey. ACM Comput. Surv. 41 (2009). https://doi.org/10.1145/1541880.1541882
4. Chugh, T., Jain, A.K.: Fingerprint presentation attack detection: generalization and efficiency. In: 2019 International Conference on Biometrics (ICB), pp. 1–8. IEEE (2019)
5. Chugh, T., Jain, A.K.: Fingerprint spoof generalization. ArXiv abs/1912.02710 (2019)
6. Connell, R., Pankanti, S., Ratha, N., Senior, A.: Guide to Biometrics (2003). https://doi.org/10.1007/978-1-4757-4036-3
7. Dalal, N., Triggs, B.: Histograms of oriented gradients for human detection. In: Proceedings of the 2005 IEEE Computer Society Conference on Computer Vision and Pattern Recognition (CVPR 2005) - Volume 1, CVPR 2005, vol. 01, pp. 886–893. IEEE Computer Society, Washington (2005). https://doi.org/10.1109/CVPR.2005.177
8. Ding, Y., Ross, A.: An ensemble of one-class SVMs for fingerprint spoof detection across different fabrication materials. In: 2016 IEEE International Workshop on Information Forensics and Security (WIFS), pp. 1–6. IEEE (2016)
9. Engelsma, J.J., Jain, A.K.: Generalizing fingerprint spoof detector: learning a one-class classifier. arXiv preprint arXiv:1901.03918 (2019)
10. Faundez-Zanuy, M.: Biometric security technology. IEEE Aerosp. Electron. Syst. Mag. 21, 15–26 (2006). https://doi.org/10.1109/MAES.2006.1662038

11. Freund, Y., Schapire, R.E.: A decision-theoretic generalization of on-line learning and an application to boosting. J. Comput. Syst. Sci. **55**(1), 119–139 (1997). https://doi.org/10.1006/jcss.1997.1504. http://www.sciencedirect.com/science/article/pii/S002200009791504X
12. Gajawada, R., Popli, A., Chugh, T., Namboodiri, A.M., Jain, A.K.: Universal material translator: towards spoof fingerprint generalization. In: 2019 International Conference on Biometrics (ICB), pp. 1–8 (2019)
13. Galbally, J., Fierrez, J., Cappelli, R.: An introduction to fingerprint presentation attack detection. In: Marcel, S., Nixon, M.S., Fierrez, J., Evans, N. (eds.) Handbook of Biometric Anti-Spoofing. ACVPR, pp. 3–31. Springer, Cham (2019). https://doi.org/10.1007/978-3-319-92627-8_1
14. Gomez-Barrero, M., Kolberg, J., Busch, C.: Multi-modal fingerprint presentation attack detection: analysing the surface and the inside. In: 2019 International Conference on Biometrics (ICB), pp. 1–8 (2019)
15. Gomez-Barrero, M., Kolberg, J., Busch, C.: Towards multi-modal finger presentation attack detection. In: 2018 14th International Conference on Signal-Image Technology & Internet-Based Systems (SITIS), pp. 547–552 (2018)
16. González-Soler, L.J., Chang, L., Hernández-Palancar, J., Pérez-Suárez, A., Gomez-Barrero, M.: Fingerprint presentation attack detection method based on a bag-of-words approach. In: Mendoza, M., Velastín, S. (eds.) CIARP 2017. LNCS, vol. 10657, pp. 263–271. Springer, Cham (2018). https://doi.org/10.1007/978-3-319-75193-1_32
17. Haralick, R.M., Shanmugam, K., Dinstein, I.: Textural features for image classification. IEEE Trans. Syst. Man Cybern. **SMC-3**(6), 610–621 (1973)
18. He, K., Zhang, X., Ren, S., Sun, J.: Deep residual learning for image recognition. In: 2016 IEEE Conference on Computer Vision and Pattern Recognition (CVPR), pp. 770–778 (2016)
19. Hussein, M., Spinoulas, L., Xiong, F., Abd-Almageed, W.: Fingerprint presentation attack detection using a novel multi-spectral capture device and patch-based convolutional neural networks, pp. 1–8, December 2018. https://doi.org/10.1109/WIFS.2018.8630773
20. Jégou, H., Perronnin, F., Douze, M., Sánchez, J., Pérez, P., Schmid, C.: Aggregating local image descriptors into compact codes. IEEE Trans. Pattern Anal. Mach. Intell. **34**(9), 1704–1716 (2012)
21. Madhun, A.S.M.: FiPrAD - A Guideline for Fingerprint Presentation Attack Database Creation (2018). http://hdl.handle.net/11250/2595890. Accessed 09 May 2020
22. Marasco, E., Sansone, C.: An anti-spoofing technique using multiple textural features in fingerprint scanners. In: 2010 IEEE Workshop on Biometric Measurements and Systems for Security and Medical Applications, pp. 8–14 (2010)
23. Marasco, E., Ross, A.: A survey on antispoofing schemes for fingerprint recognition systems. ACM Comput. Surv. **47**(2) (2014). https://doi.org/10.1145/2617756
24. Marasco, E., Sansone, C.: On the robustness of fingerprint liveness detection algorithms against new materials used for spoofing, pp. 553–558, January 2011
25. Marcel, S., Nixon, M.S., Fierrez, J., Evans, N.: Handbook of Biometric Anti-Spoofing (2019). https://doi.org/10.1007/978-3-319-92627-8_1
26. Matyáš, V., Říha, Z.: Biometric authentication — security and usability. In: Jerman-Blažič, B., Klobučar, T. (eds.) Advanced Communications and Multimedia Security. ITIFIP, vol. 100, pp. 227–239. Springer, Boston, MA (2002). https://doi.org/10.1007/978-0-387-35612-9_17

27. Mehrotra, K.G., Mohan, C.K., Huang, H.M.: Introduction. Anomaly Detection Principles and Algorithms. TSC, pp. 3–19. Springer, Cham (2017). https://doi.org/10.1007/978-3-319-67526-8_1

28. Moon, Y.S., Chen, J.S., Chan, K.C., So, K., Woo, K.C.: Wavelet based fingerprint liveness detection. Electron. Lett. **41**(20), 1112–1113 (2005)

29. Mura, V., Ghiani, L., Marcialis, G.L., Roli, F., Yambay, D., Schuckers, S.: LivDet 2015 fingerprint liveness detection competition 2015. In: 2015 IEEE 7th International Conference on Biometrics Theory, Applications and Systems (BTAS), pp. 1–6 (2015)

30. news, B.: Doctor 'used silicone fingers' to sign in for colleagues (2016). https://www.bbc.com/news/world-latin-america-21756709. Accessed 29 Mar 2020

31. Nikam, S., S., A.: Curvelet-based fingerprint anti-spoofing. Signal Image Video Process. **4**, 75–87 (2010). https://doi.org/10.1007/s11760-008-0098-8

32. Ojala, T., Pietikainen, M., Maenpaa, T.: Multiresolution gray-scale and rotation invariant texture classification with local binary patterns. IEEE Trans. Pattern Anal. Mach. Intell. **24**(7), 971–987 (2002). https://doi.org/10.1109/TPAMI.2002.1017623

33. Ojansivu, V., Heikkilä, J.: Blur insensitive texture classification using local phase quantization. In: Elmoataz, A., Lezoray, O., Nouboud, F., Mammass, D. (eds.) ICISP 2008. LNCS, vol. 5099, pp. 236–243. Springer, Heidelberg (2008). https://doi.org/10.1007/978-3-540-69905-7_27

34. Park, E., Cui, X., Kim, W., Liu, J., Kim, H.: Patch-based fake fingerprint detection using a fully convolutional neural network with a small number of parameters and an optimal threshold, March 2018

35. Ramachandra, R., Busch, C.: Presentation attack detection methods for face recognition systems: a comprehensive survey. ACM Comput. Surv. (CSUR) **50**(1), 1–37 (2017)

36. Rattani, A., Scheirer, W.J., Ross, A.: Open set fingerprint spoof detection across novel fabrication materials. IEEE Trans. Inf. Forensics Secur. **10**(11), 2447–2460 (2015)

37. Rattani, A., Ross, A.: Automatic adaptation of fingerprint liveness detector to new spoof materials. In: IEEE International Joint Conference on Biometrics, pp. 1–8 (2014)

38. Rattani, A., Ross, A.: Minimizing the impact of spoof fabrication material on fingerprint liveness detector, October 2014. https://doi.org/10.1109/ICIP.2014.7026011

39. Simonyan, K., Zisserman, A.: Very deep convolutional networks for large-scale image recognition. arXiv:1409.1556, September 2014

40. Soler, L.J.G., Gomez-Barrero, M., Chang, L., Suárez, A.P., Busch, C.: Fingerprint presentation attack detection based on local features encoding for unknown attacks. ArXiv abs/1908.10163 (2019)

41. Sousedik, C., Busch, C.: Presentation attack detection methods for fingerprint recognition systems: a survey. IET Biometrics **3**(4), 219–233 (2014)

42. Szegedy, C., et al.: Going deeper with convolutions. In: 2015 IEEE Conference on Computer Vision and Pattern Recognition (CVPR), pp. 1–9 (2015)

43. Sánchez, J., Mensink, T., Verbeek, J.: Image classification with the fisher vector: theory and practice. Int. J. Comput. Vision **105** (2013). https://doi.org/10.1007/s11263-013-0636-x

44. Tan, B., Lewicke, A., Yambay, D., Schuckers, S.: The effect of environmental conditions and novel spoofing methods on fingerprint anti-spoofing algorithms. In: 2010 IEEE International Workshop on Information Forensics and Security, WIFS 2010, December 2010. https://doi.org/10.1109/WIFS.2010.5711436
45. Tan, B., Schuckers, S.: Liveness detection using an intensity based approach in fingerprint scanners (2005)
46. Thomson, I.: German minister fingered as hacker 'steals' her thumbprint from a photo (2014). https://www.theregister.co.uk/2014/12/29/german_minister_fingered_as_hackers_steal_her_thumbprint_from_a_photo/. Accessed 29 Mar 2020
47. Tolosana, R., Gomez-Barrero, M., Busch, C., Ortega-Garcia, J.: Biometric presentation attack detection: beyond the visible spectrum. IEEE Trans. Inf. Forensics Secur. **15**, 1261–1275 (2020)
48. Tolosana, R., Gomez-Barrero, M., Busch, C., Ortega-Garcia, J.: Biometric presentation attack detection: beyond the visible spectrum. IEEE Trans. Inf. Forensics Secur. **PP**, 1–1 (2019). https://doi.org/10.1109/TIFS.2019.2934867
49. Tolosana, R., Gomez-Barrero, M., Kolberg, J., Morales, A., Busch, C., Ortega-Garcia, J.: Towards fingerprint presentation attack detection based on convolutional neural networks and short wave infrared imaging. In: 2018 International Conference of the Biometrics Special Interest Group (BIOSIG), pp. 1–5 (2018)
50. Toto, S.: Woman uses tape to trick biometric airport fingerprint scan (2009). https://techcrunch.com/2009/01/02/woman-uses-tape-to-trick-biometric-airport-fingerprint-scan/. 29 Mar 2020
51. Zhang, L., Zhou, Z., Li, H.: Binary Gabor pattern: an efficient and robust descriptor for texture classification, pp. 81–84, September 2012. https://doi.org/10.1109/ICIP.2012.6466800

Hierarchical Interpolation of Imagenet Features for Cross-Dataset Presentation Attack Detection

Jag Mohan Singh$^{(\boxtimes)}$, Raghavendra Ramachandra, and Christoph Busch

Norwegian Biometrics Laboratory, Norwegian University of Science and Technology
(NTNU), Trondheim, Norway
{jag.m.singh,raghavendra.ramachandra,christoph.busch}@ntnu.no

Abstract. Face Recognition Systems (FRS) are vulnerable to spoofing attacks (a.k.a presentation attacks), which can be carried out by presenting a printed photo (print-photo), displaying a photo (display-photo), or displaying a video (replay-video). The issue of presentation attacks can be alleviated by algorithms known as presentation attack detection (PAD) mechanisms. In this paper, we propose a novel framework based on Hierarchical Cosine/Spherical Linear Interpolation of deep learning feature vectors followed by training a Linear SVM for PAD Classification. The deep learning feature vectors are extracted from existing networks trained on the Imagenet dataset. Our proposed approach hierarchically interpolates the extracted feature vectors using Cosine/Spherically Linear Interpolation, followed by using a Linear SVM for classification, and sum-rule fusion for generating final scores. We show our results on cross-dataset PAD for the classifier trained on OULU P1 Dataset and tested on Replay Mobile Dataset. We compare it with the current state-of-the-art (SOTA) algorithms published in the literature and achieve considerably lower detection error-rate (D-EER). The extraction of features from pre-trained networks makes our approach simple to use, apart from it, giving highly accurate results, which are much better than current SOTA.

Keywords: Hierarchical cosine interpolation · Hierarchical spherical linear interpolation · Face spoofing · Presentation attack detection

1 Introduction

Face Recognition Systems are highly accurate, which is especially true with current mobile phones. One of the first face recognition systems (FRS) called face ID launched by Apple in 2017 [1]. Apple Face ID worked by projecting around 30,000 infrared dots on the person's face and comparing it with a face stored in the secure enclave. Face ID was much more robust and accurate as compared to previous approaches for FRS. Jain et al. [8] have verified the accuracy of Apple Face ID, and mention that it is close to 99.99% when the face is in a frontal pose, with uniform lighting, and neutral expression. FRSs are used in border

© Springer Nature Switzerland AG 2021
S. Yildirim Yayilgan et al. (Eds.): INTAP 2020, CCIS 1382, pp. 203–214, 2021.
https://doi.org/10.1007/978-3-030-71711-7_17

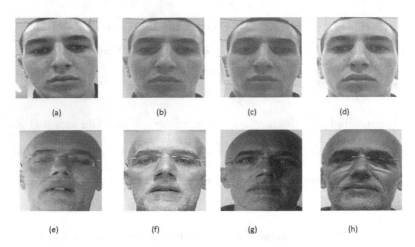

Fig. 1. Illustration showing bona fide presentations, and presentation attack images from OULU Dataset Protocol 1 [22] and Replay Mobile Dataset [2] shown in two rows. The top row shows OULU Dataset Protocol 1, bona fide in ((a)), and presentation attack images in ((b), (c), & (d)). The bottom row shows Replay Mobile Dataset, bona fide in ((e), & (f)), and presentation attack images in ((g), & (h)). The images illustrate the challenges in cross-dataset presentation attack detection due to illumination and image quality changes.

control, both attended and unattended, or automated border control (ABC) due to their high accuracy. The accuracy of FRS has increased with the advent of deep learning algorithms, which include Facenet [18] in 2015, or more recently with ArcFace [4] in 2019. However, FRS are vulnerable to spoofs or presentation attacks [13]. The presentation attacks can be performed by presenting a biometric artefact (Presentation Attack Instrument (PAI)) such as a printed photo (print photo attack), displaying a photo on an electronic medium (display photo attack), displaying a face video (display video/replay attack) or using a rigid silicone mask (mask attack). Thus, it is an important security problem to detect PAs due to its threat to security infrastructures. Presentation Attack Detection (PAD), a countermeasure to PA, is done by mechanisms implemented in hardware or software. PAD is an active research area with several papers published in this area, including books [10], and survey papers [12]. There are several public databases for PAD, which means that they are available for the biometric community to evaluate their PAD methods. The public databases include the Replay Mobile Dataset [2], OULU Database [22], CASIA FASD dataset [21], and more recently the SWAN Database [15]. The public databases define protocols that can test PAD methods' accuracy, which is usually for intra-dataset, and inter-dataset. Intra-dataset protocols have the training & the evaluation samples are from the same dataset, whereas Inter-dataset (cross-dataset) is where the training and the evaluation samples are from different datasets. Intra-dataset is mostly a solved problem with several papers pointing to this for many datasets such as CASIA-FASD [9], and especially OULU-NPU [14] was solved recently. Research direction in presentation attack detection has thus moved to the area of intra-dataset (cross-dataset) PAD, which will be the focus of this paper. Cross-dataset PAD is a challenging area as classifier trained on one PAD dataset has poor generalization on a different PAD dataset, as shown in Fig. 1, which is mainly due to illumination, and image-quality changes. Our proposed method uses pre-trained networks on the Imagenet [3] for cross-dataset PAD. It has the following advantages over other approaches in SOTA:

– Use of pre-trained features from deep-networks trained on Imagenet, without any need for fine-tuning. This eventually overcomes the need of large database for face PAD.
– A new hierarchical fusion operator is proposed, which is based on cosine interpolation, and spherical linear interpolation (SLERP) [19] for PAD.
– Achieved results better than SOTA with training on OULU-NPU Protocol 1 and testing Replay-Mobile grandtest protocol.

In the rest of the paper, we summarize the literature for related work in Sect. 2, followed by the proposed method in Sect. 3, which is followed by Sect. 4 summarizing the experimental setup, & results, and finally we present conclusions & future work for cross-dataset PAD in Sect. 5.

2   Related Work on Fusion and Cross-Dataset Face PAD

In this section, we review the related work in the area of Fusion in Biometrics and Face PAD. Biometric Fusion can be performed at different levels, which are feature-level, score-level, and decision-level, and is usually performed for multi-biometric systems [17]. Raghavendra et al. [16] performed optimal Fusion of biometric scores based on the Gaussian Mixture Model and Monte-Carlo method. Vishi et al. [20] evaluated different fusion techniques for score-level fusion, which included maximum, minimum, sum-rule, & weighted sum-rule. The score-level fusion was followed by score-normalization, which included min-max, z-score, & tan hyperbolic methods. The authors concluded that tan hyperbolic performed the best for their score-level Fusion of fingerprint and finger-vein biometric modalities. We now review the related work in the area of cross-dataset Face PAD. Liu et al. [9] proposed a two-stream convolutional neural network (CNN) architecture where one-stream is based on patch-based CNN from the patches extracted from the color image, and the second stream is based on depth estimated from the color image with a depth-based CNN. This is followed by a score-fusion of patch-based scores obtained from the color image stream and scores derived from the SVM classifier trained on features extracted from depth-based CNN. The main advantage of this approach is that it does not require explicit depth-supervision. The authors report extensive results for intra-dataset, which includes CASIA-FASD, Replay-Attack, and OULU. However, for cross-dataset, they mentioned the Half-Total-Error-Rate (HTER) of their proposed model trained on Replay-Attack and tested on CASIA-FASD to be 23.2%, and for a model trained on CASIA-FASD, and tested on Replay-Attack to be 15.4%. George et al. [5] proposed using deep pixel-wise binary supervision, along with the regular binary supervision available to a PAD method during training. The pixel-wise binary supervision means giving different feature-maps as input to their proposed network (DeepPixBiS) during training. During, test-time, they use the mean of the estimated feature-map as the score. The network architecture used by DeepPixBiS is that of pre-trained DenseNet [6], followed by a 1×1 convolution, and sigmoid activation layer to produce a binary feature map. A fully connected layer follows the previous layers, and finally, a sigmoid output produces the final binary output. DeepPixBis achieves the HTER of 12.4% for training on OULU Protocol 1 dataset, & testing on the Replay Mobile grandest dataset. They accomplish an HTER of 22.7% for training on Replay Mobile dataset, & testing on OULU Protocol 1 dataset.

Amir et al. [11] proposed using an autoencoder or a thresholded autoencoder to extract the input image's noise pattern. This is followed by using the DeepPixBiS architecture based network for the classification of extracted noise for PAD. It is to be noted that the authors reject a few samples based on loglikelihood. They train the proposed approach on OULU Protocol 1 and test it on the Replay Mobile dataset, SWAN dataset, and WMCA dataset. Their algorithm is the current SOTA for cross-dataset Face PAD.

3   Proposed Method

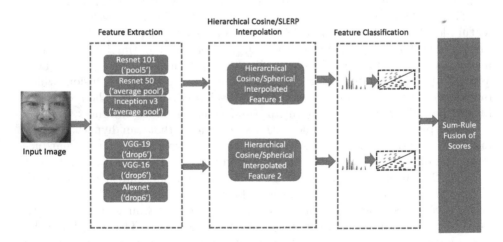

Fig. 2. Block Diagram of the proposed method for face presentation attack detection

This section presents the proposed method, which is shown in a block diagram form in Fig. 2. The proposed method mainly consists of following steps: feature extraction, Hierarchical Cosine/Spherical linear interpolation of extracted features, feature classification & sum-rule score-fusion. The stages in the proposed method are explained in the following subsections:

3.1 Feature Extraction

We extract features from deep-learning networks trained on the Imagenet database. The deep-networks are chosen in such a manner that they generate feature-vectors of the same dimension, as this is required for the subsequent step of feature interpolation. We specifically look at image classification networks trained on Imagenet dataset where the feature-vector dimension at a layer is the same for eg Resnet-101 (pool5 layer), & Resnet-50 (average pool layer). To this end, we extract features from the deep-networks in two sets, wherein each set the feature vector is of the same dimension. In the first set, we extract features from Resnet-18 (pool5 layer), from Resnet50 (average pool layer), and Inception$-$v3 (average pool layer), giving a 2048-dimensional feature vector. In the second set, we extract features from VGG$-$19 (drop6 layer), from VGG$-$16 (drop6 layer), and Alexnet (drop6 layer), giving a 4096-dimensional feature vector.

3.2 Hierarchical Cosine/SLERP Interpolation

Algorithm 1. Hierarchical Interpolation of Multiple Deep Features

Input: $F_0 \ldots F_N$
Output: Interpolated Feature F

1: **function** INTERPOLATE SLERP($F, factor$)
2:     $F \leftarrow 0$
3:     $Base \leftarrow F_0$
4:     $N \leftarrow length(F)$
5:     $L \leftarrow \log_2(N)$
6:     **for** $k \leftarrow 1$ to L **do**
7:         Compute $\frac{N}{2^L}$ features as $F_k \leftarrow$ InterpMethod($F_0, F_k, factor$)
8:     **end for**
9:     Repeat the above combination till we get one interpolated feature vector.
10:     **return** F
11: **end function**

Algorithm 2. Cosine Interpolation of Two Deep Features

Input: $F_0, F_1, factor$
Output: Cosine Interpolated Feature F

1: **function** COSINE INTERPOLATED(F_0, F_1)
2:     $NormF_0 \leftarrow$ Unit-Normalized(F_0)
3:     $NormF_1 \leftarrow$ Unit-Normalized(F_1)
4:     $dotproduct \leftarrow$ dotproduct($NormF_0, NormF_1$)
5:
6:     **if** $dotproduct > 0$ **then**
7:         $F \leftarrow$ Unit-Normalized($F_0 + F_1$)
8:     **else**
9:         $F \leftarrow$ Unit-Normalized($F_1 - F_0$)
10:     **end if**
11:     **return** F
12: **end function**

Algorithm 3. SLERP Interpolation of Two Deep Features

Input: F_0, F_1, t
Output: SLERP Interpolated Feature F

1: **function** SLERP INTERPOLATED(F_0, F_1, t)
2:     $NormF_0 \leftarrow$ Unit-Normalized(F_0)
3:     $NormF_1 \leftarrow$ Unit-Normalized(F_1)
4:     $dotproduct \leftarrow$ dotproduct($NormF_0, NormF_1$)
5:     **if** $dotproduct < 0$ **then**
6:         $NormF_0 \leftarrow -NormF_0$
7:     **end if**
8:     $\Omega \leftarrow$ Angle-Between($NormF_0, NormF_1$)
9:     $F \leftarrow \frac{\sin[(1-t)\Omega]}{\sin \Omega} NormF_0 + \frac{\sin[t\Omega]}{\sin \Omega} NormF_1$
10:     **return** F
11: **end function**

Given the two sets of extracted features, and three feature vectors in each set wherein the first set consists of features from Resnet 101, Resnet 50, &, Inception v3, and the second set consists of features from VGG-16, VGG-19, & Alexnet. We combine the three feature vectors from each set into a single interpolated feature vector. To this end, we employ two interpolation schemes, the first being cosine interpolation, and the second being spherical linear interpolation (SLERP). The combination is shown as an Algorithm 1. Algorithm 2 is the cosine interpolation algorithm, and Algorithm 3 is the SLERP interpolation algorithm that is adapted to vectors, which were initially proposed for Quaternions [19]. Thus, we obtain two-interpolated vectors, one from each set after using the combination algorithm from Algorithm 1. It should be noted that the choice of base-feature vector is important for Algorithm 3 which is Inception–v3 for the first set, and VGG-19 for the second set with a factor $= 0.45$ for interpolation which is chosen in an ad-hoc fashion.

3.3   Feature Classification and Score-Fusion

We now have two interpolated features, for which we train two Linear SVM classifiers as shown in Fig. 2. During, test time we apply a sum-rule based score fusion to generate the final score for Face PAD.

4   Experimental Setup and Results

In this section, we describe the experimental setup and the results obtained while evaluating the proposed method. We follow the metrics defined in the International Standard ISO/IEC 30107-3 [7] described as follows:

- Attack Presentation Classification Error Rate (APCER), which is the misclassification rate of attack presentations.
- Bona fide Presentation Classification Error Rate (BPCER), which is the misclassification of bona fide presentation as attacks.

Table 1. Details of Cross-dataset with OULU P1 as Train Dataset, and Replay Mobile Grandtest as Development, & Test Dataset.

	Bona fide	Attack
Videos		
OULU P1 Train	240	960
RM Development	160	256
RM Test	110	192
Images		
OULU P1 Train	31440	127560
RM Development	3200	5120
RM Test	2192	3840

4.1   Cross-Dataset OULU Protocol 1 Dataset Train, Replay Mobile Grandtest Development/Test Set

The OULU dataset consists of videos, where Protocol 1 is devised to test the generalization of face PAD under previously unseen conditions: illumination and background [22]. The dataset is divided into Train, Development, and Test in the form of videos. OULU Protocol 1 train set consists of 1200 videos (240 bona fide, 960 attacks), development set consists of 900 videos (180 bona fide, and

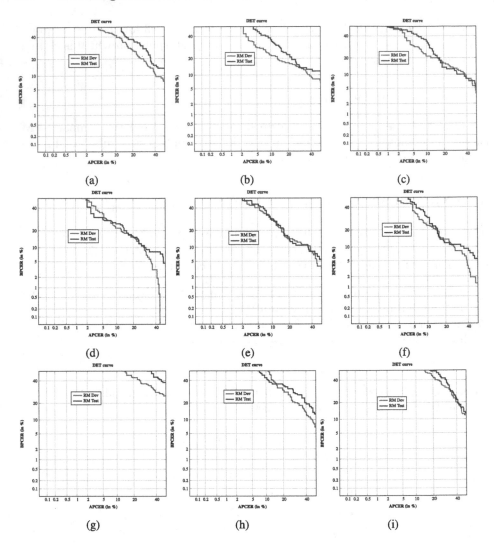

Fig. 3. DET Curves for Cross-Dataset trained on OULU Protocol 1 [22], and test of Replay Mobile (RM [2]) Development and Test Sets (a) Minimum of Deep Features, (b) Maximum of Deep Features, (c) Mean of Deep Features, (d) Median of Deep Features, (e) Proposed Hierarchical Cosine Interpolated Deep Features, (f) Proposed Hierarchical SLERP Interpolated Deep Feature, (g) Thresholded Auto Encoder [11], (h) Auto Encoder [11], and (i) DeepPixBis [5]. Notice that EER is the lowest for Proposed Hierarchical SLERP Interpolated Feature.

720 attacks), and the test set consists of 600 videos (120 bona fide, and 480 attacks). Replay-Mobile Dataset [2] consists of 312 videos (120 bona fide and 192 attacks), the development set consists of 416 videos (160 bona fide, and 256 attacks), and the test set consist of 302 videos (110 bona fide, and 192 attacks).

We use the frames from these videos described in work by George et al. [5], where we use all the frames of each video during training and 20 frames of each video during development testing. Cross-dataset evaluation with OULU Protocol 1 as training, and Replay Mobile as development, and test set with this methodology of dividing videos result into 31440 bona fide images, 127560 attack images for training for the OULU P1 Protocol, 3200 bona fide images, 5120 attack images for the development set of Replay Mobile Grandtest Protocol, and 2192 bona fide images, 3840 attack images for the test set of Replay Mobile Grandtest Protocol. The cross-dataset details are summarized in Table 1.

Table 2. Cross-Dataset Performance of the proposed method: Train OULU P1 and Test RM. Note Hierarchical SLERP gives lowest D-EER for both Development & Test Set.

Development set			
Algorithm	D-EER (%)	BPCER @ APCER = 5%	BPCER @ APCER = 10%
DeepPixBis [5]	31.9531	73.7500	59.3750
Thresholded Auto Encoder [11]	35.0781	70.6250	60.6250
Auto Encoder [11]	25.5078	60.6250	52.5000
Min Feature	23.2812	46.8750	41.2500
Max Feature	17.5391	**28.7500**	**21.8750**
Mean Feature	18.0469	30	21.2500
Median Feature	16.8359	34.3750	**21.8750**
Proposed Cosine Interpolated	17.0312	40	29.3750
Proposed SLERP Interpolated	**16.1328**	35	23.1250
Test set			
Algorithm	D-EER (%)	BPCER @ APCER = 5%	BPCER @ APCER = 10%
DeepPixBis [5]	32.7699	57.2727	47.2727
Thresholded Auto Encoder [11]	42.0028	86.3636	80
Auto Encoder [11]	28.1534	75.4545	70.9091
Min Feature	28.8684	40	37.2727
Max Feature	21.1316	34.5455	28.1818
Mean Feature	17.4905	39.0909	29.0909
Median Feature	17.2301	30.9091	23.6364
Proposed Cosine Interpolated	16.5152	31.8182	17.0312
Proposed SLERP Interpolated	**15.5398**	**16.3636**	**11.8182**

4.2   Features and Scores

Table 1 shows the training, development, and testing images used. Since we obtain one feature from a single image. We generate 31440 bona fide training features, 127560 attack training features for the first SVM, and 31440 bona fide training features, 127560 attack training features for the second SVM. We average all the scores from images of a single video and obtain 160 bona fide scores, 256 attack scores for the development set from the first SVM, 160 bona fide scores, and 256 attack scores from the development set from the second SVM. We obtain 110 bona fide scores, and 192 attack scores for the test set from the first SVM, and 110 bona fide scores, and 192 attack scores for the test set from the second SVM.

4.3 Results and Analysis

Table 2 shows the minimum, maximum, mean, median, hierarchical cosine interpolated, and hierarchical SLERP interpolated deep features in tabular-form and as DET-Curves in Fig. 3. It needs to be pointed out that Hierarchical SLERP gives the lowest error rate, which is mainly since the SLERP operation increases the correlation among deep features as it inverts the direction of a feature if it is pointing in the opposite direction as one can observe from Algorithm 3. SLERP additionally provides an interpolated vector, which is almost mid-way due to the choice of the interpolation factor of 0.45. Median and mean features give better performance than the minimum and maximum, which indicates the deep features' variance is more, especially on the minimum side. It needs to be noted that the results of the proposed method are better than the current SOTA. It is pointed out by George et al. [5] in their architecture DeepPixBis that for PAD, training from scratch of deep networks data samples is not sufficient, and does not yield good generalization due to overfitting.

5 Conclusions and Future-Work

In this paper, we presented a new method for combining deep features for biometrics, namely, Hierarchical Interpolation. We compared the Hierarchical Interpolation results with existing methods of feature interpolation such as minimum, maximum, median, and mean specifically. Hierarchical SLERP has provided the best results for the cross-dataset of OULU P1 train, and test on RM. Our approach's main advantage is that being in feature space of pre-trained deep features from Imagenet does not require fine-tuning. It has been pointed out by previous authors that the main issue with CNNs, when used for PAD, is having less data, and poor generalization [5]. The limitations for CNNs for PAD can be overcome to a certain extent by auxiliary supervision, and to a further extent by Hierarchical Interpolation in feature space. We evaluated interpolation methods of cosine and SLERP in the current work. We want to evaluate more interpolation operators and provide more results on cross-dataset in the future.

References

1. Apple Face ID (2017). https://en.wikipedia.org/wiki/Face_ID. Accessed May 2020
2. Costa-Pazo, A., Bhattacharjee, S., Vazquez-Fernandez, E., Marcel, S.: The replay-mobile face presentation-attack database. In: International Conference of the Biometrics Special Interest Group (BIOSIG), pp. 1–7, September 2016. https://doi.org/10.1109/BIOSIG.2016.7736936
3. Deng, J., Dong, W., Socher, R., Li, L.J., Li, K., Fei-Fei, L.: ImageNet: a large-scale hierarchical image database. In: 2009 IEEE Conference on Computer Vision and Pattern Recognition, pp. 248–255. IEEE (2009)

4. Deng, J., Guo, J., Xue, N., Zafeiriou, S.: ArcFace: additive angular margin loss for deep face recognition. In: The IEEE Conference on Computer Vision and Pattern Recognition (CVPR), June 2019
5. George, A., Marcel, S.: Deep pixel-wise binary supervision for face presentation attack detection. In: 2019 International Conference on Biometrics, ICB 2019, Crete, Greece, pp. 1–8, 4–7 June 2019. IEEE (2019). https://doi.org/10.1109/ICB45273. 2019.8987370
6. Huang, G., Liu, Z., Van Der Maaten, L., Weinberger, K.Q.: Densely connected convolutional networks. In: Proceedings of the IEEE Conference on Computer Vision and Pattern Recognition, pp. 4700–4708 (2017)
7. ISO/IEC JTC1 SC37 Biometrics: ISO/IEC IS 30107-3. Information Technology - Biometric presentation attack detection - Part 3: Testing and Reporting. International Organization for Standardization (2017)
8. JV Chamary: How Face ID works on iPhone X (2017). https://www.forbes.com/ sites/jvchamary/2017/09/16/how-face-id-works-apple-iphone-x/. Accessed May 2020
9. Liu, Y., Stehouwer, J., Jourabloo, A., Atoum, Y., Liu, X.: Presentation attack detection for face in mobile phones. In: Rattani, A., Derakhshani, R., Ross, A. (eds.) Selfie Biometrics. ACVPR, pp. 171–196. Springer, Cham (2019). https:// doi.org/10.1007/978-3-030-26972-2_8
10. Marcel, S., Nixon, M.S., Li, S.Z.: Handbook of Biometric Anti-Spoofing: Trusted Biometrics Under Spoofing Attacks. Springer, New York (2014). https://doi.org/ 10.1007/978-1-4471-6524-8. Incorporated
11. Mohammadi, A., Bhattacharjee, S., Marcel, S.: Improving cross-dataset performance of face presentation attack detection systems using face recognition datasets. In: 45th International Conference on Acoustics, Speech, and Signal Processing (ICASSP 2020), p. 125 (2020)
12. Raghavendra, R., Busch, C.: Presentation attack detection methods for face recognition systems: a comprehensive survey. ACM Comput. Surv. (CSUR) 50(1), 1–37 (2017)
13. Raghavendra, R., Raja, K.B., Busch, C.: Presentation attack detection for face recognition using light field camera. IEEE Trans. Image Process. 24(3), 1060–1075 (2015)
14. Ramachandra, R., Singh, J.M., Venkatesh, S., Raja, K., Busch, C.: Face presentation attack detection using multi-classifier fusion of off-the-shelf deep features. In: Nain, N., Vipparthi, S.K., Raman, B. (eds.) CVIP 2019. CCIS, vol. 1148, pp. 49–61. Springer, Singapore (2020). https://doi.org/10.1007/978-981-15-4018-9_5
15. Raghavendra, R., et al.: Smartphone multi-modal biometric authentication: Database and evaluation. arXiv preprint arXiv:1912.02487 (2019)
16. Raghavendra, R., Ashok, R., Kumar, G.H.: Multimodal biometric score fusion using gaussian mixture model and Monte Carlo method. J. Comput. Sci. Technol. 25(4), 771–782 (2010). https://doi.org/10.1007/s11390-010-9364-7
17. Ross, A., Poh, N.: Multibiometric systems: overview, case studies, and open issues. In: Tistarelli, M., Li, S.Z., Chellappa, R. (eds.) Handbook of Remote Biometrics. Advances in Pattern Recognition. Springer, London (2009). https://doi.org/10. 1007/978-1-84882-385-3_11
18. Schroff, F., Kalenichenko, D., Philbin, J.: FaceNet: a unified embedding for face recognition and clustering. In: Proceedings of the IEEE Conference on Computer Vision and Pattern Recognition, pp. 815–823 (2015)

19. Shoemake, K.: Animating rotation with quaternion curves. In: Proceedings of the 12th Annual Conference on Computer Graphics and Interactive Techniques, pp. 245–254 (1985)
20. Vishi, K., Mavroeidis, V.: An evaluation of score level fusion approaches for fingerprint and finger-vein biometrics. arXiv preprint arXiv:1805.10666 (2018)
21. Zhang, Z., Yan, J., Liu, S., Lei, Z., Yi, D., Li, S.Z.: A face antispoofing database with diverse attacks. In: 2012 5th IAPR International Conference on Biometrics (ICB), pp. 26–31. IEEE (2012)
22. Zinelabidine, B., Jukka, K., Li, L., Feng, X., Hadid, A.: OULU-NPU: a mobile face presentation attack database with real-world variations. In: IEEE International Conference on Automatic Face & Gesture Recognition (AFGR), pp. 1–7. IEEE (2017)

Cross-lingual Speaker Verification: Evaluation on X-Vector Method

Hareesh Mandalapu[1(✉)], Thomas Møller Elbo[1,2], Raghavendra Ramachandra[1], and Christoph Busch[1]

[1] Norwegian University of Science and Technology, Gjøvik, Norway
{hareesh.mandalapu,raghavendra.ramachandra,christoph.busch}@ntnu.no
[2] Technical University of Denmark, Lyngby, Denmark
s144825@student.dtu.dk

Abstract. Automatic Speaker Verification (ASV) systems accuracy is based on the spoken language used in training and enrolling speakers. Language dependency makes voice-based security systems less robust and generalizable to a wide range of applications. In this work, a study on language dependency of a speaker verification system and experiments are performed to benchmark the robustness of the x-vector based techniques to language dependency. Experiments are carried out on a smartphone multi-lingual dataset with 50 subjects containing utterances in four different languages captured in five sessions. We have used two world training datasets, one with only one language and one with multiple languages. Results show that performance is degraded when there is a language mismatch in enrolling and testing. Further, our experimental results indicate that the performance degradation depends on the language present in the word training data.

Keywords: Speaker recognition · Biometrics · Cross-lingual

1 Introduction

Biometrics characteristics are used to recognize or verify the identity of a person and to provide access to the security sensitive applications. The biometric characteristics are of two different kinds: physical and behavioral. Face, fingerprint, iris are popular physical characteristics that have been in research for many years. Behavioral biometrics are based on the way humans perform certain tasks like speaking and walking. Speaking characteristics of humans are a well-known biometric modality used to perform accurate recognition. Automatic Speaker Verification has been a famous topic in biometric applications for many years now.

The advancement of computational abilities in the recent decades encouraged applications to use biometric algorithms in many fields. Due to he wide variety of users, devices, and applications, many kinds of vulnerabilities and dependencies are evolved in operational biometric systems. The popular vulnerabilities

S. Yildirim Yayilgan et al. (Eds.): INTAP 2020, CCIS 1382, pp. 215–226, 2021.
https://doi.org/10.1007/978-3-030-71711-7_18

are anomalies in the samples and presentation attacks on the biometric devices. The dependencies are caused due to data capturing methods, change in devices, aging of the subject, and many more. There are more dependencies on behavioral biometric modalities because the behavior of the subject changes often. In speaker recognition, apart from the capturing conditions like microphone and transmission channel, background noise, the biometric algorithms also depend on the text, language, and emotion which impact the voice sample [8].

Text-dependent speaker recognition has been in use for many years [4]. In these kinds of approaches, the set of words used in testing is a subset of the words used in enrolment. Further, text-independent speaker recognition methods using Gaussian mixture models are introduced [14], and more algorithms were proposed to exclude the dependency caused by the text [6]. Language dependency is another challenging problem that emerged due to multilingual subjects and wide usage of the same biometric algorithm across the world. Language-independent approaches have been proposed on top of text-independent speaker recognition methods [1] by including multiple languages in enrolment. The National Institute of Standards and Technology Speaker Recognition Evaluation (SRE) series has been including multiple languages in their evaluation protocols over the years[1].

In this work, cross-lingual speaker verification is evaluated on a smartphone based dataset with different languages. The objective is to benchmark the performance of the state-of-the-art algorithms when different languages are mismatched in training, enrolling, and testing phases of automatic speaker verification. Thus, the following are the main contributions of this paper:

- Experiments on state-of-the-art methods that use advanced deep neural networks, like x-vector method, to check the language dependency.
- Experiments on multiple languages and multiple session datasets are included in this work.
- The dependency of trained languages used in world training data is evaluated.
- Results and discussions are presented using ISO/IEC standardized metrics for biometric performance [5].

The rest of the paper is organised as follows: Sect. 1.1 discusses the previous works on cross-lingual speaker recognition approaches and challenges. Section 2 describes the state-of-the-art approaches chosen for our experiments. In Sect. 3, the multilingual dataset is described, and Sect. 4, the cross-lingual experiments are presented with results and discussed. Finally, Sect. 5 concludes the work with the presentation of future work.

1.1   Related Work

The Automatic speaker verification as a biometric modality has emerged into many applications. The initial problems in speaker recognition have leaned over the text-dependency of the speeches in different speaker verification modules.

---

[1] https://www.nist.gov/itl/iad/mig/speaker-recognition.

Later, the language dependency has emerged into a challenging problem in text-independent speaker verification [1]. The early works on language mismatch evaluation are performed by comparing speaker verification with world models trained on only one language and multiple languages. One could observe that when provided with all languages and enough data for world model training, there is no degradation of performance [1]. It is important to note that the enrolled and tested speaker's language are the same in these experiments. Further, the authors have also pointed out the need for new databases from different languages.

Subsequently, the research work focused on bilingual speakers and performed cross-lingual speaker verification. In the investigation of combining the residual phase cepstral coefficients (RPCC) with Mel-frequency cepstral coefficients (MFCC) work from [10], it is observed that RPCC has improved the performance of traditional speaker verification methods. The residual phase characterizes the glottal closure instants better than the linear prediction models like MFCC. The glottal closure instants are known to contain speaker-specific information [3,12]. Considering the advantages of residual phase and glottal flow, Wang *et al.* [17] proposed a bilingual speaker identification with RPCC and glottal flow cepstral coefficients (GLFCC) as features. The experiments on NIST SRE 2004 corpus, RPCC features show the highest accuracy when compared to MFCC features.

In [9], Mishra *et al.* examined the language mismatch in speaker verification over i-vector system. When all the parameters are kept consistent, and by changing the language, there is performance degradation in EER by 135%. Also, including a phoneme histogram normalization method using a GMM-UBM system improves the EER by 16%. Li et al. [7] have proposed a deep feature learning for cross-lingual speaker verification in comparison with i-vector based method. Two deep neural networks (DNN) based approaches are proposed with the knowledge of phonemes, which is considered as a linguistic factor. The DNN feature with linguistic factor and PLDA scoring shows better performance than i-vector based method and DNN without linguistic factor.

2 X-Vector Based Speaker Verification System

The X-vector based speaker verification, which is a Deep Neural Network-based approach, proposed by Snyder *et al.* in [15] has the improved performance from data augmentation as suggested in [16]. The model is a feed-forward Deep Neural Network (DNN) which works on cepstral features that are 24-dimensional filter banks and has a frame length of 25 ms with mean-normalization over a sliding window of up to 3 s. The model consists of eight layers. The first five layers work on the speech frames, with an added temporal context that is gradually built on through the layers until the last of the five layers. A statistics pooling layer aggregates the outputs and calculates the mean and standard deviation for each input segment. The mean and standard deviation are concatenated and propagated through two segment-level layers and through the last layer, a softmax output layer. The block diagram of x-vector based automatic verification system is show in Fig. 1.

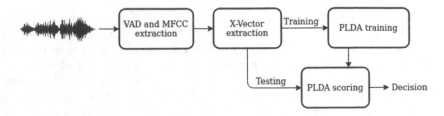

Fig. 1. Block diagram of X-vector based automatic speaker verification system

The x-vector method is used with two pre-trained variants, one trained on the combined dataset of five Switchboard datasets, SRE datasets from 2004 to 2010, and the Mixer 6 dataset and the second one is trained on the VoxCeleb 1 and VoxCeleb 2 datasets. The two models are different in multiple directions including the data capturing mechanism, languages spoken in data and variance in acquisition channels. The pre-trained models have been obtained from the Kaldi webpages namely the SRE16 model from http://kaldi-asr.org/models/m3, and the VoxCeleb model from http://kaldi-asr.org/models/m7.

2.1   NIST-SRE16 Trained Model

The NIST-SRE16 pre-trained model uses a total of 15 different datasets, containing a total of 36 different languages. The combined amount of speakers from the Switchboard, SRE, and Mixer datasets totals 91k recordings from over 7k speakers. Data augmentation is done, adding noise and reverberation to the dataset, and combining two augmented copies to the original clean training set. The augmentation of the recording was chosen randomly between four possible types, either augmenting with babble, music, noise, or reverb. Augmenting with babble was done by appending three to seven speakers from the MUSAN speech to the original signal, augmenting with music was selecting a music file randomly from MUSAN, trimmed or repeated to match the duration of the original signal. Noise augmentation was done by adding one-second intervals to the original signal, taken from the MUSAN noises set. Reverb augmentation was done by artificially reverberating via convolution with simulated RIRs.

The SRE16 x-vector model training is employed with two PLDAs. The first PLDA is trained on the same datasets as the x-vector model trained, but not fitted to the evaluation dataset. As the PLDA is only trained on out-of-domain data, this PLDA is called out-of-domain (OOD) PLDA. The second PLDA (ADT) is fitted to the same datasets and has been adapted to SRE16 data by using the SRE16 major dataset, containing utterances in Cantonese and Tagalog. Therefore, this PLDA is in-domain adapted (ADT) PLDA. The evaluation set of SRE16 is used to test the trained model. The performance of the x-vector method is observed as equal error rate (EER) of 11.73% with OOD PLDA and 8.57% with ADT PLDA.

2.2 VoxCeleb Trained Model

The VoxCeleb model used has been trained on the datasets VoxCeleb 1 and VoxCeleb 2 created by Chung *et al.* in [11] and [2], respectively. The development set of VoxCeleb 1 contains over 140k utterances for 1211 speakers, while the VoxCeleb 2 contains over a million utterances for 6112 speakers. All utterances in VoxCeleb1 are in English but VoxCeleb2 contains multiple languages and have been extracted from videos uploaded to YouTube. The training set size has been increased by using Data Augmentation by adding noise and reverberation to the datasets. In the same fashion as done in Sect. 2.1. The test set of VoxCeleb1 with 40 speakers is used to evaluate the training process and the performance is observed as EER of 3.128%.

3 Smartphone Multilingual Dataset

The SWAN (Secured access over Wide Area Network) dataset [13] is part of the SWAN project funded by The Research Council of Norway. The data has been gathered using an Apple iPhone6S and has been captured at five different sites. Each site has enlisted 50 subjects in six sessions, where eight individual recordings have been recorded. Depending on the capture site, four of the utterances are in either Norwegian, Hindi, or French, while the remaining four are in English. The utterances spoken are predetermined with alphanumerical speeches. The speakers have pronounced the first utterances in English and then in a national language depending on the site.

The six sessions of data capture are present at each site with a time interval of 1 week to 3 weeks between each session. Session 1 and 2 are captured in a controlled environment with no noise. Session 1 is primarily used to create presentation attack instruments. Therefore, we did not use session 1 data in our experiments. Session 3,4 and 6 are captured in a natural noise environment, and session five is captured in a crowded noise environment. In our experiments, we have enrolled session 2 data in all languages, and other sessions data are used for testing. This way, we can understand the session variance and the impact of noise on ASV methods. A sample of single utterance (sentence 2 in English with duration 14 s) is presented in Fig. 2 indicting the intra-subject variation between different sessions. The Fig. 2 shows the utterances of the sentence "My account number is *fake account number*" by the same subject in all sessions.

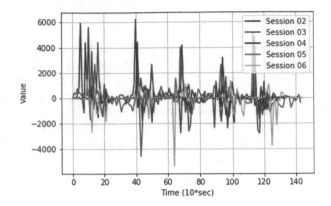

Fig. 2. A sample signal from SWAN dataset from each session.

4   Experiments and Results

We have four different sets of languages in our dataset, where English is the common language in all the sets. Experiments on four sets of different language combinations are performed. Also, we have five sessions of data capturing in each of the sets. We have followed the same protocol among all the sets by enrolling session two samples and using the rest of the sessions data for testing. To study the cross-lingual speaker recognition results, we have enrolled each language separately and tested the other languages present in that set.

The results are presented using the ISO/IEC standardized metrics for biometric performance [5]. Equal error rate (EER) is the error rate at which the false match rate (FMR) and false non-match rate (FNMR) are equal. We have plotted detection error trade-off (DET) curves, which represent the performance of the recognition of the biometric system in terms of FNMR over FMR.

4.1   Experiment 1

The first experiment is carried out on NIST-SRE16 trained model for x-vector extraction and PLDA scoring. This experiment includes two types of PLDA scoring approaches. The first type (OOD PLDA) is an out-of-domain model trained on combined data that contains the Switchboard database, all SREs prior to 2016, and Mixer 6. The second type of PLDA (ADT PLDA) is an in-domain PLDA that is adapted to the SRE16 major partition.

Table 1 represents the cross-lingual speaker recognition with English as the enrolment language in all four sessions. The highest error is highlighted among the block of same enrolled language in each PLDA method. It can be clearly seen that the EER values are lower when the enroll language and test languages are the same compared to different languages in test data. Similar results are obtained with Norwegian, Hindi, and French. The highest difference can be observed in the case of English-French combination with a degradation in performance of more than 350% on Session 6 data.

Table 1. Results from SRE16-trained X-vector Model with two types of PLDAs and different sessions.

Enrolment	Test	S3		S4		S5		S6	
Language	Language	OOD	ADT	OOD	ADT	OOD	ADT	OOD	ADT
English	English	3.21	3.20	1.65	1.76	4.05	4.15	1.78	1.83
English	Norwegian	6.45	6.65	5.89	5.61	**8.60**	**8.32**	6.16	6.11
English	Hindi	6.83	6.37	5.68	4.96	7.48	7.27	6.33	6.13
English	French	7.76	7.21	5.65	5.08	5.13	4.96	6.13	5.73
Norwegian	Norwegian	3.12	3.21	1.28	1.44	4.98	4.42	1.70	1.77
Norwegian	English	5.56	5.17	3.62	3.42	**8.46**	**7.34**	3.76	2.95
Hindi	Hindi	5.26	4.39	5.01	4.23	4.35	4.46	4.77	4.58
Hindi	English	**7.50**	**7.51**	6.18	5.73	5.45	5.49	5.23	4.72
French	French	5.33	4.32	2.45	2.40	2.62	2.35	1.88	2.06
French	English	6.13	**6.10**	3.41	3.18	**6.44**	5.22	4.63	4.64

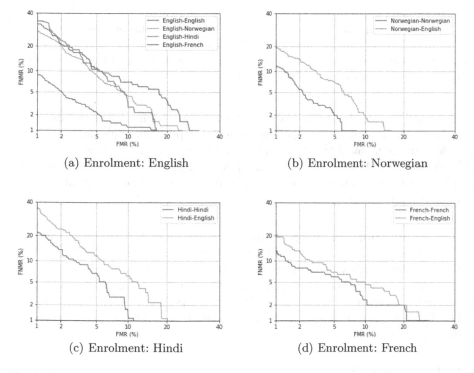

(a) Enrolment: English   (b) Enrolment: Norwegian

(c) Enrolment: Hindi   (d) Enrolment: French

Fig. 3. DET curves showing the performances of Session 3 with trained model on NIST-SRE16 and out-of-domain adapted PLDA (OOD).

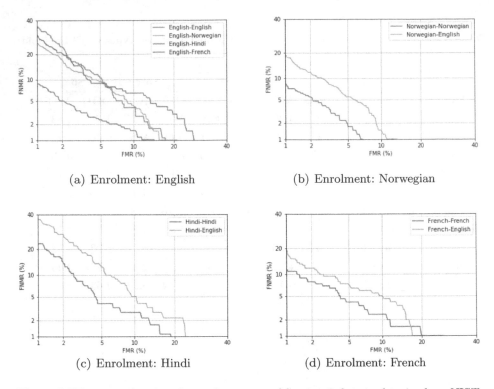

Fig. 4. DET curves showing the performances of Session 3 data and trained on NIST-SRE16 with in-domain adapted PLDA (ADT).

Session 5 has displayed the least accuracy in recognizing speakers among all language combinations. The main reason for this problem could be due to the crowded environment of the data captured. The Figs. 3 and 4 show the plots of DET curves from different languages used in enrolment and testing from Session 3. The error rates can be clearly seen increasing when cross-lingual speaker recognition is performed.

PLDA Adaptation. The adaptation of PLDA training does not show a regular trend among different languages. Although the out-of-domain PLDA adaption (OOD) displays higher error rates in many cases, in-domain adapted PLDA (ADT) does not improve the performance for some same-language and cross-language evaluations. In the future works, more experiments on different models of OOD and ADT will be studied along with multiple languages included in the data.

4.2   Experiment 2

VoxCeleb trained model is used in the second experiment. The PLDA used in this model is trained on VoxCeleb1, and Voxceleb2 combined. A similar protocol from

Experiment 1 is followed here also but with only one type of PLDA model. Table 2 shows the EER values among different language combination with highest EER value highlighted. The equal error rate is increased in all cases when there is a language mismatch between enrolment and testing. However, it is interesting to observe that the difference in the drop of EER is higher than for Experiment 1.

Figure 5 shows the comparison of DET curves between the same language and cross-language speaker recognition from Session 3 of the dataset. It can be clearly seen that the performance of the system has decreased when language mismatch has happened. The difference between the same language and cross-language is much higher in the VoxCeleb model than that of the NIST-SRE16 trained model.

Table 2. Results from VoxCeleb X-vector Model from different sessions.

Enrolment language	Test language	S3	S4	S5	S6
English	English	9.90	7.69	10.01	7.99
English	Norwegian	11.83	10.31	**15.01**	10.48
English	Hindi	13.84	13.12	12.75	12.05
English	French	11.21	9.06	11.28	9.46
Norwegian	Norwegian	8.04	6.44	10.91	6.74
Norwegian	English	11.92	9.32	**13.71**	9.55
Hindi	Hindi	12.16	10.68	11.88	10.66
Hindi	English	**14.77**	11.70	13.11	12.72
French	French	7.64	6.58	8.29	6.94
French	English	**11.83**	9.71	8.57	9.41

The speaker recognition accuracy is consistently lower than for the NIST-SRE16 trained model in all the cases. The reason for this could be that the world training dataset in the NIST-SRE16 model contains multiple languages which attributes for cross-lingual speaker recognition robustness. On the other hand, the VoxCeleb2 dataset contains multiple languages, there is a huge variance in data and bias in the number samples per subject which could be reason that limits the ability of the system to recognize different languages in enrolling and testing.

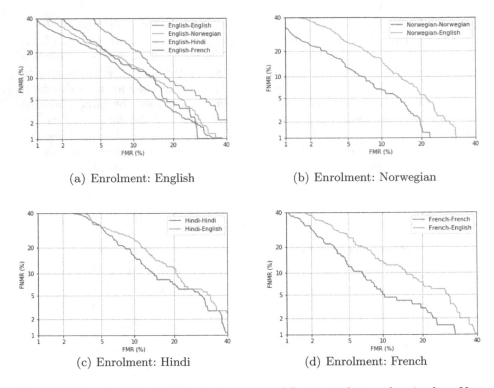

(a) Enrolment: English   (b) Enrolment: Norwegian

(c) Enrolment: Hindi   (d) Enrolment: French

Fig. 5. DET curves showing the performances of Session 3 data and trained on Vox-Celeb data.

5   Conclusion

Behavioral biometric recognition methods have multiple dependencies due to high intra-class variation caused by environmental factors and the human factors impacting the capture process. In the speaker recognition community, dependencies of samples like the text used in the speech and language in which speech is delivered needs to be investigated. The dependency due to language has been a problem when there is a mismatch between enrolment and tested language. In this work, we have focused on evaluating the problem of language mismatch on the state-of-the-art speaker recognition method, namely the x-vector method, which uses a deep neural network-based approach. We have chosen a multilingual dataset with four different languages and four different sessions. For the world training dataset, we included two popular publicly available datasets NIST-SRE16 and VoxCeleb.

The experiments on cross-lingual speaker recognition displayed the performance degradation when there is a mismatch in languages in enrolment and testing. Further, the dependency on the languages included in the world training dataset is observed. If there are multiple languages used in the world training dataset, which is the case of NIST-SRE16, performance degradation is less compared to the one language model VoxCeleb. In future works, a speaker recognition approach is implemented to overcome the problem of language dependency.

References

1. Auckenthaler, R., Carey, M.J., Mason, J.S.: Language dependency in text-independent speaker verification. In: Proceedings of 2001 IEEE International Conference on Acoustics, Speech, and Signal Processing (Cat. No. 01CH37221), vol. 1, pp. 441–444. IEEE (2001)
2. Chung, J.S., Nagrani, A., Zisserman, A.: VoxCeleb2: deep speaker recognition. In: INTERSPEECH (2018)
3. Gupta, C.S.: Significance of source features for speaker recognition. Master's thesis, Indian Institute of Technology Madras, Dept. of Computer Science and Engineering., Chennai, India (2003)
4. Hébert, M.: Text-dependent speaker recognition. In: Benesty, J., Sondhi, M.M., Huang, Y.A. (eds.) Springer Handbook of Speech Processing. SH, pp. 743–762. Springer, Heidelberg (2008). https://doi.org/10.1007/978-3-540-49127-9_37
5. ISO/IEC JTC1 SC37 Biometrics: ISO/IEC 19795–1:2006. Information Technology - Biometric Performance Testing and Reporting - Part 1: Principles and Framework. International Organization for Standardization and International Electrotechnical Committee, March 2006
6. Kinnunen, T., Li, H.: An overview of text-independent speaker recognition: from features to supervectors. Speech Commun. **52**(1), 12–40 (2010)
7. Li, L., Wang, D., Rozi, A., Zheng, T.F.: Cross-lingual speaker verification with deep feature learning. In: 2017 Asia-Pacific Signal and Information Processing Association Annual Summit and Conference (APSIPA ASC), pp. 1040–1044. IEEE (2017)
8. Lu, X., Dang, J.: An investigation of dependencies between frequency components and speaker characteristics for text-independent speaker identification. Speech Commun. **50**(4), 312–322 (2008)
9. Misra, A., Hansen, J.H.L.: Spoken language mismatch in speaker verification: an investigation with NIST-SRE and CRSS bi-ling corpora. In: 2014 IEEE Spoken Language Technology Workshop (SLT), pp. 372–377 (2014)
10. Murty, K.S.R., Yegnanarayana, B.: Combining evidence from residual phase and MFCC features for speaker recognition. IEEE Signal Process. Lett. **13**(1), 52–55 (2006)
11. Nagrani, A., Chung, J.S., Zisserman, A.: VoxCeleb: a large-scale speaker identification dataset. In: Lacerda, F. (ed.) Interspeech 2017, 18th Annual Conference of the International Speech Communication Association, Stockholm, Sweden, 20–24 August 2017, pp. 2616–2620. ISCA (2017). https://doi.org/10.21437/Interspeech. 2017. http://www.isca-speech.org/archive/Interspeech_2017/abstracts/0950.html
12. Plumpe, M.D., Quatieri, T.F., Reynolds, D.A.: Modeling of the glottal flow derivative waveform with application to speaker identification. IEEE Trans. Speech Audio Process. **7**(5), 569–586 (1999)
13. Raghavendra, R., et al.: Smartphone multi-modal biometric authentication: database and evaluation. arXiv preprint arXiv:1912.02487 (2019)
14. Reynolds, D.A., Rose, R.C.: Robust text-independent speaker identification using gaussian mixture speaker models. IEEE Trans. Speech Audio Process. **3**(1), 72–83 (1995)

15. Snyder, D., Garcia-Romero, D., Povey, D., Khudanpur, S.: Deep neural network embeddings for text-independent speaker verification. In: Proceedings of the Annual Conference of the International Speech Communication Association, INTERSPEECH, vol. 2017, pp. 999–1003, August 2017. www.scopus.com
16. Snyder, D., Garcia-Romero, D., Sell, G., Povey, D., Khudanpur, S.: X-vectors: robust DNN embeddings for speaker recognition. In: ICASSP, IEEE International Conference on Acoustics, Speech and Signal Processing - Proceedings, vol. 2018, pp. 5329–5333, April 2018. www.scopus.com
17. Wang, J., Johnson, M.T.: Vocal source features for bilingual speaker identification. In: 2013 IEEE China Summit and International Conference on Signal and Information Processing, pp. 170–173 (2013)

Fusion of Texture and Optical Flow Using Convolutional Neural Networks for Gender Classification in Videos

Jag Mohan Singh[✉], Raghavendra Ramachandra, and Patrick Bours

Norwegian Biometrics Laboratory, Norwegian University of Science and Technology
(NTNU), Trondheim, Norway
{jag.m.singh,raghavendra.ramachandra,patrick.bours}@ntnu.no

Abstract. Automatic Gender Classification (AGC) is an essential problem due to its growing demand in commercial applications, including
social media and security environments such as the airport. AGC is a
well-researched topic both in the field of Computer Vision and Biometrics. In this paper, we propose the use of decision-level fusion for AGC
in videos. Our approach does a decision-level fusion of labels obtained
from two fine-tuned deep-networks based on a color image and optical-
flow image, respectively, based on Resnet-18 architecture. We compare
our proposed method with handcrafted features, which includes the concatenation of the Histogram of Optical Flow (HOF) and Histogram of
Oriented Gradients (HOG). We compare it with deep-networks, which
includes pre-trained & fine-tuned Resnet-18 based on a color image, and
pre-trained & fine-tuned Resnet-18 based on optical flow image. Our
fusion-based approach considerably outperforms both the handcrafted
features, and the deep-networks previously mentioned. Another advantage of our proposed method is that it can work when the visual features are hidden. We used 98 videos from the HMDB51 action recognition dataset, specifically from the cart-wheel action with an almost
50% training, and testing split without validation set. We achieve an
overall accuracy of 79.59% with Resnet-18 network architecture with the
proposed method, compared to fine-tuned single-stream Resnet-18 for
Color-Stream at 65.30%, and Optical-Flow at 55.10% respectively.

Keywords: Automatic Gender Classification · Histogram of Optical
Flow · Histogram of Oriented Gradients · Resnet-18 · Fine-tuning

1 Introduction

Biometrics recognizes individuals by their biological attributes, which include
modalities such as the face, fingerprint, and iris. There are soft/behavior
attributes derived from these hard biological attributes, for instance, age, gender, and ethnicity [6]. The identification/deduction of behaviour attributes
falls under Biometrics, amongst which age & gender are the two most widely

© Springer Nature Switzerland AG 2021
S. Yildirim Yayilgan et al. (Eds.): INTAP 2020, CCIS 1382, pp. 227–236, 2021.
https://doi.org/10.1007/978-3-030-71711-7_19

Fig. 1. Hidden visual features in the image especially face in some of the frames, makes gender classification based on face difficult (taken from HMDB51 Action Recognition Dataset [15] with "cart-wheel" action.

used [6,16,20,22,24,33]. Automatic Gender Classification (AGC) is an important problem that is especially required with the rise in commercial applications such as social media, which in turn is mainly due to the increase in video content [3], and it is required in unattended security scenarios such as the airport [6]. Gender classification is usually done using facial geometric attributes [21], facial textural attributes [28], genetic algorithms [31], walking patterns (gait) [33], or more recently deep-learning [16]. These approaches give high-accuracy on the datasets used by them. However, most of them work on visual features, and some of them on walking-patterns alone. The main limitations of choosing only one amongst visual features and walking-pattern are two-fold. The limitations are occlusion when the visual-feature is hidden, and the key-points for walking-patterns do not have enough resolution for recognition. An example can illustrate this, suppose a person is wearing loosely fitted clothing [27], such as a traditional dress, or the visual features being hidden due to body pose as shown in Fig. 1, in both these scenarios AGC, becomes a difficult task. Given the recent advances in deep learning, especially the two-stream network convolutional neural network [26] combines the information from optical flow, and color image stream for a video for action recognition in a video. Thus, our proposed approach combines decision from optical-flow based deep-learning network and color-image stream-based deep-learning network for the gender classification task in a video. The following are the main advantages of our approach:

- Novel proposed approach for gender classification using the decision-level fusion of color-image stream, and optical-flow stream based on Resnet-18 [9] architecture.

- Proposed approach achieves better results than handcrafted Spatio-temporal image features [15] of Histogram of Oriented Gradients, and Optical Flow on 98 videos from HMDB51 action recognition dataset [15] with "cart-wheel" action.
- The proposed approach achieves a better accuracy than deep-learning approaches of Resnet-18, including pre-trained & fine-tuned on the same dataset.

In the rest of the paper, we provide an overview of deep-learning in Sect. 2 and literature-review of existing methods in Sect. 3. Section 4 presents the proposed method, and Sect. 5 summarizes the experimental setup, & results. Finally we present conclusions & future-work in Sect. 6.

2 Overview of Deep-Learning Architectures

In this section, we briefly review the popular deep learning architectures and provide background about them. Before the advent of deep learning, handcrafted features were being devised for the Image Classification task, which means that the input image has to be classified into an object category. Popular algorithms for hand-crafted features included Scale Invariant Feature Transform (SIFT) [19], Histogram of Oriented Gradient (HOG) [4], Local Binary Pattern (LBP) [23], and Binarized Statistical Image Features (BSIF) [13]. We now briefly review the HOG algorithm by Dalal et al. [4] for image classification, which is mainly based on the idea that local intensity gradients can characterize object appearance and shape. The authors divide the image into spatial regions called 'cells' of C×C (8×8) pixels, where the gradients are quantized into B(9) orientations to generate orientation histograms. The orientation histograms from the neighboring cells (2×2) are grouped into one block to generate a block-feature, normalized by its euclidean norm. The block features are concatenated into a single HOG feature by first clipping large gradients and performing contrast normalization. Histogram of Optical Flow (HOF) [5], works in a similar manner where it uses Optical Flow instead of Color Stream. These algorithms are now commonly called as Handcrafted Features, and are still efficient of smaller datasets [25] in biometrics. The main method of using handcrafted features is to compute the features for the training set, followed by training a classifier such as a Support Vector Machine (SVM) to classify test data.

In 2009, a challenge called Imagenet was posed to the computer vision community by Fei-Fei Li et al. [7], which mainly consisted of categorizing images into 10,000 object categories. This was considered a challenging problem, and Alex Krizhevsky et al. [14], introduced in 2012 a deep-learning-based approach which considerably outperformed the state-of-the-art approaches at that time. The main advantage of a deep learning approach is that the researcher does not have to define the features. The deep-learning network, which is an extended version of a multi-layer perceptron with different layers, including convolution and pooling, drop-out, and fully-connected layers, as shown in Fig. 2 learns the features. A deep-learning model is trained after the architecture is defined,

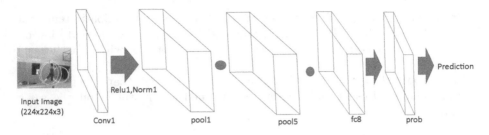

Fig. 2. Illustration of Alexnet Architecture [14] where different layers such as convolution, pooling , fully-connected, and softmax are shown

as described previously using a backpropagation algorithm such as Stochastic Gradient-Descent [14], which learns the features from the dataset, and is called a data-driven approach. Deep-learning models then became a norm for image classification task and networks such as VGG [30], and Inception [29] which had more layers than Alexnet, and were able to perform better. However, they suffered from the vanishing gradient problem, which means that the gradient of hyperparameters used in the network during training becomes 0, which results in a network not learning anything. The issue of vanishing gradients was solved by Kiameng He et al. [10], which added skip-connections to the network design, which is taking input of the one previous layer to the current layer. This resolution in network architecture resulted in the Resnet architecture to large numbers of layers, including variations of 18, 34, 50, 152, and 1000.

To use the deep-learning architectures on a new dataset trained on imagenet fine-tuning/transfer-learning needs to be performed, which means training only a few layers of these networks [12], which is tricky as the layers chosen to be fine-tuned makes a lot of difference in the performance. Usually, handcrafted features perform better on smaller datasets than deep-learning methods [25].

3 Gender Classification Methods

Given the overview of deep-learning methods previously, we overview the related-work for Gender Classification in this section. Makinen et al. [20], in their survey paper, reviewed 120 techniques for gender classification. The main steps for gender classification, according to them, are face-detection, followed by face-alignment, and using a classifier such as SVM, or Adaboost [8]. Makinen et al. concluded that automatic face alignment does not increase gender-classification rates, manual face alignment increases it to a certain extent, and that SVM is the best classifier for this task. Ng et al. [22] pointed out that facial-features extracted using descriptors such as LBP, and SIFT gave an excellent performance, which is able to perform the gender-classification task when the subject is at a distance. On evaluation, Ng et al. [22] mentioned that the approach by Zheng et al. [34] using Local Gabor Binary Mapping Pattern(LGBP) [32], and an SVM Classifier on CAS-PEAL dataset. An alternative technique to perform gender classification is to use gait or walking-style of a person. The method can be either model-based (joint-locations), or appearance-based (silhouettes) [22], and concluded after evaluation that used a novel Radon Transform of Gait Energy Image [1] resulted in the best performance of 98.94% on CASIA B dataset. Ng et al. [22] further concluded that amongst the HOG-based variants [2] approach gave the best results of 82.4% on the unconstrained dataset of attributes of people, and indicated that there is a room for improvement in these techniques.

Liew et al. [17] proposed a CNN architecture for gender classification in facial images, where they replaced convolution operation with cross-correlation. They used a second-order backpropagation learning algorithm with annealed global learning rates and achieved an accuracy of 98.75% and 99.38% on the SUMS and AT&T face datasets. Levi et al. [16] proposed a CNN architecture with three convolutional layers, each followed by a rectified linear layer, & pooling layer, and finally 2-fully connected layers. They performed both age estimation and gender classification on an unconstrained dataset and achieved a good accuracy of 86.8% ± 1.4% on Adience Benchmark. Chen et al. [3] proposed Multi-Branch Voting CNN (MBV-CNN) which detects, & extracts human face images from a video, followed by adaptive brightness enhancement, & then feeds them into three CNN branches followed by majority voting. Their method achieves state of the art performance on the labeled faces in the wild (LFW [11]) dataset of 98.11%, and Gender Classification for Live Videos (GCLV) dataset of 95.36%. In summary, we would like to point out that in handcrafted features, texture-based methods, and gait give excellent performance. The main reason for these handcrafted methods performing good is that they correspond to the surface and the contour/silhouette of an individual. In deep-learning, multi-stream CNN methods, such as MBV-CNN [3], give high accuracy as the decision is made by combining many smaller decisions.

4   Proposed Method

In this section, we describe the proposed method, which mainly consists of these steps, Input Data Preparation, Feature Extraction, Classification & Fusion, and is shown as an illustration in Fig. 3. We now describe the proposed method in the following sub-sections:

4.1   Input Data Preparation

Input Data Preparation is done by extracting the color stream and the video's optical flow stream. We use a deep learning-based optical flow extraction method [18], as it is one of the state of the art methods.

4.2   Feature Extraction

To compute the feature-vector, which will be later on used for classification, we fine-tune the Resnet-18 [10] architecture for both the color stream and the

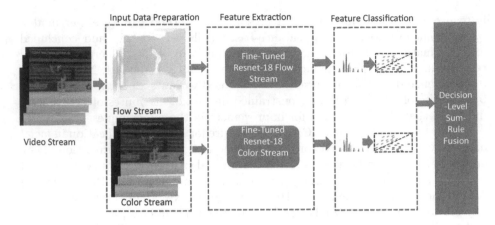

Fig. 3. Illustration shows Block Diagram of the proposed approach, which includes video stream as an input

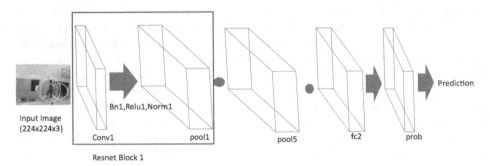

Fig. 4. Illustration of Fine-tuned Resnet-18 Architecture where the blocks shown as Resnet Block 1 are repeated five times, which are followed by pool5 (average pooling), fc2 (fully-connected layer with two classes), and fc (soft-max) layer. The features are extracted from pool5 after fine-tuning.

optical flow stream separately. The layer which is fine-tuned includes the fully-connected layer, softmax layer, and cross-entropy predictions layer. We then extract the features from both the fine-tuned networks from the 'pool5' layer. The fine-tuned architecture is shown as an illustration in Fig. 4.

4.3 Classification and Fusion

Given the feature extraction in the previous step, we train a Linear SVM classifier to obtain frame-level prediction labels in the video during testing. We then perform majority voting on the binary frame-level labels to get video-level prediction labels. This is followed by decision-level fusion using sum-rule (bit-wise 'OR') on the labels obtained from the color-stream video, and optical-flow video to generate the final classification labels.

Table 1. Details of Training and Testing Set from HMDB51 "cart-wheel", used in the form of images, and videos.

	Male	Female
Videos		
Train	22	27
Test	22	27
Frames		
Train	1550	1964
Test	1575	2000

5 Experimental Setup and Results

In this section, we explain the experimental setup and results obtained during the proposed method's evaluation. The results are reported in the form of overall accuracy and the confusion matrix.

5.1 Training and Testing Protocol

We now describe the training and testing protocol for the proposed method, shown in Table 1. We have 22 male videos with 1550 frames during training, and 27 female videos with 1964 frames, which results in 1550 color stream/optical-flow Resnet-18 features for the male category, and 1964 color-stream/optical-flow Resnet-18 features for the female category. We have 22 male videos with 1575 frames during testing, and 27 female videos with 2000 frames, which results in 1575 color stream/optical-flow Resnet-18 scores for the male category, and 2000 color stream/optical-flow Resnet-18 scores for the female category. During testing, majority voting frame-level scores are fused to give video-level scores, which results in 22 color stream/optical-flow scores for the male category and 27 color stream/optical-flow scores for the female category. The final decision is generated by fusing the video-level color stream's predictions and optical-flow stream by sum-rule.

5.2 Results and Analysis

Table 2 shows the results of the proposed method, and Hand-Crafted Features which includes Concatenated HOG&HOF Features [4,5] which Mean, Median, & Max filters, and Pre-trained/Fine-tuned Resnet-18 [10] features. The proposed method achieves better accuracy than the methods in comparison, mainly because Optical-Flow and Color-Stream fine-tuned Resnet-18 are uncorrelated, which can be seen as the accuracy of FResnet-18 Color-Stream is at 63.6% for the male category. In contrast, the accuracy of FResnet-18 Optical-Flow is at 22.7%. Our approach of fusion of multiple-streams is similar to MBV-CNN [3], which is the published state of the art for gender classification on LFW [11]. However, we do a fusion of color-stream, and optical-flow, unlike their approach.

Table 2. Results on HMDB51 with cart-wheel action, where CHOGHOF is Concatenated HOG& HOF Feature [4,5], PResnet-18 is Pre-trained Resnet-18 [10], FResnet-18 is Fine-tuned Resnet-18. Notice the accuracy is highest for the proposed method.

Algorithm	Overall accuracy (%)	TP,FP,FN,TN%	Accuracy male%	Accuracy female%
CHOGHOF mean	59.1837	18,9,11,11	50	66.6667
CHOGHOF median	55.102	18,9,13,9	40.9091	66.6667
CHOGHOF max	46.9388	13,14,12,10	45.4545	48.1481
PResnet-18 color-stream	46.9388	9,18,8,14	63.6364	33.3333
FResnet-18 color-stream	65.3061	18,9,8,14	63.6364	66.6667
PResnet-18 optical-flow	44.8980	17,10,17,5	22.7273	62.9630
FResnet-18 optical-flow	55.1020	22,5,17,5	22.7273	81.4815
Fusion PResnet-18 color stream/optical-flow	71.4286	20,7,7,15	68.1818	74.0741
Proposed method	**79.5918**	**25,2,8,14**	**63.6364**	**92.5926**

6   Conclusions and Future-Work

In summary, we presented a novel method for the gender classification of live videos based on the decision-level fusion of multiple CNNs. Our approach's main novelty uses different kinds of information, namely the color-stream, and the optical-flow stream, which helps us achieve better accuracy than handcrafted methods used in the comparison, and deep-learning methods based on a single stream used in the comparison. We evaluated our approach on public dataset HMDB51 precisely the "cart-wheel" action. The "cart-wheel" action was chosen as it had a high amount of motion, and HOG & HOF handcrafted features were selected as they are texture and motion features, respectively. We would want to experiment with more deep-learning architectures, evaluate our method on more public datasets, and take more actions in future work. We will want to know if some actions are more suitable for gender classification than others, for instance, dancing being more suitable than jumping. In terms of deep-learning architectures, we would like to evaluate the two-stream fusion architecture [26].

References

1. Bagher Oskuie, F., Faez, K.: Gender classification using a novel gait template: radon transform of mean gait energy image. In: Kamel, M., Campilho, A. (eds.) Image Analysis and Recognition, pp. 161–169. Springer, Berlin Heidelberg, Berlin, Heidelberg (2011)
2. Bourdev, L., Maji, S., Malik, J.: Describing people: a poselet-based approach to attribute classification. In: 2011 International Conference on Computer Vision, pp. 1543–1550. IEEE (2011)
3. Chen, J., Liu, S., Chen, Z.: Gender classification in live videos. In: 2017 IEEE International Conference on Image Processing (ICIP), pp. 1602–1606. IEEE (2017)
4. Dalal, N., Triggs, B.: Histograms of oriented gradients for human detection. In: 2005 IEEE Computer Society Conference on Computer Vision and Pattern Recognition (CVPR 2005), vol. 1, pp. 886–893. IEEE (2005)

5. Dalal, N., Triggs, B., Schmid, C.: Human detection using oriented histograms of flow and appearance. In: Leonardis, A., Bischof, H., Pinz, A. (eds.) ECCV 2006. LNCS, vol. 3952, pp. 428–441. Springer, Heidelberg (2006). https://doi.org/10.1007/11744047_33

6. Dantcheva, A., Elia, P., Ross, A.: What else does your biometric data reveal? a survey on soft biometrics. IEEE Trans. Inf. Forensics Secur. **11**(3), 441–467 (2015)

7. Deng, J., Dong, W., Socher, R., Li, L.J., Li, K., Fei-Fei, L.: ImageNet: a large-scale hierarchical image database. In: 2009 IEEE Conference on Computer Vision and Pattern Recognition, pp. 248–255. IEEE (2009)

8. Freund, Y., Schapire, R.E.: A decision-theoretic generalization of on-line learning and an application to boosting. J. Comput. Syst. Sci. **55**(1), 119–139 (1997). https://doi.org/10.1006/jcss.1997.1504. http://www.sciencedirect.com/science/article/pii/S002200009791504X

9. He, K., Zhang, X., Ren, S., Sun, J.: Deep residual learning for image recognition. In: Proceedings of the IEEE Conference on Computer Vision and Pattern Recognition, pp. 770–778 (2016)

10. He, K., Zhang, X., Ren, S., Sun, J.: Deep residual learning for image recognition. In: The IEEE Conference on Computer Vision and Pattern Recognition (CVPR), June 2016

11. Huang, G.B., Ramesh, M., Berg, T., Learned-Miller, E.: Labeled faces in the wild: a database for studying face recognition in unconstrained environments. Technical Report 07–49, University of Massachusetts, Amherst, October 2007

12. Huh, M., Agrawal, P., Efros, A.A.: What makes imagenet good for transfer learning? arXiv preprint arXiv:1608.08614 (2016)

13. Kannala, J., Rahtu, E.: BSIF: binarized statistical image features. In: Proceeding of 21st International Conference on Pattern Recognition (ICPR 2012), Tsukuba, Japan, pp. 1363–1366 (2012)

14. Krizhevsky, A., Sutskever, I., Hinton, G.E.: Imagenet classification with deep convolutional neural networks. In: Pereira, F., Burges, C.J.C., Bottou, L., Weinberger, K.Q. (eds.) Advances in Neural Information Processing Systems 25, pp. 1097–1105. Curran Associates, Inc. (2012). http://papers.nips.cc/paper/4824-imagenet-classification-with-deep-convolutional-neural-networks.pdf

15. Laptev, I., Marszalek, M., Schmid, C., Rozenfeld, B.: Learning realistic human actions from movies. In: 2008 IEEE Conference on Computer Vision and Pattern Recognition, pp. 1–8. IEEE (2008)

16. Levi, G., Hassner, T.: Age and gender classification using convolutional neural networks. In: Proceedings of the IEEE Conference on Computer Vision and Pattern Recognition Workshops, pp. 34–42 (2015)

17. Liew, S.S., Hani, M.K., Radzi, S.A., Bakhteri, R.: Gender classification: a convolutional neural network approach. Turkish J. Electr. Eng. Comput. Sci. **24**(3), 1248–1264 (2016)

18. Liu, P., Lyu, M., King, I., Xu, J.: Selflow: self-supervised learning of optical flow. In: Proceedings of the IEEE Conference on Computer Vision and Pattern Recognition, pp. 4571–4580 (2019)

19. Lowe, D.G.: Distinctive image features from scale-invariant keypoints. Int. J. Comput. Vis. **60**(2), 91–110 (2004)

20. Makinen, E., Raisamo, R.: Evaluation of gender classification methods with automatically detected and aligned faces. IEEE Trans. Pattern Anal. Mach. Intell. **30**(3), 541–547 (2008)

21. Moghaddam, B., Yang, M.H.: Gender classification with support vector machines. In: Proceedings Fourth IEEE International Conference on Automatic Face and Gesture Recognition (Cat. No. PR00580), pp. 306–311. IEEE (2000)

22. Ng, C.B., Tay, Y.H., Goi, B.-M.: Recognizing human gender in computer vision: a survey. In: Anthony, P., Ishizuka, M., Lukose, D. (eds.) PRICAI 2012. LNCS (LNAI), vol. 7458, pp. 335–346. Springer, Heidelberg (2012). https://doi.org/10.1007/978-3-642-32695-0_31

23. Ojala, T., Pietikainen, M., Maenpaa, T.: Multiresolution gray-scale and rotation invariant texture classification with local binary patterns. IEEE Trans. Pattern Anal. Mach. Intell. **24**(7), 971–987 (2002). https://doi.org/10.1109/TPAMI.2002.1017623

24. Rai, P., Khanna, P.: Gender classification techniques: a review. In: Wyld, D.C., Zizka, J., Nagamalai, D. (eds.) Advances in Computer Science, Engineering & Applications, pp. 51–59. Springer, Berlin Heidelberg (2012)

25. Ramachandra, R., Busch, C.: Presentation attack detection methods for face recognition systems: a comprehensive survey. ACM Comput. Surv. (CSUR) **50**(1), 1–37 (2017)

26. Simonyan, K., Zisserman, A.: Two-stream convolutional networks for action recognition in videos. In: Advances in Neural Information Processing Systems, pp. 568–576 (2014)

27. Singh, A., Kumar, A., Jain, A.: Bayesian gait-based gender identification (BGGI) network on individuals wearing loosely fitted clothing. In: Proceedings of the IEEE International Conference on Computer Vision Workshops (2019)

28. Sun, N., Zheng, W., Sun, C., Zou, C., Zhao, L.: Gender classification based on boosting local binary pattern. In: Wang, J., Yi, Z., Zurada, J.M., Lu, B.-L., Yin, H. (eds.) ISNN 2006. LNCS, vol. 3972, pp. 194–201. Springer, Heidelberg (2006). https://doi.org/10.1007/11760023_29

29. Szegedy, C., et al.: Going deeper with convolutions. In: Computer Vision and Pattern Recognition (CVPR) (2015). http://arxiv.org/abs/1409.4842

30. Tammina, S.: Transfer learning using VGG-16 with deep convolutional neural network for classifying images. Int. J. Sci. Res. Publ. (IJSRP) **9**, p9420, October 2019. https://doi.org/10.29322/IJSRP.9.10.2019.p9420

31. Sun, Z., Yuan, X., Bebis, G., Louis, S.J.: Neural-network-based gender classification using genetic search for eigen-feature selection. In: Proceedings of the 2002 International Joint Conference on Neural Networks. IJCNN 2002 (Cat. No. 02CH37290), vol. 3, pp. 2433–2438 (2002)

32. Zhang, W., Shan, S., Gao, W., Chen, X., Zhang, H.: Local gabor binary pattern histogram sequence (LGBPHS): a novel non-statistical model for face representation and recognition. In: Proceedings of the Tenth IEEE International Conference on Computer Vision (ICCV 2005) Volume 1 - Volume 01, pp. 786–791. ICCV 2005. IEEE Computer Society, USA (2005). DOIurl10.1109/ICCV.2005.147. https://doi.org/10.1109/ICCV.2005.147

33. Zhang, Z., Hu, M., Wang, Y.: A survey of advances in biometric gait recognition. In: Sun, Z., Lai, J., Chen, X., Tan, T. (eds.) Biometric Recognition, pp. 150–158. Springer, Berlin Heidelberg, Berlin, Heidelberg (2011)

34. Zheng, J., Lu, B.L.: A support vector machine classifier with automatic confidence and its application to gender classification. Neurocomputer **74**(11), 1926–1935, May 2011. https://doi.org/10.1016/j.neucom.2010.07.032. https://doi.org/10.1016/j.neucom.2010.07.032

Intelligent Environments

A PM 2.5 Forecasting Model Based on Air Pollution and Meteorological Conditions in Neighboring Areas

Muhammad Adrezo[1,2], Yo-Ping Huang[1(✉)], and Frode Eika Sandnes[3] ⓘ

[1] Department of Electrical Engineering, National Taipei University of Technology, Taipei 10608, Taiwan
muhammad.adrezo@gmail.com, yphuang@ntut.edu.tw
[2] Department of Computer Science, UPN Veteran Jakarta, Jakarta 12450, Indonesia
[3] Faculty of Technology, Art and Design, Oslo Metropolitan University, Oslo, Norway
frodes@oslomet.no

Abstract. Air pollution has received much attention in recent years, especially in the most densely populated areas. Sources of air pollution include factory emissions, vehicle emissions, building sites, wildfires, wood-burning devices, and coal power plants. Common and dangerous air pollutants include nitrogen dioxide (NO_2), ozone (O_3), carbon dioxide (CO_2), particulate matter 10 (PM 10) and particulate matter 2.5 (PM 2.5). This study focused on PM 2.5 because it has an aerodynamic diameter less than or equal to 2.5 μm. The small size of this pollutant makes it easily inhaled by humans and may end up deep in the lungs or even the bloodstream. Such pollutants can trigger health problems such as asthma, respiratory inflammation, reduced lung function and lung cancer. The purpose of this work was to forecast the next hour of PM 2.5 based on air pollution concentrations and meteorological conditions. The approach also uses station location data to cluster the area and to determine the neighboring areas of each station. Forecasting is based on the Long Short-Term Memory (LSTM). The result shows that the proposed approach can effectively forecast the next hour of PM 2.5 pollution.

Keywords: Air pollution · PM 2.5 · Forecasting · Long Short-Term Memory (LSTM)

1 Introduction

Air pollution has received much attention in recent years, especially in densely populated areas. The American Lung Association [1] estimated that nearly 134 million people in the US, that is, over 40% of the population, are at risk of disease and premature death because of air pollution. Bad outdoor air quality caused an estimated 4.2 million premature deaths in 2016. According to the World Health Organization [2] about 90% of premature deaths due to poor air quality occurred in low GDP per capita countries. Indoor smoke is an ongoing health threat to the 3 billion people who cook and heat their homes by burning biomass, kerosene, and coal. Examples of common pollutants include soot, smoke,

© Springer Nature Switzerland AG 2021
S. Yildirim Yayilgan et al. (Eds.): INTAP 2020, CCIS 1382, pp. 239–250, 2021.
https://doi.org/10.1007/978-3-030-71711-7_20

mold, pollen, nitrogen dioxide (NO_2), ozone (O_3), carbon dioxide (CO_2), particulate matter 10 (PM 10), and particulate matter 2.5 (PM 2.5). High concentrations of such substances may cause health problem to people in the affected area. Researchers have unearthed many health effects which are believed to be associated with exposure to air pollution. Effects caused by air pollution include respiratory diseases (including asthma and reduced lung function), cardiovascular diseases, cancers, and adverse pregnancy outcomes (such as preterm birth).

Throughout history, there has been many tragedies caused by air pollution resulting in diseases and deaths. Some of the worst tragedies caused by air pollution during the 19th century includes The Donora Smog of 1948 (Pennsylvania), The Great Smog of 1952 (London), The 1983 Melbourne dust storm and The 1997 Southeast Asian haze. The Donora Smog affected almost half of the population of Donora, killed 20 people and caused respiratory problems for 6000 people [3]. The Great Smog of London caused reduced visibility and even penetrated indoor areas. At least 4000 people were killed, and many more become ill [4]. Causes of air pollution includes factory emissions, vehicle emissions, building construction, wildfires, wood-burning devices, and coal-fired power plants.

One of the most dangerous air pollutants includes particulate matter 2.5 (PM 2.5). PM 2.5 is one of the primary indicators of air pollution because it affects more people than any other pollutant. PM 2.5 has an aerodynamic diameter of 2.5 μm or less. Common components of PM include sulfate, nitrates, sodium chloride, ammonia, mineral dust, black carbon, and water. High concentrations of PM is related to human health as it can easily be inhaled by humans and thereby affect the respiratory system and the cardiovascular system, and even damage the blood and nervous system and ultimately may cause death [7].

As PM 2.5 cause several diseases the Environment Protection Agencies (EPA) of several countries around the world are monitoring and forecasting PM 2.5. Prediction is important to issue early pollution warnings, for decision making and pollution control, thereby improving the life quality of the population. Traditional techniques and artificial intelligence (AI) techniques have both been applied to forecast PM 2.5. Mathematical and statistical techniques are used for traditional PM 2.5 forecasting in which a physical model was designed, and then data was calculated using mathematical differential equations. However, the traditional techniques have several shortcomings such as difficulties of processing large data sizes, long computation time and limited accuracy and inability to predict extreme points. However, with the advancement in technology, many researchers moved from mathematical and statistical techniques to computational techniques and AI techniques. AI techniques can overcome some of the challenges faced by the traditional techniques. Specific approaches include artificial neural network (ANN), machine learning, and deep learning.

This study focused on forecasting PM 2.5 concentrations using AI techniques based on air pollutants (NO_2, CO, and O_3,) and meteorological conditions (wind speed, wind direction, and rain) in each area and its neighboring areas. Air pollutants and meteorological conditions such as wind from neighboring areas are needed because PM 2.5 is a tiny particle that is easily carried by the wind from one area to other areas. This study used two datasets from the EPA of Taiwan. The first dataset is a station location dataset consisting of longitude and latitude of each station. The second dataset is an air pollution dataset consisting of air pollutant measurements and meteorological observations.

2 Related Work

Researchers and EPAs around the world have focused on air pollution, especially PM 2.5 concentrations. The research attention is in line with the public concern about the dangers of air pollution, especially PM 2.5 concentrations. PM 2.5 has received more attention than other air pollutants as it can easily be inhaled and cause many health problems. Researchers and the governments of many countries have deployed many systems to forecast PM 2.5 concentrations to be able to issue early PM 2.5 concentration warnings. Several engines and system architectures have been proposed for forecasting air pollution, especially PM 2.5 concentrations.

Ganesh et al. [5] focused on forecasting air quality index, not air pollutant concentrations such as PM 2.5, PM 10, CO, and O_3. They presented different regression models such as Support Vector Regression (SVR) and linear models such as multiple linear regression consisting of stochastic gradient descent, mini-batch gradient descent, and gradient descent to forecast air quality index based on air pollution index data. Shaban and Rezk [6] collected air quality data wirelessly from monitoring motes that were equipped with an array of gaseous and meteorological sensors. They focused on the monitoring system and the forecasting module. They investigated three machine learning models, namely Support Vector Machine (SVM), M5P model tree, and ANN.

Gu, Qiao and Lin [7] proposed a heuristic recurrent air quality predictor to infer air quality using SVR. The authors forecasted air pollution using air pollutant concentrations and the meteorological conditions in the local area. The authors compared the proposed approach to three popular predictors (Voukantsis, Vlachogianni, and Kaboodvandpour). Meteorological condition and air pollutant data were also used by Tsai, Zheng and Cheng [8]. Recurrent Neural Network (RNN) with Long Short-Term Memory (LSTM) was proposed by the authors as an approach to forecast PM 2.5 concentrations. Oprea, Mihalache and Popescu [9] tried to compare two computational intelligence techniques, namely ANNs and adaptive neuro-fuzzy inference system (ANFIS) to forecast PM 2.5 concentrations based on air pollutant concentrations and meteorological conditions.

Utilizing the data of surface meteorological observation and air pollution PM 2.5 concentrations in Wuhan City was conducted by Chen, Qin and Zhou [10]. They used multiple regression analysis and back-propagation neural network to develop an air pollution PM 2.5 index forecasting model. According to previous research we know that air pollutant concentrations correlates with meteorological conditions. The wind can carry small particles including PM 2.5 that has a size of 2.5 μm from one area to another. It can also affect PM 2.5 concentrations in other areas. Therefore, the conditions in neighboring areas is also important as an indicator for forecasting PM 2.5 concentrations.

3 Proposed Approach

The proposed approach involves two primary processes to forecast PM 2.5 concentrations. The first process involves selecting neighboring areas of each station. The second process involves making a PM 2.5 forecasting model. The system framework for the PM 2.5 forecasting is shown in Fig. 1.

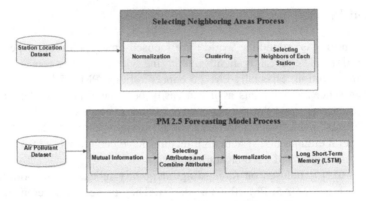

Fig. 1. System framework for PM 2.5 forecasting.

3.1 Data

Our study relied on two datasets (station location dataset and air pollution dataset) from 67 stations in Taiwan that were collected by the EPA in Taiwan. The station location dataset was used for selecting neighboring areas. The air pollution dataset was used for building the PM 2.5 forecasting model. The air pollution dataset contains hourly data in 6 years from 2012 to 2017. The data were divided into training data, validation data and testing data with ratios of 4:1:1, respectively. Training and validation data were used to build the PM 2.5 forecasting model. Testing data were used to measure the quality of the PM 2.5 forecasting model. To forecast the next hour of PM 2.5 concentrations, this study used three-hour window of observations.

3.2 Selecting Neighboring Areas

This phase involves determining the neighboring areas of each station. The flowchart of this process is shown in Fig. 2. First, the data is normalized using min-max normalization. Next, the data is clustered using the X-means method. Finally, the neighboring areas of each station is selected using the radius of each station using the Euclidean distance. However, using clustering results from only the locations which have a closer distance are not selected as neighboring areas if such stations lie on the edge of a cluster. To overcome this issue, we determined neighboring areas based on the radius of each station as shows in Fig. 3. The radii were determined as follows:

1. Based on the clustering result, the distance is calculated using Euclidean distance (1) between the station and the center cluster of each cluster:

$$EU(a, b) = \sqrt{\sum_{i=1}^{n} (x_i - y_i)^2} \tag{1}$$

$EU(a, b)$ is the distance between vector a and vector b, where vector a is the location station coordinate and vector b is the cluster center coordinate.

2. The mean distance of all clusters is calculated based on the result from step 1.

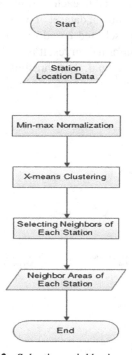

Fig. 2. Selecting neighboring areas.

3. To determine neighboring areas of the station the cluster of the station is checked.
4. The mean distance of the cluster is set as a radius of the station.
5. The Euclidean distance between the station and other stations is calculated. Then,

$$\begin{cases} dist \leq radius; & True \\ dist > radius; & False \end{cases} \tag{2}$$

If True, then the station is selected as the neighboring area. If False, the station is not selected as the neighboring area.

6. Steps 3 and 4 are repeated until neighboring areas of all stations are determined.

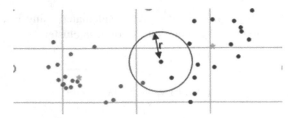

Fig. 3. Neighboring areas of the station based on radius.

3.3 PM 2.5 Forecasting Model

A PM 2.5 forecasting model is applied to each station. Figure 4 illustrates the process. First, mutual information of air pollutant dataset of each station is calculated. After that, the attributes of each station are selected based on the mutual information result by setting a threshold. The mutual information result is used for determining the attributes for the next step by setting a threshold. The threshold is based on the mean mutual information score of the attributes.

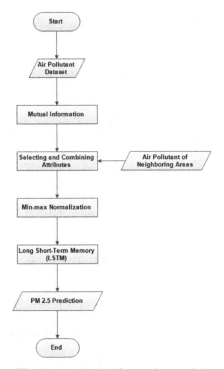

Fig. 4. The PM 2.5 forecasting model.

The threshold is determined using Eq. (3)

$$T = \frac{1}{2}avg\_MI \tag{3}$$

where *avg_MI* is the mutual information score mean of the attributes. The attributes that have a mutual information score equal to or above the threshold are selected. After that, neighboring areas determined in the previous steps are used. The selected attributes of the station combined with PM 2.5, PM 10, wind speed and the wind direction in neighboring areas. After combining the data, the data is normalized. Finally, the normalized data is used as input to the Long Short-Term Memory (LSTM) for making PM 2.5 forecasts. Our approach uses a one-to-one LSTM architecture. This architecture consists of one input, one LSTM layer, and one output. Inside the LSTM layer we used 64 LSTM units and an Adam optimizer. Root mean square error was used as a loss function during training. To measure the quality of the PM 2.5 forecasting model, RMSE and MAE were used. The proposed LSTM structure is shown in Fig. 5.

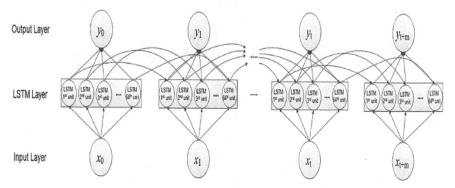

Fig. 5. Proposed LSTM structure.

4   Experimental Evaluation and Results

Figure 6 shows the results of experiment with different learning rates. Figures 6(a–f) show learning rates of 0.005, 0.001, 0.0005, 0.0001, 0.00005 and 0.00001, respectively. These experiments used 150 iterations and 32 LSTM units. The air pollution dataset from the Annan measurement station was used for these experiments. These experiments aimed to determine the effect when the learning rate decreases.

Based on the results of the experiments with different learning rates, learning rates of 0.005, 0.001, and 0.0005 showed fluctuations in training loss and validation loss. On the other hand, learning rates of 0.0001, 0.00005, and 0.00001 exhibited stable training loss and validation loss even though the error is higher with a learning rate of 0.00001. This happens because, with a small learning rate, more iterations are needed to reach the optimal model.

Table 1 shows the experiment with three different numbers of LSTM units (32 units, 64 units and 128 units). A PM 2.5 forecasting model was built for each station and the quality of the model was based on the mean error of the results from the 67 stations. A learning rate of 0.00005 with 350 iterations was used. This experiment aimed to determine the effect of number of LSTM units on the model. The experiments showed

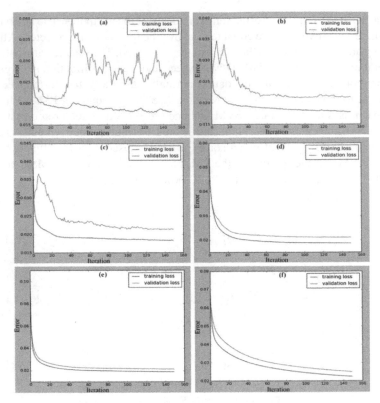

Fig. 6. Training loss and validation loss with different learning rates

Table 1. Mean RMSE and mean MAE of different LSTM units

	Mean RMSE of 67 stations	Mean MAE of 67 stations
32 LSTM units	4.2022	3.1421
64 LSTM units	4.1936	3.1309
128 LSTM units	4.2147	3.1588

that the LSTM model with 64 units yielded the best result based on the mean error of the 67 stations with a mean RMSE of 4.1936 and MAE of 3.1309. But, several units in the LSTM model did not have any significant effects. This assessment was based on the limited reduction in errors.

Also 350 iterations was used to forecast the next hour of PM 2.5 concentrations with a learning rate of 0.00005 and 64 LSTM units. The result is shown in Table 2.

The 72-h data window gave the best result with a mean RMSE of 4.1474 and mean MAE of 3.0973. However, more time was needed to train the model. Using a 3-h window of data to predict the next hour of PM 2.5 concentrations yielded a mean RMSE of 4.1936 and mean MAE of 3.1309. The difference of errors when using 3-h windows and 72-h

Table 2. Mean RMSE and mean MAE of different number of data

Input data window	Mean RMSE of 67 stations	Mean MAE of 67 stations
1-h	4.4541	3.3472
3-h	4.1936	3.1309
6-h	4.2731	3.2019
12-h	4.1698	3.1117
24-h	4.1831	3.1202
48-h	4.1750	3.1348
72-h	4.1474	3.0973

windows was 0.0462. Even though the difference was small, the processing time was very different.

We also explored the use of data from neighboring areas. This experiment was configured with 3-h data windows, 350 iterations, 64 LSTM units and a learning rate of 0.00005. The results are shown in Table 3.

Table 3. Result of the model with neighbors and without neighbors

	Mean RMSE of 67 stations	Mean MAE of 67 stations
With neighbors	4.1936	3.1309
Without neighbors	4.3926	3.2466

The results show that including data about the neighboring areas gave more beneficial results than without data about neighboring areas. Clearly, air pollution in one area can affect neighboring areas.

Finally, an experiment was conducted using only PM 2.5 data. This experiment was configured with a 3-h data windows, 350 iterations, 64 LSTM units and a learning rate of 0.00005. The results are shown in Table 4.

Table 4. Result of the model that only used PM 2.5 and other important attributes

	Mean RMSE of 67 stations	Mean MAE of 67 stations
Use important attributes	4.1936	3.1309
Only use PM 2.5 attributes	4.3709	3.2443

The mean results of the 67 stations showed that the model which included the important attributes gave a better performance than the model that only used PM 2.5 attributes.

Table 5. Station results.

Station	RMSE	MAE	Station	RMSE	MAE
Annan	4.2382	3.2652	Puli	3.2002	2.3662
Banqiao	3.0229	2.3447	Puzi	4.3750	3.3637
Cailiao	2.4441	1.8586	Qianjin	5.4130	4.1601
Changhua	5.4659	4.2174	Qianzhen	7.8106	5.6956
Chaozhou	6.5018	4.7824	Qiaotou	3.4655	2.5891
Chiayi	5.9012	4.5605	Renwu	5.0395	3.8873
Dali	4.5240	3.4289	Shalu	4.0696	2.9086
Daliao	4.1197	3.1172	Shanhua	5.0095	3.8823
Dayuan	4.1146	3.0850	Shilin	3.4324	2.6421
Dongshan	4.2207	3.0046	Sinyin	4.7020	3.5364
Douliu	5.6606	4.3191	Songshan	4.0920	3.0924
Erlin	4.5393	3.3183	Tainan	4.5315	3.4037
Fengshan	5.1525	3.8981	Taitung	2.3378	1.7630
Fengyuan	4.6981	3.6365	Taixi	4.4863	3.0750
Fuxing	4.1323	3.0565	Taoyuan	3.9041	3.0017
Guanshan	1.9509	1.3213	Toufen	3.0393	2.1690
Guanyin	4.2012	3.0137	Tucheng	2.5527	1.9375
Guting	3.3802	2.5774	Wanhua	3.8678	3.0053
Hengchun	2.9969	2.1382	Wanli	2.9183	2.0894
Hsinchu	2.9843	2.1693	Xianxi	3.4886	2.5272
Hualian	2.7852	2.1597	Xiaogang	6.6636	4.9729
Hukou	3.6707	2.7523	Xindian	3.1038	2.2755
Jilong	4.5794	3.0979	Xingang	4.5044	3.3591
Linkou	3.3532	2.4243	Xinzhuang	2.5083	1.9533
Linyuan	9.1869	6.4073	Xitun	3.8740	3.0217
Longtan	3.7045	2.9059	Xizhi	2.5024	1.8857
Lunbei	4.7674	3.5696	Yonghe	2.8041	2.1042
Mailiao	4.1385	2.9405	Zhongli	4.1864	3.1976
Meinong	4.7848	3.5040	Zhongming	4.1473	3.2268
Miaoli	4.5506	2.9245	Zhongshan	3.8098	2.9349
Nantou	3.4589	2.4960	Zhudong	3.4594	2.6179
Nanzi	5.4725	4.1397	Zhushan	4.2792	3.3270
Pingtung	5.0589	3.8742	Zuoying	5.6663	4.3459
Pingzhen	3.9752	3.1446	Mean	4.1936	3.1309

This means that other attributes such as meteorological conditions and other air pollutants played an important role in the PM 2.5 forecasts.

The results of the 67 stations are shown in Table 5. These results show that Guanshan station achieved the best result with an RMSE of 1.9509 and a MAE of 1.3213. This was followed by Taitung and Cailiao stations with an RMSE of 2.3378 and 2.4441, respectively. Some of the stations exhibited higher error rates such as Linyuan station, Qianzhen station and Xiaogang station. Linyuan station yielded an RMSE of 9.1869 and a MAE of 6.4037. Qianzhen yielded an RMSE of 7.8106 and a MAE of 5.6956. These were followed by Xiaogang with an RMSE of 6.6636 and a MAE of 4.9729. Overall, the proposed method demonstrated good performance with a mean RMSE of 4.1936 and a mean MAE of 3.1309.

5 Conclusion

PM 2.5 particles in the air can affect human health. The PM 2.5 concentration correlates with other pollutants and meteorological conditions in neighboring areas as PM 2.5 is easily carried by the wind from one area to another.

This study used air pollutant concentrations and meteorological conditions to make one-hour forecasts of PM 2.5 concentrations. Neighboring areas are determined based on station location clustering using X-means clustering. Then, we calculated the radius of each station based on the mean distance of each cluster. LSTM was applied as a forecasting engine to make one-hour PM 2.5 concentration forecasts.

Experimental results demonstrated that the proposed approach could effectively make one-hour PM 2.5 concentration forecast for 67 stations. The model achieved a RMSE of 1.9509 and a MAE of 1.3213 for Guanshan station. The overall result also showed a relatively low mean RMSE and MAE for the 67 stations all around Taiwan. The mean RMSE was 4.1936 and the mean MAE was 3.1309.

Acknowledgments. This study was funded by the Ministry of Science and Technology, Taiwan, under Grants MOST107–2221-E-027–113-, MOST108–2321-B-027–001- and MOST108–2221-E-027–111-MY3.

References

1. MacMunn, A.: More than 4 in 10 Americans live with unhealthy air according to 2018 'state of the air' report. American Lung Association (2018). https://www.lung.org/about-us/media/press-releases/2018-state-of-the-air.html. Accessed 2 May 2019
2. WHO: Ambient (outdoor) air quality and health (2018). https://www.who.int/en/news-room/fact-sheets/detail/ambient-(outdoor)-air-quality-and-health. Accessed 2 May 2019
3. Jacobs, E.T., Burgess, J.L., Abbott, M.B.: The Donora smog revisited: 70 years after the event that inspired the clean air act. Am. J. Public Health **108**, 85–88 (2018)
4. Wilkins, E.T.: Air pollution aspects of the London fog of December 1952. Q. J. Roy. Meteorol. Soc. **80**(344), 267–271 (1954)
5. Ganesh, S.S., Modali, S.H., Palreddy, S.R., Arulmozhivarman, P.: Forecasting air quality index using regression model: a case study on Delhi and Houston. In: Proceedings of the International Conference on Trends in Electronics and Informatics, pp. 248–254. IEEE (2017)
6. Shaban, K.B., Kadri, A., Rezk, E.: Urban air pollution monitoring system with forecasting models. IEEE Sens. J. **16**(8), 2598–2606 (2016)
7. Gu, K., Qiao, J., Lin, W.: Recurrent air quality predictor based on meteorology- and pollution-related factor. IEEE Trans. Ind. Inform. **14**(9), 3946–3955 (2018)
8. Tsai, Y., Zheng, Y., Cheng, Y.: Air pollution forecasting using RNN with LSTM. In: Proceedings of the IEEE 16th International Conference on Big Data Intelligence and Computing and Cyber Science and Technology Congress, pp. 1074–1079. IEEE (2018)

9. Oprea, M., Mihalache, S.F., Popescu, M.: A comparative study of computational intelligence techniques applied to PM 2.5 air pollution forecasting. In: Proceedings of the 6th International Conference on Computers Communications and Control, pp. 103–108. IEEE (2016)
10. Chen, Y., Qin, H., Zhou, Z.: A comparative study on multi-regression analysis and BP neural network of PM2.5 index. In: Proceedings of the 10th International Conference on Natural Computation, pp. 155–159. IEEE (2014)
11. Han, J., Kamber, M., Pei, J.: Data Mining: Concepts and Techniques, 3rd edn. Morgan Kaufmann, Burlington (2011)
12. Imamura, K., Kubo, N., Hashimoto, H.: Automatic moving object extraction using x-means clustering. In: Proceedings of the 28th Picture Coding Symposium, pp. 245–249. IEEE (2010)
13. Nathanson, J.A.: Air pollution. Encyclopaedia Britannica (2018). https://www.britannica.com/science/air-pollution. Accessed 9 May 2019
14. Liu, L., He, G., Shi, X., Song, H.: Metadata extraction based on mutual information in digital libraries. In: Proceedings of the First IEEE International Symposium on Information Technologies and Applications in Education, pp. 209–212. IEEE (2007)
15. Goodfellow, I., Bengio, Y., Courville, A.: Deep Learning. MIT Press, Cambridge (2017)
16. Willmott, C.J., Matsuura, K.: Advantages of the mean absolute error (MAE) over the root mean square error (RMSE) in assessing mean model performance. Clim. Res. **30**(79), 79–82 (2005)
17. Lv, B., Cai, J., Xu, B., Bai, Y.: Understanding the rising phase of the PM 2.5 concentration evolution in large china cities. Sci. Rep. **7** (2017). Article number: 46456
18. Niharika, M.V., Padma, S.R.: A survey on air quality forecasting techniques. Int. J. Comput. Sci. Inf. Technol. **5**(1), 103–107 (2014)

The Aquatic Surface Robot (AnSweR), a Lightweight, Low Cost, Multipurpose Unmanned Research Vessel

Filippo Sanfilippo[1,2]([✉]) [iD], Min Tang[3], and Sam Steyaert[4]

[1] Department of Engineering Sciences, University of Agder (UiA),
Jon Lilletuns vei 9, 4879 Grimstad, Norway
filippo.sanfilippo@uia.no
[2] Department of Mechanical, Electronic and Chemical Engineering,
Oslo Metropolitan University (OsloMet), PO box 4, St. Olavs plass,
0130 Oslo, Norway
[3] Department of Science and Industry Systems, University of South-Eastern Norway
(USN), Post box 235, 3603 Kongsberg, Norway
[4] Faculty of Biosciences and Aquaculture, Nord University, Universitetsalléen 11,
8026 Bodø, Norway

Abstract. Even though a few examples of aquatic surface robots exist, they are generally expensive, relatively large and heavy and tailored to custom-made hardware/software components that are not openly available to a broad public. In this work, the Aquatic Surface Robot (*AnSweR*), a newly-designed, lightweight, low cost, open-source, multipurpose unmanned research vessel is presented. The *AnSweR* features a lightweight and compact design that makes it fit in a backpack. Low-noise operation (in and above the surface) is achieved with a propulsion system based on two water-jets. Only affordable commercial-off-the-shelf (COTS) components are adopted. The primary goal of the *AnSweR* is to map underwater landscapes and to collect bathymetry data in lakes, rivers, and coastal ecosystems. A modular hardware and software architecture is adopted. This architecture allows the *AnSweR* to be equipped with a customisable add-on set of sensors and actuators to enable a variety of research activities, such as measuring environmental variables (e.g., salinity, oxygen, temperature) and sampling operations (e.g., sediment, vegetation, microplastics). The software architecture is based on the Robot Operating System (ROS). This paper describes the design of *AnSweR* as the main scientific contribution and presents preliminary simulation and experimental results which illustrate its potential.

Keywords: Aquatic surface robots · Unmanned surface vehicles · Robotics

This work is supported by the Top Research Centre Mechatronics, University of Agder (UiA), Jon Lilletuns vei 9, 4879, Grimstad, Norway.

S. Yildirim Yayilgan et al. (Eds.): INTAP 2020, CCIS 1382, pp. 251–265, 2021.
https://doi.org/10.1007/978-3-030-71711-7_21

1   Introduction

The monitoring of ambient environmental conditions in aquatic ecosystems is essential to ecological management and regulation. However, collecting environmental data in such aquatic environments is a challenging process [1]. It typically requires human-operated research vessels or equipment, which are time and cost-inefficient, and can expose operators to dangerous situations (i.e., scuba diving for sample collection). Unmanned surface vehicles (USVs), which started to make their appearance predominantly for military and marine purposes [25], are also becoming increasingly relevant for research purposes. USVs are remotely controlled rafts that can be equipped with various cameras and sensors to collect environmental data [2]. Commercially available USVs are fairly large, heavy (usually 1–10 m, 30 kg - several tons) and considerably expensive [2]. As a result, they are generally inaccessible to a broad public and are not practical to transport and operate in difficult to reach environments (e.g., most rivers and lakes).

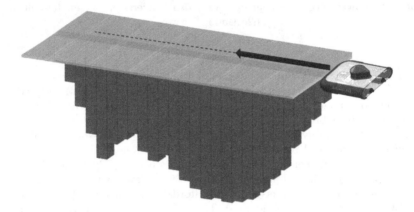

Fig. 1. The Aquatic Surface Robot (*AnSweR*) is a newly-designed, lightweight, low cost, open-source, multipurpose unmanned research vessel. The primary goal of the *AnSweR* is to map underwater landscapes and to collect bathymetry data in lakes, rivers, and coastal ecosystems. A modular hardware architecture is adopted.

Nowadays, different commercial off-the-shelf (COTS) aquatic surface robots exist [5, 11, 13, 16, 20, 22]. However, most of the existing robots are typically costly, relatively large and heavy and custom-built to specific hardware/software modules that are not openly available. Moreover, they are typically not easy to maintain, change or extend as research tools, by adding new hardware/software components and features. Therefore, the integration of these robots with other research tools still requires a significant effort. Consequently, this process can often be a tedious and time-consuming task, which may prevent researchers from fully focusing on the tasks necessary to achieve the core experimental objectives.

To give researchers and other users a robotic solution that is inexpensive, easily customisable, and fast to fabricate, a newly-designed, lightweight, low cost, open-source, multipurpose unmanned research vessel is introduced in this work.

The presented robot is named Aquatic Surface Robot (*AnSweR*) and is shown in Fig. 1. The *AnSweR* is characterised by a lightweight and compact design that makes it fit in a backpack. Exclusively low-cost commercially available components are employed. The robot mechanical components can be easily manufactured, thus making the rapid-prototyping process very economical and fast. The robot's primary purpose is to map underwater environments and to gather data on bathymetry in lakes, rivers and coastal habitats. A modular hardware architecture is adopted. In particular, the (*AnSweR* is equipped with a hardware interface that includes all sensors and actuators which are absolutely necessary for achieving guidance, navigation, and control (GNC) functions [9]. A propulsion system with two water-jet thrusters, a depth camera, a global positioning system (GPS), and a sonar are adopted to enable the robot's external system independence (ESI), adaption to environmental complexity (EC) and to mission complexity (MC). Furthermore, the *AnSweR* may be fitted with a versatile collection of sensors and actuators to allow for a range of research activities, such as measuring environmental variables (e.g., salinity, oxygen, temperature), sampling and monitoring operations (e.g., sediment, vegetation, microplastics). The concept of modularity is also applied to the software architecture. The *AnSweR* is equipped with a core control software that make it possible to achieve the required GNC functions. Moreover, an add-on software layer makes it possible to integrate extra software functionalities that can be developed/added on-demand to perform the desired research activities. The software architecture is based upon the Robot Operating System (ROS) [18]. The design of the *AnSweR* is presented as the main scientific contribution of this work. Preliminary simulation and experimental results are outlined to demonstrate potential applications.

The paper is organised as follows. A review of the related research work is given in Sect. 2. In Sect. 3, we focus on the description of the mechanical overview. A hardware/software overview is described in Sect. 4. In Sect. 5, some preliminary simulation and experimental results are outlined. Finally, conclusions and future works are discussed in Sect. 6.

2   Related Research Work

A diverse range of aquatic surface robots exist [12,15,17,21,23,24]. The focus of this paper is on introducing the (*AnSweR*) robot that can easily be transported and operated to conduct research activities in ecosystems with difficult access. Therefore, small size USVs with no more than 2 m length are briefly reviewed in this section. A more detailed review is described in [19]. For the investigated small size USVs, two types of hull are generally adopted: catamaran type or single hull type. Both of these different types of hull are easily carried and deployed by one man. Electric actuators, such as thrusters represent the most prevalent actuation systems for propelling these vehicles. These systems are used for shallow water surveillance, bathymetric survey and water monitoring, by remote control with telemetry [5,11,13,16,20,22].

Regarding catamaran type hulls, different USVs are available. For instance, Maritime Robotics produces the Otter USV [13], which is a hydrographic survey tool for mapping of sheltered and enclosed waters. With close integration between the on-board control system that enables autonomy and the multibeam echo-sounder, a bathymetric survey can be carried out with a quick, seamless workflow. The closely integrated bathymetric survey system makes the Otter a cost-effective solution for bathymetric surveys in sheltered waters such as small lakes, canals, rivers, ponds, and harbour areas. Another example with similar hull typology is the SR-Surveyor M1.8 USV, which is a highly capable man-portable autonomous hydrographic survey vessel developed by Sea Robotics [20]. It is tightly integrated with multiple high-resolution hydrographic sensors and a topographical mapping LiDAR. Thanks to its unique sensor suite, it is very suitable for collecting a wide range of hydrographic data in inland and coastal waters. Its small form factor, light weight, and shallow draft enable the SR-Surveyor M1.8 to be rapidly deployed in difficult to access areas. One more example with catamaran type hull is the Heron USV, which is a portable, mid-sized surface vessel developed by Clearpath Robotics [5]. Its design comprises anti-fouling thrusters, a remarkably shallow profile, and built-in GPS. Submerged sensors or equipment on deck can be mounted on a specifically designed payload bay. Folding pontoons and a quick swappable battery make transport, launch and retrieval a quick and easy process.

Regarding single type hulls, various example exist. For instance, the GeoSwath 4R USV is developed by Kongsberg Maritime [11]. It offers efficient simultaneous swath bathymetry and side scan mapping. It features closely integrated ancillary sensors and communication links into a proven remote-controlled platform for quick and easy deployment and operation. This remote hydrographic survey boat allows surveying in locations and situations in which deployment of conventional platforms is not practicable or hazardous. Another example with similar hull typology is the SL20 USV, which is developed by OceanAlpha [16]. Its compact and portable form factor makes it suitable for hydrographic and bathymetry surveying. It supports flexible deployment of different instruments like an Acoustic Doppler Current Profiler (ADCP) and an echo sounder. With the size of 1 m long and weight of 17 kg, it is easy for one man to operate and transport. Its powerful battery and low power consumption provide 6 h of endurance at 3 knots. One more example with single type hull is the Z-Boat 1800 RP USV. It is developed by Teledyne Marine [22] and it is a high performance portable remotely-operated hydrographic survey boat. It offers 8kt maximum operating speed, an ADCP, a side scan, and multibeam sonar payloads, with autonomous waypoint navigation.

Commercial applications of these USVs provides an indication that most of the necessary technology is mature and available, including sensors, communication and control principals. However, a robotic solution that is inexpensive, easily customisable, and fast to fabricate is still missing to the best of our knowledge.

3   Mechanical Overview

In this section, the modular mechanical design of the *AnSweR* is presented.

3.1   Hull Design

A monohull-shaped design is adopted, as shown in Fig. 2. The *AnSweR* is extremely compact in size (L 360 mm × W 285 mm × H 135 mm), and lightweight (3 Kg). The draft or draught of the robot's hull is 50 mm, with the thickness of the hull included. While computerised numeric cut (CNC) and 3D-printing fabrication processes and materials could be employed for the fabrication process, low-cost COTS components are used to fast-prototyping the *AnSweR*. In particular, polyvinyl chloride (PVC) pipes are adopted to build the hull frame. PVC pipes are non-toxic and are most commonly used for plumbing and drainage. PVC has many benefits for fast-prototyping processes. Its strength, waterproofness and durability along with low cost and easy availability make it the go to material for the fast construction of the hull. Moreover, the smooth surface of PVC material results in an efficient flow rate and reduces energy use. PVC is easy to machine, cut and connect allowing close tolerances to be achieved with either push fit or threaded compression style fittings. Leak-free PVC fittings are adopted for eliminating water loss and obtaining round corners at the front of the hull. The hull provides room for the hardware interface that includes all sensors and actuators which are strictly required to achieve all the vital GNC functions. Moreover, the hull modular design provides additional room for a payload that may be fitted with a versatile set of sensors and actuators to allow for a variety of research activities, such as measuring environmental variables (e.g., salinity, oxygen, temperature), sampling and monitoring operations (e.g., sediment, vegetation, microplastics). The payload is limited to 1 Kg.

To enable a see-through capability, the bottom, rear and top of the hull are fitted with transparent plexiglass sheets. Compared to tempered glass, plexiglass

Fig. 2. The *AnSweR* is extremely compact in size (L 360 mm × W 285 mm × H 135 mm), and lightweight (3 Kg).

holds up better in harsh weather conditions and is more shatter resistant while still allowing 90% of light to pass through it and reach sensors that might require it. One of the biggest advantages of plexiglass panels is the ability to easily cut and form them. This is especially relevant for speeding up the prototyping process. The inner side of the bottom panel provides specifically designed slots to enclose all internal electronic components. The rear panel is set up with the needed cut-outs to enclose the propulsion system. The top panel is equipped with a specifically designed cut-out to enable the fitting of a thru-hull sensor. A 3D-printed top cup encapsulates the thru-hull sensor. The top panel is provided with a custom-made edge profile that makes it possible to easily remove it to access the inner compartment and reach all internal electronic components. Silicon-based glue is adopted to ensure seal that maintains a strong hold against harsh weather conditions. The design of all components will be made publicly available.

3.2 Propulsion

The *AnSweR* is actuated by two water-jets that are simmetrically allocated onto the rear panel of the hull. Water-jets operate differently than propellers. Propeller attempt to minimise the velocity change and rely on generating pressure differences. Alternatively, water-jets designedly increase the velocity change between inlet and outlet. That change in momentum creates thrust. By multiplying the thrust with a consistent flow rate, propulsion is achieved [4]. A water-jet is fundamentally a pump inside a very short pipe. Pumps have some advantages over propellers. Pump efficiencies around 90% or more are regularly attainable. In comparison, conventional propellers are limited to 60%–72% efficiency. Each water-jet is embedded inside the hull, with just one outlet. At speed, the exit nozzles completely clear the water. This reduces the total resistance on the robot. The absence of a propeller shaft or shaft brackets makes it possible to reduce drag through the water. Moreover, water-jets do not require a rudder, because they direct the thrust through changing the direction of the outlet stream. These characteristics make it possible for the *AnSweR* to achieve low-noise operationn (in and above the water surface). Finally, water-jets also provide great manoeuvring control and enable the *AnSweR* for avoiding getting stuck with floating debris or vegetation. Two brushless waterproof motors (*Racerstar 2440*) run the two water-jet thrusters. The *AnSweR* can reach a max speed of 2 m/s.

4   Hardware/Software Overview

In this section, the modular hardware/software design of the *AnSweR* is presented.

4.1   Computation and Communications

An *Arduino Mega 2560* micro-controller is embedded in the *AnSweR* to enable an efficient low-level interface with the propulsion system and the sensors. Moreover, on-board computation is provided by an *Odroid XU4*. The *Odroid*

XU4 is a powerful single-board computer (SBC) that features an energy-efficient hardware and a small form-factor. In particular, the *Odroid XU4* is composed of an octa-core ARM Cortex-A7 CPU clocked at 2 Ghz, 2 GB RAM, 2 Universal Serial Bus (USB) 3.0 ports, 1 USB 2.0 port, and 30-pin general purpose input/output (GPIO) expansion header supporting diverse protocols such as universal asynchronous receiver/transmitter (UART), inter-integrated circuit (I2C), serial peripheral interface (SPI) and One-Wire, which facilitates integration with different electronic components and modules. The form-factor of the *Odroid XU4* (83 mm × 58 mm × 20 mm) is a crucial parameter for the selection of this specific micro-controller for the *AnSweR*, given the limited physical space. The *Odroid XU4* offers open source support and runs *Ubuntu MATE 16.04*, a *Linux* distribution based on *Debian*. The *Odroid XU4* is located in the main electronics enclosure. To enable data communication between the *Arduino Mega 2560* micro-controller and the *Odroid XU4*, an *Arduino* USB 2 Serial converter is adopted. To enable communication between the *AnSweR* and the ground/control station, a USB wireless fidelity (Wi-Fi) module for the *Odroid XU4* is used. Alternatively, a radio communication (RC) controller can be interfaced with the *Arduino Mega 2560* micro-controller for long range communication (operating range of up to 1000 m).

4.2 Sensors Required to Achieve All the GNC Functions

Fig. 3. The most relevant *AnSweR* hardware components: 1) two water-jets; 2) two brushless waterproof motors; 3) an *Arduino Mega 2560* micro-controller; 4) an *Odroid XU4* single-board computer (SBC); 5) a *DST800* smart transducer multisensor; 6) an *Intel RealSense D435 RGBD* camera; 7) two battery packs.

As shown in Fig. 3, various sensors are included in the *AnSweR*. To achieve all the vital GNC functions the following sensors are considered:

- a *STMicroelectronics LSM303D* magnetometer, which is a system-in-package featuring a 3D digital linear acceleration sensor and a 3D digital magnetic sensor. It includes an I2C serial bus interface that supports standard and fast mode (100 and 400 kHz) and an SPI serial standard interface. The sensor can be configured to generate an interrupt signal for free-fall, motion detection and magnetic field detection;
- a *DST800*, which is a smart transducer multisensor that offers depth, speed, and temperature functions in one compact thru-hull fitting. This is a low-profile, retractable sensor. The signals from the sensors are processed right inside the housing itself. The sensor is integrated into the system thanks to a specifically designed cut-out of the hull top panel;
- an *Intel RealSense D435 RGBD* camera, which is a stereo tracking device that offers quality depth for a variety of applications. It provides a wide field of view and a range up to 10 m. Thanks to its small form-factor, the camera is integrated into the inner side of the hull bottom panel, with the lens facing down to the water;
- an *Adafruit Ultimate* GPS breakout, which provides GPS signals. The breakout is built around the *MTK3339* chipset, a high-quality GPS module that can track up to 22 satellites on 66 channels, has an excellent high-sensitivity receiver, and a built in antenna. It can do up to 10 location updates a second for high speed, high sensitivity logging or tracking. Power usage is remarkably low, only 20 mA during navigation.

4.3   Battery Packs

Two battery packs are fitted into the hull enabling the *AnSweR* for an operating time of up to 6 h.

4.4   Open-Source Software

In line with the overall low-cost approach of the *AnSweR*, an open-source software framework is designed for the low-level control. To design the software architecture, the Robot Operating System (ROS) [18] is selected. ROS is a meta-operating system designed for robotic applications. The primary aim of ROS is to provide a generic interface for quicker and simpler design of capable robotic applications. Some of the ROS features comprise hardware abstraction, device drivers, message-passing and package management. The Gazebo 3D simulator [10] can be adopted in combination with ROS to simulate robots accurately and efficiently in complex indoor and outdoor settings. Gazebo also offers a robust physics engine, high-quality graphics, and convenient programmatic and graphical interfaces. In this perspective, ROS serves as the interface for the robot model of the *AnSweR*, while Gazebo is used to simulate both the robot and its operational environment. In addition to ROS and Gazebo, the RViz (ROS visualisation) [8] tool can be adopted to visualise and monitor sensor information retrieved in real-time from both the simulated scenario as well as from the real world. Other advantages for developers are the ROS community-driven support and the stable release-cycle of distributions (a new version is released every year, while a new long-term support (LTS) version is released every second year). In addition, ROS offers an excellent interface for hardware modules, such as various micro-controllers and other peripheral devices, such as actuators and sensors. The choice of ROS for the design of the control architecture makes it possible to extend the modular concept to both the hardware as well as the software of the *AnSweR*.

4.5 Framework Architecture

The proposed control framework is hierarchically organised, as shown in Fig. 4. The carrier layer is the layer that is strictly needed for achieving the standard functions and capabilities of guidance, navigation, and control (GNC) [9]:

- Guidance: this level is responsible for performing the functions of sensing, mapping and localisation. The *AnSweR*'s sensor data are used to produce a representation of the surrounding environment. This level performs parsing or segmenting of low-level sensor data (e.g., point-clouds) into higher-level and more manageable information;
- Navigation: this level is responsible for decision making in terms of where, when and how the robot should ideally move. External system commands (e.g., a remote controller operated by a human operator or an external system) and the *AnSweR*'s perception data represent the input to this level. The expected output from this level is the robot's desired trajectory (e.g., path and velocity information);
- Control: this level is the core of the proposed control framework. It allows researchers for developing their own alternative control methods. The level does not enforce any limitations with respect to its internal implementation. Each possible control method, however, must comply with the framework's given interfaces. The inputs to this level are the desired trajectory, as well as any relevant information from the above guidance level (perception data). The goal of the control level is to obtain the required setpoints for the robot actuators in order to follow the desired trajectory. This control action will preferably be based on the high-level information from the guidance level, but lower-level information like the actual position might be necessary depending on the actual algorithm employed in the control level.

Note that only the control layer is currently implemented, while the navigation and guidance levels will be implemented in the future.

The add-on layer makes it is possible to add extra sensors, actuators and software apps that are not strictly needed for achieving the GNC functions but are rather used for performing different research activities, i.e. water sampling, data collection and data processing. This layer includes the following components:

- Add-on sensors. These are extra sensors that can be added on-demand according to the specific research activity to be performed;

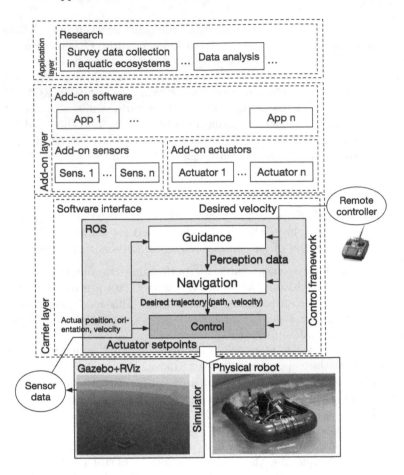

Fig. 4. The proposed framework architecture for the *AnSweR*.

- Add-on actuators. These are extra actuators that can be added on-demand according to the specific task to be achieved. For instance, a gripper or a robotic arm could be connected to the robot to collect water samples;
- Add-on software. These are extra software apps that can be developed/added on-demand to perform the desired operations.

An application layer is a supplementary abstraction level that makes it possible to develop additional and more complex research tasks, such as survey data collection, data analysis and other activities.

The proposed framework can be extended to the possibility of controlling multiple cooperative aquatic surface robots [6,7,14].

5   Simulations and Experimental Results

As depicted in Fig. 4, the proposed control framework is implemented in ROS, while Gazebo is used to provide seamless simulations, and RViz is selected to

Fig. 5. The *AnSweR* model with a basic box-shaped hull and two thrusters.

Fig. 6. A simulation scenario is built in Gazebo reproducing an aquatic environment.

visualise and monitor sensor information retrieved in real-time from the simulated scenario. The *AnSweR* is implemented as a digital twin according to the Universal Robotic Description Format (URDF) into a model with a basic box-shaped hull and two thrusters, as shown in Fig. 5. The rigid body dynamics implemented in Gazebo are augmented with environmental forces via a set of *Gazebo USV Plugins* [3]. These plugins simulate the effects of dynamics (e.g., manoeuvring - added mass, drag, etc., ave field - motion of the water surface), thrust (e.g., vehicle propulsion) and wind (e.g., windage). A simulation scenario is built in Gazebo reproducing an aquatic environment, as shown in Fig. 6.

In this preliminary study, the *AnSweR* is teleoperated from the ground station by adopting the standard ROS teleoperation package, *teleop_twist_keyboard*. The corresponding ROS topic graph is shown in Fig. 7. The node *teleop_twist_keyboard* reads keyboard inputs and publishes commands to the topic *cmd_vel*. Then the node *twist2drive* subscribes to the topic *cmd_vel* and publishes commands in topic *cmd_drive*. Finally, the node gazebo (simulator) subscribes to the topic *cmd_drive* and sets throttle commands to the left and right thrusters accordingly. A graphical user interface is also implemented to control linear and angular velocities, as shown in Fig. 8. A time plot of the *AnSweR* linear velocity is shown in Fig. 9. A preliminary in-water teleoperation test for the *AnSweR* is shown in Fig. 10.

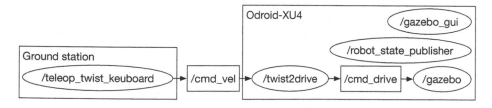

Fig. 7. The ROS topic graph for teleoperating the *AnSweR*.

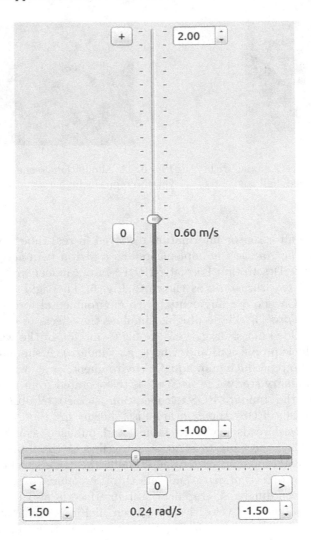

Fig. 8. A graphical user interface is implemented for the *AnSweR* to control linear and angular velocities.

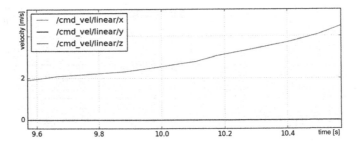

Fig. 9. A time plot of the *AnSweR* linear velocity.

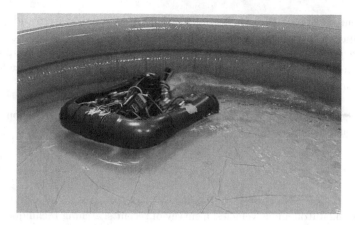

Fig. 10. A preliminary in-water teleoperation test for the *AnSweR*.

6   Conclusions and Future Work

The Aquatic Surface Robot (*AnSweR*), a newly-designed, lightweight, low cost, open-source, multipurpose unmanned research vessel was introduced in this work. The *AnSweR* is characterised by a lightweight and compact design that makes it transportable inside a backpack. With its ultra-low draught, the *AnSweR* can operate in very shallow waters. Thanks to its water-jet propulsion, the *AnSweR* is characterised by low-noise operation (in and above the surface). The design of the robot relies exclusively on low-cost commercial-off-the-shelf (COTS) components. The robot's primary purpose is to monitor aquatic environments and to gather data on bathymetry in lakes, oceans, and coastal habitats. A modular hardware and software architecture is adopted, which makes it possible for the *AnSweR* to be customised with a payload of sensors and actuators for enabling a range of research activities, such as measuring environmental variables (e.g., salinity, oxygen, temperature) and sampling operations (e.g., sediment, vegetation, microplastics). The principle of modularity is also adopted for the software architecture. The robot is fitted with a core control software, which allows the necessary guidance, navigation and control (GNC) functions to be accomplished. In addition, an add-on software layer enables the incorporation of additional software functionalities which can be developed/added on-demand to conduct the desired research activities. The software architecture is based on the Robot Operating System (ROS) [18]. The choice of ROS for the implementation of the control framework enables researchers to develop different control algorithms in a simulated environment with the Gazebo 3D simulator [10]. This integration makes the development of control algorithms more safe, rapid and efficient. Preliminary simulations and experimental results were presented to illustrate the potential of the proposed design.

As future work, the design of reliable control algorithms for navigation and guidance will be investigated. Moreover, the possibility of gradually increment the autonomy levels of the *AnSweR* in terms of external system independence (ESI), adaption to environmental complexity (EC) and to mission complexity (MC). The possibility of advancing the *AnSweR* from being a simple stand-alone aquatic surface robot to becoming part of a swarm of cobots will also be considered in the future.

Acknowledgements. The authors gratefully acknowledge the contribution of Erlend Helgerud, Sondre Lieblein Aronsen and John Mulholland.

References

1. Bayat, B., Crasta, N., Crespi, A., Pascoal, A.M., Ijspeert, A.: Environmental monitoring using autonomous vehicles: a survey of recent searching techniques. Current Opin. Biotechnol. **45**, 76–84 (2017)
2. Bertram, V.: Unmanned surface vehicles-a survey. Skibsteknisk Selskab, Copenhagen, Denmark **1**, 1–14 (2008)
3. Bingham, B.: Gazebo USV plugins, theory of operation. https://github.com/bsb 808/robotx_docs/blob/master/theoryofoperation/theory_of_operation.pdf. Accessed May 2020
4. Carlton, J.: Marine Propellers and Propulsion. Butterworth-Heinemann, Oxford (2018)
5. Clearpath Robotics Inc.: Heron. https://clearpathrobotics.com/heron-unmanned-surface-vessel/. Accessed Jan 2020
6. Curcio, J., Leonard, J., Patrikalakis, A.: Scout-a low cost autonomous surface platform for research in cooperative autonomy. In: Proceeding of OCEANS 2005 MTS/IEEE, pp. 725–729 (2005)
7. Duarte, M., et al.: Evolution of collective behaviors for a real swarm of aquatic surface robots. PLoS ONE **11**(3), e0151834 (2016)
8. Kam, H.R., Lee, S.H., Park, T., Kim, C.H.: RVIZ: a toolkit for real domain data visualization. Telecommun. Syst. **60**(2), 337–345 (2015)
9. Kendoul, F.: Towards a unified framework for UAS Autonomy and Technology Readiness Assessment (ATRA). In: Nonami, K., Kartidjo, M., Yoon, K.J., Budiyono, A. (eds.) Autonomous Control Systems and Vehicles, pp. 55–71. No. 65 in Intelligent Systems, Control and Automation: Science and Engineering, Springer Japan (2013). http://link.springer.com/chapter/10.1007/978-4-431-54276-6_4. https://doi.org/10.1007/978-4-431-54276-6_4
10. Koenig, N., Howard, A.: Design and use paradigms for gazebo, an open-source multi-robot simulator. In: Proceeding of the IEEE/RSJ International Conference on Intelligent Robots and Systems (IROS), vol. 3, pp. 2149–2154 (2004)
11. KONGSBERG: GeoSwath 4R USV. https://www.kongsberg.com/maritime/prod ucts/marine-robotics/autonomous-surface-vehicles/geoswath-4r-USV/. Accessed Jan 2020
12. Liu, Z., Zhang, Y., Yu, X., Yuan, C.: Unmanned surface vehicles: an overview of developments and challenges. Ann. Rev. Control **41**, 71–93 (2016)
13. Maritime Robotics AS: The Otter. https://www.maritimerobotics.com/otter. Accessed Jan 2020
14. Mendonça, R., et al.: A cooperative multi-robot team for the surveillance of shipwreck survivors at sea. In: Proceeding of OCEANS 2016 MTS/IEEE Monterey, pp. 1–6 (2016)

15. Metcalfe, B., Thomas, B., Treloar, A., Rymansaib, Z., Hunter, A., Wilson, P.: A compact, low-cost unmanned surface vehicle for shallow inshore applications. In: Proceeding of the IEEE Intelligent Systems Conference (IntelliSys), pp. 961–968 (2017)
16. OceanAlpha: SL20. https://www.oceanalpha.com/product-item/sl20/. Accessed Jan 2020
17. Park, J., et al.: Development of an unmanned surface vehicle system for the 2014 maritime robotx challenge. J. Field Robot. **34**(4), 644–665 (2017)
18. Quigley, M., et al.: ROS: an open-source robot operating system. In: Proceeding of the IEEE International Conference on Robotics and Automation (ICRA), workshop on open source software, vol. 3, p. 5 (2009)
19. Sanfilippo, F., Tang, M., Steyaert, S.: Aquatic surface robots: the state of the art, challenges and possibilities. In: Accepted for Publication to the Proceeding of the IEEE International Conference on Human-Machine Systems (ICHMS), Rome, Italy (2020)
20. SeaRobotics Corporation: SR-Surveyor M1.8. https://www.searobotics.com/products/autonomous-surface-vehicles/sr-surveyor-m1-8. Accessed Jan 2020
21. Tanakitkorn, K., Wilson, P.: A new design concept for a fully actuated unmanned surface vehicle. Ocean Eng. (2019)
22. Teledyne Marine: Z-BOAT 1800RP. http://www.teledynemarine.com/z-boat-1800rp. Accessed Jan 2020
23. Villa, J., Paez, J., Quintero, C., Yime, E., Cabrera, J.: Design and control of an unmanned surface vehicle for environmental monitoring applications. In: Proceeding of the IEEE Colombian Conference on Robotics and Automation (CCRA), pp. 1–5 (2016)
24. Wang, G., Shi, F., Xiang, X.: Unmanned boat design for challenges and verification of unmanned surface ship intelligent navigation. In: Proceeding of the IEEE 8th International Conference on Underwater System Technology: Theory and Applications (USYS), pp. 1–5 (2018)
25. Yan, R.J., Pang, S., Sun, H.B., Pang, Y.J.: Development and missions of unmanned surface vehicle. J. Marine Sci. Appl. **9**(4), 451–457 (2010)

Intrusion and Malware Detection

Empirical Analysis of Data Mining Techniques in Network Intrusion Detection Systems

Reza Soufizadeh[1][✉] and Jamshid Bagherzadeh[2]

[1] Department of Computer Engineering, Science and Research Branch,
Islamic Azad University, West Azerbaijan, Iran
RSoufizadeh@iaurmia.ac.ir
[2] Department of Computer Engineering, Urmia University, Urmia, Iran
J.Bagherzadeh@urmia.ac.ir

Abstract. Computer networks have an essential role in modern societies which are developing extensively. Considering that the main goal of the attackers is the ability to access a huge amount of information, Intrusion detection techniques have been attracted attention to the researchers and they believe that to proffer an approach that has an optimization rate both in timing and performance recognition. Moreover, it can be also implemented in commercial devices. A complete analysis of the latest researches in anomaly detection with a high recognition rate of 98% and 2% false positive can be reported. Despite the high rate of attack detection in academic researches, looking at industry solutions that are commercially produced, fewer products can be found that implement smart methods on devices. However, cybersecurity engineers still do not believe in the performance of these new technologies. In order to find out the reason for this contradiction, NSL-KDD and KDDCUP99 Data sets with some machine learning approaches will be evaluated and the results will be compared with previous related works in this paper.

Keywords: Network Intrusion Detection System · Classification methods · Data mining and Machine learning · Feature selection

1 Introduction

Computer networks have a major role in today's modern world and they are developing and becoming inclusive rapidly. At the same time, ensuring their security, maintenance and stability require a high cost. Since the main purpose of attacks is to reach the high amount of information, intrusion detection techniques, have attracted researchers attention. They attempt to find a way that is efficient from both aspects of time and detection ability, and at the same time the technique should be capable of being implemented in network security devices. Network attacks as a group of destructive activities are known for fragmentation, denial and destruction of the information and services in computer networks. For example, network attacks are viruses attached to e-mails, system's probe for collecting information, internet worms, unauthorized use of a system and denial of services with abuse of system's attributes or exploiting a bug in software in order to change the system's information.

© Springer Nature Switzerland AG 2021
S. Yildirim Yayilgan et al. (Eds.): INTAP 2020, CCIS 1382, pp. 269–279, 2021.
https://doi.org/10.1007/978-3-030-71711-7_22

An intrusion detection system (IDS) can be either a device or a software application by which a network or a system is monitored for malicious activity or policy violations. Any malicious activity or violation is typically reported either to an administrator or collected centrally using a security information and event management (SIEM) system. A SIEM system combines outputs from multiple sources, and then uses alarm filtering. Intrusion detection typically refers to tools for detecting efforts which want to unauthorized access to a system or to decline its efficiency. In other words, these systems with checking the saved information of user's loggings do not permit to any unauthorized login to the system and meanwhile they detect the users' activities while they are doing something on a system in order to inform the system's manager if there is an unauthorized activity by a user. A simple model for network intrusion detection system has shown in Fig. 1:

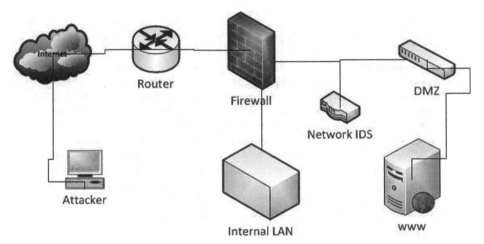

Fig. 1. A simple model of exposure IDS in computer networks

2 Network Intrusion Detection Systems

Network intrusion detection systems (NIDS) like other network equipment are developing in attacks' detection aspect. For a long time, intrusion detection systems have been focusing on anomaly detection and misuse detection. Meanwhile, commercial manufacturers concentrate highly on misuse detection for high level of detection ability and high amount of precision. Anomaly detection is being developed in academic researches for the existence of high level of theoretical background. This method as a general analysis features like; CPU consumption, input and output, traffic network card, number of file access, user's identity, machines that a user want to access, all of the opened files, read pages and page fault. Then with being far from the threshold, by using statistical or intelligent techniques, it will be detected as anomaly [1]. In misuse detection methods, patterns that are clear in data course are first encoded then corresponded with intrusive procedures like special signatures [2]. At the same time, anomaly detection, a model of data flow, is being monitored by statistical analysis to detect whether in normal situations, intrusive procedures, abnormal traffic, and an unusual activity happened as intrusion or not [1]. In addition, it is difficult to recognize signatures that include different types of possible attacks. All the mistakes in detecting these signatures cause the increase of false alarm rate and decrease of detection technique's efficiency. Therefore, techniques which are based on rules can be used. Thus, the security expert can form the policies as rules then it is corresponded with data flow model. It is imperative that the methods based on rules in corresponding patterns be updated by security experts [2].

3   KDDCUP99 and NSL-KDD Datasets

Different data sets with various classifications have been presented for attacks up to now, but the [3] classification seems to be more complicated and more complete than the others and at the same time includes the whole qualities and capabilities of other classifiers. If there is a better description of attacks, the detection of them can be easily done by machine learning techniques. Since 1999, KDDCUP99 data set has been used in order to evaluate the anomaly detection method widely. This data set was prepared at Lincoln laboratory of MIT University by Stolfo et al. during 7 weeks with approximately 5 million records of data and the capacity of 4 GB in which each record had 100 bites capacity; this data set also constituted 41 features [4].

As regards with having a comprehensive analysis of the recent process in anomaly detection and according to previously reported researches which has been mentioned above, the highest detection rate of 98% and false detection rate of 2% can be obtained [5]. Despite highest rate of attack detection in academic researches, you can't see any machine learning methods in produced commercial devices. That's the reason, cyber security equipment manufacturers do not believe to efficiency of recently introduced technologies. In order to find out the reason of this contradiction, A.A. Ghorbani et al. [6] investigated the details of accomplished studies in anomaly detection domain and its different aspects, including: training, learning, testing and evaluation of data sets with variety methods. Their studies reveal that there are intrinsic problems in KDDCUP99 data set. Nevertheless, most of the researchers use this data set which is one of the prevalent data sets for anomaly detection and obtain unreliable results for ages. The first shortcoming of KDDCUP99 data set is the large amounts of data redundancy.

As regards with analyzing, training and testing data sets, it can be realized that nearly 78% and 75% of records of these sets are duplicated [6]. This large amount of data redundancy in the training set causes the machine learning algorithms don't have a good performance. As a result, having duplicated records in both testing and training sets has been reported a high percentage of detection by previous researchers in this area. While studying different machine learning algorithms and randomly selected instances from data sets as mentioned before, a high detection rate of 98% can be obtained. This amount is declined to approximately 86% in the worst conditions. A.A. Ghorbani et al. in [6] their research, by presenting KDDCUP99 problems acknowledged that the evaluated results in this area are unreliable. On the other hand, the existence of redundant, duplicated and repeated records in both testing and training tables is harmful and in reported papers the detection rates of these attacks are lower than other ones. Nevertheless, there is only a few numbers of such attacks in both tables and they do not follow a normal distribution. Thus, as the first step the redundancy of the training and testing data set records are eliminated and then the train records are eliminated which are repeated in the test table.

A new data set is presented as NSL-KDD in [8]. Although this new data set does not have the above mentioned problems, it still has the problems asserted by McHugh [7].

4   Related Works

Nowadays with the extensive development of computer networks and the rapid increase of special applications running in these networks, the importance of the security of these networks is being concerned. During the last decade, misuse and anomaly detections have been more concerned. The researchers about overcoming the flaws of misuse detection in novel attacks, and KDDCUP99 data set is highly being used for evaluation systems. For a long time, researches on intrusion detection range had been concentrated on anomaly and misuse detections. Since misuse detection is concentrated by commercials manufacturers for high level of detection ability and high amount of precision, anomaly detection is developing for the existence of high level of theoretical background in academic researches.

4.1   Naïve Bayes Method in Anomaly Detection

Conditional probability P(HjE) is used to compute the probability of H given E. H can be sampled as a column feature vector and can be considered as $X = x_1, x_2,...$ We calculate: P(Xjclass = Normal).P(Normal) and P(Xjclass = Attack).P(Attack), each part that becomes maximum, indicates that input data is Normal or Attack respectively. Adebayo et al. [9] has eliminated these features with using fuzzy methods but he has not given a clear explanation of how he did it: 0, 1, 8, 14, 15, 16, 17, 18, 19, 20, 21, 36 features from their test and carried out their evaluations based on only 22 features and used Naïve Bayes method with 5924 training data and 12130 test data, and finally the results were the same as those obtained from the whole features equal to 96.67%. Ben Amor et al. [10] for *DoS, U2R, R2L* and *Probe* attacks as well as for the normality of input packets using Naïve Bayes method obtained the accuracy of 96.38%, 11.84%, 7.11%, 78.18% and 96.64% respectively. At the same time the precision of 98.48% and 89.75% was reported for normal and abnormal detections respectively.

4.2   Decision Trees Method in Anomaly Detection

In artificial intelligence, trees are used for different concepts such as: sentences structures, equations, game modes, and so on. Decision trees learning is a way for approximation of the objective functions of discrete values. This method, which is resistant to noise of data, is able to learn the disjunction predicate conjunction. Pachghare et al. [11] detected the level of packet's normality about 99% without any preprocessing only by using decision trees and 1000 instances. In [13], with using "Feature Selection" technique and "InfoGain" method, the accuracy rate of 95% was obtained.

4.3   Support Vector Machine Method in Anomaly Detection

The main idea of the support- vector machines, [12, 13] is to increase the samples size as they can be separated. Hence, despite the fact that there is a common process in order to reduce the dimensions in the support vector machines, in reality the dimensions increase. The aim is to find a very dimensions, it may seem excessive as a volume). Teng et al.

[15] using the fuzzy and SVM methods and also dividing test dataset and train dataset to three groups performed their tests based on TCP, UDP, ICMP protocols and at the end they obtained 82.5% accuracy rate for a Single SVM and 91.2% of accuracy for a Multi SVM. In [15] article, Rung-Ching et al. obtained 89.13% of accuracy using SVM and Rough Set methods.

4.4   Artificial Neural Networks Method in Anomaly Detection

Multilayer perceptron (MLP) [12] is one of the most common algorithms being used in neural networks classification. Researchers use multilayer perceptron for detection of the attacks in KDDCUP99 data set [16]. Their structure consists of Feed-Forward, three-Layer neural networks: an input layer, a hidden layer and an output layer. Unipolar sigmoid transfer functions for each neuron in both hidden and output layers are used with deviation value of 1. The applied detection algorithm is a random descending gradient with the mean square error function. As a whole, there are 41 neurons in the input layer (pattern with 41 input features) and 5 neurons (one for each group) in the output layer. The reported results show that 88.7% of attacks are *probe*, 97.2% are *DoS*, 13.2% are *U2R* and 5.6% of attacks are *R2L* [16]. In [17], Abdulkader et al. using neural networks for some special *DoS* attacks with 24 neurons and a hidden layer, obtained 91,42% detection rate with 8,57% false detection rate. Their test revealed that even if they increased the number of neurons, the above ratios would not change. While Mukhopadhyay et al. used the back propagation neural network [18] with all 41 features; they used corrected data set as learned and test. As a result, from 311030 records of this data set, they used 217720 records for train and 46655 records as test and finally they reported 95.6% detection rate with 4.4% false detection rate.

5   Evaluation Made by Intelligence Algorithms on KDDCUP99 and NSL-KDD Datasets

As already mentioned, different tables have been extracted from KDDCUP99. Generally, in the published papers, random samples are used from kddcupdata10percent table, for training and testing, which finally give unreliable results. In this research, first of all the tables are selected using KDDCUP99 data set for evaluation and then they are compared with similar related works. In the next step, evaluations are done based on NSL-KDD Data Set as follows and finally the results are compared.

5.1   Preprocessing and Analysis of Various Methods on KDDCUP99 Data Set

First of all, from KDDCUP99 data set 10% of the corrected table is selected randomly as testing data with 17 novel attacks, and 10% of *kddcup.data_10_percent* table as training data. Analyzing the information in the tables with SQL Servers facilities (see Table 1), it can be clearly seen that *num_outbound_cmds* feature has the value of zero in all rows. Therefore, this feature is not used in our computations using machine learning techniques and the following results can be obtained:

Table 1. Random sample selection from KDDCUP99

Instances to Test	Instances to Train	R2L	U2R	DoS	Probe	Normal
31103	49402	988	3	23627	809	5676

We evaluated various methods on KDDCUP99 and compared them with [13–16] which are shown in Table 2 and Table 3.

Table 2. Comparison of accuracy various methods on KDDCUP99

Method	Accuracy	Attack	Normal
Ref [13] Decision tree feature selection	95.02%	–	–
Ref [16] Hybrid methods with 41 feature	95.06%	–	–
Decision Tree with 40 feature	96.32%	95.7%	99%
Naïve Bayes with 40 feature	96.42%	96%	97%
Neural Networks with 40 feature	96.56%	–	–
Ref [14] SVM	91.2%	–	–
Ref [15] SVM Feature Selection	95.65%	–	–
Single SVM with 40 feature	95.71%	–	–

Table 3. Analysis of various methods on KDDCUP99

Category of attacks	Ref [10] Naïve Bayes with 41 features	Naïve Bayes 40 features	Decision tree 40 features	Ref [16] Hybrid methods 41 features	Neural Networks 40 Features	Multi SVM 40 features	Naïve Bayes + DT 41 features
DoS	96.38%	99.4%	99.5%	97.2%	97.2%	99.81%	96.25%
U2R	11.84%	75.9%	66.7%	13.2%	0	0	23.68%
R2L	7.11%	0,09%	0,06%	5.6%	0	0	0,014%
Probe	78.18%	93.7%	99%	88.7%	95.67%	94.8%	60.37%
Normal	96.64%	95.8%	99.4%	–	98.90%	99.43%	94.12%

5.2 Preprocessing and Analysis of Various Methods on NSL-KDD Data Set

According to invalid results mentioned before, in order to obtain reliable and acceptable results, NSL-KDD data set will be used in this research. Generally, for obtaining high percentages in researches by using this data set, only the training table is used and unreliable results are obtained. For this reason in this research, from NSL-KDD data set

50% of records are extracted from two NSL-Train and NSL-Test tables randomly with an appropriate distribution of *Protocol*, *Service* and *Flag* features, by using a simple SQL command, then we will compare the results of learning machines with related works. When different researches are reviewed, it can be realized that the only valid and reliable research that corroborates our method of study is the research of A.A. Ghorbani et al. in [6]. According to the analysis on the tables in SQLServer, it is revealed that the *num_outbound_cmds* feature, in both tables has the value of zero for all rows. The nature of this field is used in ftp and has nothing to do with IDS. Accordingly, this feature is not used in our computations using machine learning methods. The results are shown by Table 4 and Table 5:

Table 4. Analysis of various methods on NSL-KDD

Category of attacks	Naïve Bayes 40 features	Decision tree 40 features	Neural networks 40 features	Multi SVM 40 features	Naïve Bayes + DT 41 features
DoS	70%	80%	72%	70%	70%
U2R	14%	0,08%	0.01%	0	0.045%
R2L	17.5%	16.2%	0.01%	0.09%	0.065%
Probe	86.5%	66.8%	49.7%	50%	65.2%
Normal	91.8%	98.5%			
Attack	71.9%	75.8%			

Table 5. Comparison with 40 features and Ref [6]

Methods	Ref [6] All features	With 40 features
Naïve Bayes	76.56%	78.24%
Decision Tree	81.05%	83.78%
Multi-Layer Perceptron	77.41%	78.4%
SVM	69.52%	70.8%

It can be concluded from Table 2, Table 3 and Table 4, Table 5 that:

1- The Naïve Bayes classification method for the detection of *U2R* and *R2L R2L* and *Probe* attacks is better than other approaches.
2- The Decision Trees classification method for the detection of *DoS* and *Probe* attacks is better than other approaches.
3- The Neural Networks classification method for the detection of *DoS* attacks is better than other approaches.
4- The Support Vector Machine classification method for the detection of *Normal* packets is better than other approaches.
5- The accuracy of Neural Networks for indicating of Normal/Attack is better than other approaches.

6   Feature Selection

Some studies on KDDCUP99 NSL-KDD data sets' showed researchers among feature selection techniques, select features that are important in the computation of accuracy and false positive and false negative detection. Moreover, they select the features most relevant to each other. Indeed, unnecessary features that decrease accuracy are ignored. These techniques increase the performance and reduce the time compared to normal situation (without selecting feature). InfoGain method is used for selection of features. Using this method has some problems in some attacks which will be discussed later. In this research, InfoGain method is used for selection of the most relevant features and then based on Naïve Bayes.

6.1   InfoGain

Suppose S is the set of labels with the corresponding labels and there are m classes and the sample s_i content from class I and s the number of samples in the train set. The expected information needed to classify a given set is calculated according to the following formula [19]:

$$I(s_1, s_2, \ldots, s_n) = -\sum_{i=1}^{m} \frac{s_i}{s} \log_2 \frac{s_i}{s} \tag{1}$$

The property F with values of $\{f_1, f_2, \ldots, f_v\}$ can be added to the training set inside v with subsets $\{S_1, S_2, \ldots, S_v\}$ so that S_j is a subset which has the value f_j for the attribute F. Furthermore, S_j is include S_{ij} samples of class i. The entropy of the attribute F is obtained by the following formula:

$$E(F) = \sum_{j=1}^{v} \frac{s_{1j} + \ldots + s_{mj}}{s} * I(S_{1j}, \ldots, S_{mj}) \tag{2}$$

Therefore:

$$InfoGain(F) = I(s_1, s_2, \ldots s_n) - E(F) \tag{3}$$

In this case, If we accomplish InfoGain algorithm on NSL-KDD data set we obtain this features: *Duration, service, src-bytes, dst-bytes, land, hot, num-failed-login, logged-in, num-compromised, Root-shell, su-attemped, num-root, num-file-creation, num-shells, num-access-files, is-host-login, is-guest-login.* So, when these features are used with Naïve Bayes, we can obtain results which have been represented in Table 6:

Table 6. Analysis InfoGain + Naïve Bayes on NSL-KDD

Attacks	InfoGain + Naïve Bayes	Naïve Bayes with 40 features
U2R	**57%**	14%
R2L	**19%**	17.5%
DoS	**73.4%**	70%
Probe	74%	**86.5%**

In these experiments, various tests with using different feature selection methods to select the best features are accomplished. However, when the evaluation is done based on "SVM", "Decision Trees", "Neural Networks" for the detection of Probe and DoS Attacks, have no good results are obtained.

7   Conclusion

Regardless of KDDCUP99 data sets defects, such as data redundancy and duplicated records, among the mentioned techniques based on McHugh and A.A.Ghorbani et al. reports in [6] and [7] respectively and also according to investigation conducted on KDDCUP99, it is concluded that decision trees and SVM work outperform other methods for detecting the normality of input packet. Also, Neural Networks have a better performance than other methods for detection of *DoS* attacks. Similarly, for the *Proble* attacks, "Decision Trees" are much better than the other methods. Meanwhile, "Naïve Bayes" is also the most effective method for detecting *U2R* and *R2L* attacks. The result of conducted evaluations on NSL-KDD data set shows that Feature Selection techniques in NSL-KDD data set cause problems at detection of *probe* attacks. It can be concluded that among mentioned techniques and investigations that have been conducted for the detection of normality of input packet and also detection of *DoS* attacks, decision trees report a better result than other techniques. For *Probe* attacks, "Naïve Bayes" technique is better than the others and for *U2R* and *R2L* attacks; "InfoGain" and "Naïve Bayes" techniques have better results. For detecting *DoS, Probe,* normality input packets all the features except feature *num_outbound_cmds* should be used. This summary is shown in Fig. 2:

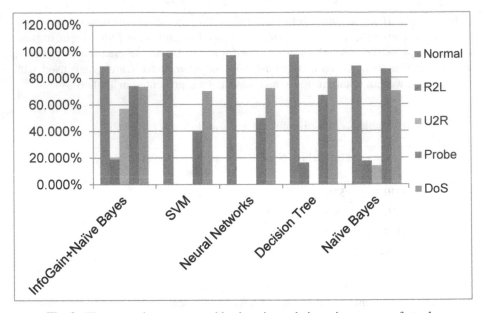

Fig. 2. The comparison some machine learning techniques in category of attacks

References

1. Lazarevic, A., Ertoz, L., Ozgur, A., Srivastava, J., Kumar, V.: A comparative study of anomaly detection schemes in network intrusion detection. In: Proceedings of Third SIAM Conference on Data Mining (2003)
2. Sabhnani, M., Serpen, G.: Application of machine learning algorithms to KDDCUP99 intrusion detection dataset within misuse detection context. In: International Conference on Machine Learning Models, Technologies and Applications Proceedings, pp. 209–215 (2004)
3. KDDCUP99 Dataset. https://kdd.ics.uci.edu/databases/kddcup99
4. Stolfo, S.J., Fan, W., Lee, W., Prodromidis, A., Chan, P.K.: Cost based modeling for fraud and intrusion detection: Results from the jam project, discex, vol. 02, p. 1130 (2000)
5. Shyu, S., Chen, K., Sarinnapakorn, K., Chang, L.: A novel anomaly detection scheme based on principal component classifier. In: Proceedings of the IEEE Foundations and New Directions of Data Mining Workshop, in conjunction with the Third IEEE International Conference on Data Mining (ICDM 2003), pp. 172–179 (2003)
6. Tavallaee, M., Bagheri, E., Lu, W., Ghorbani, A.: A detailed analysis of the KDDCUP99 data set. In: Submitted to Second IEEE Symposium on Computational Intelligence for Security and Defense Applications (CISDA) (2009)
7. McHugh, J.: Testing intrusion detection systems: a critique of the 1998 and 1999 Darpa intrusion detection system evaluations as performed by lincoln laboratory. ACM Trans. Inf. Syst. Secur. **3**(4), 262–294 (2000)
8. Nsl-kdd data set for network-based intrusion detection systems. https://nsl.cs.unb.ca/NSL-KDD
9. Adetunmbi Adebayo, O., Shi, Z., Shi, Z., Adewale, O.S.: Network anomalous intrusion detection using fuzzy-bayes. In: Shi, Z., Shimohara, K., Feng, D. (eds.) IIP 2006. IIFIP, vol. 228, pp. 525–530. Springer, Boston, MA (2006). https://doi.org/10.1007/978-0-387-44641-7_56

10. Amor, N.B., Benferhat, S., Elouedi, Z.: Naïve Bayesian Networks in Intrusion Detection Systems. In: 14th European Conference on Machine Learning (Dubrovnik) (2003)
11. Pachghare, V.K., Kulkarni, P.: pattern based network security using decision trees and support vector machine, Department of Computer Engineering And Information Technology College of Engineering, Pune, India. IEEE (2011)
12. Werbos, P.J.: Beyond regression. New tools for prediction and analysis in the behavioral sciences, Ph.D. thesis, Harvard University (1974)
13. Rajesh, R., Sheen, S.: Network Intrusion Detection using Feature Selection and Decision tree classifier (2008)
14. Teng, S., Du, H., Wu, N., Zhang, W., Su, J.: A cooperative network intrusion detection based on fuzzy SVMs. J. Networks 5(4), 475, Academy Publisher (2010)
15. Chen, R.-C., Cheng, K.-F., Hsieh, C.F.: Using rough set and support vector machine for network intrusion detection. Int. J. Network Secur. Appl. (IJNSA) 1(1) (2009)
16. Sabhnani, M., Serpen, G.: Application of machine learning algorithms to KDDCUP99 intrusion detection dataset within misuse detection context. In: International Conference on Machine Learning, Models, Technologies and Applications Proceedings, pp. 209–215 (2004)
17. Alfantookh, A.A.: DoS Attacks Intelligent Detection using Neural Networks, Department of Computer Science, College of Computer and Information Sciences King Saud University, P.O. Box 51178, Riyadh 11543, Saudi Arabia (2005)
18. Mukhopadhyay, I., Chakraborty, M., Chakrabarti, S., Chatterjee, T.: Back propagation neural network approach to intrusion detection system. In: International Conference on Recent Trends in Information Systems, Department of Information Technology, Institute of Engineering and Management (2011)
19. Kayacık, H.G., Zincir-Heywood, A.N., Heywood, M.I.: Selecting Features for Intrusion Detection: A Feature Relevance Analysis on KDDCUP 99 Intrusion Detection Datasets (2005)

Deep Neural Network Based Malicious Network Activity Detection Under Adversarial Machine Learning Attacks

Ferhat Ozgur Catak$^{(\boxtimes)}$ (ID) and Sule Yildirim Yayilgan

Department of Information Security and Communication Technology,
NTNU Norwegian University of Science and Technology, 2815 Gjøvik, Norway
{ferhat.o.catak,sule.yildirim}@ntnu.no

Abstract. Machine learning-based computational intelligence methods are used more often recently in the cybersecurity area, especially for malicious network activity detection. ML based solutions have been used and discussed by a significant number of authors in literature. Several methods, including deep learning, are used to develop models for solving this issue. So far, attackers try to generate malicious activities in a network to put down several system services or steal some information from the databases. More recent designs of security components use predictive modeling approach to detect such kind of attacks. Thus, the new target for the attackers is machine learning algorithm itself. Previous studies in cybersecurity have almost exclusively focused on attack detection in a network. Another promising line of attack detection research would be machine learning algorithm protection. There are some attacks against deep learning models in the literature, including fast-gradient sign method (FGSM) attack. This attack is the purest form of the gradient-based evading technique that is used by attackers to evade the classification model. This paper presents a new approach to protect a malicious activity detection model from the FGSM attack. Hence, we explore the power of applying adversarial training to build a robust model against FGSM attacks. Accordingly, (1) dataset enhanced with the adversarial examples; (2) deep neural network-based detection model is trained using the KDDCUP99 dataset to learn the FGSM based attack patterns. We applied this training model to the benchmark cyber security dataset.

Keywords: Cyber security · Machine learning · Adversarial attacks · Adversarial machine learning

1 Introduction

Machine learning (ML) has been part of the cybersecurity area, especially in malicious activity detection since the 2000s, and its applications are increasing day by day [2,12]. Predictive modeling in cybersecurity is attracting considerable

© Springer Nature Switzerland AG 2021
S. Yildirim Yayilgan et al. (Eds.): INTAP 2020, CCIS 1382, pp. 280–291, 2021.
https://doi.org/10.1007/978-3-030-71711-7_23

interest due to its flexibility to detect the different patterns of the same attack type. For the future, ML is considered as the de facto solution for security components, especially for the distributed denial of service attacks detection [5,13].

Intrusion detection systems (IDS) and intrusion prevention systems (IPS) are commonly used for preventing different cyber-attacks types. Early IPS/IDS components used signature-based attack detections. Thus, they are not capable of detecting changes in the attack pattern. When the attacker changes the signature of the attack, such as adding some bits to a network packet's payload, the attacker can evade its attack [1,8,11].

Some early studies focus on descriptive statistics to detect malicious network flow. A most known type of network attack is distributed denial of service (DDoS). In a typical DDoS attack, hackers utilize the compromised computers that hacked earlier, to generate significant network traffic to a victim system or computer. Such unusual differences could be discovered using descriptive-analytical techniques. Feinstein et al. [9] use Chi-Square statistics to classify network flow volume irregularities, is correct. The keyword is *volume* for DDoS attacks. The authors introduced time window based entropy fluctuations in a flow volume to detect malicious traffic.

Descriptive statistics based discovery schemes have relied on previously recorded data. A distinct disadvantage of this type of method is that network flux irregularities are a timely fluid target [4]. It is essential to discriminate against the set of malicious traffic precisely. On the other hand, attackers continue to develop a new type of malicious traffic. Consequently, a malicious traffic classification model needs to bypass the overfit problem to any predefined set of malicious traffic types.

Even if such overfitting problems are solved, the attackers always try to find other evading techniques for the security components. One of the most powerful evading techniques against ML-based detection method is adversarial machine learning. The adversarial machine learning has been used to describe the attacks to machine learning models, which tries to mislead models by malicious input instances. Figure 1 shows the typical adversarial machine learning attack.

A typical machine learning model basically consists of two stages as training time and decision time. Thus, the adversarial machine learning attacks occur in either training time or decision time. The techniques used by hackers for adversarial machine learning can be divided into two, according to the time of the attack:

- *Data Poisoning*: The attacker changes some labels of training input instances to mislead the output model.
- *Model Poisoning*: The hacker drives model to produce false labeling using some perturbated instance after the model is created.

The main contributions of this research are to detect network attacks using window-based training input instances according to deep neural networks under adversarial machine learning attacks for model poisoning by hackers. We per-

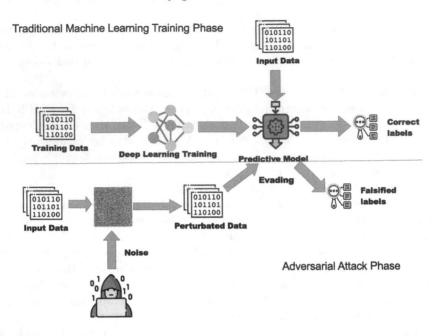

Fig. 1. A typical adversarial machine learning attack.

formed adversarial training based model building and deep neural network algorithm based classification to detect normal network behavior and malicious activities, including denial of service (DOS), probe, remote-to-local (r2l), and normal behavior. The primary purpose of the introduced design is to use a mixture model strategy [15,19] for precise classification of malicious network flow from several network packets. The adversarial training part of the proposed model increase robustness against adversarial instances. The deep neural network model layer tries to find out the exact malicious activity class. Our model is able to respond to the model attacks by hackers who use the adversarial machine learning methods. Figure 2 illustrates the system architecture used to protect the model and to classify correctly.

Our system consists of three main parts, data enhancing, algorithm training, and classification.

The rest of the paper is organized as follows: The related work is presented in Sect. 2. Section 3 gives brief preliminary information. Our model evaluation and real system test results are presented in Sect. 4. The concluding remarks are given in Sect. 5.

2 Related Work

In recent years, with the rise of the machine learning attacks, various researches have been submitted to build preventive actions against this kind of attacks.

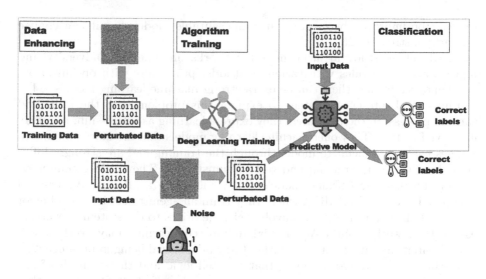

Fig. 2. General system architecture. Architecture consists of 3 parts; data enhancing, algorithm training, and classification.

Data infertility and learning resistance are suggested as countermeasures in fixing a machine learning training phase [20]. Most of the researches in these areas has been adjusted on particular adversarial attacks and usually showed the theoretical analysis of the adversarial machine learning area [10,14].

Bo Li et al. present a binary domain and classifications. In their work, the proposal begins with mixed-integer linear programming (MILP) with constraint generation and provides instructions on top of these techniques. They further practice the Stackelberg game multi-adversary model algorithm and the other algorithm that feeds back the produced adversarial examples to the training phase, which is called as RAD (Retraining with Adversarial Examples) [16]. Contrarily, their research is individual and operates only in particular systems. It is offered as a comprehensive protection scheme. They have suggested a system that achieves healthy outcomes.

Furthermore, Xiao et al. present a technique to enhance the speed of defense training toward the rectified linear unit (ReLU) [21]. They apply weight sparsity and RELU confidence for reliable confirmation. Their methodology does not present a comprehensive proposal.

Yu et al. suggest a study that can decide the neural network's features under opposed attacks. In their study, the relationship between the input training data and malicious instances is presented. Furthermore, the relationship between the network strength and the decision surface geometry as a sign of the malicious strength of the neural network is presented. By spreading the loss surface to decision surface and other several ways, they provide adversarial robustness by decision surface. The geometry of the decision surface cannot be confirmed mostly, and there is no exact decision border between right or faulty prediction. Robustness can be improved by creating an immeasurable model, but it can change with attack strength [25].

Mardy et al. study artificial neural networks immune with adversity and improve accuracy scales with various methods, principally with optimization, and demonstrate that there can be extra strong machine learning models [24].

Pinto et al. present a system to explain this problem with the promoted learning process. In their research, they express learning as a zero-sum, minimax objective function. They offer machine learning models that are more immune to changes that are difficult to model through the training and are strongly influenced by changes in training and test circumstances. They induce reinforced learning on machine learning models. They introduce a "Robust Adversarial Reinforced Learning" (RARL), where they train an agent to act in the behavior of a destabilizing adversary that involves change drives to the system. Nevertheless, in their work, Robust Adversarial Reinforced Learning may overfit itself, and seldom it can miss predicting without any adversarial being in presence [22].

Carlini et al. propose a model that the self-logic and the strength of the machine learning model with a strong attack can be affected. They prove that these types of attacks can often be used to evaluate the effectiveness of potential defenses. They propose defensive distillation as a general-purpose procedure to increase robustness [6].

Harding et al. similarly investigate the effects of malicious input instances generated from targeted and non-targeted attacks in decision making. They provide that non-targeted samples are more effective than targeted samples in human perception and categorization of decisions [3].

Bai et al. present a convolutional autoencoder model with the adversarial decoders to automate the generation of adversarial samples. They produce adversary examples by a convolutional autoencoder model and use pooling computations and sampling tricks to achieve these results. After this process, an adversarial decoder automates the generation of adversarial samples. Adversarial sampling is useful, but it cannot provide adversarial robustness on its own, and sampling tricks are too specific [18].

Sahay et al. propose an FGSM attack and use an autoencoder to denoise the test data. They have also used an autoencoder to denoise the test data, which is trained with both corrupted and healthy data. Then they reduce the dimension of the denoised data. These autoencoders are specifically designed to compress data effectively and reduce dimensions. Hence, it may not be wholly generalized, and training with corrupted data requires many adjustments to get better test results [17].

I-Ting Chen et al. also provide with FGSM attack on denoising autoencoders. They analyze the attacks from the perspective that attacks can be applied stealthily. They use autoencoders to filter data before applied to the model and compare it with the model without an autoencoder filter. They use autoencoders mainly focused on the stealth aspect of these attacks and used them specifically against FGSM with specific parameters [7].

Gondim-Ribeiro et al. propose autoencoders attacks. In their work, they attack 3 types of autoencoders: Simple variational autoencoders, convolutional variational autoencoders, and DRAW (Deep Recurrent AttentiveWriter). They propose to scheme an attack on autoencoders. As they accept that "No attack can both convincingly reconstruct the target while keeping the distortions on the input imperceptible". This method cannot be used to achieve robustness against adversarial attacks [23].

3   Preliminary Information

In this section, we will briefly describe adversarial machine learning, attack environments, and adversarial training that we have used in this study.

3.1   Adversarial Machine Learning

Machine learning model attacks have been utilized mostly by attackers to evade security components that protect a network. Attackers also apply model evasion attacks for phishing attacks, spams, and executing malware code in an analysis environment. There are also some advantages to hackers in misclassification and misdirection of models. Such attacks, the attacker does not change training instances. Instead, he tries to make some small perturbations in input instances in the model's decision time to make this new input instance seem safe (normal behavior). We mainly concentrate on this kind of adversarial attacks in this study. There are many attacking methods for deep learning models, and FGSM is the most straightforward and powerful attack type. We only focus on the FGSM attack, but our solution to prevent this attack can be applied to other adversarial machine learning attacks.

Fast-Gradient Sign Method (FGSM). FGSM works by utilizing the gradients of the neural network to create an adversarial example to evade the model. For an input instance $\mathbf{x}$, the FGSM utilizes the gradients ∇_x of the loss value ℓ for the input instance to build a new instance $\mathbf{x}_{adv}$ that maximizes the loss value of the classifier hypothesis h. This new instance is named the adversarial instance. We can summarize the FGSM using the following explanation:

$$\eta = \epsilon * sign(\nabla_x J(\theta, \mathbf{x}, y)) \tag{1}$$

3.2   Adversarial Training

Adversarial training is a widely recommended defense that implies generating adversarial instances using the gradient of the victim classifier, and then retraining the model with the adversarial instances and their respective labels. This technique has demonstrated to be efficient in defending models from adversarial attacks.

Let us first think a common classification problem with a training instances $X \in \mathbb{R}^{m \times n}$ of dimension d, a label space Y We assume the classifier h_θ has been trained to minimize a loss function ℓ as follows:

$$min_{\theta} \frac{1}{m} \sum_{i=1}^{m} \ell(h_\theta(\mathbf{x}_i, y_i)) \tag{2}$$

Given a classifier model $h_\theta(\cdot)$ and an input instance x, whose responding output is y, an adversarial instance x^* is an input such that:

$$h_\theta(x^*) \neq y \quad \wedge \quad d(x, x^*) < \epsilon \tag{3}$$

where $d(\cdot, \cdot)$ is the distance metric between two input instances original input x and adversarial version x^*. Most actual adversarial model attacks transform Eq. 3 into the following optimization problem:

$$\underset{x}{\operatorname{argmax}} \, \ell\left(h_\theta(x^*), y\right) \tag{4}$$

$$s.t. d(x, x^*) < \epsilon \tag{5}$$

where ℓ is loss function between predicted output $h(\cdot)$ and correct label y.

In order to mitigate such attacks, at per training step, the conventional training procedure from Eq. 2 is replaced with a min-max objective function to minimize the expected value of the maximum loss, as follows:

$$\underset{\theta}{min} \, \underset{(x,y)}{\mathbb{E}} \left(\underset{d(x,x^*)<\epsilon}{max} \ell(h(x^*), y) \right) \tag{6}$$

4   Experiments

In this section, we conduct experiments on the KDDCUP99 dataset from the publicly available data set repositories. We implemented the proposed mitigation method using Keras and TensorFlow libraries in the Python environment.

In Fig. 3a, the training history of the model, which uses normal input instances, is shown. As it can be seen in history, the graph of loss and accuracy progresses smoothly. Figure 3b shows the confusion matrix of the test data set using the trained model. As can be seen from the Figure, the classification performance of the model for normal instances is quite good. Figure 3c shows the confusion matrix of adversarial samples. As can be seen from the graph, the classification performance of the model decreases considerably.

In order to show the effect of adversarial samples on the model in more detail, we have shown the results of the classification reports in Table 1–2. According to these tables, the weighted average $F1$ value of the benign test dataset is 0.997379. The weighted $F1$ value of the adversarial dataset, which was created from the same model and created from the test dataset, dramatically decreased up to 0.176636. As one can see here, a classification model created by applying only the training data is highly vulnerable to adversarial attacks.

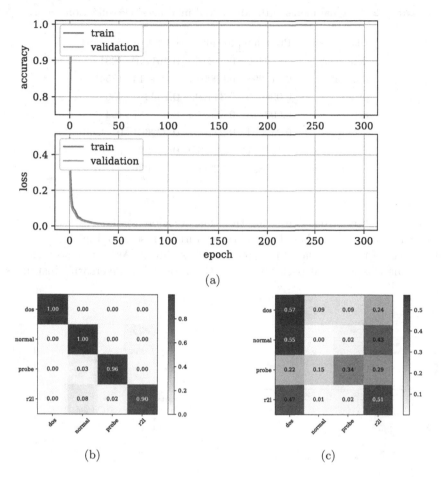

Fig. 3. Original classifier model for KDDCUP99 dataset. (a) accuracy and loss plot with epoch, (b) test dataset confusion matrix, (c) adversarial instances confusion matrix.

Table 1. Original model with normal instances' classification report

Classes	Precision	Recall	F1-score	Support
dos	0.998901	0.999450	0.999175	10911
normal	0.997949	0.998119	0.998034	17546
probe	0.971239	0.962719	0.966960	456
r2l	0.920635	0.896907	0.908616	194
accuracy	0.997389	0.997389	0.997389	0.997389
macro avg	0.972181	0.964299	0.968196	29107
weighted avg	0.997372	0.997389	0.997379	29107

Table 2. Original model with adversarial instances' classification report

Classes	Precision	Recall	F1-score	Support
dos	0.388392	0.569150	0.461710	10911
normal	0.014298	0.000912	0.001714	17546
probe	0.098680	0.344298	0.153395	456
r2l	0.009416	0.505155	0.018487	194
accuracy	0.222661	0.222661	0.222661	0.222661
macro avg	0.127697	0.354879	0.158827	29107
weighted avg	0.155820	0.222661	0.176636	29107

Figure 4a shows the history of the classification model trained using the adversarial training method for the train and test set. In Fig. 4b, the confusion matrix of the adversarial training model is shown. As can be seen from the Figure, the classification performance of the model for adversarial instances is quite good.

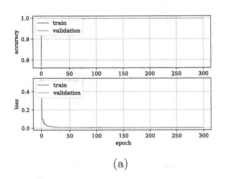

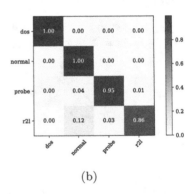

(a)   (b)

Fig. 4. Adversarial trained classifier model for KDDCUP99 dataset. (a) accuracy and loss plot with epoch, (b) adversarial instances confusion matrix.

In order to show the effect of adversarial training on the model in more detail, we have shown the results of the classification report in Table 3. According to these tables, the weighted average $F1$ value of the benign test dataset is 0.996858.

According to the table, the original vulnerable model's $F1$ metric decreases up to 0.176636 with adversarial input instances, while the original $F1$ value was 0.996858. With our protection methods, the new classification model's $F1$ metric is 0.996858, almost the same as the original $F1$ metric. As can be seen, the malicious network traffic classification model shows high classification performance with only a small loss.

Table 3. Adversarial trained model with adversarial instances' classification report

Classes	Precision	Recall	F1-score	Support
dos	0.998901	0.999542	0.999221	10911
normal	0.997493	0.997948	0.997721	17546
probe	0.975281	0.951754	0.963374	456
r2l	0.873684	0.855670	0.864583	194
accuracy	0.996874	0.996874	0.996874	0.996874
macro avg	0.961340	0.951229	0.956225	29107
weighted avg	0.996848	0.996874	0.996858	29107

5   Conclusion

In this study, we explained the methods of developing model robustness to adversarial instances during the detection of malicious network attacks. The malicious network traffic detection methods is a mature research subject in the literature, but how the model itself behaves under adversarial attack is not much researched. Attackers want to continue their malicious activities by evading network security components by applying adversarial machine learning techniques. With the increasing use of machine learning models in cybersecurity soon, there will be an increase in such attacks. In this study, we would have recommended a method to detect malicious network traffic by keeping the classification performance almost identical even under the attack of the model itself that detects network attacks. Attackers can reduce the $F1$ value of a model used without this precaution from 0.997379 to 0.176636. With our method, the $F1$ value decreases only to 0.996858, detecting malicious network traffic at very high rates.

In this study, we examined the FGSM attack. In future studies, we plan to improve our robustness method by analyzing other attack methods such as the basic iterative method and DeepFool.

References

1. Abeshu, A., Chilamkurti, N.: Deep learning: the frontier for distributed attack detection in fog-to-things computing. IEEE Commun. Mag. **56**(2), 169–175 (2018)
2. Ben-Asher, N., Gonzalez, C.: Effects of cyber security knowledge on attack detection. Comput. Hum. Behav. **48**, 51–61 (2015). https://doi.org/10.1016/j.chb.2015.01.039, http://www.sciencedirect.com/science/article/pii/S0747563215000539
3. Harding, S., Rajivan, P., Bertenthal, B.I., Gonzalez, C.: Human decisions on targeted and non-targeted adversarial sample, August 2018. https://mindmodeling.org/cogsci2018/papers/0103/index.html
4. Bhuyan, M.H., Bhattacharyya, D., Kalita, J.: An empirical evaluation of information metrics for low-rate and high-rate DDoS attack detection. Pattern Recogn. Lett. **51**, 1–7 (2015). https://doi.org/10.1016/j.patrec.2014.07.019, http://www.sciencedirect.com/science/article/pii/S016786551400244X

5. Cappers, B.C.M., van Wijk, J.J.: Snaps: Semantic network traffic analysis through projection and selection. In: 2015 IEEE Symposium on Visualization for Cyber Security (VizSec), pp. 1–8, October 2015. https://doi.org/10.1109/VIZSEC.2015.7312768

6. Carlini, N., Wagner, D.A.: Towards evaluating the robustness of neural networks. CoRR abs/1608.04644, August 2016. http://arxiv.org/abs/1608.04644

7. Chen, I., Sirkeci-Mergen, B.: A comparative study of autoencoders against adversarial attacks. International Conference on Image Processing, Computer Vision, and Pattern Recognition, August 2018. https://csce.ucmss.com/cr/books/2018/LFS/CSREA2018/IPC3651.pdf

8. Diro, A.A., Chilamkurti, N.: Distributed attack detection scheme using deep learning approach for internet of things. Future Gener. Comput. Syst. **82**, 761–768 (2018). https://doi.org/10.1016/j.future.2017.08.043, http://www.sciencedirect.com/science/article/pii/S0167739X17308488

9. Feinstein, L., Schnackenberg, D., Balupari, R., Kindred, D.: Statistical approaches to DDoS attack detection and response. In: Proceedings DARPA Information Survivability Conference and Exposition, vol. 1, pp. 303–314, April 2003. https://doi.org/10.1109/DISCEX.2003.1194894

10. Isakov, M., Gadepally, V., Gettings, K.M., Kinsy, M.A.: Survey of attacks and defenses on edge-deployed neural networks, November 2019. https://arxiv.org/abs/1911.11932

11. Han, F., Xu, L., Yu, X., Tari, Z., Feng, Y., Hu, J.: Sliding-mode observers for real-time DDoS detection. In: 2016 IEEE 11th Conference on Industrial Electronics and Applications (ICIEA), pp. 825–830, June 2016. https://doi.org/10.1109/ICIEA.2016.7603695

12. Jasiul, B., Szpyrka, M., Śliwa, J.: Detection and modeling of cyber attacks with petri nets. Entropy **16**(12), 6602–6623 (2014). https://doi.org/10.3390/e16126602, http://www.mdpi.com/1099-4300/16/12/6602

13. Jiang, D., Xu, Z., Zhang, P., Zhu, T.: A transform domain-based anomaly detection approach to network-wide traffic. J. Netw. Comput. Appl. **40**, 292–306 (2014). https://doi.org/10.1016/j.jnca.2013.09.014, http://www.sciencedirect.com/science/article/pii/S1084804513002038

14. Guo, J., Zhao, Y., Han, X., Jiang, Y., Sun, J.: RNN-test: adversarial testing framework for recurrent neural network systems, November 2019. https://arxiv.org/abs/1911.06155

15. Latif, S., Rana, R., Qadir, J.: Adversarial machine learning and speech emotion recognition: utilizing generative adversarial networks for robustness. CoRR abs/1811.11402 (2018), http://arxiv.org/abs/1811.11402

16. Li, B., Vorobeychik, Y.: Evasion-robust classification on binary domains. ACM Trans. Knowl. Discov. Data **12**(4), 50:1–50:32 (2018). https://doi.org/10.1145/3186282, https://doi.org/10.1145/3186282

17. Mahfuz, R.S.R., Gamal, A.E.: Combatting adversarial attacks through denoising and dimensionality reduction: a cascaded autoencoder approach. CoRR abs/1812.03087, December 2018. http://arxiv.org/abs/1812.03087

18. Quan, W.B.C., Luo, Z.: Alleviating adversarial attacks via convolutional autoencoder, pp. 53–58, June 2017. https://doi.org/10.1109/SNPD.2017.8022700

19. Ren, K., Zheng, T., Qin, Z., Liu, X.: Adversarial attacks and defenses in deep learning. Engineering **6**(3), 346–360 (2020). https://doi.org/10.1016/j.eng.2019.12.012, http://www.sciencedirect.com/science/article/pii/S209580991930503X

20. Huang, L., Joseph, A.D., Nelson, B., Rubinstein, B.I., Tygar, J.D.: Adversarial machine learning. In: Proceedings of the 4th ACM Workshop on Security and Artificial Intelligence, AISec 2011, pp. 43–58. ACM, New York, October 2011. https://doi.org/10.1145/2046684.2046692, http://doi.acm.org/10.1145/2046684.2046692
21. Xiao, K.Y., Tjeng, V., Shafiullah, N.M., Madry, A.: Training for faster adversarial robustness verification via inducing ReLU stability. CoRR abs/1809.03008, September 2018. http://arxiv.org/abs/1809.03008
22. Pinto, L., Davidson, J., Sukthankar, R., Gupta, A.: Robust adversarial reinforcement learning. CoRR abs/1703.02702, March 2017. http://arxiv.org/abs/1703.02702
23. Tabacof, G.G.P., Valle, E.: Adversarial attacks on variational autoencoders. CoRR abs/1806.04646, June 2018. http://arxiv.org/abs/1806.04646
24. Madry, A., Makelov, A., Schmidt, L., Tsipras, D., Vladu, A: Towards deep learning models resistant to adversarial attacks. CoRR abs/1706.06083, June 2017. http://arxiv.org/abs/1706.06083
25. Yu, F., Liu, C., Wang, Y., Zhao, L., Chen, X.: Interpreting adversarial robustness: a view from decision surface in input space. CoRR abs/1810.00144, September 2018. http://arxiv.org/abs/1810.00144

Towards Low Cost and Smart Load Testing as a Service Using Containers

Berrak Alara Baransel, Alper Peker, Hilmi Omer Balkis, and Ismail Ari[(✉)]

Özyegin University, Istanbul, Turkey
ismail.ari@ozyegin.edu.tr

Abstract. Providing end-users with high quality e-commerce, online communication, education services requires careful performance monitoring, tuning and prediction under heavy traffic loads. To address this issue, we propose and evaluate a novel methodology using Docker containers for load testing. Our experience over several benchmarks, local machines vs. Cloud, and web servers suggest that load testing as a service requires a multi-dimensional optimization over slave counts, network latencies, bandwidth, and traffic patterns and there are opportunities for learning these parameters that can later be modelled into a smart load testing algorithm, with machine learning at the driver seat. Beyond the ease and speed of deployment, containers and cloud also provide a low cost alternative to load testing; we completed our cloud experiments by spending only $10. The only disadvantage of public clouds can be their centralized nature and distance to real customer bases.

Keywords: Load testing · Container · Docker · Cloud · Jmeter · Kubernetes · Django

1 Introduction

Today, all global activities including communication, finance, commerce and education run through the world wide web (WWW) and modern cloud computing services. One of the biggest problems of online service providers is to handle the heavy traffic on their sites by predicting and provisioning accordingly. Both under-provisioning and over-provisioning of computing resources are very costly, leading to business interruption in the former and bankruptcy in the latter cases. In certain scenarios, the business (*e.g.* e-commerce) owner and the IP service provider may be two different entities contracted through Service-Level Agreements (SLA). In that case, simple and smart load testing via contained services will be an essential tool for the businesses to cross-examine their providers for compliance to their SLA.

Creating hi-fidelity test environments that fully represent real customer experience over multi-tier systems is hard. There are lots of platform dependencies and variabilities that affect the end result, *e.g.* differences in hardware capacities, operating systems, virtualization and container technologies used, web servers – browsers and/or public cloud

S. Yildirim Yayilgan et al. (Eds.): INTAP 2020, CCIS 1382, pp. 292–302, 2021.
https://doi.org/10.1007/978-3-030-71711-7_24

service details. Configuring and testing all possible combinations requires tremendous time, which is a luxury in today's fast moving world.

Containerization [1], is a recent term that refers to packaging related applications and their dependencies together so that they can be replicated, migrated, shared, deployed, started, scaled up & down dynamically. This flexibility caused containers to be strongly associated with software development and operations (DevOps) architectures. Recent surveys of Chief Information Officers (CIO) reveal that adoption rate of containers is more than 70% globally among IT professionals and developers. Thus, the distinction between the development, integration and deployment environments will diminish over time. This practice is also called Continuous Integration and Continuous Delivery (CI/CD). However, different dimensions of containerized load testing have not been extensively explored in prior work.

2 Background and Related Work

Automatic load testing using containers has recently attracted attention of many software and systems companies including Oracle [2], Broadcom (CA, Inc.) [3] and Huawei (Futurewei) [4] as can be seen from their recent patent applications. In general terms, these proposals containerize applications, create a workload profile, orchestrate the deployment and monitor the results. Yet, they do not differentiate between local or cloud-based deployment and use machine learning to train models over load testing benchmarks whereas in this paper we execute and highlight these aspects as well.

Table 1 summarizes main tiers involved in load testing, different test parameters for each tier, and possible values they can take. On the client side there can be different browsers and HTTP versions, different workload generators to record & replay tests [5] and replicate them at scale [6]. Selenium [5] is a functional testing tool for web applications, which helps UI/Web developers save clicks and movements on a web site and then playback at scale. Jmeter [6] is a Java application that allows load testing with simple test plans; we prepared Dockerized and distributed (master-slave) test environments with Jmeter. Implementation details and results will be given in Sect. 3 and Sect. 4, respectively.

Whether workers (*a.k.a* slaves) are physical, virtual or container-based as well as their allocated capacities (cores, MB) are important parameters. The client side performance results are measured in terms of latency, APDEX index [7], throughput and error rates. APDEX (Application Performance Index) provides unified measure for satisfied and unsatisfied users [7–9]. Responses under user's toleration threshold are considered satisfied (S), counted and given a full score (1), requests that are not satisfied but tolerated (T) are given a half (0.5) score and requests that caused frustration (F) are given no (0) score.

$$APDEX = (SatisfiedCount * 1 + ToleratingCount * 0.5 + F * 0)/TotalRequests \quad (1)$$

We used the default Toleration threshold (Tt = 0.5 s) and Frustration threshold (Ft = 1.5 s) values in Jmeter. The static nature of APDEX thresholds has been a subject of criticism claiming that users can be more patient with different applications. However,

Table 1. Summary of tiers and parameters effecting load testing as a service.

Tiers	Test parameter	Possible tools & values (Categorical or Scalar)
Client side	Browser, HTTP protocol	Chrome, IE, Firefox, Safari, Opera, Netscape, wget, curl and HTTP 1.x, 2.x, 3.x (QUIC)
	Workload generation	Selenium, Jmeter (# Slaves/Workers, Thread count, Ramp-up time, Hold time)
	HW and OS technology	Physical, VM (Local or IaaS), Docker
	Max. & Utilized capacity	# CPU cores, Memory GB, I/O MB/sec
	Performance results	Latency, APDEX (T, F), Throughput, Error Rate
Network	Distance and capacity	Latency (ms), Bandwidth (Mbps, Gbps)
	Intermediaries	If Exists? (Proxy, Load balancer, Firewall, CDN)
Server side	Scale	Thread pool size (# threads/server)
	Web, App, DB servers	Apache, IIS, Node.js, NGINX, Django, React, SQL, NoSQL

we argue that user patience has diminished drastically over years to these selected values, whether the application is an e-commerce site or a news channel. People can *and will* find alternatives to slow web sites very quickly. In the future, APDEX may be replaced by more elaborate SLA definitions. Other client perceived performance values include throughput for bulk data transfers and HTTP errors. We observe that a system under test (SUT) can respond with HTTP error codes (500) and finding those limits is a part of the learning here.

The network performance parameters such as latency and bandwidth, and whether there are any intermediaries (proxy, balancer, firewall, CDN) between clients-servers can also be important in load testing. Server side parameters include number of web servers and their multi-threading capacity. Apache, IIS, Node.js, NGINX are among the top web servers and Django, React are among the top web frameworks supporting news portals, e-commerce sites and educational systems. Django [10] follows the MVC (Model-View-Controller) architectural design pattern. In this paper, we focus on load testing and do not consider other types of software tests including unit, functional or acceptance tests.

Other orthogonal, but related topics include cost of running the loads tests in terms of capital and operational expenses (CAPEX, OPEX) and related security issues such as the "load test as a service" being mistaken as a Denial of Service (DoS) attack on the server side. During our load tests we did not encounter any firewall or security blockage.

3   Implementation and Initial Trials

The preparation for application containment (*i.e.* Dockerization) simply includes writing a Dockerfile for selecting the apps and using "docker build" to create the docker images. Next, we push images to the DockerHub [11] repository using "docker push", so that they can be easily pulled over to different machines on which the load tests will be executed, as shown in Fig. 1. DockerHub is similar to the Github, but for sharing containers instead of software. Load testing providers can build their private repositories to accumulate their images containing different software, libraries, plugins, versions, patches, *i.e.* overall know-how gained from different customer experiences over time. Finally, we use "docker compose" (YAML) to bind images to web ports and other services.

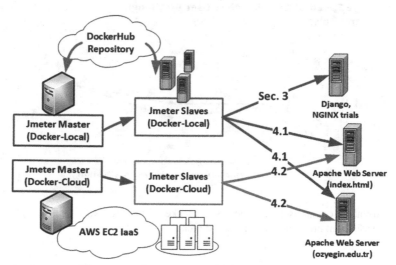

Fig. 1. Load testing architecture and summary of test executions show Dockerization of load tests and dispatching of HTTP requests from local (laptop) and Amazon AWS EC2 cloud slave instances onto different web servers and web sites.

To test the ease of DevOps with containers, we first Dockerized a Django web application written in Python (Fig. 1-Sec 3.), which reads RSS feeds from various sites and presents them to the clients. Next, we created test plans using Selenium. Finally, we replicated the Django container using Kubernetes [12], which simplifies management and orchestration of containers on different computers.

We compared performance of a containerized Django application using different browsers (Opera, Chrome, Firefox) as shown in Fig. 2. We measured the response time (speed in seconds) of "creating a new user from the admin panel" by using a Python test script that uses Selenium. We executed this script 100 times and averaged results. We found that opening and closing the browsers for each user creation operation was the biggest overhead. However, there was no significant performance difference among browsers otherwise and therefore we excluded browser parameter from our ongoing load test experiments. We also repeated our local trials with a simple web server, called NGINX. Our goal was to set a closed, black-box performance reference before including the effects of the open Internet. As shown in Fig. 3, we could adjust the "ramp up" and "hold" times to create different load profiles. One slave was used to create 25 "concurrent users" each minute (ramp = 15 s, hold = 45 s) until 100 concurrent users were loading the server; we utilized "ultimate thread group" feature in Jmeter. NGINX performance results were briefly as follows: APDEX value was 1.0 (Error rate: 0.0%) as all responses fell within the toleration time (avg. Latency = 17.31 ms, throughput = 1460 KB/s). About 850,000 requests were completed within 5 min. We attribute this low-latency and high throughput to the lack of any other traffic and NGINX's caching mechanism [13].

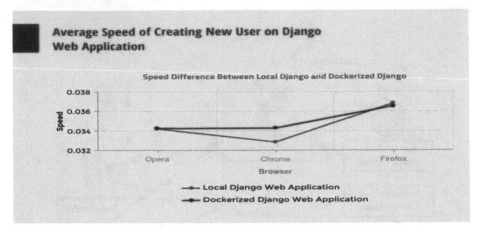

Fig. 2. Performance comparison of Local OS vs. Dockerized Django RSS application saved and replayed over different browsers via Selenium driver.

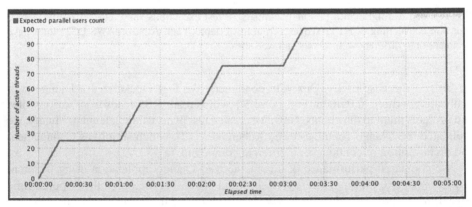

Fig. 3. A controlled loading profile using "ramp up" and "hold" times in Jmeter that tested the performance of a local NGINX server.

4 Experiments and Results

In this section, we report detailed performance analysis and comparison of load tests from Jmeter slaves over the Internet. As shown in Fig. 1 setup 4.1, we first push load onto a dedicated Apache web server serving a simple index.html page and accepting no other loads. Next, we test the Apache web server for our university's active web site (www.ozyegin.edu.tr), which is also open to public. Finally, we repeat the experiments using Amazon AWS EC2 VM instances as shown in Fig. 1 setup 4.2. We report the performance results in Sects. 4.1 and 4.2, respectively.

Our main goal here, is to understand the effect of change in number of slaves, while fixing the total number of requests/second. Thus, we add another dimension for load testing into the equation, which was not done by previous work. We select a maximum thread (user) count of 1050 requests and distribute this load over 1-to-15 slaves: 1 slave generating 1050 requests, 3 slaves each generating 350 requests, and so on until 15 slaves each generating 70 requests. If all the slaves were started to push the load instantaneously (ramp-up = 0 s), then the load could be spurious.

Our local machine has Intel i7-8 core CPU, 8 GB DRAM and 128 GB SSD capacity on host machine. We install and use Docker 19.03 and Jmeter 3.3 inside Ubuntu Linux OS version 18.04. Docker slaves use 2–4 vCPU and ~100–200 MB DRAM; we report maximum memory usage below. For cloud tests, we used one Amazon EC2 t2.large instance per slave which had 2 vCPU cores and 8 GB RAM. On the server side, Apache web servers use default FIFO scheduling.

Jmeter dashboard reports the following parameters: response time and percentiles, active threads, bytes, latencies and connect times over time; throughput in transactions per second, latency vs. requests, time vs. threads. Jmeter reports error percentages as OK% and KO% (Not OK). For the erroneous responses, we received HTTP "500/Service Unavailable with Message" code, where the internal message was "java.net.ConnectException/Non HTTP response message: Connection timed out".

4.1 Load Testing with Local Slaves

Table 2 shows load tests from local (non-cloud) Dockerized JMeter containers onto Apache web server. We can observe the following results: APDEX value can be less than 1.0 even if there are no errors. As we push load from increased number of slaves, the average latency will generally increase. The maximum upload bandwidth of Apache web server is around 485 KB/sec. During our experiments, we carefully observed that each Docker image uses around 60–70 MB memory at rest before the Jmeter loads are started. The maximum memory (MB) used per slave drops from 186 MB to 121 MB, since the workload is shared among slaves.

Table 3 shows load tests from local (non-cloud) Dockerized Jmeter containers onto www.ozyegin.edu.tr (Apache web server). In general, we observe higher latencies (average, min, max) that Table 2, due to existence of other traffic. APDEX value is less than 1.0 (0.483–0.000) even if there are no errors, but even a small increase in error rate will reduce APDEX to 0.0 (i.e. fully frustrated). Throughput (KB/sec) performance will increase to ~500–600 KB/sec, but the latencies perceived by each user will also drastically increase starting at 7 slaves. At 10 slaves that error rate increases to 27.81% and latency is around 25.2 s (close to HTTP timeouts). Then, at 15 slaves the average latency decreases slightly to 17.7 s possibly because of (a) load distribution over web server connections and (b) due to the quickly rejected HTTP requests (34.2%) which cannot be handled by the server anymore. These interesting phenomena can be observed under heavy loads when the server starts rejecting all new requests, completes the ones it was

Table 2. Loading from local Jmeter slaves onto Apache web server.

Workload	Average Lat. (ms)	Min/Max Lat. (ms)	Max. Mem. (MB)	APDEX	Error rate (%)	Throughput (KB/Sec)
1 slave × 1050 req.	44.28	38/299	186	1.000	0.0	108.80
3 slave × 350 req.	129.95	38/3738	148	0.966	0.0	301.25
5 slave × 210 req.	280.85	38/5217	131	0.897	0.0	424.81
7 slave × 150 req.	389.83	38/5094	131	0.850	0.0	485.34
10 slave × 105 req.	976.10	38/9292	121	0.692	0.0	377.65
15 slave × 70 req.	887.41	38/6700	121	0.656	0.0	320.51

serving, and timely serves a small percentage of new requests (APDEX = 0.013). We can name this phenomena "opportunity window in load testing". When our goal is to find the breaking points, we can use a sharp jump in average latency, max/min ratio, or a sharp drop in the APDEX value in our machine learning algorithms (see Sect. 4.3).

Table 3. Loading from local Jmeter slaves onto www.ozyegin.edu.tr domain.

Workload	Average Lat. (ms)	Min/Max Lat. (ms)	Max. Mem (MB)	APDEX	Error rate (%)	Throughput (KB/Sec)
1 slave × 1050 req.	825.79	526/7951	233	0.487	0.0	82.58
3 slave × 350 req.	1057.89	510/15916	153	0.466	0.0	237.14
5 slave × 210 req.	1605.09	517/32269	142	0.431	0.0	397.76
7 slave × 150 req.	7960.94	3014/23545	140	0.000	0.0	528.89
10 slave × 105 req.	25240.29	64/51948	122	0.000	27.81	500.13
15 slave × 70 req.	17771.25	59/40726	122	0.013	34.29	636.53

4.2 Load Testing with AWS EC2 Slaves

For cloud tests, we used Amazon EC2 t2.large instances which have 2 vCPU cores and 8GB RAM. These experiments took about 160 CPU/hours including setup and multiple trials and cost us $10 to execute. Therefore, we believe providing load testing as a service (SaaS or PaaS) can be a feasible IT business. Amazon's Elastic Container Service (ECS) also uses Docker images and launches them in Amazon EC2 instances.

In Table 4, we observe higher latencies than local slave experiments, but the load pattern (latency jump at 7–10 slaves) is similar to the experiment in Sect. 4.1 and results in Table 2. So, additional round-trip latency is incurred by all the requests causing slightly lower APDEX values, starting close to 1.0 and reducing to 0.0 even if there are no errors. The maximum upload bandwidth of Apache web server is around 718 KB/s. Similarly, maximum memory use of 1 slave starts from 218 MB and drops until 118 MB as the load gets shared among 15 slaves.

Table 4. Loading from AWS EC2 Jmeter Slaves onto Apache web server.

Workload	Average Lat. (ms)	Min/Max Lat. (ms)	Max. Slave Mem. (MB)	APDEX	Error rate (%)	Throughput (KB/Sec)
1 slave × 1050 req.	414.36	381/540	218	0.999	0.0	109.26
3 slave × 350 req.	416.02	381/695	146	0.996	0.0	322.88
5 slave × 210 req.	437.40	384/558	129	0.996	0.0	527.61
7 slave × 150 req.	444.61	388/556	123	0.996	0.0	718.42
10 slave × 105 req.	2340.82	421/9924	123	0.236	0.0	710.72
15 slave × 70 req.	4347.76	427/16413	118	0.137	0.0	622.37

Figure 4 shows the result of this experiment from another perspective. For the 1 slave × 1050 req. Configuration in part (a), we see the latency distribution percentiles (left part) to be between 380 ms–540 ms and number of active threads goes up to 7 threads (right). As the number of active threads increase the latency increases as expected. For the 15 slave × 70 req. Configuration in part (b), we see the latency distribution percentiles (left part) to be between 0 ms–17500 ms and number of active threads goes up to 50 threads. As the number of active threads increases the latency decreases. Since we don't have any errors in this benchmark, the only plausible way to explain this is to refer to caching effect.

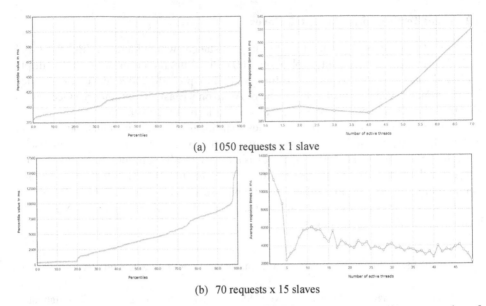

(a) 1050 requests x 1 slave

(b) 70 requests x 15 slaves

Fig. 4. (**Left**) Latency distribution percentiles and (**Right**) Average response time per number of active threads for (**a**) 1050 requests × 1 slave load and (b) 70 requests × 15 slaves load.

4.3   Load Test Classification Using Weka

In this section, we investigate if experimental data from load tests can be used to train machine learning algorithms and obtain experimental models, which can later be used for designing load testing benchmarks, i.e. model-based testing. We converted performance results from previous sections into a Weka [14] ARFF file and classified results using various classifiers including J48 decision tree, Naïve Bayesian classifier and Multi-layer perceptron (MLP) as shown in Fig. 5. The highest precision-recall values were achieved by the MLP with a weighted-average F-measure value of 0.747 over all load test setups (labeled as: Local2Apache, Local2OzU, Cloud2Apache, Cloud2OzU). The weighted average F-measure for J48 and Naive Bayesian were 0.660 and 0.541, respectively. We used default values for all the algorithms and 10-fold cross validation. The confusion matrix for 30 sample dataset shows that 23 samples were correctly classified and 7 samples were misclassified. These models can be utilized in Model-Based Testing (MBT). One of the future goals is to predict the correct load testing configurations for different web sites on the fly. The confusion matrix clearly shows which experiments had misclassified values.

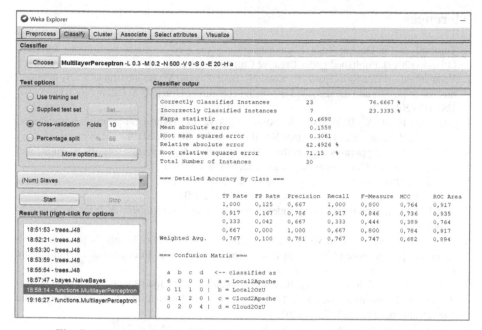

Fig. 5. Weka classification results for load tests using multi-layer perceptron.

5   Conclusions

In this paper, we evaluated and compared performances of local vs. Cloud-based web load testing using Docker, Jmeter and various other web & application server technologies. We found that containerization reduces differences among local and cloud deployments in establishing a correct, representative profile of the server side performance. While the cloud services are fully-elastic and can scale to thousands of instances easily compared to local resources, their limit on data center locations and distances to real customers (of e-commerce, online bank, online open course site) can be determining criteria for the business. Docker provides a higher network mobility and decentralization to load tests, compared to centralized public clouds. Turning CAPEX into OPEX for load testing and competitive pricing is an advantage of cloud.

In the future, we plan to extend our tests with HTTP POST messages, involve more browsers, servers, web frameworks to collect more data and train advanced machine learning algorithms to develop better load testing and parameter estimation models.

Acknowledgements. We would like to thank Suayip Ozmen, Erdi Olmezogullari, Selcuk Sozuer and Zeynep Ozdemir Guler from Saha Information Technologies and Doga Yilmaz from Ozyegin University for their valuable technical comments and support.

References

1. Turnbull, J.: The Docker Book: Containerization is the New Virtualization. James Turnbull, Orlando (2019). Published under Creative Commons License
2. Vedurumudi, P.V., Morusupalli, P., Kota, N., Beerakayala, V., Balakrishna, A.: System and method to execute and manage load tests using containers. Oracle U.S. Patent No. 10,445,207. USPTO (2019).
3. Arad, D., Haiut, A., Bykhovsky, V., Atias, D., Arye, G.: Hybrid on-premises/software-as-service applications. CA U.S. Patent No. 10,521,612. USPTO (2019)
4. Zhu, X., et al.: Apparatus and method for application deployment assessment. FutureWei Technologies Inc. U.S. Patent Application 15/648,204 (2019)
5. Selenium. https://www.selenium.dev. Accessed 20 May 2020
6. Jmeter. https://jmeter.apache.org. Accessed 20 May 2020
7. APDEX Application Performance Index. https://www.apdex.org/overview.html. Accessed 20 May 2020
8. Chhetri, M.B., Chichin, S., Vo, Q.B., Kowalczyk, R.: Smart CloudMonitor - providing visibility into performance of black-box clouds. In: 2014 IEEE 7th International Conference on Cloud Computing, pp. 777–784. IEEE (2014)
9. Chhetri, M.B., Chichin, S., Vo, Q. B., Kowalczyk, R.: Smart CloudBench - automated performance benchmarking of the cloud. In: 2013 IEEE Sixth International Conference on Cloud Computing, pp. 414–421. IEEE (2013)
10. Django Project. https://www.djangoproject.com. Accessed 20 May 2020
11. Docker Hub. https://hub.docker.com/. Accessed 20 May 2020
12. Kubernetes. https://kubernetes.io. Accessed 20 May 2020
13. Data, M., Luthfi, M., Yahya, W.: Optimizing single low-end LAMP server using NGINX reverse proxy caching. In IEEE International Conference on Sustainable Information Engineering and Technology (SIET), pp. 21–23 (2017)
14. Hall, M., Frank, E., Holmes, G., Pfahringer, B., Reutemann, P., Witten, I.H.: The WEKA data mining software: an update. ACM SIGKDD Explor. Newsl. **11**(1), 10–18 (2009)

SecurityGuard: An Automated Secure Coding Framework

Yasir Javed[1](✉) [iD], Qasim Ali Arian[2] [iD], and Mamdouh Alenezi[1] [iD]

[1] Prince Sultan University, Riyadh, Kingdom of Saudi Arabia
{yjaved,malenezi}@psu.edu.sa
[2] Mehran University of Engineering and Technology, Jamshoro, Pakistan

Abstract. The security of software systems is becoming extra vulnerable as new software is being created. It is due to several reasons such as security exploiters are becoming much smarter while the majority of developers are usually not aware of a new set of attacks or even using previous codes that are known to be vulnerable. It's quite challenging to build secure software with limited time and budget. This work presents a framework called SecurityGuard which is an automated secure coding framework that will allow auto-code fixes based on recommendations from experts as well as learning from best practices. The proposed framework can be used as a plugin to the Integrated Development Environment. The framework is based on three important segments along with a user-friendly interface and an adaptable dashboard providing useful statistics. SecurityGuard will ensure that developers can focus on business logic development without worrying about the implementation of security components.

Keywords: Software bugs · Security · Automated bug fixing · Secure coding · Software vulnerabilities

1 Introduction

Cyber-attacks can be seen as a serious threat to all aspects of our lives. Hackers and attackers exploit weaknesses in software systems to achieve their goals. If these attackers can get access to the system, they can make use of the critical infrastructure and sensitive data. The importance and awareness of securing software systems, has increased as society is getting dependent on technology [1]. Secondly, every day there are hundreds of solution that are released in the form of software, application, or tools that contains security bugs. The reason for these security bugs are dependencies of previously released versions (bug forwarding), using open-source codes and meeting deadlines are often on top [2].

Finding security vulnerabilities is a very difficult task, particularly in these days software systems size and complexity as well as the number of used technologies and their vulnerabilities. Secure coding is a very important aspect of designing and building resilient and secure software systems. Still, many developers are not aware of secure coding practices. Therefore, it is very important to use the advances of artificial intelligence and data science techniques to create smart automated tools that address these

© Springer Nature Switzerland AG 2021
S. Yildirim Yayilgan et al. (Eds.): INTAP 2020, CCIS 1382, pp. 303–310, 2021.
https://doi.org/10.1007/978-3-030-71711-7_25

issues. Most software engineers do not believe that existing static analysis tools are very efficient since they produce a high number of false-positive alerts [3]. Furthermore, these static analysis tools are designed to find potential vulnerabilities but not ways of fixing them.

One of the ways to secure information is by removing security vulnerabilities in the software code. Inattention, complexity, or lack of primitive knowledge can lead to the unintentional inclusion of security vulnerabilities by developers [4, 5]. To address these kinds of vulnerabilities number of efforts have been made by researchers as well as professionals that is to automate finding security vulnerabilities at the Integrated Development Environment (IDE) level, it will help developers fixing these issues while they are developing solutions as they are getting real-time feedback. Another solution often adapted for fixing vulnerabilities is static analysis tools that are integrated into the IDE. However, these tools are not formally compared and recommended which makes it a difficult choice for developers for choosing an optimally correct mitigation solution [6, 7]. The second approach is a code review that requires expert opinion from experienced developers requiring a lot of time and making it hard to adapt. To be effective, the code review needs to be done by experienced senior developers with the help of modern source code analysis tools. Code review provides great insights into finding security anomalies [8].

Some of the processes of SDLC are based on manual coding that can be automated and provided as IDE plugins. It will allow developers to detect and fix security vulnerabilities during development. One of the examples of such plugins is ASIDE (Application Security plugin for Integrated Development Environment) from Open Web Application Security Project (OWASP) that is an Eclipse Plugin to help developers to write secure code by spotting potentially vulnerable code segments and providing suggested fixes for them [9]. One of the other examples is SecureAssist is a commercial static analysis tool that finds security-related vulnerabilities and provides informative guidance to enable the developers to fix the issue [10]. FindSecBugs is another open-source static code analysis plugin that spots and finds potentially vulnerable code segments and provides informative fixes.

Thus, there is a need for an automated tool that can incorporate all kinds of vulnerabilities at the commonplace and present it in a common language that can be adapted by any tool. The tool can be used as standalone or can be incorporated in IDE. This research addresses two challenges (1) a need for common vulnerability representation (2) automated tools to identify and fix security vulnerabilities by presenting a blueprint of the automated secure coding framework. Upcoming sections present literature, proposed solution along with detailed parts ending with the conclusion. This proposed framework is addressing these challenges.

2   Related Works

Most of the research studies propose various ways of automating the process of finding and fixing security vulnerabilities. Baset and Denning [11] compared different plugins from the informational level by using coverage measures. Charest et al. [12] investigated the security plugins coverage for only four different vulnerabilities. Oyetoyan et al. [13]

studied 112 CWE entries in the Juliet Test Suite. However, their study did not reveal the results per CWE entry. They just aggregated the results into categories which made it hard to know which plugin covers which vulnerability. Xie et al. [14] evaluated the usability of ASIDE with only nine students. Their usability evaluation was focusing on the functionality without comparing other similar tools. Christakis and Bird [15] studied developers' needs from static analysis tools. Johnson et al. [16] studied why the number of developers using static analysis tools is so low. Sadowski et al. [17] showed the guiding philosophy of Google concerning the usability of static analysis tools.

FindBugs is a Java-based static analysis tool that finds coding defects by employing bug patterns on Java byte code [18]. FindSecBugs is a FindBugs extension plugin, which is specialized in security audits of web applications [19]. Li et. al. [20] evaluated several open-source IDE plugins for detecting security issues namely ASIDE, ESVD, LAPSE+, SpotBugs, and FindSecBugs. The evaluation criteria used were a coverage that is finding how many vulnerabilities of different categories can be detected by a plugin, performance that is computed using recall, precision, and discrimination rates, and usability that is calculated and analyzed in terms of false-positive rate, prioritized output, quick fixes, and early or late detection. They found that there are still many categories of vulnerabilities that are not covered by any of the plugins. The documentation of these plugins is often misleading since there is a lot of claimed coverage that does not exist. Most plugins have a high false-positive rate and are not user-friendly for developers.

DeepCode [21] is a vulnerability-searching tool for Java, JavaScript, TypeScript, and Python software code that features machine learning as a component. The tool contains more than 250,000 rules. This tool learns from changes, made by developers in the source code of open-source projects. The company building the tool claims it to be some kind of Grammarly for developers. Infer [22] a tool built by a startup that is later bought by Facebook. The tool is a static analyzer based on machine learning for projects in Java, C, C++, and Objective-C. It is also used in Amazon Web Services, Oculus, Uber, and other popular projects. Infer can find errors related to a null pointer dereference and memory leaks. Infer is based on Hoare's logic, separation logic, and bi-abduction, as well as abstract interpretation theory. Usage of these approaches allows the analyzer to break the program into chunks and analyze them independently. SapFix [23] is an automated editing tool that receives information from Sapienz, a testing automation tool, and the Infer static analyzer. In some cases, SapFix rolls back all changes or parts of them. In other cases, it tries to solve the problem by generating a patch from its set of fixing patterns. This set is formed from patterns of fixes collected by programmers themselves from a set of fixes that were already made.

Some of the work focused on prioritizing alerts or vulnerabilities to make it easier to manage these issues [24]. Autobugs [24] is a tool that uses historic alert data from static analysis tools and combines the alert-data with complexity metrics to build a classifier that predicts the actionability of an alert from data and unit properties [21]. Unfortunately, the empirical experiments showed that the tool potentially misleads developers to believe they have no security issues. VULCON [25], a vulnerability management strategy is proposed to prioritize vulnerabilities for patching. Using two metrics (total vulnerability exposure and time-to-vulnerability remediation), the framework ingests vulnerability scan reports from code analyzers and outputs security exposure metrics and vulnerability management plans to managers, operators, analysts, and engineers, so they can decide on which vulnerabilities to mediate [26].

Literature shows that there are several solutions proposed that provide a guideline to automate security bug detection and correction but most of them lack all sources as they obtain information through a few sources. Several research works identify major security sources such as OSSIndex, National Vulnerability Database (NVD), Common Vulnerabilities and Exposures (CVE), Common Weakness Enumeration (CWE) managed by National Institute of Standards and Technology (NIST). All these databases report vulnerabilities of different types and different formats. While OWASP, Common Platform Enumeration (CPE), and Common Vulnerability Scoring System (CVSS) are one of the sources for ranking. This research included all these sources. The second issue that is found in previous researches is to create a recommendation system that includes advice from major sources as well as experts. This research addressed that. Thirdly feedback system is required that allows correction of previous recommendation if any of this research includes that. It is quite a challenge to integrate the information from all sources such as source managed by NIST and other open bug repositories. To address this challenge this research borrows the idea of having a common representation of data to a bug where it recommended to convert all the bugs to common information set explained later in Table 1.

3   The Proposed Framework

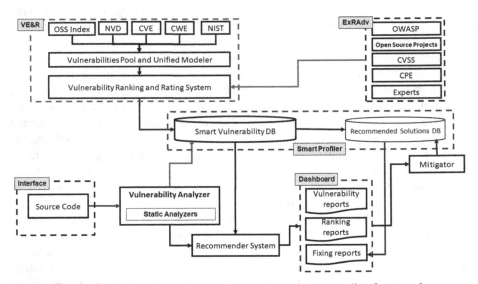

Fig. 1. The proposed securityguard: an automated secure coding framework

This research proposes a detailed framework for vulnerability extraction, profiling, ranking, and automatic vulnerability fixing system. Figure 1 shows a high-level description of the proposed framework. The proposed system works on input from most reliable sources while getting feedback from new analysis approaches as well as solutions adapted to provide the best adaptable solution. The details of the proposed system architecture are as the following:

Vulnerability Extractor and Ranker (VE&R). The first module is referred to as Vulnerability Extractor and Ranker (VE&R) that holds the responsibility of extracting the vulnerabilities from major vulnerability sources such as NVD, CVE, NIST and OSS Index. All these vulnerabilities are collected in a common source called Vulnerability Pool and Unified Modler. This module serves two purposes (1) extraction of vulnerabilities and (2) transforming all vulnerabilities to a unified template allowing a common and unified pooling mechanism of vulnerability collection and allowing reading from any other operating source. All these vulnerabilities are pooled into a common module and unified template the Ranking module will take action that will rank vulnerabilities according to various factors such as defined in Expert Ranker Advisor (EXRAdv).

Expert Ranker Advisor (EXRAdv). This Scalable Module Consists of Major Ranking Systems Such as CVSS, CPE, and OWASP but also Takes Feedback from Vulnerabilities and Weaknesses in Open-Source Projects as Well as Feedback from Experts. This Module Fuse Data from Multiple Sources and Present It as Unified Ranking Criteria. The Ranking System also Allows the Solution of Data to Be Adopted by Developers or Automated Correction System for Optimal and Recommended Solutions. Weightage of Expert Experience, Contribution, and Confidence Among Peers Will Play a Key Role in the Ranking of Solutions. Thus, an Adaptive Ranking System Will Have More Confidence Compared to Several Likes or Approvals.

Interface. This is where the developer writes his/her code. The interface acts as an input to the system where the source code is parsed then read to be sent to the Vulnerability Analyzer. The interface currently will be similar to Eclipse as the proposed solution will be integrated with Eclipse. Integration with IDE will allow adaptive development as well as bug fixes there and then.

Vulnerability Analyzer. This module will run a static analysis tool on the code. It acts as a first filtering block to scan the code and look for potential problems in the code. Static analysis can provide very useful information about the written code. To have an effective vulnerability analyzer, this module will take advice from EXRAdv for recommending the optimal solution and implementing it wherever applied. This module will also serve as a new vulnerability identifier for the system.

Dashboard. This module presents insights about the security of the source code. These insights can be in the form of vulnerabilities report, ranking reports, and fixing reports. Vulnerability reports are the one that will list all vulnerabilities according to specific categories such as security vulnerabilities, software vulnerabilities along with other reports that will rank the vulnerabilities according to their score achieved from Smart Vulnerabilities DB. The third report that it will get is the Fixing report that will be obtained from Recommended Solution DB that will get its solutions from the recommender system.

Database Details. The Most Common Details that Are Obtained from Sources Are Vulnerability ID, Vulnerability Description, Source of Vulnerability, Ranking, Solution

Reference, Link to Other Vulnerabilities, and Status. The Scheme of the Table is as Shown in Table 1. This Table Shows the Information that Can Be Obtained from All Vulnerabilities Sources and Storing Them in the Following Format to Allow Universalization of Information. These Fields Are Selected Based on Finding the Union Between All Bug-Repositories that Are Shown in Fig. 1.

Table 1. Database schema for storing vulnerabilities from multiple sources

Sr. No	Field name	Field description
1	vulnerability_id	The ID of Vulnerability given by source
2	vulnerability_description	Description of vulnerability
3	source_of_vulnerability	From which source vulnerability is coming such as CVE, CWE, NIST, etc.
4	Operating_system_of_vulnerability	Which Operating system has this kind of vulnerability such as Windows, Linux, Ubuntu
5	Ranking	Ranking of vulnerability calculated or given at sources such as OWASP, CPE, CVSS and Expert System
6	solution_reference	List of all solutions that are reported to be correct. The detailed table consists of all solutions along with details about which solution is widely adapted and reported to be successful
7	link_to_other_vulnerablities	Link to other vulnerabilities allows the unification of different vulnerabilities to one level so that the solution to one will lead to a solution to all
8	Status	Status can be open, solved, reported to be solved

4 Conclusion

This research focuses on addressing the issues of secure development that may be related to lack of knowledge of developers, strict deadlines, using old vulnerable codes, or relaying on open-source systems that have proven vulnerabilities. Awareness about secure development cannot encircle the amount of development that has been occurred in the current decade and is being contributed daily. To support secure development by identifying all the latest vulnerabilities and fixing them by adopting best practices. The proposed framework will ensure secure development as well as save time for development. SecurityGuard grabs the vulnerabilities from all common sources such as CVE, CWE, NVD, and NIST, it also supports the integration of any new vulnerability database as well as create a unified system for using vulnerabilities in any recommender or security testing system.

References

1. Torten, R., Reaiche, C., Boyle, S.: The impact of security awareness on information technology professionals' behavior. Comput. Secur. **79**, 68–79 (2018)
2. Chou, T.S.: Security threats on cloud computing vulnerabilities. Int. J. Comput. Sci. Inf. Technol. **5**(3), 79 (2013)
3. Johnson, B., Song, Y., Murphy-Hill, E., Bowdidge, R.: Why don't software developers use static analysis tools to find bugs? In: 2013 35th International Conference on Software Engineering (ICSE), pp. 672–681. IEEE (2013)
4. Dowd, M., McDonald, J., Schuh, J.: The Art of Software Security Assessment: Identifying and Preventing Software Vulnerabilities, 1st edn. Pearson Education, USA (2006)
5. Li, J., Beba, S., Karlsen, M.: Evaluation of open-source IDE plugins for detecting security vulnerabilities. In: Proceedings of the Evaluation and Assessment on Software Engineering, pp. 200–209 (2019)
6. Takanen, A., Demott, J.D., Miller, C., Kettunen, A.: Fuzzing for Software Security Testing and Quality Assurance, 1st edn. Artech House, USA (2018)
7. Yang, J., Tan, L., Peyton, J., Duer, K.A.: Towards better utilizing static application security testing. In: IEEE/ACM 41st International Conference on Software Engineering: Software Engineering in Practice, pp. 51–60. IEEE (2019)
8. De Cremer, P., Desmet, N., Madou, M., De Sutter, B.: Sensei: enforcing secure coding guidelines in the integrated development environment. Wiley Practice and Experience, Software (2020)
9. Sampaio, L., Garcia, A.: Exploring context-sensitive data flow analysis for early vulnerability detection. J. Syst. Softw. **113**, 337–361 (2016)
10. Murthy, N.: Codiscope SecureAssist™: The Developer's Security Assistant. In: IEEE Cybersecurity Development (SecDev), pp. 162. IEEE (2016)
11. Baset, A. Z., Denning, T.: IDE plugins for detecting input-validation vulnerabilities. In: 2017 IEEE Security and Privacy Workshops, pp. 143–146, IEEE (2017)
12. Charest, T., Rodgers, N., Wu, Y.: Comparison of static analysis tools for Java using the Juliet test suite. In: 11th International Conference on Cyber Warfare and Security, pp. 431–438. Academic Conferences Limited, USA (2016)
13. Oyetoyan, T.D., Milosheska, B., Grini, M., Soares Cruzes, D.: Myths and facts about static application security testing tools: an action research at Telenor digital. In: Garbajosa, J., Wang, X., Aguiar, A. (eds.) XP 2018. LNBIP, vol. 314, pp. 86–103. Springer, Cham (2018). https://doi.org/10.1007/978-3-319-91602-6_6
14. Xie, J., Chu, B., Lipford, H.R., Melton, J.T.: ASIDE IDE support for web application security. In: Proceedings of the 27th Annual Computer Security Applications Conference, pp. 267–276. ACM (2011)
15. Christakis, M., Bird, C.: What developers want and need from program analysis: an empirical study. In: Proceedings of the 31st IEEE/ACM International Conference on Automated Software Engineering, pp. 332–343. IEEE (2016)
16. Johnson, B., Song, Y., Murphy-Hill, E., Bowdidge, R.: Why don't software developers use static analysis tools to find bugs? In: 35th International Conference on Software Engineering, pp. 672–681. IEEE (2013)
17. Sadowski, C., Van Gogh, J., Jaspan, C., Söderberg, E., Winter, C.: Tricorder: building a program analysis ecosystem. In: 2015 IEEE/ACM 37th IEEE International Conference on Software Engineering, pp. 598–608. IEEE (2015)

18. Ayewah, N., Pugh, W., Hovemeyer, D., Morgenthaler, J.D., Penix, J.: Using static analysis to find bugs. IEEE Softw. **25**(5), 22–29 (2008)
19. Alenezi, M., Javed, Y.: Developer companion: a framework to produce secure web applications. Int. J. Comput. Sci. Inf. Secur. **14**(7), 12 (2016)   ・
20. Li, J., Beba, S., Karlsen, M.: Evaluation of open-source IDE plugins for detecting security vulnerabilities. In: Proceedings of the Evaluation and Assessment on Software Engineering, pp. 200–209, Denmark (2019)
21. Kim, H., Jiang, Y., Kannan, S., Oh, S., Viswanath, P.: Deepcode: feedback codes via deep learning. In: Advances in Neural Information Processing Systems, pp. 9436–9446, Canada (2018)
22. Calcagno, C., Distefano, D.: Infer: an automatic program verifier for memory safety of C programs. In: Bobaru, M., Havelund, K., Holzmann, G.J., Joshi, R. (eds.) NFM 2011. LNCS, vol. 6617, pp. 459–465. Springer, Heidelberg (2011). https://doi.org/10.1007/978-3-642-20398-5_33
23. Marginean, A., et al.: Sapfix: automated end-to-end repair at scale. In: IEEE/ACM 41st International Conference on Software Engineering: Software Engineering in Practice, pp. 269–278. IEEE (2019)
24. Nembhard, F., Carvalho, M., Eskridge, T.: Extracting knowledge from open source projects to improve program security. In: SoutheastCon 2018, pp. 1–7. IEEE (2018)
25. Farris, K.A., Shah, A., Cybenko, G., Ganesan, R., Jajodia, S.: Vulcon: a system for vulnerability prioritization, mitigation, and management. ACM Trans. Priv. Secur. **21**(4), 1–28 (2018)
26. Alenezi, M., Javed, Y.: Open source web application security: a static analysis approach. In: 2016 International Conference on Engineering & MIS, pp. 1–5. IEEE (2016).

The Multi-objective Feature Selection in Android Malware Detection System

Anahita Golrang[1]([✉]), Sule Yildirim Yayilgan[2], and Ogerta Elezaj[2]

[1] Department of Computer Science, Norwegian University of Science
and Technology, 2815 Gjøvik, Norway
Anahitam@stud.ntnu.no
[2] Department of Information Security and Communication Technology, Norwegian
University of Science and Technology, 2815 Gjøvik, Norway
{sule.yildirim,ogerta.elezaj}@ntnu.no

Abstract. The Android operating system boosts a global market share over the previous years, which has made it the most popular operating system in the world. Recently, Android has become the target of attacks by cybercriminals because of its open-source code and its progressive growth. Many machine learning techniques have been used to address this issue in the Android operating system. However, a limited range of feature selection methods has been used in these systems. This paper, therefore, aims to address and evaluate the impact of a multi-objective feature selection approach called NSGAII in Android malware detection systems. To improve the diversity of solutions offered by this method, we have modified the standard NSGAII approach. Experimental results show that the proposed method can lead to better malware classification.

Keywords: Feature selection · Android malware detection system · Multi-objective optimization

1 Introduction

Android has dominated the mobile device industry. Just in 2019, the percentage of mobile devices using the Android operating system was around 76 % [1]. This operating system is supported by various types of applications in different markets which provides grateful functionality to its users. However, the total number of malware applications on the android market has boomed catastrophically, due to being an open-source software and also being one of the most used mobile operating systems. Moreover, many malicious applications are found on unofficial Android markets, where security issues receive less attention. Furthermore, as mentioned formerly, the market share for Android is considerably high compared to other operating systems. Therefore, Android is the hot target of attackers to gain more control of the system. The machine learning approaches have been proposed in recent years as one of the effective solutions in Android malware detection systems [2]. However, data mining researchers consider high-dimensional data analysis as a challenge. Feature selection known as the process

© Springer Nature Switzerland AG 2021
S. Yildirim Yayilgan et al. (Eds.): INTAP 2020, CCIS 1382, pp. 311–322, 2021.
https://doi.org/10.1007/978-3-030-71711-7_26

of selecting a subset of features that contribute most to the classification process in machine learning activities brings many advantages in the reduction of the data dimensionality and enhancement of classifier efficiency [3]. The effectiveness of these methods has been established in improving the learning performance as well as the high- dimensional data processing. The feature selection technique aims at reducing the irrelevant features, reducing the computation cost, increase prediction performance and gaining a better understanding or representation of the data [4]. Although feature selection methods have been used widely in other fields such as intrusion detection systems [5], the majority of papers in the area of Android malware detection tend to select the essential features by rationalizing which require a deep understanding of the nature of the features involved in Android applications. The research in [2] and [6] have provided review papers on various types of features which have been applied in Android malware detection systems. The results of their investigations demonstrate that despite the advantages of feature selection approaches they have been applied in around 8% to 13% of the reviewed papers. To the best of our knowledge, the majority of feature selection approaches currently used in Android malware detection systems encounter difficulties concerning the nature of the problem. The feature selection problem can be modelled as two conflicting objectives which are to minimize the number of features while offering a higher classification performance (minimize classification error). The single objective feature-selection approaches applied in Android malware detection systems are not able to confront both objectives simultaneously while the multi-objective techniques could be considered as a potential solution to the aforementioned issue [7]. Hence, we would attempt to assess the impact of multi-objective feature selection techniques compared to single-objective approaches in Android malware detection systems. To achieve this objective, the following research questions are defined:

1. Can multi-objective techniques perform better compared to single-objective feature selection approaches in Android malware detection systems?
2. Is there any special deficiency in current multi-objective approaches which could be improved?

Consequently, the gap mentioned is hoped to be filled by using multi-objective techniques as a feature selection method. To address the first question, the proposed framework applies the multi-objective genetic algorithm, namely NSGAII, for the feature selection purpose. The research done in [8] introduces the redundancy issue as one of the intrinsic issues in NSGAII algorithm. Hence, a modified version of the NSGAII method which removes the redundant solutions have been proposed in this paper which has been tested on two well-known datasets in the field of Android malware detection systems. The most significant contributions of this paper can be folded as follows:

1. To the best of our knowledge, there is no other research in the literature assessing the impact of the multi-objective feature selection approaches in malware detection in Android systems.

2. The multi-objective feature selection technique used in this research is a modified version of the standard NSGAII method, which improves the diversity of the solutions.

The rest of this paper is constructed as follows, wherein Sect. 2, we give a brief overview of related works. Section 3 describes the methodology used in the proposed Android malware detection system by defining the dataset in use, the modified feature selection, and the malware detection approach, respectively. The experimental results are discussed in Sect. 4, where the evaluation metrics are defined prior to the results achieved in the experiments. Finally, the conclusions of the research are outlined in Sect. 5.

2   Background

As this study is aimed at improving feature selection approaches used in Android malware detection systems, the literature is explored on this subject. Coronado-De-Alba et al. [9] examined the impact of two different feature selection methods called chi-square and relief approach. The malware samples in this dataset are derived from the Drebin dataset. However, the benign samples are gathered from Google Play, and third-party stores after evaluation by the Virustotal tool [10]. The features used in this experiment are divided into permissions, intents, hardware, and software categories. They have introduced Random Forest and random committee as the most efficient meta learner classifiers. In the next step, Random Forest with 200 random trees is selected while using the random committee as the base classifier, which showed the best outcomes on an unbalanced dataset and without feature selection. However, they report these feature selection methods with the ensemble of classifiers to show better efficiency compared to single classifiers. As a result, they suggest these methods in situations where velocity plays a vital role to cope with the dataset size. Zhao et al. [11] proposed a novel feature selection method called FrequenSel. In this research, more than 32000 features have been gathered before feature selection. These features are divided into APIs, permissions, actions, IP, and URLs. They have mentioned the distribution bias in favor of benign apps features and the long-tail effect as the main issues regarding traditional feature selection methods such as information-gain and chi-square. To solve this problem, the features selected by their algorithm should follow two conditions. First of all, its usage percentage should be higher in malware compared to benign samples. Next, a threshold has been introduced that ensures the proper occurrence of features in all malware samples. The proposed framework depicts better results compared to information gain and chi-square. The research done in [12] has proposed a novel architecture in Android malware detection systems. They have gathered permissions, and API function calls from the Android app samples. In the experiments, the benign app is gathered by Google Play, and the malware data are taken from the Malgenome project. The results of their experiments show that the API calls have a higher impact on the efficiency of the models compared to the permission features. As a result, they have selected a higher range of API calls after the feature selection process. In the feature selection step, ANOVA and SVM-RFE approaches have been applied to rank the features. Finally, they have chosen the first 300 API calls features in the sorted list as well as the top 80 features in the permission set.

3   Methodology

In this section, the datasets used to evaluate the proposed method are described initially. Next, we have defined the feature selection approach and the two-step modifications applied to the feature selection technique, and we would explain how These modifications are done to improve the diversity of the solutions. Finally, the malware detection approach, which divides the samples into benign and malware categories, is discussed in detail.

3.1   Dataset

The experiments have been conducted on two datasets consists of real-world Android application samples, details of which are presented in Table 1. Each of this dataset contains 215 features. We have selected these datasets as they are widely used in the research community. During the dataset generation process, AXMLprinter2 is used to extract permissions and intents from the manifest file. Moreover, the extra features in API calls are derived from the .dex files using reverse engineering by Baksmali disassembler. Finally, the most important ad libraries introduced in [13] have been excluded to improve the quality of API call feature extraction.

Table 1. The sample distributions in Drebin [14], and Malgenome [15] datasets

Dataset	#Samples	#malware	#benign	#features
Malgenome-215	3799	1260	2539	215
Drebin-215	15036	5560	9476	215

3.2   Feature Selection

In order to remove the irrelevant features, we have applied feature selection approaches which lead to the dimensionality reduction of the datasets and potential improvement of the classification performance. As mentioned previously, the majority of the projects in this field of study have chosen the list of features based on rationalizations which requires a deep understanding regarding the nature of features available in the datasets. To the best of our knowledge, the multi-objective approaches have not been used for feature selection purposes in

Android malware detection systems. This provides a gap for further investigation. In our previous research [5], we proposed an intrusion detection framework based on a modified multi-objective feature selection approach called NSGAII. Hence, it provides enough motivation to assess the effectiveness of this method for feature selection purpose in Android malware detection systems. The modification which was applied to the aforementioned research was improving the diversity of solutions by removing the identical redundant solutions. In this research, two levels of modification have been applied to the standard NSGAII technique. Algorithm 1 demonstrates the steps involved in the modification process where the duplicate solutions referring to exactly the same feature sets are removed in the first level. In the second step, the solutions referring to various feature sets are evaluated to ensure that they report distinct objective functions. In the following paragraphs, we would describe the modification process in detail.

Algorithm 1: MODIFIED NSGAII technique

Input: pop population
Output: Rank(S) for each solution S in pop
C = the array from CFS method
Step 1. Remove all duplicate solutions in the initial population
Step 2. **for** *each solution i and j* **do**
> **if** *objective function (i) = objective function (j)* **then**
>> A= correlation (i, C) and B=correlation (j, C)
>> **if** *if (A < B)* **then**
>>> remove A
>> **else**
>>> remove B

Modified NSGAII

Step 1: The presence of duplicate solutions in standard NSGAII techniques have been mentioned as a significant threat to diversity [16] and convergence speed [8] of this algorithm. In our previous research [5], we modified the NSGAII technique to remove the duplicate solutions in the merged population. Hence, we applied the same modification technique to remove the duplicate solutions and improve the diversity and convergence speed of the NSGAII algorithm in the first modification step in this research as well.

Step 2: Although in step 1, we have removed the identical solutions referring to the exactly the same solutions, there is still the possibility that the solutions with other degrees of similarity are still present in the offered solutions. In Step 2, we would attempt to remove the solutions reporting exactly the same objective-functions since we would consider these solutions as redundant solutions that their presence is not adding any extra value to the quality of the proposed solution, and this fact provides the motivation to apply the modification in the second step. To ascertain which of the overlapping solutions may provide higher value, we have attempted to discover which one has the highest similarity with a single objective method available in the Weka environment, namely CFS. The reason for choosing a feature selection method is the fact that these solutions are referring to various feature sets proposed by the NSGAII technique. It should be mentioned that the CFS technique could be replaced by any other feature selection approach available in the state-of-the-art. To achieve the highest similarity degree, the linear association between each of the overlapping solutions (i and j) and the array achieved by CFS is calculated using the correlation-coefficient concept. The linear association between the two- vectors, $A_1 = (A_1, A_2, \ldots, A_n)$ and $B = (B_1, B_2, \ldots, B_n)$, is called the Pearson correlation, and can be calculated according to Eq. 1.

$$correlation(A, B) = \frac{\sum_{i=1}^{n}(A_i - \overline{A})(B_i - \overline{B})}{\sqrt{\sum_{i=1}^{n}(A_i - \overline{A})^2}\sqrt{\sum_{i=1}^{n}(B_i - \overline{B})^2}} \tag{1}$$

Finally, the solution which reports higher degree of correlation using Eq. 1 is chosen and the other one is eliminated from the list of offered solutions.

3.3   Malware Detection

In the malware detection step, we would like to divide the solutions into a binary classification of malware and benign categories. The feature selection technique defined in Sect. 3.2 provides a list of solutions which provide various feature subsets. Among all of these solutions, we would select the solution with minimum f_2 value which is equivalent to the error rate reported for the corresponding feature set. Next, we would reduce the size of the dataset according to the proposed list of feature sets. Afterwards, the Random Forest classifier, as an ensemble method and peered review machine learning technique found in literature [9], would be applied on the datasets to evaluate the efficiency of the proposed solution and divide the samples into benign and malware categories.

4   Experimental Results

In this section, we would initially describe the evaluation metrics used to assess the effectiveness of the proposed feature sets. Afterwards, the results of two experiments on Drebin and Malgenome datasets are reported according to the aforementioned metrics.

4.1   Evaluation Metrics

Weighted F Measure is applied in the research conducted in [17] to evaluate the efficiency of the method. The dataset used in this research is extracted from this research. Hence, we apply the same metric as described in Eq. 2 by WFM.

$$WFM = \frac{(F_m * N_m) + (F_b * N_b)}{(N_m + N_b)} \tag{2}$$

Where the F_m, F_b, N_m, and N_b used in the evaluation process refer to the F Measure and number of instances in malware and benign instances, respectively. The F value in this equation correlates with the F Measure value where it can be calculated according to the Eq. 3.

$$F\ Measure = 2 * \left(\frac{Precision * Recall}{Precision + Recall}\right) \tag{3}$$

While the Precision and Recall are formulated as follows:

$$Precision = \frac{TP}{TP + FP} \tag{4}$$

$$Recall = \frac{TP}{TP + FN} \tag{5}$$

where TP, TN, FP, and FN are equal to the following values:

- **True Positive (TP):** the number of correctly classified malware files.

- **True Negative (TN):** the number of correct classification of benign samples as benign.

- **False Negative (FN):** Malicious applications wrongly classified as benign.

- **False Positive (FP):** the number of misclassified legitimate applications.

4.2   Results

This section describes the experimental results obtained with the improved NAS-GII over the datasets selected for these experiments. The proposed feature selection solution was implemented using Matlab R2019a. Next, the Random Forest algorithm is applied to the reduced dataset in the Waikato Environment for Knowledge Analysis (Weka 3.8). The data analyses are performed using a PC with Intel Core i7 processor, 2.1 GHz speed and 8 GB RAM. To evaluate the performance of each model, a 10-fold cross-validation resampling method was applied. This method is selected for the advantages it has in guaranteeing the independence of the validation set from the training one and the validity of the trained classifier against any unseen sample.

Experiment One on Drebin Dataset: Figure 1 demonstrates the feature sub-set solutions proposed by the modified multi-objective NSGAII. Each * symbol in this fig is considered as the demonstration of an individual solution. Further detail about these solutions can be found in Table 2 where the Num, NF, MSE, and ratio refer to the order of solution on the Pareto front, the number of selected features, Mean-square-error (MSE) of the solution achieved by the artificial neural network (ANN), and the percentage of the selected features in each solution compared to the full features available in the original datasets. We have chosen the last solution with the minimum MSE value, which corresponds to 186 features of total 215 features available in Drebin dataset.

Table 2. Pareto front in Drebin

Num	NF	MSE	Ratio
1	81	0.023	37%
2	84	0.023	39%
3	87	0.021	40.4%
4	88	0.019	40.9%
5	89	0.018	41%
6	93	0.018	43.2%
7	94	0.018	43.7%
8	95	0.017	44%
9	97	0.016	45%
10	100	0.016	46.5%
11	101	0.013	46.9%
12	112	0.013	52%
13	117	0.013	54%
14	122	0.011	56%
15	121	0.012	56.2%
16	168	0.011	78%
17	186	0.0094	86%

Table 3. Pareto front in Malgenome

Num	NF	MSE	Ratio
1	78	0.019	36%
2	80	0.018	37.2%
3	81	0.010	37.6%
4	83	0.005	38%
5	88	0.005	40%
6	90	0.004	41%
7	91	0.004	42%
8	94	0.0042	43%
9	105	0.0040	48%
10	106	0.003	49%
11	113	0.003	52%
12	115	0.002	53%

Next, the features unavailable on the feature subset solution are eliminated from the dataset, and the dataset is fed into the malware detection step where the Random Forest technique available in Weka environment would classify the samples into malware and benign categories. Table 4 demonstrates the confusion matrix derived from the classification approach on Drebin dataset. We have compared the proposed method with two single objective feature- selection techniques called CFS and FilterSubsetEval. To achieve a uniform structure for comparison, we have initially applied each of these techniques on Drebin dataset. Afterwards, the malware detection approach is applied to the reduced

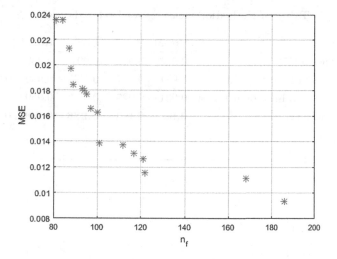

Fig. 1. Pareto front derived from Drebin

size datasets using Random Forest. Moreover, the proposed method results are compared to another research called Droid-Fusion [17], in which they have published the final version of Drebin and Malgenome datasets used in our research. Table 5 reports the results of this comparison, where the proposed method shows higher efficiency in all performance metrics compared to both single objective feature selection approaches. However, it demonstrates better results in three out of five metrics in comparison with Drebin. To evaluate the efficiency of the method in both benign and Malware samples, the precision and recall factors have been reported in malware and benign classes separately instead of a single average factor in all samples.

Table 4. Drebin confusion matrix

	Malware	Benign	Total
Malware	5429	131	5560
Benign	39	9437	9476
Total	5468	9568	15036

Experiment Two on Malgenome Dataset: The proposed feature selection has been applied on Malgenome dataset as well. Figure 2 demonstrates the feature subset solutions offered by the proposed multi-objective approach in this research. Twelve distinct solutions have been offered by this technique where the solution with the least MSE rate has been chosen to be used to reduce the

Table 5. Evaluation measures for Drebin dataset

	Pre-M	Rec-M	Prec-B	Rec-B	W-FM
Droid-Fusion [17]	0.981	0.984	0.991	0.989	0.9872
CFS-Random Forest	0.931	0.927	0.957	0.959	0.949
FilterSubsetEval-Random Forest	0.931	0.927	0.957	0.959	0.949
Proposed-Method	**0.993**	**0.976**	**0.986**	**0.996**	**0.989**

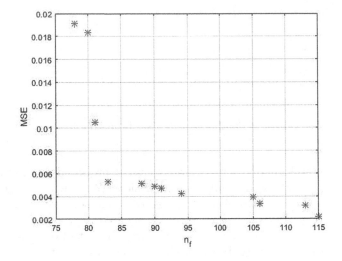

Fig. 2. Pareto front derived from Malgenome

feature subset size of the Malgenome dataset. Table 3 demonstrates the details of the offered solutions by the multi-objective technique. We have chosen the last solution in this table where 115 features out of 215 features available on Malgenome dataset have been chosen which is equivalent to 53% of the total features. Next, the reduced size dataset is classified using Random Forest classifier. The confusion matrix derived from this process can be found in Table 6. We have compared the proposed method with the same state-of-the-art mentioned in the Drebin experiment. The evaluation results of our experiment demonstrate the superiority of the proposed multi-objective feature selection technique compared to two single objective feature selection methods, namely CFS and FilterSubsetEval in all factors and its improvement in three out of five metrics compared to Droid-Fusion [17] (Table 7).

Table 6. Malgenome confusion matrix

	Malware	Benign	Total
Malware	1239	21	1260
Benign	10	2529	2539
Total	1249	2550	3799

Table 7. Evaluation measures for Malgenome dataset

	Pre-M	Rec-M	Prec-B	Rec-B	W-FM
Droid-Fusion [17]	0.984	0.968	0.984	0.992	0.984
CFS-Random Forest	0.968	0.948	0.974	0.985	0.972
FilterSubsetEval-Random Forest	0.975	0.980	0.960	0.988	0.978
Proposed-Method	**0.992**	**0.983**	**0.992**	**0.996**	**0.992**

5 Conclusion

By selecting the relevant features and by applying different machine learning algorithms, it is possible to effectively detect Android malware. The aim of this study was to explore the use of a multi-objective function for feature-selection purpose on Android malware detection systems in order to create the optimal feature subsets. Hence, a NSGAII-ANN method is applied to construct the basis for the feature-selection stage. To improve the proposed framework, we have modified the traditional NSGAII method to solve one of the most significant deficiencies in NSGAII algorithm by a redundant solution removal approach in two stages. Moreover, the Random Forest method is applied in order to evaluate the selected subsets. Experimental results show that the proposed method is superior to other methods found in literature in terms of improving the classification metrics for both datasets. In the future, we would like to test our proposed solution on other real datasets covering a broader range of malware, and we would like to apply and compare different machine learning algorithms. As Android malware detection techniques are mostly applied on imbalanced network traffic datasets, different experiments should be performed applying oversampling and downsampling techniques, expecting to achieve higher accuracy on both the minority class and the entire datasets.

References

1. Mobile Operating System Market Share Worldwide. https://gs.statcounter.com/os-market-share/mobile/worldwide. Accessed 13 Apr 2020
2. Feizollah, A., Anuar, N.B., Salleh, R., Wahab, A.W.A.: A review of feature selection in mobile malware detection. Digital Invest. **13**, 22–37 (2015)
3. Cai, J., Luo, J., Wang, S., Yang, S.: Feature selection in machine learning: a new perspective. Neurocomputing **300**, 70–79 (2018)

4. Chandrashekar, G., Sahin, F.: A survey on feature selection methods. Comput. Electr. Eng. **40**(1), 16–28 (2014)

5. Golrang, A., Golrang, A.M., Yayilgan, S.Y., Elezaj, O.: A novel hybrid IDS based on modified NSGAII-ANN and random forest. Electronics **9**(4), 577 (2020)

6. Wang, W., et al.: Constructing features for detecting android malicious applications: issues, taxonomy and directions. IEEE Access **7**, 67602–67631 (2019)

7. Xue, B., Zhang, M., Browne, W.N., Yao, X.: A survey on evolutionary computation approaches to feature selection. IEEE Trans. Evol. Comput. **20**(4), 606–626 (2015)

8. Huang, B., Buckley, B., Kechadi, T.M.: Multi-objective feature selection by using NSGA-II for customer churn prediction in telecommunications. Expert Syst. Appl. **37**(5), 3638–3646 (2010)

9. Coronado-De-Alba, L.D., Rodr'ıguez-Mota, A., Escamilla-Ambrosio, P.J.: Feature selection and ensemble of classifiers for Android malware detection. In: 2016 8th IEEE Latin-American Conference on Communications (LATIN- COM), pp. 1–6. IEEE, November 2016

10. VIRUSTOTAL. https://www.virustotal.com/gui/home/upload. Accessed 13 Apr 2020

11. Zhao, K., Zhang, D., Su, X., Li, W., Fest: a feature extraction and selection tool for Android malware 373 detection. In: IEEE Symposium on Computers and Communication (ISCC), vol. 2015, pp. 714–720. IEEE (2015)

12. Qiao, M., Sung, A.H., Liu, Q.: Merging permission and API features for Android malware detection. In: 2016 5th IIAI International Congress on Advanced Applied Informatics (IIAI-AAI), pp. 566–571. IEEE, July 2016

13. Cen, L., Gates, C.S., Si, L., Li, N.: A probabilistic discriminative model for android malware detection with decompiled source code. IEEE Trans. Dependable Secure Comput. **12**(4), 400–412 (2014)

14. Arp, D., Spreitzenbarth, M., Hubner, M., Gascon, H., Rieck, K., Siemens, C.E.R.T.: DREBIN: effective and explainable detection of Android malware in your pocket. In: NDSS, vol. 14, pp. 23–26, February 2014

15. Zhou, Y., Jiang, X.: Dissecting android malware: characterization and evolution. In: 2012 IEEE Symposium on Security and Privacy, pp. 95–109. IEEE, May 2012

16. Chaiyaratana, N., Piroonratana, T., Sangkawelert, N.: Effects of diversity control in single-objective and multi-objective genetic algorithms. J. Heuristics **13**(1), 1–34 (2007)

17. Yerima, S.Y.; Sezer, S. DroidFusion: a novel multilevel classifier fusion approach for Android malware 384 detection. IEEE Trans. Cybern. **49**(2), 453–466 (2018)

AIRLEAs

Border Management Systems: How Can They Help Against Pandemics

Georgios Stavropoulos[1,2]([✉]), Dimitra Triantafyllou[2], Elpiniki Makri[2],
Zoltán Székely[3], and Dimitrios Tzovaras[2]

[1] Department of Electrical and Computer Engineering, University of Patras, Patras, Greece
stavrop@ece.upatras.gr
[2] Information Technologies Institute, Centre for Research and Technology Hellas,
Thessaloniki, Greece
[3] Szekely Family & Co., Budapest, Hungary

Abstract. The presented work proposes ways that modern and upcoming border management systems can be utilized to help the authorities mitigate the spread of infectious diseases. This work was inspired by the latest COVID-19 pandemic that spread all around the world forcing governments to apply restrictions and bans on international travels. The paper presents the case of how the border management solution proposed and extended by the H2020 projects SMILE and ITFLOWS respectively, can be utilized to (i) allow the travellers to make a self-assessment before their travel, (ii) be notified of potential health-related alerts at their destination or transit and (iii) provide to the border authorities advanced information on the travel history of each passenger allowing them to better and faster assess their entry or exit of a country. To the best of the authors' knowledge, the proposed methods are not yet implemented in any border management system and would provide a valuable mean to help mitigate a pandemic from spreading.

Keywords: Border management · Biometrics · E-health · Border checks · Public health

1 Introduction

The introduction of recent pandemics such as Covid-19, Zika, SARS and H1N1 prove the necessity of coping mechanisms that mitigate their spread and reduce the sweeping consequences they may have on affected populations. The severity of such situations and their effect on the lives, health, psychology, and economy has led to an increasing scientific interest and prolific literature regarding epidemic modelling, optimization, and control.

Restrictions of human activities have been utilized as a drastic countermeasure for disease spread mitigation, nevertheless their extensive use can have huge economic and societal consequences. Therefore, purposeful strategies that minimize the spread of infection with the least possible sacrifices are deployed. The World Health Organization (WHO) considers cross-border interactions a determining factor that characterizes a

© Springer Nature Switzerland AG 2021
S. Yildirim Yayilgan et al. (Eds.): INTAP 2020, CCIS 1382, pp. 325–334, 2021.
https://doi.org/10.1007/978-3-030-71711-7_27

country's readiness to cope with a health or biological emergency, such as a pandemic [1]. Hence, border control is considered a vital measure against pandemics, especially during the emerging of the outbreaks, since it prevents the spread between different countries and populations [2, 3]. In the Schengen Border Code of the European Union, if checks conclude that an individual poses a threat to the public health, it may not be admitted to the country. Until latest pandemics this condition of entry and stay was merely an administrative filter for people arriving from countries with underdeveloped health systems and basically meant the requirements of presenting their vaccination booklet.

This paper presents an effort to accommodate an H2020 project that developed a border control system, namely SMILE (Smart mobILity at the European land borders), to the additional requirements occurring for border crossing during pandemic situations. Until now, SMILE's aim is to leverage border control through mobile applications that ensure trusted and secure authentication through biometric control, while enabling faster control procedures, providing to the travellers the capability to declare their trip in advance (similar to the air borders using Advance Passenger Information and/or Passenger Name Records for long time). In this paper, supplementary features that can be easily incorporated to SMILE's structure and constitute valuable assets to border control during pandemics are proposed. The suggested features include communication of the problem and any requested measures that a traveller should be aware of before their departure, accelerated and safer border control procedures by submitting in advance recent health and travel history, preparedness of border control officers to cope with suspicious cases. To our knowledge, there is no other system offering such thorough support for border control that includes both common security control and health control in regard to pandemics. It is especially important however, to ensure the proportionality between requested health data and the actual pandemic threat, as personal health data is a sensitive personal data. SMILE is capable to dynamically follow these requirements, changing requested data and allocated risk indicators by country or by time period according to actual decisions of policymakers.

The remainder of the paper is organized as follows. Section 2 describes related work regarding border control systems and technologies utilized to cope with pandemics. In Sect. 3, the SMILE system is presented while updates that can leverage it to a tool for health border control during outbreaks are introduced. In Sect. 4, the application scenarios for the updated system are analysed while examples depicting the new features of SMILE's applications are provided in Sect. 5. Finally, the paper concludes in Sect. 6.

2 Related Work

Related work is divided in two subsections in order to cover the topic on measures and technologies developed to handle pandemic situations but also to describe existing border control systems.

2.1 Technologies and Measures for Pandemic Situations

Due to their deep impact on humanity, pandemics have gained scientists interest. Literature covers tools that calculate the outbreaks' spread, measures that mitigate them and technological tools aiming at informing the public on the situation and facilitate them to recognize possible symptoms. The existence of large-scale datasets [1, 2] providing information on pandemics' spread has facilitated the study of network topology, meta-population and disease diffusion models and patterns [4–6]. Furthermore, computational and visualization tools made their appearance so as to provide accurate spread predictions and the capability of measuring the impact of control strategies [7, 8]. Moreover, mobile applications are developed in order to gather data on social interactions and predict the progress of a contagious disease [9, 10].

Multiple measures are deployed at borders for pandemic mitigation. Their goal is to inform travellers on the pandemic, filter suspected cases, detect the infected ones, manage them and probably apply a health follow up [11–13]. In this scope, usual tactics are entry screening with thermal scanners, self-reporting of travellers on health and travel history, further lab tests on symptomatic cases, quarantine and health follow up by means of telecommunication.

A very powerful strategy against the pandemic spread is proven to be the communication of the problem, by providing notices on disease outbreaks to the travellers, information on practices that will help them to protect their health, legislations and rules of the country to be visited regarding ongoing pandemics. In [14], the effect of the information is considered to be more effective and valuable than entry screening with thermal sensors, highlighting its importance. Various ways of communications have been utilized until now; from leaflets, posters and informational videos to announcements to social media, mobile apps [15, 16] and websites such as the Center's for Disease Control (CDC) website [17]. In this site, travel notices on disease outbreaks are posted and each notice is assigned with a risk level while for each country there is specified information on contagious diseases, ways to protect oneself and vaccines that are needed depending on the visit duration. Furthermore, personalized traveller notifications based on criteria such as age, pregnancy, immune compromise, and chronic disease are provided. Furthermore, apps like Mo-Buzz and Mozify [15, 16] provide real-time worldwide news on a specific disease (dengue), have educational videos, dynamic hotspot maps and symptoms checker.

2.2 Border Control Systems

There are several mechanisms for exchanging information in European border management cooperation. In recent years, the EU has sought to implement new technologies and develop large-scale IT systems to improve the tools already in use. They allow European authorities throughout the Schengen area to make efficient use of and use the data required to perform their tasks. The European Agency eu-LISA has major role for the operational management of large-scale IT systems. Eu-LISA actively supports and promotes effective cooperation and ex-change of information between EU law enforcement authorities, ensuring the uninterrupted operation of large-scale IT systems, thereby contributing to the free movement of persons within and across the Schengen area. The Agency currently manages EURODAC, the Visa In-formation System (VIS) and the second-generation Schengen Information System (SIS II). The SIS II database enables the exchange of information on criminal matters in order to ensure a coordinated investigation of offenses that no longer respect national borders. The VIS ensures fair, efficient and secure processing of procedures for applying for visas and foreign visitors to the EU, while the Eurodac system allows for the monitoring of asylum applications, submitted by those protected under EU values and norms. In addition, both the Europol Information System (EIS) and the European Criminal Records Information System (ECRIS) are used in border control mechanisms. These systems are extended with two new systems under introduction process. First is the European Entry-Exit System (EES), recording third country citizens entering and leaving the Schengen Area at EU level instead of the previous individual Member State entry-exit systems such as HERR in Hungary. Second is the European Travel Authorization System (ETIAS), requesting pre-registration from third country citizens before traveling to the EU, similar to existing ESTA in the US or ETA in Canada.

3   Smile System Description

SMILE proposes a novel mobility concept for the accurate verification, automated control, monitoring and optimization of people's flows at Land Border Crossing Points (BCP), requiring much less infrastructure than traditional border gates with fixed workstations. It leverages the capabilities of the smart mobile devices in biometric control for secure and trusted authentication while enabling faster control procedures. The traveller declares to SMILE's application the Border Crossing Point (BCP) they are going to visit providing any information that is required for border control procedures and risk analysis based on the traveller's data. The border check is completed at the BCP by using biometrics to validate the user's identity.

In particular, two different mobile applications, one for the user and one for the officers at border control, are utilized. The user fills in any required information regarding their identity and their trip. Important documents, such as the identity card, are scanned while biometrics, like facial photos, are provided. The reported trip information notifies the Border Crossing Point (BCP) officers of the travellers' arrival so that any essential checks in border control systems databases are completed before they reach the border. In this way, travellers are submitted to risk analysis regarding security issues in advance, accelerating control procedures. Once the travellers have reached the border, authorized control officers verify their identity through a designated SMILE application that has access to all the a priori submitted traveller information. Biometric features from the travellers are matched to the submitted ones and further procedures are followed according to related legislation.

SMILE's structure can easily accommodate to border control needs during pandemics. Based on advanced knowledge of the travel plan, SMILE application can alert travellers on information on the outbreak condition to their destination and any necessary actions they have to take before travelling. Moreover, during registration any additional information required due to pandemics, such as travel history or health symptoms, can be submitted along with the rest data in the registration form. In this way, the authorities at the BCPs have advanced knowledge on cases that require special attention. Furthermore, biometrics that facilitate the detection of symptomatic travellers can be included to the existing ones to provide supplementary assistance to the detection of the suspected cases.

4 Application Scenarios

Border control has proven to be an essential measure against pandemics spread with extreme importance and severity. Travelers visiting different countries might be the reason a contiguous disease enters and infects different populations while people with the intention to visit an infected country should be aware of the disease and the necessary measures to protect themselves. Therefore, a complete border control apparatus for pandemics comprises the intention and the measures to protect both travellers and visited countries.

In this scope, there are two main actors in the border control application scenarios: (i) travellers, and (ii) border authorities. Furthermore, the two major factors that determine the application scenarios are: 1) the state of the country to be visited regarding the pandemic, i.e. if it is already affected or not; 2) the infection status of the country(-ies) the visitor has visited over the affection window. Based on these factors, four application scenarios are analysed comprising each actor facing the two aforementioned states.

All of those scenarios assume that the corresponding policy has provided a legal basis on processing such sensitive data as a form of response to the pandemic situation and issued proper legal order to travellers making provision of such data compulsory for them. Therefore, the scenarios described in the paper does not include proportionality test or impact assessment related to process of health data and sensitive personal data or restriction of fundamental rights such as a citizen's right to leave or return.

4.1 Traveller Entering a Country with a Health-Related Alert

During the pre-registration stage, a traveller will enter his/her origin and destination countries, along with any transit countries. In case of a health-related alert or ban of entrance in any of the countries to be visited or transit, the system sends a notification to the traveller providing information on the nature of the alert as well as the level of the security alert (according to CDC there are 3 levels: (1) usual precautions, (2) alert for enhanced precautions, (3) warning to avoid nonessential travel). Moreover, further instructions for actions required or suggested for a health wise safer trip are provided. For example, necessary vaccinations or tests required for admission to destination countries are listed, while more personalized information on precautions also provided, such as supplementary measures in cases of pregnancy or underage children can be offered.

4.2 Traveller Exiting a Country with a Health-Related Alert

In cases where a traveller comes from an infected country or when there is an outbreak at one of the transit countries of their trip, the application offers them the opportunity to do a self-assessment of their condition. Hence, a questionnaire where the travellers report their symptoms and any possible contact they had with infected persons is provided. This allows the travellers to acknowledge their situation, take measures, and even postpone their trip if possible and necessary. Moreover, an additional benefit is that, by providing a priori their health history, border checks can be accelerated.

Another service provided by the application, in the case a traveller comes from an infected country, is to provide notifications on the policies applied by the destination country regarding the pandemic. Such examples may be a quarantine for a certain period, required health tests before entering the country, the provision of healthcare in case the traveller's symptoms suggest infection etc.

4.3 Border Control to Mitigate Pandemic Entering a Country

The existence of an application that allows a traveller to notify the border authorities of their arrival and provide a priori the required information, such as health and travel history, facilitates and accelerates the border control. In this way, authorities have advanced knowledge that travellers from affected countries arrive at particular BCPs while they are notified on the existence of any suspicious symptoms. Furthermore, in cases that a traveller has already crossed other BCPs, they can be notified on the control checks and their remarks on the specific traveller. Hence, once the traveller reaches the border, the officers have already made a risk analysis based on the reported statements and facts. Cases that indicate possible infection are treated with special attention following the anticipated procedures as they are defined by each country's legislation. In addition, procedures regarding travellers of low infection risk can be accelerated.

Another measure adopted during outbreaks is the use of unobtrusive means that acquire soft biometrics related to the pandemic's symptoms. Since fever is usually a symptom in pandemics two widely used means are thermal cameras and infrared thermometers. Therefore, border control can utilize thermal cameras in travellers' passages, so that the authorities are alerted when higher body temperatures are detected while non-contact thermometers can provide more accurate results in detected cases or in high-risk travellers regarding their travel and health history.

4.4 Border Control to Mitigate Pandemic Exiting a Country

Although it is not a common tactic, WHO suggests border control for detection of infected or suspicious cases at BCPs while travellers exit a country, especially in cases that multiple people are going to use a common transport mean, such as airplane, train or bus. The technical procedures are common with the checks made while travellers enter a country.

5 SMILE Examples

In this section, several examples depicting the adjustments that can transform SMILE apparatus into a powerful tool for border control during pandemic situations are analysed. The presented examples are based on use cases that occur from the application scenarios and their goal is to further clarify the adaptability of SMILE to the new pandemic scenarios and to highlight the easiness of the application use for the travellers.

5.1 SMILE Traveller Application

The registration to SMILE application requires filling a form with identity data, providing biometric data, such as close face photos, and information on the user's trip (BCP's to be crossed, approximate time schedule, data of the vehicle to be utilized etc.). In cases that the country of departure is affected from a pandemic, the application displays a supplementary form to be filled with questions regarding the appearance of symptoms related to the pandemic and recent travel history (Fig. 2).

Fig. 1. Travel history

Fig. 2. Traveller self-assessment

In cases that the destination or transit countries are affected, the application alerts the user on the situation by displayed messages (Figs. 3 and 4). Apart from the appearance of the outbreak, the messages include information on bans and important legislations regarding the pandemic (e.g. a potential quarantine that will be applied to travellers in when entering specific countries). Moreover, the users can have access to useful instructions they should be aware of before beginning their trip, e.g. required vaccinations or tests (Fig. 5). Since the gender and the age of the traveller is submitted to SMILE's system, personalized information can be displayed as well. For example, the application could display specific measures required for pregnant women or underage children.

5.2 SMILE BCPs' System

Since the user provides a priori information on the trip and answers a questioner on their recent health history and symptoms, a risk analysis regarding the pandemic can be made by the SMILE's BCP system. In the SMILE's application for the BCP officer, the officer has a clear view of the travellers that are expected over the next time period at the BCP of his/her interest along with their risk profiles (Fig. 6). For each traveller, the officer can have access to more detailed information (Fig. 7). The results of the analysis can be displayed to the SMILE application that is implemented to be used by

Fig. 3. Alert for transit country   **Fig. 4.** Ban of travel alert   **Fig. 5.** Vaccinations and Medicines required for travel

the authorized control officers. The officer, among other issues that require risk analysis, such as criminal activities, can be informed on the risk level of a traveller regarding the pandemic (Fig. 8). In this way, the officer knows in advance when suspicious cases are arriving at the BCP so that extensive control can be applied. Moreover, cases that have passed the control in other BCPs in a recent time period and the results of the control can be acknowledged to the designated officers (Fig. 9).

Fig. 6. List of expected travellers   **Fig. 7.** Traveller profile

Moreover, SMILE system can provide a more thorough examination for symptoms using soft biometrics. Since a very common symptom of pandemics is fever, thermal cameras and infrared thermometers can facilitate SMILE officers to detect suspicious cases. Therefore, thermal cameras can be used to travellers' passages to detect high body temperatures even in cases that were not analysed as high-risk travellers. On the other hand, infrared thermometers can measure the temperature of random travellers, travellers that were indicated by the thermal cameras or travellers that were evaluated

Fig. 8. Traveller risk profile details   **Fig. 9.** Travel history with comments

as of high-risk by SMILE system. Depending on the measurements and the risk level reported by SMILE system additional measures and procedures (e.g. tests for the disease or quarantine) are followed according to each country legislation. The control results are reported to SMILE officers' application so that they are available to other BCPs in case the traveller is intending to cross them.

6   Conclusions

This paper presents an effort to accommodate SMILE border control system to the additional requirements occurring for border crossing during pandemic situations. SMILE's structure provides the capability of information exchange between the travellers and the border control authorities in advance of their arrival at the border crossing point. Based on this feature, extra functionalities that can be proved critical during pandemics can be easily added to SMILE's mobile applications. Therefore, information on the disease's spread, the measures taken at each country, the required procedures to bulletproof the one's health via vaccines and tests can be notified to the travellers before their departure providing them the time to prepare themselves appropriately. Moreover, border officers can be a priori aware of the arrival of travellers with suspicious symptoms and travel history and conduct a risk analysis in advance, achieving accelerated control procedures and increased preparedness to cope with infected travellers.

Another feature of SMILE is the use of soft biometrics and their integration to the mobile applications to facilitate the user identification. In this sense, biometrics indicative of a human's health, such as body temperature, can be easily incorporated to SMILE's application in order to make a better evaluation of the travellers' health condition.

The goal of this paper is to demonstrate ways that SMILE border control system can easily adjust, due to its structure, to pandemic situations. The presented use cases show that both travellers and authorities can benefit from the proposed additional features that accelerate border procedures, improve the evaluation and the detection of suspected cases and provide valuable information to travellers to achieve a safer and more organized trip.

Acknowledgement. This work is co-funded by the European Union (EU) within the SMILE project under Grant agreement number 740931 and the ITFLOWS project under Grant agreement number 882986. The SMILE and ITFLOWS projects are part of the EU Framework Program for Research and Innovation Horizon 2020.

References

1. https://data.humdata.org/dataset/2019-novel-coronavirus-cases
2. https://www.kaggle.com/de5d5fe61fcaa6ad7a66/pandemic-2009-h1n1-swine-flu-influenza-a-dataset
3. Wang, L., Li, X.: Spatial epidemiology of networked metapopulation: an overview. Chin. Sci. Bull. **59**(28), 3511–3522 (2014). https://doi.org/10.1007/s11434-014-0499-8
4. Sun, G.Q., Jusup, M., Jin, Z., Wang, Y., Wang, Z.: Pattern transitions in spatial epidemics: mechanisms and emergent properties. Phys. Life Rev. **19**, 43–73 (2016)
5. Wang, Y., Ma, J., Cao, J., Li, L.: Edge-based epidemic spreading in degree correlated complex networks. J. Theor. Biol. **454**, 164–181 (2018)
6. Balcan, D., Gonçalves, B., Hu, H., Ramasco, J.J., Colizza, V., Vespignani, A.: Modeling the spatial spread of infectious diseases: the GLobal epidemic and mobility computational model. J. Comput. Sci. **1**, 132–145 (2010)
7. Douglas, J.V., et al.: STEM: an open source tool for disease modeling. Health Secur. **17**(4), 291–306 (2019)
8. Burki, T.K.: App to model pandemic influenza. Spotlight **6**(1), 17–18 (2018)
9. Günther, C., Günther, M., Günther, D.: Tracing contacts to control the COVID-19 pandemic. Social and Information Networks (2020)
10. WHO: Joint external evaluation tool-International health regulations. WHO Press, Geneva, Switzerland (2016)
11. Wells, C.R., et al.: Impact of international travel and border control measures on the global spread of the novel 2019 coronavirus outbreak. In: Proceedings of the National Academy of Sciences, vol. 117, no. 3, pp. 7504–7509 (2020)
12. Zlojutro, A., Rey, D., Gardner, L.: A decision-support framework to optimize border control for global outbreak mitigation. Sci. Rep. **9**(1), 1–4 (2019)
13. Ho, L.L., Tsai, Y.H., Lee, W.P., Liao, S.T., Wu, L.G., Wu, Y.C.: Taiwan's travel and border health measures in response to Zika. Health Secur. **15**(2), 185–192 (2017)
14. Sakaguchi, H., et al.: Assessment of border control measures and community containment measures used in Japan during the early stages of pandemic (H1N1) 2009. PLoS ONE **7**(2), e31289 (2012)
15. Cohen, N.J.: Travel and border health measures to prevent the international spread of ebola. MMWR **65**(3), 57–67 (2016)
16. Selvey, L.A., Antão, C., Hall, R.: Entry screening for infectious diseases in humans. Emerg. Inf. Dis. **21**(2), 197–201 (2015)
17. Karita, T., Francisco, M.E.: Watanabe, K,: An Integrated mHealth App for dengue reporting and mapping, health communication, and behavior modification: development and assessment of mozzify. JMIR **4**(1), e16424 (2020)
18. Lwin, M.O., Ng, J.S., Jayasundar, K., et al.: Visual design for a mobile pandemic map system for public health. AI Soc. (2020). https://doi.org/10.1007/s00146-020-00939-7
19. https://wwwnc.cdc.gov/travel

Translating Ethical Theory into Ethical Action: An Ethic of Responsibility Approach to Value-Oriented Design

Zachary J. Goldberg[✉] [iD]

Trilateral Research, Waterford, Ireland
zachary.goldberg@trilateralresearch.com

Abstract. Calls for ethics by and in design of new technologies are now commonplace in academic literature, private businesses such as Microsoft and Google, and the European Commission's Horizon 2020 and Horizon Europe research projects. This emphasis on ethics is necessary owing to the ways in which new technologies are embedded in our every day practices, can radically affect these practices, and have the potential for transgressing or promoting important values. Despite this importance, there is a lack of clarity concerning how designers can translate ethical theories and ethical values into ethical action. In this paper, I canvass some of the most prominent ethical theories and explain their connection to action. Finding these wanting, I propose an ethic of responsibility as a first step in a more ethically sensitive approach to value-oriented design. This approach internalizes responsibility for ethical action into the actor, rather than seeking ethical characteristics in the external act or value. The reader should keep in mind that this is only the first step given constraints on time and space of this paper. The following step of identifying concrete design suggestions will follow in a subsequent article.

Keywords: Responsibility · Value-Oriented Design · Ethical Theory

1 Introduction

Calls for ethics by and in design of new technologies are now commonplace in academic literature, in private businesses such as Microsoft and Google, and in the European Commission's Horizon 2020 and Horizon Europe research projects. This emphasis on ethics is necessary owing to the ways in which new technologies are embedded in our every day practices, can radically affect both these practices and human interaction more generally, and have the potential for transgressing or promoting important values. Despite this importance, there is a lack of clarity concerning how designers of new technologies can translate ethical theories and ethical values into ethical action. As a result of this lack of clarity, new technologies might be designed in ways that elicit ethical concerns, harms or wrongs, or fail to promote ethical opportunities. In this paper, my objective it to identify obstacles inherent in past approaches attempting to translate ethical theory into ethical action, and offer the initial steps of a new approach focused on responsibility. First, I canvass some of the most prominent ethical theories and explain their connection

© Springer Nature Switzerland AG 2021
S. Yildirim Yayilgan et al. (Eds.): INTAP 2020, CCIS 1382, pp. 335–343, 2021.
https://doi.org/10.1007/978-3-030-71711-7_28

to action. Next, finding these wanting, I propose an ethic of responsibility as a first step in a more ethically sensitive approach to value-oriented design. This approach internalizes responsibility for ethical action into the actor, rather than seeking ethical characteristics in an external act or abstract value. The reader should keep in mind that this is only the first step given constraints on time and space of this paper and presentation. The following step of identifying concrete design suggestions will follow in a subsequent article.

2   Ethical Theories

In this section, I will canvass ethical theories and the ways in which each is tied to ethical action.

2.1   Consequentialism and Deontology

The most prominent ethical theories both in the Western philosophical tradition as well in diverse approaches to ethics by and in design are deontology and consequentialism. Although they differ in their methodologies as well as in how each prioritizes the right and the good, I have grouped them together in a single category because they are similar in how they relate to ethical action.

As its name communicates, consequentialists argue that choices—acts and/or intentions—are to be morally assessed solely by the states of affairs they bring about. Consequentialists thus need to specify initially the states of affairs that are intrinsically valuable—often called, collectively, "the Good." They are then in a position to assert that whatever choices increase the Good, that is, bring about more of it, are the choices that it is morally right to make and to execute.

Consequentialism strikes many as reflecting our ordinary moral thinking. When we think about what we ought to do, we often think about the risks, consequences, and the benefits our actions could bring about. We weigh these considerations against one another and often choose the course of action that produces "the best" consequences. We see commitments to consequentialist principles when companies and people urge to "Do no harm". The H2020 ethics requirements explicitly require project partners to assess the risks of their work and as well as the impact that the development of new technologies could have for the wellbeing of society.

Deontology identifies the locus of ethical action not in good consequences, but in terms of what is right. In contrast to consequentialist theories, deontological theories judge the morality of choices by criteria different from the states of affairs those choices bring about. The most familiar forms of deontology, and also the forms presenting the greatest contrast to consequentialism, hold that some choices cannot be justified by their effects—that no matter how morally good their consequences, some choices are morally forbidden. For such deontologists, what makes a choice right is its conformity with a moral norm. In this sense, for such deontologists, the Right is said to have priority over the Good. If an act is not in accord with the Right, it may not be undertaken, no matter the Good that it might produce [2].

The deontological approach is reflected in directives to protect persons' autonomy and human dignity, and the promotion of the values of equality and fairness (although these values are not excluded from consequentialism). From the deontological perspective, a person's autonomy cannot be infringed upon for the sake of producing good consequences or states of affairs. It would be wrong to do so even if the result would be good. Like consequentialism, the deontological perspective is also embedded into European value systems, and we see appeals to protect such values in the calls for the design and development of new technologies in H2020 calls.

Both theories can teach us about the nature of ethical action. Nevertheless, neither theory is without its share of conceptual and ethical problems. It is widely discussed by philosophers that consequentialism can obligate acts that are clearly unethical [3]. If consequences are all that matter ethically, then values such as autonomy, dignity, and privacy could be transgressed for the sake of producing a great deal of good consequences for others. For example, some simple versions of consequentialism could obligate enslaving a small portion of the population if doing so were to produce a great deal of good consequences for the majority. Such a conclusion is ethically horrendous.

Additionally, it is notoriously complicated to predict good states of affairs, especially for the long term and especially in the contexts of technology design and scientific discovery. Who could have known that the invention of the combustible engine would irrevocably accelerate global warming? Who could have known that splitting the atom would result in the production of a bomb with a destructive force virtually unimaginable at the time of its creation?

Deontological theories also run up against ethical issues. One intractable problem arises when values conflict. It seems fairly straightforward to claim that a person's autonomy and privacy ought to be protected and promoted. However, these values might come into conflict with one another making it difficult if not impossible to know which value to prioritize simply on the basis of deontological theory alone. For example, in order offset algorithmic bias in a facial recognition tool to avoid significant problems identifying and misidentifying people of color, we might ask designers to train the algorithm on as vast a dataset as possible with the hope of designing diversity recognition into the tool. However, we may find that collecting such a large dataset would require us to violate individuals' privacy. How should AI designers adjudicate this conflict relying upon deontological principles alone?

Moreover, deontological theories completely forbid the transgression of its values. Is it always the case that important values ought never to be violated? What if the good consequences indeed outweigh the value in question? For example, deontologists claim that one ought not lie. Lying to another uses the other person as a means to one's own goal, whereas one ought to recognize each person as an autonomous agent worthy of making decisions without being manipulated through false information. However, I think it is a fair guess that every one of us in this room has lied or been tempted to lie to spare someone's feelings. More ethically serious examples include whether it is always impermissible to sacrifice the life of one person for the lives of many others. I do not argue that it is not. But it is a question worthy of reflection and discussion that cannot be ignored due to commitment to a particular theory or rule.

Finally, and despite these differences, consequentialism and deontology share the manner in which each theory is related to ethical practice. Both theories include a deductive relation to action. Deductive views are ones under which "the moral theory is related to practice as premises are to conclusions" [9]. That is, the by combining the moral rule with the details of the particular circumstances, we can deduce the right, or good, thing to do.

The principal problem with deductive views is that they do not always translate into clear action directives. Particular circumstances can be so complex that the moral rule is either too vague to be helpful, or requires a vast amount of qualifications. For example, when designing AI algorithms for facial recognition, the principle to promote well-being is far too vague. The principle to protect persons' autonomy is as well. Or, the principle that it is always wrong to violate another's privacy confronts challenges from the need for security. Hence, we must alter the principle to read, "It is always wrong to violate another's privacy unless (a), (b)....(z), when these variables stand for various exceptions or particular circumstances. Consequently, deductive views do not translate easily into ethical action in complex scenarios.

In what follows, I canvass additional methods for translating theory into action before presenting an ethic of responsibility as an alternative.

2.2 Balancing with Intuitions

The model of balancing is based on intuitions [9, 22]. This approach acknowledges that we are often confronted with conflicting values without a clear method for adjudicating priority. In such cases, Rawls invites us to attempt and find "reflective equilibrium" by which we try to strike a balance among competing values by way of intuition.

The main objection to balancing is that it renders the agent incapable of giving reasons for an ethical decision or action other than that it "strikes him/her" to be right or good. And since the decision is based on intuitions there does not appear to be an acceptable way of determining whether the decision was ethically correct after the fact. Finally, moral intuitions will vary depending on culture and even differ according to the individual. Consequently, it is not a reliable method to translate theory into action[1].

2.3 Casuistry

This method often appears in the field of applied ethics. Issues in medical ethics, business ethics, and the ethics of technology can be highly complex making it unclear how to translate theories and values into concrete action. The casuist approaches such complexities with a series of paradigmatic cases that reflect an accepted ethical rule or value. The casuist approach then calls for slightly changing various variables of the paradigmatic case to make a case more ethically problematic. We then conclude that the adapted case is similar enough to the original one such that the value or ethical rule with which we began is still present, or that the case is dissimilar for a particular reason. This reason provides us ethical insight into which features of a situation have ethical significance and why.

---

[1] For more on the role of moral intuitions in technology design, see Umbrello [27].

This approach has its merits and can lead to concrete ethical decision making. However, this process of reasoning does not allow us to question and justify our original assessment. At most it can show that we are consistent with our first judgment of the original case. Furthermore, without a substantive moral theory behind it, there is no clear method for preferring certain values over others.

2.4 Value-Oriented Design Approaches

Different value-oriented approaches have been developed for application to intelligent technology design and HCI more widely, including Values at Play [11, 12], Values in Design [8, 18], and Worth-Centered Computing [6]. Participatory design has traditionally attended to participants' values [17], although the term "values" does not always appear in the corresponding literature. Within this wide-ranging field, Value Sensitive Design [14] is considered by many scholars to be the most comprehensive approach to addressing human values in technology design [e.g. 1, 5, 10]. Other scholars work in the area of values and technology design, but do not present a particular account of how to do so [13], often focusing on specific values such as privacy, autonomy, or dignity [e.g., 4, 21].

These varying approaches to values-oriented design are noble attempts to embed ethics into the design of new technology. Nevertheless, despite attempts to make concrete ethical action more clear, each of these approaches has been subject to criticisms that they share many of the problems already discussed above [7].

Of course there remain other methodological approaches to translating ethical theory and values into ethical action (e.g. principlism, particularism), but they also share the problems translating values and theory into action. I now present an ethic of responsibility, which can be more successful in translating values into action than these other approaches. Further, owing to its flexibility (that we will see), it complements the rapidly changing world of technology design and development.

3 An Ethic of Responsibility

As we have seen so far there are many disparate approaches to ethical theory generally, translating theory into action, and value-oriented design. Each has conceptual and ethical advantages that are worth retaining in any new theory or approach. My view is that there is a coherent and highly plausible theoretical perspective which unites many of the desirable aspects belonging to cotemporary writings on ethics and values, but which shifts the focus from external values to personal and social responsibility. Such a coherent conception of responsibility is well suited especially for professional cases and the rapidly changing world of technology design and development.

The initial impetus behind an ethic of responsibility is to move away from commitment to a particular principle or rule such as those that characterize consequentialism or deontology. Rather than focusing on a sense of obligation one has to a universal moral principle, one focuses on the kinds of responsibilities one has owing to the relationships one has formed or finds oneself in [15, 19, 25].

The most developed philosophical treatments concerning an ethic of responsibility appeared originally in feminist philosophical literature [e.g. 16, 20, 23, 26], but have since been taken up by non-feminist philosophers as well including Christopher Gowans [15], Larry May [19], and Michael Slote [24]. I draw on these sources and present several interrelated aspects characterizing an ethic of responsibility. They are:

1. A responsiveness to those whom we could help, especially concerning those who are in relationships with us or toward whom we have taken on a certain role;
2. a sensitivity to the peculiarities of a person's concrete circumstances and contexts;
3. a motivation to respond to another which grows out of the needs of others, especially those who depend on us;
4. a wide discretion concerning what is required to be a responsible person, rather than an emphasis on keeping an abstract commandment or rule;
5. a respect for the legitimacy of emotions as a source of moral knowledge, and especially for the feelings of guilt, shame, and remorse that are central to people's actual moral experiences;
6. a sense of who we are as responsible people that is tied more to who we are, and what we can do, than to what we have done [19].

This ethic of responsibility can reply to the three main categories of objection that we canvassed earlier. First, we said that consequentialism and deontology can require us to take ethical action that it is unethical. Consequentialism could require us to kill one person to save many, and deontology could require us to tell someone the truth even if that truth would be devastating to them psychologically. Because an ethic of responsibility does not follow an abstract principle or rule that is purported to be universal, it allows us to take seriously the nuances of the moral landscape acknowledging that it is often quite difficult to act in an ethical manner. Acting ethically often means paying heed to others' needs and vulnerabilities, and not being obligated to an abstract rule no matter the particulars of the situation and the individual with whom we interact.

Secondly, it was shown that values can conflict and deontology does not provide a reliable methodology for adjudicating such conflicts. Such conflicts are especially problematic in professional cases when a person must make a decision. An ethic of responsibility provides a means for handling such conflicts. By focusing on the particular circumstances of an individual, a responsiveness to his/her needs, and the position one has to respond to those circumstances and needs, we can emphasize some values over others in one set of circumstances and later alter this ordering in another set of circumstances. Since we are not committed to obeying one single principle, we can adjust our ethical understanding and ethical responses to the particular circumstances we encounter.

Thirdly, we canvassed different methods for translating theory into action. An ethic of responsibility is action guiding, but it allows for some individual discretion as well. Its aspects speak to each of us but may speak to each of us in a different way. By including a focus on the importance of moral emotions, especially remorse, guilt or shame, in informing our ethical responses, it presents a realistic ethical approach that recognizes that each of us has a moral biography. We have all been faced with countless ethical decisions, some of which we have made well and some of which we have not. This ethical experience is invaluable in making future ethical decisions. Especially those decisions we did not make well, can help guide us to make better decisions in the future. As an ethic of responsibility is prospective rather than merely a responsibility for past actions and decisions, it can guide our future actions.

To illustrate: imagine a company is designing and developing a biometric corridor to be placed at border crossing points in order to collect travelers' biometrics, check the biometrics against a preregistration database to confirm the travelers' identity, and let them cross the border quickly and securely. One of the innovative features of this biometric corridor is that it can collect the travelers' biometrics "on the fly" without the traveler stopping. One of the biometrics it captures is an iris scan. In order to capture a clear image of the iris of the traveler on the fly, the camera must be within a certain close distance of the traveler as he/she walks. As a consequence, the corridor must be built narrowly, only slightly wider than the shoulders of a person. With this width as a functional requirement, several groups of people are excluded from using the biometric corridor, most obviously people in wheelchairs, parents with strollers, and elderly people with walkers.

A consequentialist approach would weigh the good consequences against the bad, and since more people would benefit from use of the corridor than would be excluded, we are obligated to proceed with its design and development. A deontological approach might consider the dignity of those excluded to be violated thereby obligating the company to refrain from design and development of the corridor despite the good consequences its implementation at the border would bring.

In contrast, an ethic of responsibility approach allows us to be more sensitive to the nuances of the particular context, to take moral emotions seriously, and to focus on how to respond to those affected. These aspects might direct our thinking in the following way: The excluded groups are not excluded from crossing the border; they are excluded from using the more efficient corridor. In this way, their right to the freedom of movement is not hindered. Further, it is regrettable that the current technical possibilities disallow certain groups from accessing the corridor, but it would also be regrettable if no one could use it as it would shorten wait lines and add an extra level of security to the identity verification process. Although it's not an ideal solution, perhaps it would be ethically acceptable to provide a public acknowledgment of the shortcomings of the current construction of the corridor, and a sincere commitment to update the system as soon as the technology allows it. Indeed, in interpersonal relationships we do not expect each other to be moral saints, but we do expect and usually accept an acknowledgment and explanation when others fall ethically short. An ethic of responsibility provides the means for ethical decision making and ethical action in an ethically complex and imperfect world.

4 Conclusion

In this paper, I have briefly presented an alternative to the traditional and prominent Western ethical theories and methods for translating theory into action. An ethic of responsibility is a first step in a more ethically sensitive approach to value-oriented design. This approach internalizes responsibility for ethical action into the actor, rather than seeking ethical characteristics in an external act or value. As an approach to value-oriented design it focuses on one's ability to respond to the needs of others while considering particular circumstances, and moral emotions. Its guidelines are flexible while remaining firmly directed at responding to others. In these ways it offers a more realistic framework for making ethical decisions and turning them into action. Since it is not tied to a specific rule or principle, it is especially appropriate for the rapidly changing environment of technology design and development where the designers carry an ethical responsibility to future users.

References

1. Albrechtslund, A.: Ethics and technology design. Eth. Inf. Technol. 1(9), 63–72 (2007)
2. Alexander, L., Moore, M.: Deontological Ethics. In: Zalta, E. (ed.) The Stanford Encyclopedia of Philosophy (Winter 2016 Edition). https://plato.stanford.edu/archives/win2016/entries/ethics-deontological/. Accessed 7 July 2020
3. Anscombe, G.E.M.: Modern moral philosophy. Philosophy 33(124), 1–19 (1958)
4. Barkhuus, L.: The mismeasurement of privacy. In: Proceedings of the SIGCHI Conference on Human Factors in Computing Systems, pp. 367–376. ACM, New York (2012)
5. Brey, P.: Values in technology and disclosive computer ethics. In: Floridi, L. (ed.) The Cambridge Handbook of Information and Computer Ethics, pp. 41–58. Cambridge University Press, Cambridge (2010)
6. Cockton, G.: Getting there: six meta-principles and interaction design. In: Proceedings of the SIGCHI Conference on Human Factors in Computing Systems, pp. 2223–2232. ACM, New York (2009)
7. Davis, J., Nathan, L.P.: Value sensitive design: applications, adaptations, and critiques. In: van den Hoven, J., Vermaas, P.E., van de Poel, I. (eds.) Handbook of Ethics, Values, and Technological Design, pp. 11–40. Springer, Dordrecht (2013). https://doi.org/10.1007/978-94-007-6970-0_3
8. Detweiler, C., Hindriks, K., Jonker, C.: Principles for value-sensitive agent-oriented software engineering. In: Weyns, D., Gleizes, M.-P. (eds.) AOSE 2010. LNCS, vol. 6788, pp. 1–16. Springer, Heidelberg (2011). https://doi.org/10.1007/978-3-642-22636-6_1
9. Dworkin, G.: Theory, practice, and moral reasoning. In: Copp, D. (ed.) Oxford Handbook of Ethical Theory, pp. 624–644. Oxford University Press, Oxford (2006)
10. Fallman, D.: The new good: exploring the potential of philosophy of technology to contribute to human-computer interaction. In: Proceedings of the SIGCHI Conference on Human Factors in Computing Systems, pp. 1051–1060 . ACM, New York (2011)
11. Flanagan, M., Howe, D., Nissenbaum, H.: Values at play. In: Proceedings of the SIGCHI Conference on Human Factors in Computing Systems, pp. 751–760. ACM, New York (2005)
12. Flanagan, M., Nissenbaum, H.: A game design methodology to incorporate social activist themes. In: Proceedings of the SIGCHI Conference on Human Factors in Computing Systems, pp. 181–190. ACM, New York (2007)
13. Flanagan, M., Howe, D., Nissenbaum, H.: Embodying values in technology: theory and practice. In: Van Den Hoven, J., Weckert, J. (eds.) Information technology and moral philosophy, pp. 322–353. Cambridge University Press, Cambridge (2008)
14. Friedman, B., Kahn, P.H., Jr., Borning, A.: Value sensitive design and information systems. In: Zhang, P., Galletta, D. (eds.) Human-computer interaction in management information systems: Foundations, pp. 348–372. Armonk, M.E. Sharpe (2006)
15. Gowans, C.: Innocence Lost: An Examination of Inescapable Wrongdoing. Oxford University Press, Oxford (1994)
16. Held, V.: Non-contractual society: a feminist view. Can. J. Philos. Supplementary 13, 111–137 (1987)

17. Iverson, O., Halskov, K., Leong, T.W.: Rekindling values in participatory design. In: Proceedings of the 11th Biennial Participatory Design Conference, pp. 91–100. ACM, New York (2010)
18. Knobel, C., Bowker, G.: Values in design. In: Communications of the ACM, vol 54, no 7, pp. 26–28. ACM, New York (2011)
19. May, L.: Social Responsibility. Midwest Studies in Philosophy XX. (2006)
20. Meyers, D.: Self & Society und Personal Choice. Columbia Press, New York (1989)
21. Palen, L., Dourish, P.: Unpacking privacy for a networked world. In: Proceedings of the SIGCHI Conference on Human Factors in Computing Systems, pp. 129–136. ACM, New York (2003)
22. Rawls, J.: A Theory of Justice. Harvard University Press, Cambridge, MA (1971)
23. Ruddick, S.: Maternal Thinking: Toward a Politics of Peace. Beacon Press, Boston, MA (1989)
24. Slote, M.: From Enlightenment to Receptivity: Rethinking Our Values. Oxford University Press, Oxford (2013)
25. Weber, M.: Reprinted in From Max Weber: Essays in Sociology. In: Translated and edited by H. H. Gerth and C. Wright Mills, Ulan Press, New York (1946/2012)
26. Whitbeck, C.: A different reality: feminist ontology. In: Gould, C. (ed.) Beyond Domination. Rowman & Allanheld, Totowa, N.J (1984)
27. Umbrello, S.: The moral psychology of value sensitive design: the methodological issues of moral intuitions for responsible innovation. J. Responsible Innov. 5(2), 186–200 (2018)

An Example of Privacy and Data Protection Best Practices for Biometrics Data Processing in Border Control: Lesson Learned from SMILE

Mohamed Abomhara[✉] and Sule Yildirim Yayilgan

Department of Information Security and Communication Technology, Norwegian University of Science and Technology, Trondheim, Norway
{mohamed.abomhara,sule.yildirim}@ntnu.no

Abstract. Biometric recognition is a highly adopted technology to support different kinds of applications, ranging from security and access control applications to low enforcement applications. However, such systems raise serious privacy and data protection concerns. Misuse of data, compromising the privacy of individuals and/or authorized processing of data may be irreversible and could have severe consequences on the individual's rights to privacy and data protection. This is partly due to the lack of methods and guidance for the integration of data protection and privacy by design in the system development process. In this paper, we present an example of privacy and data protection best practices to provide more guidance for data controllers and developers on how to comply with the legal obligation for data protection. These privacy and data protection best practices and considerations are based on the lessons learned from the SMart mobILity at the European land borders (SMILE) project.

Keywords: Privacy by design · Data protection by design · Data protection · Best practices · Biometrics

1 Introduction

The dramatic advances in computerization and personal data collection have opened doors to unprecedented opportunities in the field of law enforcement and national security applications. However, the increase in data collection, processing, retention and analysis is leading to increased surveillance and tracking of people (data subjects) in many ways [19]. When data about individual's activities is collected and analyzed, it can lead to some challenges and conflicts with fundamental human rights and can be the cause of ethical, social and legal challenges such as unauthorized and inadvertent disclosure, embarrassment and harassment, social stigma and inappropriate decisions, to name a few [2, 4, 15, 17].

© Springer Nature Switzerland AG 2021
S. Yildirim Yayilgan et al. (Eds.): INTAP 2020, CCIS 1382, pp. 344–358, 2021.
https://doi.org/10.1007/978-3-030-71711-7_29

The key challenge and the focus of this paper is related to the respect for individual privacy and the right to personal data protection.

The amount of personal data processed in the border control and its research context continues to rise every year. SMILE[1] as a proposed border control tool can help to optimize and monitor the flows of people at land borders to increase security and improve border crossing efficiency as well as to facilitate effective migration control and enforcement. Like others, SMILE also increases the tendency to collect, use and process sensitive personal data (e.g., alpha-numeric data and biometric data). Thus, SMILE system raises serious legal and policy concerns [1, 2]. Misuse of data, compromising the privacy of individuals and/or authorized processing of data may be irreversible and could have severe consequences on the individual's fundamental rights [1].

In order to prevent and mitigate privacy and data protection risks, it is paramount that data controllers comply with the European legal framework designed to protect the privacy and the personal data of individuals. It is worth mentioning that for data controller(s), it is very important to consider all laws and rules related to the developed technology. However, it is extremely difficult for the data controller(s) to implement a single technological solution or practice that must likely to be compliant with all Member States' laws and rules. Thus, the aim of this paper is to guide data controllers through a general overview of the best practices for privacy and data protection related to personal data processing. During the SMILE research and development, we investigated and critically conducted a theoretical analysis of privacy and data protection by design legal obligation [13, 18] in the European frameworks and how it can be implemented in the context of biometrics data processing at border control. The focus of this paper is only on the European Union (EU) legal obligation established by the General Data Protection Regulation (GDPR) [18].

In this paper, we present a brief summary of privacy and data protection best practices to provide more guidance for data controllers and developers on how to comply with the legal obligation for data protection. These best practices and considerations are based on the lessons learned from the SMILE project.

The remaining part of this paper is organized as following: Sect. 2 presents the proposed SMILE data governance framework including a brief summary of EU legal frameworks for data protection, privacy and data protection requirements, organizational and technical measures and data protection impact assessment. Section 3 describes privacy and data protection measures that shall be considered by controllers. Section 4 concludes the paper.

---

[1] https://smile-h2020.eu/smile/.

2   SMILE Data Governance Framework

The proposed framework for personal data processing in SMILE consists of multiple elements including the legal frameworks, entities, data protection impact assessment and compliance assessment.

2.1   Legal Frameworks: EU and National Laws

The EU has taken numerous specific legislative initiatives with regard to data protection. Currently, the most important instruments is Regulation 2016/679 (GDPR) [18] on the protection of natural persons with regard to the processing of personal data and on the free movement of such data. In additional to GDPR, most of other EU legislative initiatives are in the form of directives (e.g., Directive (EU) 2016/680 [16]) which have been implemented or transposed into national laws. This process of implementation allows Member States for some variation along national lines whilst preserving the essential context of the directive. Moreover, the European Data Protection Board (EDPB[2]) gives expert advices regarding data protection in forms of standards and guidelines such as opinions expressed by the Article 29 Data Protection Working Party. This paper focuses only on the legal framework for privacy and personal data protection (GDPR). Whilst the GDRP is a regulation (which does not require transposition to have legal effect), it still gives a room for Member States to maintain or introduce further conditions, including limitations, with regard to the processing of genetic data, biometric data or data concerning health.

Biometrics data are considered as "special categories of data" [18]. Therefore, the GDPR prohibits the processing of biometrics data in principle. However, the Regulation specifies a list of exemptions. In fact, processing biometrics data is covered by certain exemptions listed in Article 9(2) of GDPR. Firstly, there is the consent of the data subject, which must be specific, informed, given freely and explicit (Article 9(2)(a) and Article 7 of GDPR). Most of the time, the processing of biometrics data at the borders is subjected to the express consent of the travelers and it is not necessarily written. Moreover, biometrics data may be processed because of the vital interests of the data subject (travelers) or another natural person. Another possible exemption occurs when the processing is necessary for substantial public interest (Article 9(2)(g) of GDPR). For example, the COVID-19 pandemic forced Member States to reintroduce border checks on Schengen internal borders. In the end, the GDPR includes the exception for the processing related to the public interest when the data are manifestly made public by the data subject (Article 9(2)(e) of GDPR).

---

[2] The European Data Protection Board is an independent European body whose purpose is to ensure consistent application of the General Data Protection Regulation and to promote cooperation among the EU's data protection authorities.

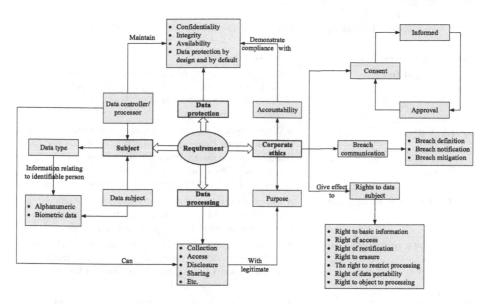

Fig. 1. Data protection requirements

Based on lessons learned during the SMILE research and development, it is argued that in the context of border crossing, even if the processing is not entirely founded on consent, the travelers have the right to take a role when and how their personal data are used. In Articles 12-23 of GDPR, the law confer on data subject's rights and prescribes the other general rules to be complied with when personal data are processed. For example, according to Article 25 of GDPR, data controllers processing personal data shall implement Data Protection by Design and by Default (DPbD) measures [18]. Moreover, to ensure compliance with all relevant legal provisions, Data Protection Impact Assessment (DPIA) [3,14] is required in case of the processing on a large scale of special categories of personal data (Article 35 of GDPR).

Biometric data processing at border control must comply with privacy and data protection provisions as prescribed in GDPR and Directive (EU) 2016/680 as well as national law. As we mentioned above, the focus of this paper is only GDPR requirements, Fig. 1 demonstrates set of requirements refer to the processing operations that the data controller must carry out during and after data collection. Moreover, Table 1 presents data protection requirements derived from GDPR.

Table 1. Data protection requirements derived from GDPR.

ID	Requirement	Biometrics system
Req01	**Legal basis**	• Data processing shall be carried out in accordance with data protection law (e.g., consent, legal obligation of the controller, fair, lawful and transparent processing)
Req02	**Consent**	• When applicable, data must collected and processed with freely given, specific, informed and unambiguous consent from the data subject and protection of its vital interests when the data subject is physically or legally incapable of giving consent
Req03	**Purpose limitation**	• Biometrics data must be processed for specific, explicitly defined and legitimate purpose and data should not be used for incompatible purposes
Req04	**Data minimization**	• Personal data collected must be adequate, relevant and limited to what is necessary for border control, and in relation to the purpose(s) (Req03) for which those data are processed
Req05	**Data accuracy**	• Biometrics data (and other personal data) must be accurate and, when necessary, kept up to date during the enrollment and matching to avoid false acceptance and/or rejection. Every reasonable step shall be taken to ensure that inaccurate personal data are either erased or rectified with-out delay
Req06	**Data storage limitation**	• Unless there is a legal basis (Req01) with appropriate safeguards (i.e., security (Req07) and privacy control) in place, personal data must not be stored more than what is necessary for
Req07	**Data security**	• Data controller(s) implement appropriate technical and organizational measures to ensure a level of security appropriate to the risk guarantee availability, integrity and confidentiality of personal data
Req08	**Right of information**	• Data subject (traveler) must have the right to obtain information about their personal data as described in Article 12, 13 and 14 of GDPR
Req09	**Right to access**	• Data subject (traveler) must have the right to request access to data related to him or her as described in Article 15 of GDPR. Keep in mind, in case of border management, such a right can be limited or restricted to some extent as stated in Article of 15 of Directive (EU) 2016/680
Req10	**Right to rectification**	• Data subject (traveler) must have the right to require a controller to rectify any errors in their personal data and o have incomplete personal data completed as described in Article 16 of GDPR
Req11	**Right to erasure**	• Data subjects must have the right to require a controller(s) to delete their personal data as described in Article 17 of GDPR

(*continued*)

Table 1. (*continued*)

ID	Requirement	Biometrics system
Req12	**The right to restrict processing**	• Data subjects must have the right to restrict the processing of personal data when accuracy of the personal data is contested, processing is unlawful, data no longer needed, or data subject has objected to processing as described in Article 18 of GDPR. • Controllers must inform the data subject in writing of any refusal of rectification (Req10) or erasure of personal data (Req11) or restriction of processing (Req12) and of the reasons for the refusal (Article 19 of GDPR)
Req13	**Right of data portability**	• Where applicable, data subjects must have the right to object, on grounds relating to their particular situation, to the processing of personal data as described in Article 20 of GDPR
Req14	**Right to object the processing**	• Data subject must have the right to transfer their personal data between controllers (e.g., to move account details from one SMILE platform to another) as described in Article 21 of GDPR
Req15	**Data disclosure to third parties/countries**	• In the case where the data needed to disclosure to third parties/countries, data controllers must en-sure (1) an adequate level of data protection before transmission and disclosure, (2) an appropriate safeguards to ensure adequate protection level provided by the third party, (3) an explicit legal permission and (4) the data subject's well informed about the identity of controller(s) in the third parties/countries (Req08)
Req16	**Data breach communication**	• Data controller must ensure an assessment of data incidents and prompt notification of breach to data subjects when there is a high risk to the rights and freedoms of natural persons and, with respect to supervisory authorities, notification when the breach is likely to result in a risk to the rights and freedoms of natural persons
Req17	**Accountability**	• Data controller must be able to demonstrate compliance with the data protection principles • Data controller and data processor must take the necessary measures to give effect to the basic principles of data protection set out in GDPR • Data controller must be accountable for complying with measures, which give effect to the principles stated above • Data controller must carry out "Data Protection Impact Assessment (DPIA)" with accordance to Article 35 of GDPR

2.2   Entity: Organizational and Technical Measures

The entity is a public or private operator of essential services. In our case, the entity is a competent authority (border/policy authority) composed of social unit of people and complementary partners (another entity) who work together to fulfill and regulate the objectives of the movement of people, animals, and goods across the borders (Regulation (EU) 2016/399 [9]). All border authority have a management structure that determines relationships between the different activities and the personnel's roles, responsibilities and authority to carry out different tasks. In order to guarantee an effective and efficient interaction and information sharing within and among entities and avoid any management difficulties, this section aims to define responsibilities and allocate roles related to data sharing in accordance with legal requirements (Sect. 2.1) and the entity's policy.

The organizational and administrative measures are expressions of data protection by design approach. Many data protection principles in GDPR are related to organizational measures: fairness, transparency, accuracy, confidentiality and accountability. The data controller should provide evidence that the processing is privacy friendly and in accordance to the legal frameworks. In the case of border control, it may be important to remember that there may be more than one data controller. Depending on exact circumstances, the competent authority might be a border authority and/or other law enforcement agencies (LEAs) where they must decide how the data is to be processed etc. Other entity such as cloud service providers might be classified as data processors. In this case, it is important for the relevant entity (competent authority) to enter into a contract with any other joint controller and processors in order to ensure that the requirements of the GDPR and other national or EU data protection laws (e.g., Directive (EU) 2016/680) are met. Also, the data controller(s) must take all measures needed to ensure that any data processor(s) and other joint controllers are indeed able to fulfil their requirements under such contract. The role of data controllers and data processors are as follows:

- Defining data collection purposes, scope, and procedures.
- Defining policies for data classification (security levels) and data access control.
- Defining the data breach reporting procedures and plans for incident response and disaster recovery.
- Perform the Data Protection Impact Assessment (DPIA) – discussed in Sect. 2.3.
- Design, create, and implement IT processes and systems that would enable the data controllers to gather personal data.
- Define the used tools and strategies to gather personal data.
- Implement security measures that would safeguard personal data.
- Transfer data from the data controller to another entity (can be data controller or data processor) and vice versa.

In the case of joint controllers or data is begin processed by a data processor(s), Article 28 of the GDPR lays down requirements that must be in place between a controller(s) and processor(s), in order to protect the rights of the data subject. Data controller shall ensure that processors are authorized to process the personal data and have committed themselves to confidentiality or are under an appropriate legal obligation of confidentiality (Articles 27-29 of the GDPR). Joint data controllers agreement must be in place and signed by data controllers and processors. The main scope of the joint data controllers and processors agreement are (in accordance to Article. 26 of the GDPR):

– The agreement must lay down the distribution of responsibilities among the joint controllers and processors in connection with all the processing of personal data.
– The agreement must lay down the rules of sharing and transferring of the personal data.

Moreover, controllers must ensure the data subject's rights are being upheld within the entity/system. Data controllers and processors are required to respect data subject' rights as defined in the GDPR (Articles 12-23 of GDPR). The data controller should give clear and documented instructions to data subjects about how to excise their rights (Req08 to Req13) as presented in Table 1. Also, the data controller may ask an opinion of a privacy expert to ensure compliance with the law. A data protection officer (DPO) shall be designated where the core activities of the data controller consists of processing on a large scale of special categories of personal data such as biometrics data. The DPO, who may or may not be the same person for several data controllers should (among others) provide advice and guidance to the controllers and processors on the requirements of the data protection, provide advice about the DPIA as well as monitor and support its performance and be the person of contact for data subjects and for consulting with national supervisory authorities.

Table 3 presents a summary of the organizational and technical measures for biometrics data processing. The measures presented in Table 3 are considered based on ISO/IEC 27001:2013 standard [11]. ISO/IEC 27001:2013 specifies the requirements for establishing, implementing, maintaining and continually improving an information security management system within the context of the organization.

Table 2. Organizational and technical measures.

Name of measure	Description	Reference to ISO/IEC 27001:2013
Policy and procedures	• Data controllers must document its security and privacy policy for privacy and data protection • The policy must be reviewed and revised by the all data controllers (in the case of joint controllers)	• A.5 Security policy
Roles and responsibilities	• Data controllers must specify and allocate role(s) and responsibilities related to data processing in accordance with the policy and procedures • Data controllers must (when applicable) appoint a Data Protection Officer (DPO) and define the role of the authorized persons to reduce opportunities for unauthorized or unintentional modification or misuse of personal data	• A.6.1.1 Information security roles and responsibilities • A6.1.2 Segregation of duty
Access control policy	• Access control policy must define the rights of access to each role(s) in the competent authority • An appropriate access control mechanism (e.g., Role based access control [10]) must be implemented to restrict access rights for specific user roles based on need-to-know principle [12]	• A.9.1 Business requirement of Access control policy • A.9.2 User access management
Resource & asset management	• System hardware, software and network resources must be reviewed and approved by controllers before any resource is put in action • Resources must be classified by the their sensitivity to limit unauthorized disclosure/modification of any sensitive information/data	• A.8 Asset management • A.8.2.1 Classification of information
Data & controllers or processors	• An agreement must define the role and responsibilities of each data controller and processor with respect to confidentiality, non-disclosure etc.	• A.15.1.1 Information security policy for supplier relationships • A.15.1.2 Addressing security within supplier agreements
Incidents handling & personal data breaches	• Incident response plan with detailed notification procedures for reporting must be defined to ensure effective and orderly response to incidents pertaining personal data	• A.16 Information security incident management
Human resources security	• Entities must ensures that responsibilities and obligations related to the processing of personal data are clearly communicated to its personnel • Entities must ensure that its personnel involved in the date processing are well trained and understand the policy related to confidentiality and non-disclosure	• A.7 Human resource security • A.7.2.2 Information security awareness, education and training
Security risk assessment & DPIA	• Data controllers must ensure the performance of security risk assessment and the performance of DPIA to map data protection and privacy requirements (described in Table 1) to threats, vulnerabilities, risks and mitigation measures for development	• A12.6 Technical vulnerability management • A.14.2 Security in development and support processes
Activity & Event logging and monitoring	• Data controllers must ensure logging and auditing record of authorized users' activities and events (read, write, view etc.) with timestamped and adequately protected against tampering and unauthorized access • Action (collection, deletion, disclosure etc.) and system operators and system administrators must be logged timestamped and adequately protected against tampering and unauthorized access	• A.12.4 Logging and monitoring
Data security	• Data controllers must ensure protecting digital data from destructive forces and from the unwanted actions of unauthorized users, such as a cyberattack or a data breach.	• A.10.1 Cryptographic control • A.12 Operations security
Backup	• Data controllers keep back-up copies in a locked and fire-proof facility and kept separate from operating equipment • Back-ups copy shall be protected against malware and incidents	• A.12.3 Back-Up
Data deletion & disposal	• Personal data must be deleted when no longer needed. This includes shredding of paper and portable media used to store personal data	• A. 8.3.2 Disposal of media • A.11.2.7 Secure disposal or re-use of equipment

2.3   Data Protection Impact Assessment (DPIA)

Article 35 of the GDPR introduces the necessity of DPIA. It is a process that helps to identify and minimize the privacy and data protection risks resulting from the processing of personal data [1, 2]. The process is designed to describe the processing, assess its necessity and proportionality and help manage the risks to the rights and freedoms of natural persons. Article 25 GDPR establishes that, both at the time of the determination of the means for processing and at the time of the processing itself, the controller shall implement appropriate technical and organizational measures which are designed to implement data protection principles in an effective manner and to integrate the necessary safeguards into the processing. The DPIA may be considered as an organizational measure. Thus, the DPIA helps data controllers to comply with legal requirements of data protection and demonstrate the appropriate measures where it is used to check compliance against data protection regulation. To ensure compliance with legal requirements of data protection and demonstrate the appropriate measures, DPIA shall include:

- A systematic description of the processing activities.
- A description of the purpose for the processing of personal data.
- An assessment of whether or not the processing of personal data is necessary and proportionate to the purpose.
- An assessment of the privacy and data protection risks for the data subject.
- Planned privacy and data protection risks mitigation in order to safeguard data and protect privacy.

Controllers shall consult with the DPO, if such an officer has been designated, in connection with the performance of DPIA. In case the processing of biometrics data and personal data entail a high risk which cannot be mitigated through reasonable measures, controllers shall request an advance discussion with the Data Protection Authority (DPA) before the processing is commenced.

It is argued that the DPIA is a preliminary step of any privacy and data protection by design process [5,13]. The loss of confidentiality, integrity and availability of data concerning biometrics data processing is a high risk. Once the risks have been identified, the appropriate solutions solutions developed according to PbD principles should balance and take into account state-of-the-art of the technology and the costs of implementation. The controller shall take into account the risks of varying likelihood and severity for rights and freedoms of natural persons posed by the processing. However, the management of the data processing and the risk assessment are crucial. The report "Privacy and Data Protection by Design, from policy to engineering" sets out some strategies for the implementation and defines eight PbD strategies and three data protection goals [8]. These recommendations are strictly related to the Hoepman et alia's PbD strategies [6]. Table 2 provides an overview of the privacy by design (PbD) strategies for biometrics data processing and the possible implementation measures in each of the phases of the data processing [7,8]. A brief overview of the strategies is as follows:

- **Inform:** Data subject should be adequately informed whenever his/her data is processed (transparency).
- **Control:** Data subjects should be provided control over the processing of their personal data (rights to data subject).
- **Minimize:** The amount of personal data should be restricted to the minimal amount possible (data minimization).
- **Hide:** Personal data and their interrelations should be hidden, not communicated in plain text.
- **Separate:** Personal data should be processed in a distributed fashion, in separate compartments whenever possible. Personal data should be stored in separate databases and areas for each purpose and process.
- **Aggregate:** Personal data should be processed at the highest level of aggregation and with the least possible detail in which it is (still) useful. This would ensure the enforceability of the data subject's rights, without prejudice to the business value and purpose of the collection and use.
- **Enforce:** A privacy policy compatible with legal requirements (e.g., GDPR requirements) should be in place and should be enforced.
- **Demonstrate:** Data controllers must be able to demonstrate compliance with privacy policy into force and any applicable legal requirements.

Table 3. Security and data protection measures.

Processing phase	PbD strategies	Implementation
	Inform	• Controller(s) must provide appropriate information to data subject about the data collection and the purpose of the data • Controller(s) must use transparency mechanisms (whenever possible) to inform data subject about the processing • Controller(s) must provide contact point that data subject can use to practice data subject rights • Controller(s) must use multiple languages if necessary and enrich information to use photographs, audio, video, etc. (when applicable)
	Minimize	• Controller(s) must define what data are needed/necessary before collection to reduce data fields, define relevant controls and avoid collection of unwanted information
	Hide	• Controller(s) must implement privacy enhancing techniques, e.g. anti-tracking techniques, encryption techniques, identity masking techniques, secure file sharing techniques, etc. to avoid unnecessary exposure of data
Data collection	Aggregate	• Controller(s) should use anonymization/pseudonymization whenever possible • Controller(s) should remove unnecessary and excessive information
	Control	• Controller(s) must implement an appropriate mechanism for data subject to express their rights includes informed consent, rights to withdraw consent, rights to give access for the rectification, blocking, or deletion of personal data and rights to submit questions or complaints relating to data protection and security • Controller(s) must have/implement mechanisms for expressing privacy preferences (e.g., which biometric data an individual prefer to use)
	Demonstrate	• Controller(s) must demonstrate that they have defined what data to be collected, why and how including documentation demonstrating the system design and security (auditing re-ports, vulnerability scanning, data breach management, etc.)

(*continued*)

Table 3. (*continued*)

Processing phase	PbD strategies	Implementation
Data storage	Hide	• Controller(s) must encrypt data at rest or in transit • Controller(s) must use authentication and access control mechanisms to process (e.g., access, read, write, copy etc.) data. • Controller(s) must use other measures (e.g., encrypted backups) for secure data storage
	Separate	• Controller(s) must use distributed/decentralized storage and analytic facilities whenever possible • Controller(s) separate sensitive personal data from less sensitive personal data (in the database, access to sites, for clients and units, etc.)
	Enforce/ Demonstrate	Controller(s) must demonstrate what type of security and privacy techniques are used as well as how these techniques are enforced?
Data use & disclosure	Aggregate	• Controller(s) must use anonymization/pseudonymization techniques whenever possible
	Hide	• Controller(s) must use searchable encryption and privacy-preserving computations, whenever possible

3   Privacy and Data Protection Best Practices

This section describes privacy and data protection best practices that shall be considered by controllers. Privacy and data protection measures shall be chosen on the basis of risk assessments and DPIA. In order to guarantee privacy and data protection, this paper presents the aspects of data protection that relate most directly to biometric data processing in border management. As discussed above, there are many factors to consider when it comes to data protection such as:

1. **Compliance with security requirements:** Privacy and data protection requirements deal with security issues, such as confidentiality, integrity and availability when processing personal data. Activities required to preserve confidentiality, integrity and availability including granting access only to authorized personnel, applying encryption to data that will be sent over the Internet or stored on digital media, performing risk assessments to uncover new vulnerabilities, building software defensively and developing a disaster recovery plan to ensure that the business can continue to exist in the event of a disaster or loss of access by personnel. Controllers ought to take the following into consideration:
   - **Confidentiality:** Controllers must ensure the security of collected data and be able to prevent data leakage. Moreover, controllers must have an access control capability that can authenticate users who want to access data and authorize eligible users to have access.
   - **Integrity:** Controllers must be able to prevent data loss and any unauthorized modifications of data as well as to verify the integrity and authenticity of the collected data.
   - **Availability:** Controllers must ensure data backup to prevent loss of data due to natural disasters (fire, flooding, storms, earthquakes, etc.) or human actions such as Denial of Service (DoS) attacks.

- **Auditing:** Controllers must allow security and data protection audits as a systematic evaluation of the security of a system hardware and software by measuring how well it conforms to a set of established criteria.
2. **Compliance with the regulation requirements:** As explained above, for border control related purposes data protection compliance essentially refers to the GDPR and Directive (EU) 2016/680. Controllers must take into consideration all the requirements and main principles presented in the GDPR and Directive (EU) 2016/680. These include:
   - **Collection limitation principle:** Aimed at limiting the collection of personal data.
   - **Lawfulness of the data processing principle:** Require for data to be obtained by lawful and fair means and when appropriate, with the individual's knowledge or consent.
   - **Accountability principle:** Requires data controllers to adhere to applicable legislation themselves, at their own initiative and best efforts, and to be able to demonstrate such compliance whenever needed.
   - **Transparency principle:** Aimed at strengthening data subjects' position while defending their right to personal data protection.
   - **Right to data subject principle:** Data subjects can make a specific request and be assured that his/her personal data is not being misused for other than the legitimate purpose for which it was originally provided. GDPR empowers data subjects with rights including the right to information, right to access, right to rectification and erasure as well as the right to be forgotten, to name a few (Article 12-23, GDPR).

4 Conclusions and Recommendations

Data protection aims at guaranteeing the individual's right to privacy. It refers to the technical and legal framework designed to ensure that personal data are safe from unforeseen, unintended or unauthorized use. Data protection therefore includes e.g., measures concerning collection, access to data, communication and conservation of data. In addition, a data protection strategy can also include measures to assure the accuracy of the data. In the context of biometrics data processing, data protection issues arise whenever data relating to persons are collected and stored.

Privacy and data protection by design are currently mandatory with the GDPR, but many entities still find difficulties with the concept, both in terms of what it exactly means and how to implement it as a system quality attribute. Moreover, the law imposes high administrative fines in case of infringements (Article 83 of GDPR). For these reasons, in the future, the aim is to investigate more about privacy and data protection measures and propose a comprehensive privacy and data protection management framework for biometrics data processing. Future work could also focus on analyzing if and how far our proposed privacy and data protection management framework could comply and adhere to other legislation.

Acknowledgements. This work is carried out in the EU-funded project SMILE (Project ID: 740931), [H2020-DS-2016-2017] SEC-14-BES-2016 towards reducing the cost of technologies in land border security applications.

References

1. Abomhara, M., Yayilgan, S.Y., Nymoen, A.H., Shalaginova, M., Székely, Z., Elezaj, O.: How to do it right: a framework for biometrics supported border control. In: Katsikas, S., Zorkadis, V. (eds.) e-Democracy 2019. CCIS, vol. 1111, pp. 94–109. Springer, Cham (2020). https://doi.org/10.1007/978-3-030-37545-4_7
2. Abomhara, M., Yayilgan, S.Y., Shalaginova, M., Székely, Z.: Border control and use of biometrics: reasons why the right to privacy can not be absolute. In: Friedewald, M., Önen, M., Lievens, E., Krenn, S., Fricker, S. (eds.) Privacy and Identity 2019. IAICT, vol. 576, pp. 259–271. Springer, Cham (2020). https://doi.org/10.1007/978-3-030-42504-3_17
3. Bieker, F., Friedewald, M., Hansen, M., Obersteller, H., Rost, M.: A process for data protection impact assessment under the European general data protection regulation. In: Schiffner, S., Serna, J., Ikonomou, D., Rannenberg, K. (eds.) APF 2016. LNCS, vol. 9857, pp. 21–37. Springer, Cham (2016). https://doi.org/10.1007/978-3-319-44760-5_2
4. Campisi, P.: Security and Privacy in Biometrics, vol. 24. Springer, London (2013)
5. Cavoukian, A., et al.: Privacy by Design: The 7 Foundational Principles. Information and Privacy Commissioner of Ontario, Canada 5 (2009)
6. Colesky, M., Hoepman, J.H., Hillen, C.: A critical analysis of privacy design strategies. In: 2016 IEEE Security and Privacy Workshops (SPW), pp. 33–40. IEEE (2016)
7. D'Acquisto, G., Domingo-Ferrer, J., Kikiras, P., Torra, V., de Montjoye, Y.A., Bourka, A.: Privacy by design in big data: an overview of privacy enhancing technologies in the era of big data analytics. arXiv preprint arXiv:1512.06000 (2015)
8. Danezis, G., et al.: Privacy and data protection by design-from policy to engineering. arXiv preprint arXiv:1501.03726 (2015)
9. European Commission: Regulation (EU) 2016/399 of the European Parliament and of the Council of 9 March 2016 on a Union Code on the rules governing the movement of persons across borders (Schengen Borders Code). Official Journal of the European Union (2016)
10. Ferraiolo, D.F., Sandhu, R., Gavrila, S., Kuhn, D.R., Chandramouli, R.: Proposed NIST standard for role-based access control. ACM Trans. Inf. Syst. Secur. (TISSEC) 4(3), 224–274 (2001)
11. International Organization for Standardization: ISO/IEC 27001: 2013: Information Technology-Security Techniques-Information Security Management Systems-Requirements. International Organization for Standardization (2013)
12. Janczewski, L.J., Portougal, V.: "need-to-know" principle and fuzzy security clearances modelling. Inf. Manage. Comput. Secur. (2000)
13. Jasmontaite, L., Kamara, I., Zanfir-Fortuna, G., Leucci, S.: Data protection by design and by default: framing guiding principles into legal obligations in the GDPR. Eur. Data Prot. L. Rev. **4**, 168 (2018)
14. Kloza, D., van Dijk, N., Gellert, R., Böröcz, I., Tanas, A., Mantovani, E., Quinn, P.: Data protection impact assessments in the European union: complementing the new legal framework towards a more robust protection of individuals. Brussels Laboratory for Data Protection & Privacy Impact Assessments Policy Brief (2017)

15. Memon, N.: How biometric authentication poses new challenges to our security and privacy [in the spotlight]. IEEE Signal Process. Mag. **34**(4), 194–196 (2017)
16. Sajfert, J., Quintel, T.: Data Protection Directive (EU) 2016/680 For Police and Criminal Justice Authorities. Edward Elgar Publishing, Cole/Boehm GDPR Commentary (2019)
17. Sutrop, M.: Ethical issues in governing biometric technologies. In: Kumar, A., Zhang, D. (eds.) ICEB 2010. LNCS, vol. 6005, pp. 102–114. Springer, Heidelberg (2010). https://doi.org/10.1007/978-3-642-12595-9_14
18. Voigt, P., von dem Bussche, A.: The EU General Data Protection Regulation (GDPR). Springer, Cham (2017). https://doi.org/10.1007/978-3-319-57959-7
19. Willoughby, A.: Biometric surveillance and the right to privacy [commentary]. IEEE Technol. Soc. Mag. **36**(3), 41–45 (2017)

Unsupervised Single Image Super-Resolution Using Cycle Generative Adversarial Network

Kalpesh Prajapati[1], Vishal Chudasama[1], Heena Patel[1], Kishor Upla[1,2(✉)], Raghavendra Ramachandra[2], Kiran Raja[2], and Christoph Busch[2]

[1] Sardar Vallabhbhai National Institute of Technology (SVNIT), Surat, India
kalpesh.jp89@gmail.com, vishalchudasama2188@gmail.com,
hpatel1323@gmail.com, kishorupla@gmail.com
[2] Norwegian University of Science and Technology (NTNU), Gjøvik, Norway
{raghavendra.ramachandra,kiran.raja,christoph.busch}@ntnu.no

Abstract. The current state-of-the-art deep learning based Single Image Super-Resolution (SISR) techniques employ supervised learning in the training process. In this learning, the Low-Resolution (LR) images are prepared by applying known degradation such as bicubic downsampling to the High-Resolution (HR) images. Unfortunately, bicubic downsampling eliminates the natural image characteristics such as sensor noise, degradation due to built-in hardware, etc., and generates smooth images and hence generated images are different from the real-world data. When deep learning model is trained using such artificially generated LR-HR pairs, they often are prone to generate better SR results for real-world images. To circumvent this problem, we propose an SR framework that can train in an unsupervised manner using Generative Adversarial Networks (GANs). It contains mainly couple of networks called SR network and degradation network which work on an unpaired data of LR-HR images. The SR network learns to eliminate noise present in the LR image and super-resolve it. While, degradation network performs inverse of SR network (i.e. down-sampling and adding degradation from real-world images). We demonstrate the effectiveness of the proposed method by conducting extensive experiments on NTIRE-2020 Real-world SR challenge dataset where it demonstrates the superior performance over state-of-the-art methods in terms of both quantitative and qualitative assessments.

Keywords: Convolutional Neural Network · Generative Adversarial Network · Single Image Super-Resolution · Unsupervised learning · No-reference quality assessment · Image restoration · Deep learning

1 Introduction

The High-Resolution (HR) images are always preferred in all the vision-based applications due to good details in the image. However, acquiring HR images

© Springer Nature Switzerland AG 2021
S. Yildirim Yayilgan et al. (Eds.): INTAP 2020, CCIS 1382, pp. 359–370, 2021.
https://doi.org/10.1007/978-3-030-71711-7_30

needs expensive imaging devises such as High-Definition (HD) cameras. The installation and maintenance cost of such devices is high and hence it is practically impossible to replace the existing Low-Resolution (LR) sensors. Thus, increasing the spatial resolution of the given LR observation is an imperative requirement for the vision community. The Single Image Super-Resolution (SISR) is an algorithmic approach to enhance the resolution of give single LR observation [2,32]. The task of Super-Resolution (SR) is to map LR image from source domain (i.e. noisy, blurry) to HR image from target domain (i.e. clean, noise-free). Despite of many research works in super-resolution problem, it is still an open research problem due to it's ill-posed nature and also due to unavailability of perceptual quantitative measurement.

In the early era, the problem of SR was tackled by many co-variants such as prediction-based methods [22], edge-based methods [10], statistical methods [14], patch-based methods [12], sparse representation methods [34] etc. In the recent years, the rapid development of deep learning techniques have led to it's use in SISR where large variety of network have been deployed ranging from early Convolutional Neural Network (CNN) based methods (i.e. SRCNN [6], VDSR [20] etc.) to recent promising SR approaches using Generative Adversarial Network (GAN) (i.e. SRGAN [18], ESRGAN [31], etc.,). However, these works need a bicubic down-sampling to create LR image from the available HR data. Unfortunately, bicubic down-sampling degrades the image and eliminates sensor noise which is always present in an acquired image [23]. Hence, the SR network trained using such dataset does not generalize on the realistic data properly.

In order to solve this problem, Cai et al. [4] introduced an RealSR dataset of true LR-HR images. However, capturing a real-world LR-HR pairs requires accurate hardware and also trained manpower which is expensive and also a cumbersome process. Alternate solution to this problem is to solve the SR problem in an unsupervised manner [9,23]. To further develop such novel idea of unsupervised learning for SR, Lugmayr et al. [23] introduced real-world SR challenge based on above concept in ICCV 2019 (*called AIM 2019 Challenge* [24]) and in conjunction with CVPR 2020 (*called as NTIRE-2020 Real-world SR Challange* [25]). In this direction, we propose a new framework that comprises of GAN architecture with cyclic-consistency loss to obtain SR of the given LR observation. Additionally, we use quality loss to improve the perceptual quality of SR image using another network called Quality Assessment (QA) network. The proposed framework is trained on NTIRE-2020 real-world SR challenge [25] and evaluated in terms of quantitative (i.e. PSNR, SSIM, LPIPS) and qualitative assessments. The key contributions of the proposed work are:

- An unsupervised SISR approach using GAN framework is proposed for real-world super-resolution of images.
- In order to improve the perceptual quality of SR results, a novel loss function based on the quality of SR images has been introduced in the proposed network.
- Extensive experiments are conducted on the NTIRE-2020 real-world SR challenge [25] dataset to indicate the improvement on the state-of-art results.

In rest of the paper, related works on the single image super-resolution have been reviewed in Sect. 2. The proposed framework is presented in Sect. 3. In the Sect. 4, we elaborate the proposed method's experimental analysis. Finally, conclusion is drawn in the Sect. 5.

2 Related Works

With the growing technology, remarkable progress has been made in terms of hardware which enables fast computing facility with storage of abundant amount of data. This has lead to use of more powerful Convolutional Neural Networks (CNNs) based methods to solve SISR problem. Dong et al. [6] attempted CNN to SISR problem with simplest network with only three convolutional layers. This effort seems as pioneering work and large number of works have been inspired to further improve the quality of SR image. To the simplest network, VDSR [16] increases the layers to make more deeper network to obtain better performance. However, deeper network suffers with vanishing gradient problem which is solved by using residual learning which is used in many of the recent works [18–20,38]. Despite residual networks which add features at particular location, it is also useful to concatenate them to keep all the features to proceed further. This idea is also employed in many works including SRDenseNet [30], RDN [39], DBPN [15] etc. Furthermore, RCAN [38] introduced channel attention module enables to attend adaptive importance on certain features only to improve the performance. However, these methods employ L_1 or L_2 based loss functions in the training process and thus they yield blurry SR image. In order to overcome such shortcoming, adversarial training [13] has been introduced and same has been successfully applied to SISR problem. Ledig et al. Attempted first adversarial training which is referred as *SRGAN* to improve the perceptual based performance of the SR results. Recently, many GAN based techniques [26,31] are reported to enhance their performance over SRGAN method.

However, all above methods have been trained using LR-HR pair prepared using bicubic down-sampling. Unfortunately, bicubic down-sampling removes the sensor noise and makes the images smooth that are different from the real-world data. The network trained using bicubically synthesized data generalizes poorly on the real-world data. Alternatively, SRMD [36] and ZSSR [28] used a synthesized LR-HR pair data using multiple degradation and perform super-resolution. However, the real-world degradation is always unknown and difficult to model it fully. In order to solve the problem, Cai et al. [4] introduced the real-world paired LR-HR data (RealSR). Additionally, based on this dataset, NTIRE-2019 challenge has been organized and number of competent works has been reported [5,7,8,11,17,27,33].

Apart from RealSR dataset [4], other alternative solution is to use unsupervised super-resolution with unpaired LR-HR data. In this approach, Lugmayr et al. [23] proposed a framework that use cycle consistency loss [40] to degrade the image first that maps natural characteristics of source domain. After degrading the image, SR network is trained using such LR-HR paired data in supervised manner. However, this approach needs two sequential training of network that consists more time for training. In order to solve the SISR problem in unsupervised manner, many works have been reported in [3,9,35]. In [9], authors learns the features related to high and low frequencies separately and proposed the SR approach which is based on ESRGAN [31]. Similarly, Yuan et al. [35] use two sets of cycle GAN to obtain noise-free LR observation and to super-resolve that LR image, respectively. Additionally, authors in [3] learn the downsampling process for face hallucination by using face prior in the network. In the similar direction, we propose an unsupervised approach for image SR using GAN framework with the novel idea of loss based quality of SR images.

3   Proposed Methodology

In the LR observation, certain degradation such as blur, noise, etc., are always present. However, on the other side, HR images are clean and rich of high-frequency details. The problem of SR is to map the given data distribution (P_X, i.e., LR observation) to the target distribution of clean HR images (i.e., P_Y). For unsupervised SR problem, input sampled data $X_{i\,i=1}^{M} \sim P_X$ and output sampled data $Y_{i\,j=1}^{N} \sim P_Y$ are available in an unpaired manner with different data distributions, respectively. Given this unpaired data, an SR technique learns a mapping S that can super-resolve a new image $X \sim p_X$ such that $S(X) \sim p_Y$. In order to train such SR network called S from unpaired dataset, we introduce an another network called degradation network F that maps $F(Y) \sim p_X$ to follow the data distribution. Since no paired data is available, we enforce cycle consistency loss to maintain original image detail into output of the network. The framework of the proposed method using cycle GAN in unsupervised manner is depicted in Fig. 1. Here, first LR image X is passed through SR network S which generates super-resolved image $S(X) \sim p_Y$ such that SR image follows the output data distribution. This super-resolved image is again passed through degradation network F to apply degradation $F(S(X)) = \hat{X}$ such that it follows original distribution p_X. The network learns the degradation from P_Y to P_X from available dataset. These X and $\hat{X}$ are discriminated using discriminator D_X which works in adversarial manner with network S and F. Similarly, HR image Y is degraded first using degradation network F which gives $F(Y) \sim p_X$. It is then enlarged using SR network S to estimate HR image back $S(F(Y)) = \hat{Y}$ which must follow distribution p_Y. This estimated $\hat{Y}$ and original Y are discriminated using another discriminator network D_Y. These two pairs $\{X, \hat{X}\}$ and $\{Y, \hat{Y}\}$ are also used to calculate cycle consistency loss.

The architecture of SR and degradation networks are depicted in Fig. 2(a, b), respectively which are inspired from ESRGAN [31]. The different modules in the architecture of SR generator network are separated into three different parts: Low-level Feature Extractor, High-level Feature Extractor and Reconstruction modules. First LR image is passed through low-level feature extractor module which is made using a single convolutional layer with 5×5 kernel size. Here, larger size of kernel helps to predict information based on more reception field.

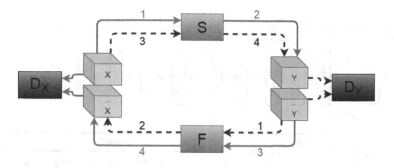

Fig. 1. The block schematic of the proposed approach.

The high-level details (e.g., finer details) are extracted using several Residual-in-Residual (RIR) blocks with one skip connection as shown in Fig. 2(a). Each RIR block has three residual blocks with one residual connection made-up with convolutional layer. In the residual block, we use four convolutional layers with a channel attention module in residual manner. The channel attention layer helps to attain several features based on their importance on final objective. In final stage, this high-level features are reconstructed into final SR image using up-sampling and convolutional layers. In up-sampling layer, we use pixel shuffler technique which is better than nearest up-sampling [18]. Furthermore, we use bicubic up-sampling in outer most skip connection that enables to retain colour information more precisely in the SR image. The architecture of degradation network (F) is similar to SR network with few modifications and same is depicted in Fig. 2(b). We first use down-sampling module and also remove up-sampling layer from last layer of SR network. We then use bicubic down-sampling in outer most skip connection instead of up-sampling layer of SR network.

The architecture of discriminator network is similar to SRGAN [18] and same is depicted in Fig. 3. We replace flattening layer with Global Average Pooling (GAP) layer which helps to reduce number of trainable parameters. The discriminator network consists of several strided convolutional layers. After such layers, GAP layer is used to reduce dimension of features and then it is followed with couple of Fully Connected (FC) layers.

Additionally, we also propose to use an another deep network called Quality Assessment (QA) network in order to improve the perceptual quality of SR image. The output of QA network is the predicted quality score of SR images which is used as a loss function in the training of SR network. The QA network learns mapping of image to quality of the same image without using any reference image which is often referred No-Reference Image Quality Assessment (NR-IQA). To train the QA network, we use KADID-10K dataset [21][1] which consists of $\sim$ 10K images with Mean Opinion Score (MOS) rating of each image. The architecture design of QA network is depicted in Fig. 4. It has two separated

---

[1] Presently, the KADID-10K dataset is the largest dataset available for such NR-IQA problem.

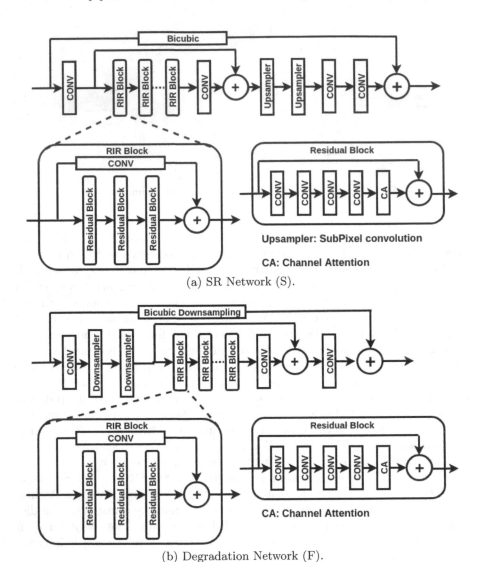

(a) SR Network (S).

(b) Degradation Network (F).

Fig. 2. The architecture of generator networks.

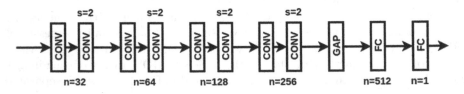

Fig. 3. The architecture of discriminator networks: D_X and D_Y.

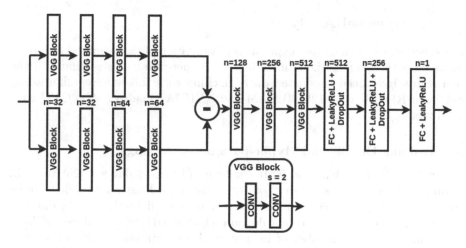

Fig. 4. The architecture design of QA network.

paths using VGG blocks and features available from both paths are subtracted which is further passed through three additional VGG blocks followed with three FC layers. The VGG block consists of couple of convolutional layers where second convolutional layer uses a strided convolution to reduce height and width of features.

Loss: As discussed earlier, the proposed network architecture consists of couple of GAN frameworks in cyclic manner. The SR and degradation networks are trained using combination of several losses as mentioned in Eq. (1).

$$L_{SR}(S, F, D_X, D_Y) = \lambda_1(L_{GAN}(S, D_Y) + L_{GAN}(F, D_X)) + \lambda_2 L_{cc}(S, F) + \lambda_3 L_{QA}(S).$$
(1)

For L_{GAN}, we use an adversarial GAN loss function as suggested by Goodfellow et al. in [13] and same can be represented as,

$$L_{GAN}(S, D_Y) = E_{Y \sim p_y}[log D_Y(Y)] + E_{X \sim p_X}[log(1 - D_Y(S(X)))].$$
(2)

$$L_{GAN}(F, D_X) = E_{X \sim p_X}[log D_X(X)] + E_{Y \sim p_Y}[log(1 - D_X(F(Y)))].$$
(3)

As we do not have paired data, we use cycle consistency loss to prevent information loss which is mentioned in Eq. (4) as,

$$L_{cc}(S, F) = E_{X \sim p_X}[\|F(S(X)) - X|_1] + E_{Y \sim p_Y}[\|S(F(Y)) - Y|_1].$$
(4)

Finally, we use an QA network for predicting quality of an SR image which is trained on KADID-10K dataset (with MOS scores in range of 1–5 values). The higher score indicates superiority of an image and *vise-versa*. To use this score as a loss function, we calculate it by subtracting score from highest value of prediction as,

$$L_{QA}(S) = E_{X \sim p_X}[5 - Q(S(X))].$$
(5)

4   Experimental Analysis

In this section, we demonstrate experimental validation of the proposed approach and along with other methods including the hyper-parameter setting. All the experiments have been conducted on a machine with following configuration: Intel Xeon(R) CPU with 128 GB RAM and NVIDIA Quadro P5000 GPU with 16 GB memory.

4.1   Training Details and Hyper-parameter Settings

We use NTIRE-2020 Real-world SR challenge (Track-1) dataset [25] to train the proposed model. This dataset consists image sets. First set is called source domain which is generated with unknown noise on Flickr-2K [20, 29] dataset. Another set of images called target domain which is DIV2K [1] dataset without any editing. The total number of images in above datasets are 2650 and 800, respectively. Additionally, the total 100 number of images from DIV2K dataset are available for validation purpose. To train the network, we use an Adam optimizer with default β_1 and β_2 values. The training is conducted upto $200,000$ number of iterations with batch size of 32. We keep learning rate of 1×10^{-4} and reduced it by half at every $50,000$ iterations. To generalize the network, we use augmentation using random cropping, flipping and rotation in the training dataset. Additionally, the weights of GAN loss (λ_1), cycle consistency loss (λ_2) and quality loss (λ_3) are set empirically to 1×10^{-2}, 1×10^{-1} and 1×10^{-6}, respectively.

4.2   Quantitative Analysis

To measure the performance of image obtained with SR approach, different degradation metrics such as PSNR and SSIM are most frequently used in the SISR task. However, these measures are less correlated with human perception and hence it is improper to judge the quality of SR images based on the values of those degradation measures. Thus, we include Learned Perceptual Image Patch Similarity (LPIPS) [37] as a perception based measure which is based on deep network. The lower LPIPS values indicates better perception quality of SR image. Table 1 shows quantitative comparison of the proposed method with other state-of-the-art methods on NTIRE-2020 Real-world SR challenge validation dataset [25]. It is observed here that despite of inferior values of PSNR and SSIM, our proposed method obtains better LPIPS value indicating better perceptual quality over other state-of-the-art methods. Additionally, we also evaluate the potential of the proposed method on the testing dataset of the NTIRE-2020 Real-world SR challenge (Track-1) and it's quantitative performance is depicted in the Table 2.

4.3   Qualitative Analysis

In order to perform the visual comparison of the proposed method with other existing methods, we use bicubic interpolation along with ESRGAN [31] methods

Table 1. The quantitative comparison of the proposed and other existing SR methods on NTIRE-2020 Real-world SR Challenge validation dataset (Track-1).

Method	PSNR ↑	SSIM ↑	LPIPS ↓
Bicubic	**25.50**	**0.6701**	0.644
ESRGAN [31]	19.04	0.2422	0.755
Proposed	25.41	0.6678	**0.634**

Table 2. The quantitative measurements obtained using the proposed method on NTIRE-2020 Real-world SR Challenge Track-1 testing dataset.

	PSNR ↑	SSIM ↑	LPIPS ↓
Proposed	25.39	0.67	0.615

and same is depicted in Fig. 5 and Fig. 6 for NTIRE-2020 Real-world SR challenge validation and testing datasets [25], respectively. To observe difference more clearly, we zoom into the patches which shows that the proposed method removes noise more efficiently than other competing methods in both the results.

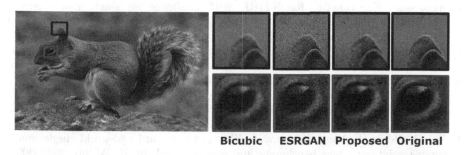

Bicubic   ESRGAN   Proposed   Original

Fig. 5. The visual comparison of the SR results obtained using the proposed and other existing methods on NTIRE-2020 Real-world SR challenge validation dataset.

Bicubic   ESRGAN   Proposed

Fig. 6. The visual comparison of the SR results obtained using the proposed and other existing methods on NTIRE-2020 Real-world SR challenge testing dataset.

5 Conclusion

As bicubic down-sampling changes the natural characteristics of acquired image, deep networks trained using such synthesized data performs poorly on real-world image for super-resolution applications. In order to solve the problem, an alternative solution of unsupervised super-resolution has been proposed in this work using adversarial training along with cycle consistency loss. Additionally, we use the quality loss to improve the perceptual quality of SR results. The proposed method is compared with other state-of-the-art methods and its shows it's superiority over the other methods using NTIRE-2020 Real-world SR challenge validation and testing datasets.

Acknowledgment. This work is supported by ERCIM, who kindly enabled the internship of Kishor Upla at NTNU, Gjøvik. Authors are also thankful to Science and Engineering Research Board (SERB), a statutory body of Department of Science and Technology (DST), Government of India for providing support for this research work (ECR/2017/003268).

References

1. Agustsson, E., Timofte, R.: NTIRE 2017 challenge on single image super-resolution: dataset and study. In: 2017 IEEE Conference on Computer Vision and Pattern Recognition Workshops (CVPRW), pp. 1122–1131 (2017)
2. Anwar, S., Khan, S., Barnes, N.: A deep journey into super-resolution: a survey. arXiv (2019)
3. Bulat, A., Yang, J., Tzimiropoulos, G.: To learn image super-resolution, use a GAN to learn how to do image degradation first. In: Ferrari, V., Hebert, M., Sminchisescu, C., Weiss, Y. (eds.) ECCV 2018. LNCS, vol. 11210, pp. 187–202. Springer, Cham (2018). https://doi.org/10.1007/978-3-030-01231-1_12
4. Cai, J., Zeng, H., Yong, H., Cao, Z., Zhang, L.: Toward real-world single image super-resolution: a new benchmark and a new model. In: ICCV, pp. 3086–3095, October 2019
5. Cheng, G., Matsune, A., Li, Q., Zhu, L., Zang, H., Zhan, S.: Encoder-decoder residual network for real super-resolution. In: CVPR Workshops, pp. 2169–2178, June 2019
6. Dong, C., Loy, C.C., He, K., Tang, X.: Image super-resolution using deep convolutional networks. IEEE Trans. Pattern Anal. Mach. Intell. **38**(2), 295–307 (2016). https://doi.org/10.1109/TPAMI.2015.2439281
7. Du, C., Zewei, H., Anshun, S., et al.: Orientation-aware deep neural network for real image super-resolution. In: The IEEE Conference on Computer Vision and Pattern Recognition (CVPR) Workshops, pp. 1944–1953, June 2019
8. Feng, R., Gu, J., Qiao, Y., Dong, C.: Suppressing model overfitting for image super-resolution networks. In: CVPR Workshops, pp. 1964–1973, June 2019
9. Fritsche, M., Gu, S., Timofte, R.: Frequency separation for real-world super-resolution. In: 2019 IEEE/CVF International Conference on Computer Vision Workshop (ICCVW), pp. 3599–3608 (2019)
10. Gajjar, P.P., Joshi, M.V.: New learning based super-resolution: use of DWT and IGMRF prior. IEEE Trans. Image Process. **19**(5), 1201–1213 (2010)

11. Gao, S., Zhuang, X.: Multi-scale deep neural networks for real image super-resolution. In: Proceedings of the IEEE Conference on Computer Vision and Pattern Recognition Workshops, pp. 2006–2013 (2019)
12. Glasner, D., Bagon, S., Irani, M.: Super-resolution from a single image. In: 2009 IEEE 12th International Conference on Computer Vision, pp. 349–356, September 2009. https://doi.org/10.1109/ICCV.2009.5459271
13. Goodfellow, I., Pouget-Abadie, J., Mirza, M., et al.: Generative adversarial nets. In: Ghahramani, Z., Welling, M., Cortes, C., Lawrence, N.D., Weinberger, K.Q. (eds.) Advances in Neural Information Processing Systems, vol. 27, pp. 2672–2680. Curran Associates, Inc. (2014)
14. Hardie, R.C., Barnard, K.J., Armstrong, E.E.: Joint MAP registration and high-resolution image estimation using a sequence of undersampled images. IEEE Trans. Image Process. 6(12), 1621–1633 (1997). https://doi.org/10.1109/83.650116
15. Haris, M., Shakhnarovich, G., Ukita, N.: Deep back-projection networks for super-resolution. In: Proceedings of the IEEE Conference on Computer Vision and Pattern Recognition, pp. 1664–1673 (2018)
16. Kim, J., Lee, J.K., Lee, K.M.: Accurate image super-resolution using very deep convolutional networks. In: 2016 IEEE CVPR, pp. 1646–1654, June 2016. https://doi.org/10.1109/CVPR.2016.182
17. Kwak, J., Son, D.: Fractal residual network and solutions for real super-resolution. In: The IEEE Conference on Computer Vision and Pattern Recognition (CVPR) Workshops, pp. 2114–2121, June 2019
18. Ledig, C., Theis, L., Huszár, F., et al.: Photo-realistic single image super-resolution using a generative adversarial network. In: Proceedings of the IEEE Conference on Computer Vision and Pattern Recognition, pp. 4681–4690 (2017)
19. Li, Y., Agustsson, E., Gu, S., Timofte, R., Van Gool, L.: CARN: convolutional anchored regression network for fast and accurate single image super-resolution. In: Leal-Taixé, L., Roth, S. (eds.) ECCV 2018. LNCS, vol. 11133, pp. 166–181. Springer, Cham (2019). https://doi.org/10.1007/978-3-030-11021-5_11
20. Lim, B., Son, S., Kim, H., Nah, S., Lee, K.M.: Enhanced deep residual networks for single image super-resolutaion. In: 2017 IEEE Conference on Computer Vision and Pattern Recognition Workshops (CVPRW), pp. 1132–1140 (2017)
21. Lin, H., Hosu, V., Saupe, D.: KADID-10k: a large-scale artificially distorted IQA database. In: 2019 Tenth International Conference on Quality of Multimedia Experience (QoMEX), pp. 1–3. IEEE (2019)
22. Lin, Z., Shum, H.Y.: Fundamental limits of reconstruction-based superresolution algorithms under local translation. IEEE Trans. Pattern Anal. Mach. Intell. 26(1), 83–97 (2004). https://doi.org/10.1109/TPAMI.2004.1261081
23. Lugmayr, A., Danelljan, M., Timofte, R.: Unsupervised learning for real-world super-resolution. In: ICCV Workshops, pp. 3408–3416 (2019)
24. Lugmayr, A., Danelljan, M., Timofte, R., et al.: AIM 2019 challenge on real-world image super-resolution: methods and results. In: ICCV Workshops, pp. 3575–3583 (2019)
25. Lugmayr, A., Danelljan, M., Timofte, R., et al.: NTIRE 2020 challenge on real-world image super-resolution: methods and results. In: CVPR Workshops (2020)
26. Park, S.-J., Son, H., Cho, S., Hong, K.-S., Lee, S.: SRFeat: single image super-resolution with feature discrimination. In: Ferrari, V., Hebert, M., Sminchisescu, C., Weiss, Y. (eds.) ECCV 2018. LNCS, vol. 11220, pp. 455–471. Springer, Cham (2018). https://doi.org/10.1007/978-3-030-01270-0_27

27. Shi, Y., Zhong, H., Yang, Z., Yang, X., Lin, L.: DDet: dual-path dynamic enhancement network for real-world image super-resolution. IEEE Sig. Process. Lett. **27**, 481–485 (2020)
28. Shocher, A., Cohen, N., Irani, M.: Zero-shot super-resolution using deep internal learning. In: 2018 IEEE/CVF Conference on Computer Vision and Pattern Recognition, pp. 3118–3126 (2018)
29. Timofte, R., Agustsson, E., Van Gool, L., Yang, M.H., Zhang, L.: NTIRE 2017 challenge on single image super-resolution: methods and results. In: Proceedings of the IEEE Conference on Computer Vision and Pattern Recognition Workshops, pp. 114–125 (2017)
30. Tong, T., Li, G., Liu, X., Gao, Q.: Image super-resolution using dense skip connections. In: Proceedings of the IEEE International Conference on Computer Vision, pp. 4799–4807 (2017)
31. Wang, X., et al.: ESRGAN: enhanced super-resolution generative adversarial networks. In: Leal-Taixé, L., Roth, S. (eds.) ECCV 2018. LNCS, vol. 11133, pp. 63–79. Springer, Cham (2019). https://doi.org/10.1007/978-3-030-11021-5_5
32. Wang, Z., Chen, J., Hoi, S.C.H.: Deep learning for image super-resolution: a survey (2019)
33. Xu, X., Li, X.: SCAN: spatial color attention networks for real single image super-resolution. In: The IEEE Conference on Computer Vision and Pattern Recognition (CVPR) Workshops, pp. 2024–2032, June 2019
34. Yang, J., Wright, J., Huang, T.S., Ma, Y.: Image super-resolution via sparse representation. IEEE Trans. Image Process. **19**(11), 2861–2873 (2010)
35. Yuan, Y., Liu, S., Zhang, J., Zhang, Y., Dong, C., Lin, L.: Unsupervised image super-resolution using cycle-in-cycle generative adversarial networks. In: 2018 IEEE/CVF Conference on Computer Vision and Pattern Recognition Workshops (CVPRW), p. 814-81409, June 2018
36. Zhang, K., Zuo, W., Zhang, L.: Learning a single convolutional super-resolution network for multiple degradations. In: Proceedings of the IEEE Conference on Computer Vision and Pattern Recognition, pp. 3262–3271 (2018)
37. Zhang, R., Isola, P., Efros, A.A., Shechtman, E., Wang, O.: The unreasonable effectiveness of deep features as a perceptual metric. In: Proceedings of the IEEE Conference on Computer Vision and Pattern Recognition, pp. 586–595 (2018)
38. Zhang, Y., Li, K., Li, K., Wang, L., Zhong, B., Fu, Y.: Image super-resolution using very deep residual channel attention networks. In: Ferrari, V., Hebert, M., Sminchisescu, C., Weiss, Y. (eds.) ECCV 2018. LNCS, vol. 11211, pp. 294–310. Springer, Cham (2018). https://doi.org/10.1007/978-3-030-01234-2_18
39. Zhang, Y., Tian, Y., Kong, Y., Zhong, B., Fu, Y.: Residual dense network for image super-resolution. In: Proceedings of the IEEE Conference on Computer Vision and Pattern Recognition, pp. 2472–2481 (2018)
40. Zhu, J.Y., Park, T., Isola, P., Efros, A.A.: Unpaired image-to-image translation using cycle-consistent adversarial networks. In: 2017 IEEE International Conference on Computer Vision (ICCV), pp. 2242–2251 (2017)

Criminal Network Community Detection in Social Media Forensics

Ogerta Elezaj[1](✉), Sule Yildirim Yayilgan[1](✉), and Edlira Kalemi[2](✉)

[1] Department of Information Security and Communication Technology,
Norwegian University of Science and Technology (NTNU), Trondheim, Norway
{ogerta.elezaj,sule.yildirim}@ntnu.no
[2] University of Tirana, Tirana, Albania
edlira.kalemi@unit.edu.al

Abstract. Nowadays, Online Social Networks (OSNs) has created a breeding ground for criminals to engage in cyber–crime activities, and the legal enforcement agencies (LEAs) are facing significant challenges since there is no consistent and generalized framework built specifically to analyse users' misbehaviour and their social activity on these platforms. Data exchanged over these platforms represent an important source of information, even their characteristics such as unstructured nature, high volumes, velocity, and data inter–connectivity, become an obstacle for LEAs to analyse these data using traditional methods in order to provide it to the legal domain. Although numerous researches have been carried out on digital forensics, little focus has been employed on developing appropriate tools to exhaustively meet all the requirements of crime investigation targeting data integration, information sharing, collection and preservation of digital evidences. To bridge this gap, in our preliminary work we presented a generic digital evidence framework, called CISMO as a semantic tool that is able to support LEAs in detecting and preventing different type of crimes happening on OSNs. This paper gives details of the knowledge extraction layer of the framework. Specially, we mainly focus on analyses criminal social graph structures proving the effectiveness of CISMO in a case study with real criminal dataset. Experimental results reveal that applying appropriate Social Network Analyses (SNA), CISMO framework should be able to query and discover the criminal networks, empowering the criminal investigator to see the connections between people.

Keywords: Criminal networks · Digital forensics · Knowledge graph · Online social networks · Social network analyses · Community detection

1 Introduction

In recent years, we have seen a sharply increase on the usage of online social networks (OSNs) by billions of people around the world and these platforms are becoming an indispensable part of their life. People use this platform to easily express and share their day-to-day activities and sentiments. The number of worldwide users reported for January 2020 is 3.8 billion users, with this number increasing by more than 9% since

© Springer Nature Switzerland AG 2021
S. Yildirim Yayilgan et al. (Eds.): INTAP 2020, CCIS 1382, pp. 371–383, 2021.
https://doi.org/10.1007/978-3-030-71711-7_31

this time last year [1]. It has been alleged that they have the power to energize collective action in social movements like Arab Spring [2].

In UK, police officers reported 32,451 Facebook-related crimes happening during 2017–2018, showing an increase in crime of 19%[1], since the time last year. Of major concern to LEAs is the fact that social media has become a useful tool for terrorism organisation used to recruit and radicalize new members [3, 7]. On the other hand, it is noted that 59% of teenagers have been target of cyberbullying or harassing on OSNs, so this type of crime becomes a major problem for police investigator to identify and manage such cases as often it goes unreported, and thus unpunished[2]. As a result, the exploitation of technology, with the internet and social media at its core, is one of, if not the, most important challenge faced by Law Enforcement Agencies (LEAs) within the EU, and worldwide, today[3]. The paring of virtual marketplaces on the dark web with cryptocurrencies such as bitcoin are increasingly being used as a means to avert authorities 'efforts to surveillance and trace the exchange of illegal goods and services [4].

A common problem for LEAs during investigation is to analyse people involved in organized crime and to identify groups and key actors [5], using clusters of correlated entities based on information about the connections between the given entities [6]. In this research, the patterns of interactions of the hacker forum can be represented as a network, the individual parts of the forum being denoted by nodes and their private interaction by edges. SNA is employed to detect influencers and communities, such as finding these leaders in such networks and removing them may defragment the criminal network or disrupt it.

The contribution of this paper is twofold. First, this paper introduces the knowledge extraction layer of CISMO framework [22], which is a knowledge graph- based framework developed at our lab originally for the purpose of providing LEAs with the possibility to process unstructured data and identify hidden patterns and relationships in crime datasets with the focus on crime investigation and prevention. Second, the research is focused on scalability and usability challenges posed by large criminal graphs to discover communities. In the experimental part we apply some traditional community detection algorithms over information from the Nulled.io5[4] forum, a recently leaked dataset collected for distributing cracked software forum, showing an effective way of processing the information aiming to detect groups with similar characteristics.

The remaining part of the paper is organized as follows. In the background section some preliminaries and notation are summarized. Section 3 describes the architecture, and steps applied in the knowledge extraction layer of the CISMO framework developed by authors for crime detection on OSNs. Section 4 represents the results obtained from applying the proposed algorithms to a real crime data set. Finally, conclusions are presented in Sect. 5.

---

[1] https://www.infosecurity-magazine.com/news/facebook-crime-rises-19-per-cent/.

[2] http://www.bullyingstatistics.org/content/cyber-bullying-statistics.html.

[3] https://www.europol.europa.eu/sites/default/files/documents/iocta2017.pdf.

[4] https://archive.org/details/nulled.io_database_dump_06052016.

2 Background

Social networks can be modelled as a graph G = (V, E). In OSNs, the nodes represent actors and the edges represent the relationships among actors. Each network represented as graph is characterised by a list of properties which provide information about the structure of the network as a whole. These properties do not provide any information related to the specific actors in the network. Here are definitions of some of popular properties which are used in this research.

- **Size:** the number of nodes within the graph. This property is important as it provides information to classify a graph as a big graph or not. When the size is big the analysing and processing of it it's a challenge.
- **Diameter:** the length of the longest shortest path among all vertices in a given graph. Diameter affects the speed of the diffusion of information within the network.
- **Average Clustering Coefficient:** the mean of local clustering of each node in a given graph calculated as a fraction of triangles that actually exist over all possible triangles in its neighbourhood.
- **Average Path Length:** the average number of steps along the shortest paths for all possible pairs of network nodes, used to measure the efficiency of information or mass transport on a network.

In order to analyse the importance of different actors in social graphs, centralization degrees are calculated. Here, in this paper we focus our analyses different centrality measures, namely, degree, weighted degree, closeness centrality, harmonic closeness centrality, betweenness centrality [13] and eigen centrality [12], given in Table 1.

Table 1. Graph based centrality measures

Centralities	Definition	Formula
Degree	Number of direct ties that involve a given node	$C_d(i) = \sum_{i=1}^{N} A_{ij}$ (1) N - number of nodes A - the adjacency matrix $A_{ij} = 1$ if there is a link between the nodes i and j and $A_{ij} = 0$ if there is not a link between these nodes
Closeness	Estimates how fast the flow of information would be through a given node to other nodes	$C_c(i) = \sum_{j=1}^{N} \frac{1}{d(i,j)}$ (2) N - number of nodes d (i, j) - the distance between node i and other nodes

(continued)

Table 1. (*continued*)

Centralities	Definition	Formula
Betweenness	Captures how much a given node is in-between others	$C_C(i) = \sum_{j \neq k} \frac{g_{jk}(i)}{g_{jk}}$ (3) $g_{jk}(i)$ - the number of shortest paths between j and k passing through i g_{jk} - the total number of shortest paths between j and k where $\neq k$.
Eigenvector	Measures a node's importance while giving consideration to the importance of its neighbors	$C_e(i) = \frac{1}{\omega} \sum_{j=1}^{N} A_{ij} C_e(j)$ (4) N - number of nodes A - the adjacency matrix

During the last decade, there has been a considerable interest in community detection in social graphs. There are different definitions of community concept in graphs. The common definition is that a community is a group of nodes densely interconnected compared to the other nodes for a given network.

For a given social network, represented by a graph G = (V, E) where V is the set of nodes and E the set of edges, the community detection is a partition of the nodes in V of the form $C = C_1, \ldots, C_k$ such that each C_i, $1 \leq i \leq k$ exhibits the community structure that presents groups of nodes so called communities [16]. There are two types of community detection, overlapping and non-overlapping (disjoint) communities. In this paper, we focus on applying some well-known non-overlapping community detection, used to find a community structure that any actor in a social network can be member of only one community. Here, we will introduce a set of algorithms we have applied in the forum graph we have created. We ignored some of algorithms that are very slow as the graph we are conducting our experiments is big.

In this research, we have used R software and the igraph library to compare community detection algorithms. This library provides mostly used community detection algorithms i.e. Infomap, Louvain, Fast greedy and Walktrap.

Walktrap
In [14] author proposed the random-walk concept to find community in a network. This method is based on node similarity and it uses the hierarchical agglomerative clustering, where random walks tend to be confined to denser region of a graph (i.e. communities). This algorithm starts from a non-clustered area and calculates distance between adjacent nodes, where two adjacent communities are chosen and merged into one updating the distance between communities. This process is repeated (N − 1) times.

Infomap
Infomap, introduced by Martin Rosvall et al. [15], it is based on the map equation to find community structure in network, which represents description length of a random walker in a network. It is based on the rule that the partitions with good modular structure have

smaller description length. The algorithm first starts with by considering each node as a separate module and then, nodes are selected randomly and are combined resulting in largest decrease in map equation. Then, modules formed in previous steps are considered as nodes and the same process is repeated until there is no further decrease in map equation.

Louvain

This algorithm, originally introduced by Blondel et al. in 2008 [17], it is considered as one of the most powerful community detection algorithms, due to the high modularity community partitions in a fast and memory-efficient manner. This algorithm has multiple phases and each phase is characterised by multiple iterations, that are running until the stopping criteria is met. This process stops when there is no change in modularity value. At the beginning of the process, each node i is going to be assigned to a unique community. In the situation of adjacent nodes, if the merging results ends up in a higher modularity gain, these nodes are merged in the same group. Once these calculations are done, the algorithms consider the communities as nodes while total of weights of inter-communities' edges are taken as weight assigned to edges among new nodes. Generally, based on the results presented in literature the method needs only tens of iterations and fewer phases to terminate on real world data, showing significant improvement in terms of computational speed.

Fast Greedy

This algorithm is an agglomerative hierarchical clustering method proposed by Clauset et al. [18]. It is recommended to use this algorithm for community detection in networks which have sparse adjacency matrix. This method maximizes the modularity function Q and starts with assigning a different community to each node in a given graph. Then, the pair of clusters that reach the maximum increase or minimum decrease of ΔQ are combined which results in higher modularity gain, until one cluster remains with all nodes in the network. As an output of this algorithm, a dendrogram, showing the order of merges is produced. The optimal community cluster can be found by cutting the dendrogram at the level of maximum Q.

Girvan-Newman

This algorithm [19] detects communities by progressively removing edges from the original network. It is a hierarchical method, based on the edge betweenness. The edges groups that are loosely connected by a few edges are removed. In this way, the groups are separated from each other and reveal the structure of communities, until the connected components of the remaining network are the communities. Instead of basing on the edges are the most central to communities, the Girvan–Newman algorithm focuses on edges that are most likely "between" communities.

Leading Eigenvector

This algorithm tries to find densely connected subgraph by moving the maximization process to the eigenspectrum to maximize modularity by using a matrix known as the modularity matrix [21]. The elements of the leading eigenvector measure how firmly each vertex belongs to its assigned community. Thus, large vector elements represent central members of their communities and small vector elements shows more ambivalent results.

In this section, we introduced some of the classic community detection algorithms that are originally designed to be generally applied to any information network. All these algorithms are recursive of high polynomial computational complexity [20]. Thus, their application in big social media networks is limited due in terms of scalability, outcome consistency, and overall reliability. Thus, their application could doubtlessly be considered infeasible.

Evaluation Metrics

In this paper, we have used modularity [23] and number of communities as the evaluation factors for community detection algorithms. Modularity (Q) is the most widely used and accepted metric, which is used for measuring the quality of community's detection. Let assume that the graph has been partitioned into k communities. Define a $k \times k$ symmetric matrix e whose element e_{ij} is the fraction of all edges in the network connecting nodes in community i to those in community j. Let $a_i = \sum_j e_{ij}$ be the fraction of edges that connect to nodes in community i. Then modularity is defined as:

$$Q = \sum_i (e_{ij} - a_i^2) \tag{5}$$

For practical purpose, a value ranging from about 0.3 to 0.7 usually appears to indicate a strong community structure.

3   Knowledge Extraction Layer

To understand the criminal behaviour of various actors, the groups they belong to, and to analyse the information shared by them on social media, the knowledge extraction layer of CISMO framework, uses the combination of machine learning, SNA and community detection on OSN to unveil the communication patterns of online users. The steps of the knowledge extraction are outlined in Fig. 1. After pre-processing the messages sent in a specific OSNs, each message is converted into feature vectors that are learnable for the machine learning models.

In the previous research, we trained multiple classifiers with the labelled data, including Bayesian network, support vector machine, neural networks and k-nearest neighbours. As the data are unlabelled, we manually labelled 5% of the data in order to build up predictive models for labelling the whole dataset. Linear SVM achieved the highest mean accuracy. Thus, we used linear SVM with the tuned parameter to machine label the rest of the corpus. Thus far, the focus has been on identifying each user's private message (i.e., as a criminal profile, or non-criminal profile), we then constructed a forum network to understand how in-group and cross-group communicate in the structural communities detected in the forum networks.

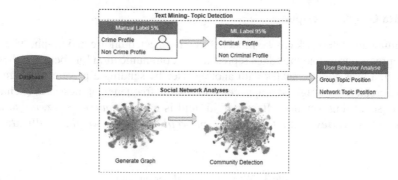

Fig. 1. Knwoledge extraction layer of CISMO framework

4 Results and Discussions

4.1 Data Source and Data Pre-processing

In this research, we use a dataset from Nulled.io, a popular dark web forum which has been hacked and its data leaked. The main reason for using this dataset in our experiments is the real life characteristics and the large number of records in it. However, we do not claim that the data found in this forum represent all different categories of crimes happening in OSNs, but this data is a treasure trove of information for investigators that could yield powerful follow-up research in the social media digital forensics, and not only. As this data contains confidential and sensitive information, the research is done after deep consideration about research ethics, and as a consequence in our results we do not provide any data that can directly or indirectly identify the users. Moreover, in legal proceedings we can find out many attempts to analyse the growth and membership of the involved communities in these networks [8, 9]. This database contains a wealth of information, 599,085 user profiles and their private and public communication, but we will limit our research on the private communication among users, where the relevant information is stored in the table message_topics, as shown in Table 2.

During the data preprocessing, the messages are processed in order to remove HTML tags. For this task an HTML parser, Beautiful Soup is used first and then to convert nouns and verbs to their lemma we applied lemmatizers in NLTK. The text messages contains special characters, punctuation marks and stop word which are removed using NLTK.

Table 2. Database information

Database	Table	Number of instances
Nulled.io	members	599,085
	message_topics	404,355
	message_posts	800,593

4.2 Data Graph Description

A communication network can be modeled as a connected undirected graph, where the nodes represent users and the edges represent the communication line between them. In the forum, a user communicates with another user by sending a private message. The graph we created is a weighted graph, considering the frequency of messages exchanged between users using weights. Mt_starter_id field is used as *source vertex, mt_to member_id as target vertex, and mt_to count + mt_replies as edge weight*, as illustrated in Table 3.

Table 3. Weighting unit determination

Table	Interaction kind	Source vertex	Target vertex	Weighting unit
Message topics	User A send a private message to user B	starter_id (User A)	member_id (User B)	count + replies

In a connected graph, the normalized closeness centrality (or closeness) of a node is the average length of the shortest path between the node and all other nodes in the graph. This adjustment allows comparisons between nodes of graphs of different sizes. In Table 4 shows only the centrality indices of the moxt 10 influential nodes of the network, due to page limitiations.

Table 4. The details of the most influential nodes selected by different methods

Name	Degree	Weighted degree	Closeness centrality	Harmonic closeness centrality	Betweenness centrality	Eigen centrality
1	281462	284984	0,934919	0,971208	52,237939	1
1471	1587	2263	0,494116	0,498154	0,055225	0,006038
1337	1504	2121	0,49395	0,497933	0,10866	0,005725
334	1321	2111	0,494808	0,498262	0,127523	0,005077
8	1260	1612	0,493564	0,497414	0,055841	0,004869
0	1259	1662	0,492575	0,496835	0,216206	0,004817
15398	1229	1819	0,49326	0,497189	0,134325	0,00473
6	1049	1289	0,33721	0,34098	0,102374	0,003722
448198	840	1237	0,493606	0,496945	0,059106	0,003372

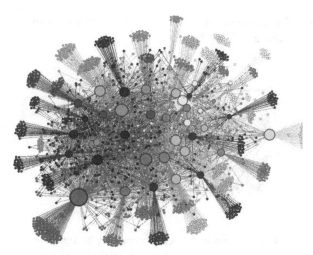

Fig. 2. Network for users in Nulled.io forum with private communication. Deep colour and big size of nodes represent users that are having many connections.

Based on the graph presentation, it is evident that one of the nodes has more connections compared to all the others, the node with bigger size belonging to the user 1. After manual checking of the private messages send and received by this node, it is evident that most of the messages are welcome messages and for this reason it can be concluded that this user is the administrator of the network. In order to define relevant criminal community, it has been deleted all the connections where the sender or receiver is user 1 and the connection weigh is equal to one. When the weight is one, it has been shared only a welcome message between the user 1 and any other user in the forum. After deleting all these welcome messages, and some other irrelevant messages, it was obtained a graph with the properties presented in Table 5.

Table 5. Graph properties

Property	Value
Nodes	25983
Edges	80671
Diameter	14
Average clustering coefficient	0.144
Average path length	4.5

Looking at Table 5, as the network of interest of Nulled.io is large, the graph has a small average path length and low clustering coefficient. Investigation done in social networks concluded a short path length between individuals, the so-called "six degrees of separation" [10], which is seen in Nulled.io. This graph has an average clustering coefficient of 0.1444, in the same range with other studies carried out for OSNs data such as Facebook. The range of this property for Facebook data varies between 0.133 and 0.211 with an average of 0.167 [11].

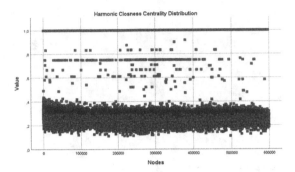

Fig. 3. Harmonic closeness centrality histogram

In order to analyse and gain a better insight of importance of individuals and their influence in the forum, we analysed the distribution of graph centralities, Between Centrality and Harmonized Closeness Centrality respectively. As illustrated in Fig. 3, in total there are 1335 nodes with a centrality over 0.8. These nodes are considered as central nodes as they have the shortest path length to other nodes. These nodes give an idea about the number of communities that can be discovered in this graph. The distribution of the Betweenness Centrality, illustrated in Fig. 4, shows that more than 13000 nodes has a value close to zero. These nodes belong to one community as they are far away from other nodes in the graph. From the graph it is evident that there are some nodes with centrality value over 500000, which means that those nodes play a central role in the spreading process in their local neighbourhood.

In this graph, we applied some community detection algorithms in order to define communities and to discover possible criminal communities.

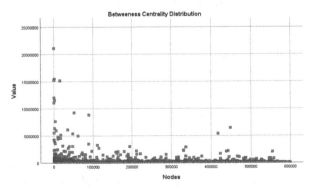

Fig. 4. Betweenness centrality histogram

4.3 Community Detection

In this section, we are evaluating some of the existing algorithms used for community detection in order to compare them. The results are compared based on the two metrics, the modularity Q and number of communities discovered, presented in Table 6.

Table 6. Modularity of the network when partitioned by each algorithm.

Algorithm	Modularity (Q)	No of communities
Louvain algorithm	0.58	861
Girvan-Newman algorithm	0.47	986
Fast Greedy	0.48	1137
Leading_eigen	0.35	730
Imfomap	0.37	2741
Walktrap	0.39	3079

Modularity reported in Table 6 varies from 0.35 (Leading Eigenvector) to 0.58 (Louvain). Regarding to the identified communities, the Walktrap algorithm obtained the highest number of communities. However, it also got low modularity; this is due to the principle of random walks that tend to fall into isolated groups of nodes. Based on the results shown in Table 6, we can conclude that partitions obtained by Louvain have consistently high modularity scores, indicating that the network partitions are more community-like. Fast Greedy, Infomap and Walktrap algorithms also have high modularity scores. These algorithms also differ in terms of the number of communities being detected. Infomap, Walktrap and Fast Greedy detect a large number of communities, result that is not surprising due to the propagation methods behind these algorithms.

Based on the achieved results, we can conclude that the Louvain algorithms for this graph model generates 861 communities with $Q = 0.49$, the highest modularity. On real world networks, Louvain algorithm achieves the detection of communities which are densely connected inside communities and sparsely connected between communities, detecting a lower number of communities compared to other algorithms.. Louvain algorithm remains both effective and efficient also when the probability of edges between communities increases (results on artificial networks). On the other hand, Infomap, Leading Eingenvector and Walktrap are weak on modularity metrics.

By using graph analysis techniques. LEAs can identify key members of different criminal communities that might be targeted to disrupt these communities. It was observed that by extracting relevant knowledge, a broad overview of some criminal activities can be obtained; however, due to the heterogeneity of private messages, it is difficult to obtain further details on different crime categories.

5 Conclusions

In this paper we presented some challenges faced by LEAS during their daily activities to fight crime happening on social media. We elaborated the knowledge extraction layer of the CISMO framework, a framework developed to semantically detect and prevent crime happening on OSNs. We focus on methodical and analytical aspects of graph analyses of criminal data in big data environments on large datasets with thousands of nodes and edges. Experimental results reveal that applying appropriate Social Network Analyses (SNA), CISMO framework should be able to query and discover the criminal networks, empowering the criminal being capable to identify key members of criminal communities and the communities they belong to. Based on the modularity used as a metric to quantitatively compare the selected community detection algorithm, we conclude that Louvain algorithm appears to be robust in terms of higher modularity and lower number of discovered communities. Our study shows that modeling the data coming from OSNs into a knowledge graph and applying SNA and community detection algorithms, LEAs can gain valuable insights into how criminal communities are organized. Future work will consist in testing the framework with real data of OSNs covering a broader range of crimes, considering both more algorithms and more networks for testing.

References

1. Digital 2020. https://wearesocial.com/digital-2020
2. Lotan, G., Graeff, E., Ananny, M., Gaffney, D., Pearce, I., Boyd, D.: The Arab spring| the revolutions were tweeted: information flows during the Tunisian and Egyptian revolutions. Int. J. Commun. **5**, 2011 (2011)
3. Eaton, R.: Digital Terrorism and Hate. Simon Wiesenthal Centre (2014). Accessed 18 Mar 2020. http://www.wiesenthal.com/site/apps/nlnet/content.aspx?c=lsKWLbPJLnF&b=8776547&ct=13928897
4. Janze, C.: Are cryptocurrencies criminals' best friends? Examining the coevolution of Bitcoin and darknet markets. In: Proceedings of the Americas Conference on Information Systems (AMCIS), Boston, MA, p. 10 (2017)
5. Décary-Hétu, D., Dupont, B.: The social network of hackers. Global Crime **13**(3), 160–175 (2012)
6. Marcus, S.M., Moy, M., Coffman, T.: Social network analysis. In: Cook, D.J., Holder, L.B. (eds.) Mining Graph Data. Wiley, New York (2007)
7. Weimann, G.: Going dark: terrorism on the dark web. Stud. Conflict Terrorism **39**(3), 195–206 (2016)
8. Bradbury, D.: Unveiling the dark web. Netw. Secur. **4**, 14–17 (2014)
9. Edwards, M.J., Rashid, A., Rayson, P.: A service-independent model for linking online user profile information. In: Proceedings of the 2014 IEEE Joint Intelligence and Security Informatics Conference, The Hague, The Netherlands, 24–26 September 2014, pp. 280–283 (2014)
10. Travers, J., Milgram, S.: An experimental study of the small world problem. Sociometry **32**, 425–443 (1969)
11. Wilson, C., Sala, A., Puttaswamy, K.P.N., Zhao, B.Y.: Beyond social graphs. ACM Trans. Web **6**(4), 1–31 (2012)
12. Bonacich, P.: Technique for analyzing overlapping memberships. Sociol. Methodol. **4**, 176–185 (1972)
13. Freeman, L.C., Roeder, D., Mulholland, R.R.: Centrality in social networks: II. Experimental results. Soc. Netw. **2**(2):119–141 (1979)

14. Pons, P., Latapy, M.: Computing communities in large networks using random walks. In: Yolum, Güngör, T., Gürgen, F., Özturan, C. (eds.) Computer and Information Sciences - ISCIS 2005. ISCIS 2005. Lecture Notes in Computer Science, vol. 3733, pp. 284–293. Springer, Heidelberg. https://doi.org/10.1007/11569596_31

15. Rosvall, M., Bergstrom, C.T.: Maps of information flow reveal community structure in complex networks. PNAS **105**, 1118 (2008)

16. Fortunato, S., Barthelemy, M.: Resolution limit in community detection. Proc. Natl. Acad. Sci. **104**(5), 36–41 (2007)

17. Blondel, V.D., Guillaume, J.-L., Lambiotte, R., Lefebvre, E.: Fast unfolding of communities in large networks. J. Stat. Mech. Theory Exp. (10), P10008 (2008)

18. Clauset, A., Newman, M.E.J., Moore, C.: Finding community structure in very large networks. Phys. Rev. E **70**, 066111 (2004)

19. Girvan, M., Newman, M.E.J.: Community structure in social and biological networks. Proc. Natl. Acad. Sci. **99**(12), 7821–7826 (2002)

20. Peel, L., Larremore, D.B., Clauset, A.: The ground truth about metadata and community detection in networks. Sci. Adv. **3**, e1602548 (2017)

21. Newman, M.E.J.: Finding community structure in networks using the eigenvectors of matrices. Phys. Rev. E **74**(3), 036104 (2006)

22. Elezaj, O., Yildirim, S., Ahmed, J., Kalemi, E., Brichfeldt, B., Haubold, C.: Crime Intelligence from Social Media Using CISMO. In: Yang, X.S., Sherratt, R.S., Dey, N., Joshi, A. (eds.) Proceedings of Fifth International Congress on Information and Communication Technology. ICICT 2020. Advances in Intelligent Systems and Computing, vol. 1183, pp. 441–460. Springer, Singapore. https://doi.org/10.1007/978-981-15-5856-6_44

23. Newman, M.E.J.: Finding and evaluating community structure in networks. Phys. Rev. E **69**, 026113 (2004)

Data Privacy in IoT Equipped Future Smart Homes

Athar Khodabakhsh$^{(\boxtimes)}$ ⓘ and Sule Yildirim Yayilgan ⓘ

Department of Information Security and Communication Technology, Norwegian University of Science and Technology, NTNU, Gjovik, Norway
{athar.khodabakhsh,sule.yildirim}@ntnu.no

Abstract. Smart devices are becoming inseparable from daily lives and are improving fast for providing intelligent services and remote monitoring and control. In order to provide personalized and customized services more personal data collection is required. Consequently, intelligent services are becoming intensely personal and they raise concerns regarding data privacy and security. In this paper data privacy requirements in a smart home environment equipped with "Internet of Things" are described and privacy challenges for data and models are addressed.

Keywords: Data privacy · IoT · Model · Pattern · Privacy · Smart home

1 Introduction

Smart home system let the individuals interact with home devices and organize their home intelligently. Heterogeneous electronic smart devices are equipped with sensors, cameras, or actuators and are connected to each other through Internet of Things (IoT) technologies [1]. These devices are able to collect information from users and home environment to support real-time monitoring, remote control, and safety for smart home. Machine learning algorithms process the collected data and train models to perform personalized and intelligent actions by utilizing techniques such as pattern extraction and speech recognition. Smart service's aim is to provide recommendation to users and bring more intelligence to daily life. Although smart homes bring many advantages in terms of control, management, and cost benefits for users and companies, but also raises concerns about personal data protection, security, and privacy. For a smart service to be reliable *data security and privacy, authorization and trust, authentication and secure communication,* and *compliance and regulations* [2] should be provided for users. In this paper we discuss data privacy challenges for individuals' activity patterns where data processing gives more insights about their natural behavior [3] therefore, they should have the rights to protect their personal data and be aware of data processing results extracted from their personal information.

© Springer Nature Switzerland AG 2021
S. Yildirim Yayilgan et al. (Eds.): INTAP 2020, CCIS 1382, pp. 384–391, 2021.
https://doi.org/10.1007/978-3-030-71711-7_32

Fig. 1. Smart home equipped with IoT devices and remote mobile access.

Moreover, some IoT devices are produced cheaper and faster by companies to capture the new trend in the market which lead to security risks. Actors with malicious intentions may exploit the vulnerabilities in IoT devices or trained models remotely. They may intrude into smart home's network and analyze internet traffic of smart devices, process user's information, track users' activities, and exploit IoT device vulnerabilities and gradually take over the control of home or lock out the actual residents.

This paper focuses on data privacy requirements in smart home environment and evolves around a research question: "what are the requirements to protect personal data and user's profile against privacy violation?" and is organized as follows. Section 2 describes IoT equipped smart home and intelligent services for users. Section 3 explores data privacy challenges and privacy violation scenarios and discusses requirements for smart home privacy policy developments. Section 4 concludes the study and highlights future research.

2   Smart Home

Smart home system provides the ability for users to interact remotely with IoT devices via mobile application and finger-print/voice-enabled home automation commands. A smart home consists of several IoT devices depicted in Fig. 1 including smart-kitchen devices, smart-meters, smart lighting, smart locks, and wearables [4]. In Table 1, their features and functionalities are listed. IoT equipment are interconnected and communicate with each other to provide intelligent services to users. They collect data and user's activities through sensors in order to learn patterns using machine learning techniques.

Table 1. IoT device functionality in smart home.

Device	Functionalities
Smart-meters	Real-time recording of electricity/water consumption and interaction with users for consumption patterns
Smart fridge	Flexible user-controlled cooling options and tracking products that are stored inside
Smart-light	Remote controlling the light requirements at home with customized and scheduled features
Surveillance camera	Monitoring home environment with motion sensors and malicious activity detection in area and sending alarms
Smart-heating	Control and set the environment temperature intelligently
Smart-air conditioning	Monitoring and customize humidity, smoke, and carbon monoxide in home environment
Smart-key/lock	Verified person can enter home or modify system and vdevice settings
Smart-garden	Home growing fresh food and flowers by automated watering, light, and nutrients
Smart-kitchen devices	Eco friendly washing machines by reducing water, time, and energy consumption
Wearable devices	Real-time tracking of the vital signs (via smart watch, etc.)
Smart-phone	Control smart home system remotely

2.1 IoT Intelligent Services

According to device functionalities described in Table 1, smart-meter can communicate with smart-heating devices to set the environment temperature, and with smart air-conditioning for setting humidity and smoke level. Smart kitchen devices can provide household services based on resident's presence at home and on holidays based on trained models. Once the pattern is modeled, it can be used for recommendations, generalization to solve problems, estimations and forecasting future requirements. The benefits from smart homes and intelligent customization features can bring automation services such as:

- In the smart home system the user can set alarm automatically at a specific time of day when all the residents are away. For instance, this can help to turn off devices that are not used for electricity optimization.
- The home can be set for warm welcome specially in winter after working hour, including setting the home temperature, boiling water for a drink, etc. based on resident's habits and behavior pattern.

- Set up camera to send alarm in case of intrusion utilizing smart and in-built motion sensors and detect frequent visitors through face recognition techniques.
- In smart home it is possible to light up the home before they arrive and turn on/off lights with respect to movement pattern inside home.
- The IoT devices at kitchen such as smart fridge, smart coffee maker, etc. can send notification when an item is finished.

In order to provide these intelligent services, personal data from user's activity are constantly collected and processed for training models and patterns extraction. Personalized models can expose highly sensitive information.

2.2 Privacy Violation Scenarios

IoT devices are connected to internet and to each other and having access to one component can lead to direct/indirect access to other smart devices and smart home system. Some of IoT devices are more critical such as smart keys and smart locks. IoT devices collect data about homeowners for better customization and personalization which are stored locally on things or on edge/cloud and unauthorized access to this information can be used for criminal or disruptive activities [5]. Many companies and smart service providers use collected data from IoT devices and train machine learning models to improve advertising and product and service recommendations for users. By using the smart services, activities of the users, their preferences, purchases, health data, transactions, voice commands, and location data are constantly recorded and processed to better understand the data generated by their operations [6]. Personal data collection and records bring two main concerns regarding personal information exposure.

- **Attack on data** can expose sensitive information about users:
  - *personal data leakage*: data is less secured when stored on data centers,
  - *false data injection attack*: attacker might attempt to change/falsify data that is used for real-time decision making,
  - *misinformation attack*: attacker may release false data reports similar to actual data.

  An intruder may gain access to home network, remotely control and exploit sensors and autonomous home devices, track user's activities, and observe smart-cameras in real-time to find out resident's activity pattern and what is going on inside users house [2]. Attackers can use the personal information to unlock the smart keys and turn off alarms during intrusion. Additionally, data processing and analytics are moved to edge for real-time services which gives the attackers an entry point to smart home network through remote-access.
- **Attack on machine learning models** can leak information about the individual data records similar to any other software systems. Privacy attack on machine learning systems such as:
  - *membership interface attacks*: whether a record was in model training dataset,

- *model inversion attacks*: use a model's output on a hidden input to infer something about this input [6].

For example, training model can uncover high correlations between a user's activities or health features. Once the correlations are known, the information can be used as public facts about the person or members of a population and is a form of privacy breach. Attackers may gain query access to the model and obtain the model's prediction vector on data records [6].

Therefore, a user's activity pattern can be profiled and may be used to predict aspects concerning natural person's behavior, health, and personal preferences. Personal data is subject to regulatory requirements for protection against violation and should be developed under General Data Protection Regulation (GDPR) standards for novel activity monitoring using machine learning techniques.

3   Data Privacy

According to *GDPR, Article.1 Subject-matter and Objectives*: "regulation to protect fundamental rights and freedoms of natural persons and in particular their right to the protection of personal data" [7] and *GDPR, Article.4 Definitions*:

Art.4.2 Data Processing: "any operation or set of operations which is performed on personal data or on sets of personal data, whether or not by automated means, such as collection, recording, organization, structuring, storage, adaptation or alteration, retrieval, consultation, use, disclosure by transmission, dissemination or otherwise making available, alignment or combination, restriction, erasure or destruction;"

Art.4.4 Profiling: "any form of automated processing of personal data consisting of the use of personal data to evaluate certain personal aspects relating to a natural person, in particular to analyze or predict aspects concerning that natural person's performance at work, economic situation, health, personal preferences, interests, reliability, behavior, location or movements;"

data collection, data processing, and model training which will lead to profiling by applying machine learning techniques are subject to regulations and protection of person's natural behavior pattern.

3.1   User's Activity Pattern

For demonstration, we used a public smart home **UMass Smart* Dataset**, from Smart* project [8] for extracting correlation. The goal of Smart* project was to optimize home energy consumption and contains data for 114 single-family apartments for the period 2014–2016. We used Home-A dataset in experiments for pattern extraction. The dataset includes electricity consumption of 11 devices at smart home such as WashingMachine, FridgeRange, KitchenLights, BedroomLights, MasterLights which are measured every 30 mins.

Correlation: is statistical relationship between two variables and can be positive or negative, where positive correlation means both variables move in same direction and negative value means when one variable increase the other variable decreases [9].

KitchenLights and BedroomLights were selected since have -0.09 correlation. As shown in Fig. 2, the BedroomLights and KitchenLights are not turned on simultaneously and it can be inferred as, the resident turns off the kitchen light when they go to bedroom. Machine learning algorithms can use this knowledge can to extract pattern for electricity consumption management.

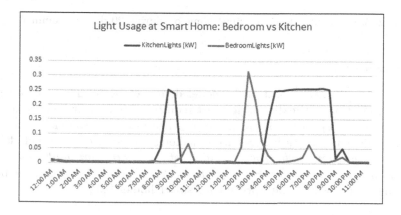

Fig. 2. Daily light usage at smart home for one day on 1/1/2014.

Another example is correlation between KitchenLights and MasterLights with values of +0.41, which is positive and relatively high correlation. It can be inferred that KitchenLights and MasterLights are turned on simultaneously. In addition, by a quick analysis, absence of the residence can be extracted. As shown in Fig. 3, the lights are not turned on for a period of 5 days by having access to only two features from smart home data. Although this knowledge is very useful for energy optimization, it can be misused if unauthorized actors gain access.

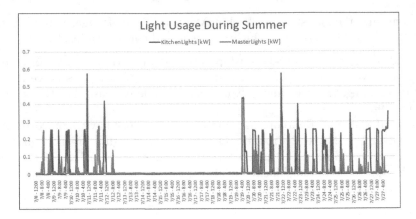

Fig. 3. Daily light usage at smart home on during 20 days in summer.

3.2 Discussion

Once a natural person's pattern is modeled, it can be used to recommendations, optimization, estimate and forecast requirements by learning relationship among features. Depending on the problem, features are fed to machine learning algorithm for data processing. Security challenges in smart home include *data security and privacy, authorization and trust, authentication and secure communication*, and *compliance and regulations* [2]. In Table 2, we defined policy requirements to preserve data privacy for smart homes [10].

Table 2. Smart home data privacy requirements.

Privacy issue	Requirements
Data privacy	It is essential to preserve authorized access to personal information. Any data access and knowledge extraction require user's consent and results from trained models should be returned to users
Authorization	It is essential to ensure that messages and commands are sent from a trusted authorized entity, rather from a malicious adversary
Authentication	Devices need to be authenticated first in order to get connected to various services on a smart home system
Regulations	Contracts are required for data privacy and security of IoT devices and smart services. Intellectual property protection clauses and cyber insurance are important for users to protect from cyber risks

For reliable smart home operation the following points should be considered:

- Device vendors should be selected based on security quality, data protection, and special features.
- Devices should have strong passwords and possibly use biometrics for critical information access and settings.
- The IoT device software and smart home services should be kept updated with latest version.
- Features that let users for remote access should be turn off if it is not needed.
- Encryption of all static data must be ensured.
- Communications must be encrypted and all the smart devices must be physically secured.

4 Conclusion and Future Work

Artificial intelligence and machine learning are tools to provide smart services however, privacy of natural person and their personal data should be preserved and sensitive training data and their models should be secured. In this paper data privacy challenges in a smart home environment equipped with IoT are addressed. We conclude that mechanisms are required to protect user's and their personal data in smart environments. The lack of security by design in IoT technology can lead to more vulnerabilities and weak security. As future work, we will investigate model protection, device-to device interactions, and data privacy regulations for smart homes.

References

1. Luo, X., et al.: A lightweight privacy-preserving communication protocol for heterogeneous IoT environment. IEEE Access **8**, 67192–67204 (2020)
2. Gupta, M., Abdelsalam, M., Khorsandroo, S., Mittal, S.: Security and privacy in smart farming: challenges and opportunities. IEEE Access **8**, 34564–34584 (2020)
3. Patil, S., Joshi, S., Patil, D.: Enhanced privacy preservation using anonymization in IoT-enabled smart homes. In: Satapathy, S.C., Bhateja, V., Mohanty, J.R., Udgata, S.K. (eds.) Smart Intelligent Computing and Applications. SIST, vol. 159, pp. 439–454. Springer, Singapore (2020). https://doi.org/10.1007/978-981-13-9282-5_42
4. Chang, Z.: IoT device security: locking out risks and threats to smart homes. Trend Micro Research (2019)
5. Srivastava, A., Gupta, S., Quamara, M., Chaudhary, P., Aski, V.J.: Future IoT-enabled threats and vulnerabilities: state of the art, challenges, and future prospects. Int. J. Commun. Syst. **33**, e4443 (2020)
6. Shokri, R., Stronati, M., Song, C., Shmatikov, V.: Membership inference attacks against machine learning models. In: 2017 IEEE Symposium on Security and Privacy (SP), pp. 3–18. IEEE (2017)
7. General Data Protection Regulation, European Union. https://gdpr-info.eu/. Accessed June 2020
8. Smart* Data Set for Sustainability. UMassTraceRepository. http://traces.cs.umass.edu/index.php/Smart/Smart. Accessed June 2020
9. Akoglu, H.: User's guide to correlation coefficients. Turk. J. Emerg. Med. **18**(3), 91–93 (2018)
10. Information Commissioner's Office. Guide to the general data protection regulation (GDPR) (2018)

Machine Learning and the Legal Framework for the Use of Passenger Name Record Data

Iva Kostov[(✉)] [ID]

Faculty of Law, Hamburg University, 20148 Hamburg, Germany
iva.simeonova@uni-hamburg.de

Abstract. The processing of passenger name records (PNR) for security purposes on a European level was officially announced in 2016. Since then, ongoing legal discussions about PNR data focus mainly on its collection and the impact on data protection. The focus of this paper lies on a less-discussed aspect of the legal framework: the processing of PNR data and the different technological approaches it allows for. The following analysis of the German implementation of the European Directive on PNR data processing shows that it is open to the use of two different technological approaches: theory-based and machine learning methods. Taking this into account can provide a perspective that is mostly lacking in current legal debates about PNR data but can be an important addition since different technological approaches might shift the focus from data protection concerns to some aspects of technologies like machine learning. The paper also addresses a need for more technical research on the topic.

Keywords: Passenger name record · Security law · Terrorism · Serious crime · Prevention · Machine learning

1 Introduction

An interesting data processing provision has been added to the European law enforcement arsenal. According to Article 6 of the European PNR Directive [1], PNR data can be processed against pre-determined criteria for the purpose of identification of any persons requiring further examination regarding any possible involvement in terrorist offences or serious crime. Such criteria, referred to in the German implementation of the PNR Directive as "patterns" (Muster), can, in turn, be created or updated by analyzing PNR data. After an outline of the legal framework of PNR data processing in Europe and Germany in the next section, two different technological approaches of its implementation are presented in Sect. 3, with a focus on machine learning methods.

2 The PNR Legal Framework: Europe and Germany

PNR data contains personal information needed from airlines, travel agencies, or tour operators to process and fulfill a flight booking request. It consists of information on,

© Springer Nature Switzerland AG 2021
S. Yildirim Yayilgan et al. (Eds.): INTAP 2020, CCIS 1382, pp. 392–403, 2021.
https://doi.org/10.1007/978-3-030-71711-7_33

e.g., destination, seat number, frequent flyer information, baggage information and can also involve meal preferences and special needs, as required by Annex I Nr. 12 of the PNR Directive. It may also include API data (Advanced Passenger Information), which contains basic identity information such as a passenger's name, date of birth, gender, nationality and travel document information (for a full list see PNR Directive Annex I, Nr. 18). All categories of PNR data are listed in Annex I of the PNR Directive [1].

2.1 Europe

The original initiative to process PNR data for national security purposes can be traced back to US legislation,[1] which required airlines flying to and from the United States, including European airlines, to provide PNR data. The European Union then took a series of steps to develop its own legal framework (for a detailed account see [2] p. 36 ff.), which, from a sociological institutionalist perspective, at least in the early stages, were perceived as the EU's attempt to provide a feasible legal basis for the American security policies [3] p. 125. Even though the EU may have gradually realized the advantages of using PNR data for security purposes, such an initiative was originally not part of the European action plan to combat terrorism and serious crime, nor was it discussed beforehand in meetings of the Justice and Home Affairs Council [3] p. 125 f. The development of a European legal framework for the processing of PNR data can, therefore, be seen as the EU's decision to establish reciprocity in the context of otherwise asymmetrical international regulatory structures in the field of PNR data.

An impact assessment of the Commission [4] considered different options for a design of the legal framework, including centralized processing of PNR data at a European level and decentralized processing by the Member States. It was decided that a decentralized collection of PNR data for the purpose of preventing, detecting, investigating and prosecuting terrorist offenses and other serious crime was the best option, as such a proposal would lead to enhanced security in the EU while limiting the impact on the protection of personal data and keeping costs to an acceptable level. In 2016, the proposal was accepted and in the following time the PNR Directive was adopted in its current form, laying the foundations of the European PNR regulatory structures.

According to the Commission PNR data may be used in a reactive, active, or proactive manner, [4] p. 4, [5] p. 11. Data use for investigation and prosecution purposes in response to requests on a case-by-case basis *after* a criminal offense was committed can be referred to as reactive. Active or real-time processing of PNR data can be used to prevent crime *before* it is committed or interrupt crime that is *currently* being committed by assessing passengers prior to their scheduled arrival in or departure from a Member State. Proactive use of PNR data occurs for the purpose of analyzing, determining and updating criteria/patterns that can be used for passenger assessment. Article 6 of the PNR directive contains all three types of data use.

---

[1] 107th Congress (2001-2002), p. 1447 – Aviation and Transportation Security Act.

2.2 Germany

The legal basis for PNR data processing in Germany is the German Passenger Name Record Act (Fluggastdatengestz: FlugDaG), which came into force in June 2017.[2] According to the National Standards Control Council, the German PNR Act is a 1:1 implementation of the European PNR directive [6]. Nonetheless, the German Act provides more detail to some provisions of the Directive.

Pattern Matching. The automated check of PNR data against certain patterns (henceforth called *pattern matching,* (Musterabgleich)), is specified in Section 4 (2) Nr. 2 FlugDaG and further specified in Section 4 (3) and (4) FlugDaG. The government presents the process as a new and innovative measure to combat the offenses listed in Section 4 (1) FlugDaG.[3] In some cases, it has even been referred to as the *"main added value of the processing of the [PNR] data"*.[4] According to the grounds of the PNR Act,[5] pattern matching is carried out for the purpose of identifying persons previously unknown to the security authorities who may have committed, or may – currently, or in the foreseeable future – commit terrorist offenses or serious crime. This is done by classifying passengers as suspicious or unsuspicious based on previously defined criteria, which form the patterns required for the process of pattern matching.[6] If a pattern matching of the PNR data of a certain passenger results in a match, they are classified as suspicious, otherwise the passenger is classified as unsuspicious.

The main purpose of pattern matching is not to secure air traffic or to facilitate border controls. Air travel is simply a convenient opportunity for the execution of such measures [7] p. 412, [8] p. 140. PNR data is a type of behavioral data that can be used in many different contexts for different purposes, from advertising to security [8] p. 140. While pattern matching could also contribute to safer air travel, the purpose of prevention and prosecution of terrorist offenses and serious crime, as stated in Section 1 (2) FlugDaG, is not limited to this context. The offenses listed in Section 4 (1) FlugDaG (for a list of the offenses see Sect. 3.2, Subsect. "Output") can, but do not have to be directly related to air travel. Rather, a flight or its details are perceived as a part of more complex behavioral structures that might happen to intertwine with such behavioral data. The basic prerequisite for pattern matching is that the flight behavior of potential offenders is – in the broadest sense – irregular and that these irregularities manifest in their PNR data, see also [9] p. 4. Such irregular flight behavior must be further able to fit behaviors usually encountered in the case of offenders. In such cases, pattern matching could link data that in and of itself merely describes neutral everyday actions and would otherwise seem unsuspicious with the offenses in Section 4 (1) FlugDaG.

---

[2] BGBl. Part 1: Nr. 34 (2017), 1484.

[3] See p. 28 of BT-Drs. 18/11501.

[4] AG *Mengozzi*, in: ECJ, Opinion 1/15, EU:C:2016:656, point 252.

[5] BT-Drs. 18/11501, p. 28.

[6] In computer sciences, the terms "features" or "attributes" are often used to describe the properties of a model. In mathematics, the term "variable" can sometimes be used for this purpose. In the following, the term "criteria" is used since it is also used in Section 4 (3) second sentence FlugDaG: "The patterns shall contain […] criteria".

Pattern Creation. The pre-defined patterns against which passenger data is being matched are composed of different, regularly reprogrammed and refined criteria (Prüfungsmerkmale). They can be based on the knowledge of experts within the German safety authorities (Section 4 (3) FlugDaG) or on the results of PNR data analysis (Section 4 (4) FlugDaG), which is the corresponding provision to the aforementioned pro-active data use. The creation and design of criteria for the purposes of the German PNR Act is henceforth called *pattern creation* (Mustererstellung).

According to the PNR Act, pattern criteria occur in two forms: the first form is exonerating criteria (verdachtsentlastend), which, occurring in a certain composition and number, result in the flight behavior being seen as unsuspicious. The second type is incriminating criteria (verdachtsbegründend), which contain different compositions of characteristics, the occurrence of which results in the suspicion of a passenger. Sentence four of Section 4 (3) FlugDaG stipulates that the ratio of exonerating and incriminating criteria should be such that as few persons as possible produce a match. The provision can, therefore, be seen as relating to the precision and recall ratio of the pattern matching classification system. Examples of pattern criteria, as cited by the Federal Criminal Police Office and the European Commission are: previously not traveling alone, now traveling alone and under eighteen, destination airport convenient for onward flight or located near specific areas, return flight follows shortly after the outbound flight, short-term booking, multiple rebookings, cash purchase of tickets, choice of longer or more expensive routes than needed, little to no baggage, a mismatch between baggage size and length of stay and destination, travel agencies or usual routes used by traffickers, use of stolen credit cards [10] p. 26, [4] p. 5, [5] p. 24. Certain combinations of various such criteria should make it possible to identify potential offenders.

3 Technological Approaches to Pattern Creation and Pattern Matching

Technical requirements of both the European and German legal framework are limited to the use of common protocols and supported data formats for data transfers. This ensures that PIUs generally receive structured and qualitative data sets, although a recent review of the Commission voiced a need for an enhancement of data reliability and quality to ensure even more targeted and efficient data processing [5], p. 41 ff. PNR data is being transmitted by all aircraft companies, travel agencies and tour operators to the German Passenger Information Unit (PIU) on a daily basis. It is worth mentioning that since the beginning of the restricted operation of the PIU on the 29.8.2018 until the 19.8.2019, a total of 31,617,068 passenger name records had been transmitted to and processed by the PIU.[7] Annually, the PIU must deal with up to 340 million passenger name records of around 170 million passengers.[8]

Germany is still at an early stage of the implementation of pattern creation and matching.[9] Neither the European nor the German framework specifies the type of technology that is to be used for data processing and analysis, therefore, offering room

---

[7] BT-Drs. 19/12858, p. 4.

[8] BT-Drs. 18/11501, p. 23.

[9] BT-Drs. 19/12975, p. 7.

for two main approaches to pattern creation and matching: theory-based and machine learning approaches. For a similar distinction of technological approaches, see [11], [12] p. 8 f. and p. 17 ff, [13] p. 196 f., similar in substance also [14] p. 23 f. There are various other descriptions for the two technological approaches, including "rule-based" and "data-driven", "expert" and "intelligent", or "traditional algorithms/programming" and "learning algorithms/programming".

3.1 Theory-Based Approaches

Regardless of the specific technological approach, patterns are always formed by the composition of criteria that make up behavioral profiles of certain offenses or offenders, see [12] p. 16. The starting point of theory-based approaches to *pattern creation* is assumptions about certain crimes, see also [13] p. 196. Such assumptions can be based on theoretical knowledge about crime patterns, which in the best-case scenario is also supported by the corresponding expertise of practitioners and vice versa. Theoretical knowledge for the creation of such patterns can be provided by the criminal sciences. Recent breakthroughs of criminological research on terrorism – an area, long considered as "undertheorized" – are illustrated in the contributions in [15], as well as the state of theoretical research on the topic, in [16] p. 6. Professional expertise for the creation of crime patterns results from the knowledge of field experts within the German security authorities [17] p. 248. The Federal Criminal Police Office, which acts as the national PIU, conducts both research and practical measures of protection, investigation and threat prevention, which results in the embedding of theoretical knowledge within the agency practice and vice versa. Given the complexity and dynamics of the field of terrorism and serious crime, more general knowledge that can otherwise play an important role in many areas of police work [17], p. 248, seems less relevant for pattern creation. For example, the creation of patterns regarding white-collar crime (Section 4 (1) Nr. 6 FlugDaG i.c.w. Annex II to the PNR-Directive, Nr. 6, 7, 8, 17, 18, 26, e.g. corruption, fraud, money laundering) would require expert knowledge of finance, organization, management, psychology, law, communication and sociology [18] p. 80. Theory-based approaches to pattern creation would, therefore, be based primarily on the knowledge of experts from science and practice. Such approaches would be mainly cause-oriented; they would be based on assumptions about causality between pattern criteria and offenses.[10]

The German PNR Act opens the possibility of exploiting such approaches by stipulating, in Section 4 (3) fourth sentence FlugDaG, that facts available to the security authorities regarding certain offenses shall be the basis in the process of pattern creation,

---

[10] Causality in this context is not understood as a definite causal link between cause and event, such as the term may be known in the natural sciences. Instead, a limited concept of causality is applied, which stands for an observed regularity between certain characteristics and certain offenses in the sense of plausible cause-and-effect relationships. Such a concept of causality stands for the assumption that certain causes make the occurrence of an event more probable and is understood, therefore, as probabilistic causality, such as described by [19], p. 87-97. When analyzing behavioral causes, it can be difficult to work with stricter concepts of causality, see [20] p. 1098, with further evidence.

which should result in greater objectivity of criminalistic expertise.[11] Therefore, such patterns can be seen as a range of collective experience of the security authorities.[12] The results of a theory-based pattern creation are thus humanly conceived, theoretically, and/or practically derived patterns. This is not in itself a "technological" approach. However, for the following automated *pattern matching*, the patterns are modeled and coded as "if-then" rules in computer software. The software's function is predictable and explainable since the reasoning behind a particular pattern can be traced back to its creators, who, in turn, can explain the reasoning behind a chosen arrangement of criteria.

3.2 Machine Learning Approaches

Pattern matching, as stipulated by Section 4 (2) Nr. 2 FlugDaG, can be seen as a binary classification task, that can also profit from technologies suited to identify previously unknown or unnoticed structures in large data sets. International academic literature on big-data analysis has highlighted some benefits and difficulties of the use of machine learning in the field of PNR data, see [21–26]. Still, technical papers with practical results remain a rarity, which points to a need for more technical research on this topic. Not only is such research important for a better understanding of the technological possibilities that the analysis of PNR data offers. Since security authorities generally do not disclose details of their systems, for legal, social and political-science scholars, such research can act as a basis on which they can build upon when analyzing their national legal frameworks. The remaining part of the text attempts to utilize such research in order to analyze the technical possibilities for the implementation of the German PNR Act.

On a national and European level, consideration from authorities and scholars regarding the application of machine learning to pattern creation and pattern matching can be accounted for, see [8] p. 140, [7] p. 410, [10] p. 23 and p. 28 f, [27], [28] p. 7. For such considerations from the Federal Office of Administration, tasked with the development of the PNR-Information System in Germany, see BVA-International Nr. 1/2019, p. 12 f. Legal discussions regarding the PNR legal framework are mainly centered around more general aspects such as the possible disruption of German police dogmatic, or data protection concerns, e.g. [29]. While such discussions are important, without an in-depth analysis of possible technological approaches within the legal framework, they can sometimes misinterpret or misjudge the legal framework or lay a disproportionate focus on data protection concerns, which can play only a partial role in the legal debate once machine learning enters the picture. The limiting effects of a data protection perspective regarding algorithms are analyzed by [30]. As far as machine learning is seen as a knowledge-generating technology, a problem with the German data protection perspective is that it is mainly concerned with input-regulation, instead of knowledge-regulation. Identifying the possibility of utilizing different technological approaches, and specifically, machine learning approaches can, in turn, activate legal debates regarding the technology in this field and lead to the consideration of other, possibly more pressing legal questions, such as the possibility of knowledge-regulation, see [30] p. 61 f. Such debates can than tap into the steadily growing body of legal literature on machine learning; for some examples

---

[11] BT-Drs. 18/11501, p. 29.

[12] For a similar description of patterns in a different context of police work, see [17] p. 250.

with a focus mainly on a single aspect of the technology, namely on its alleged black-box nature, see: [31] p. 14 ff., referring to aspects of machine learning as „obstacles to the effective application of the law"; [7], p. 377; [32] p. 494; [33] p. 5, with further evidence; [34] p. 43 ff.; [35] p. 235; [36] p. 102 f.; [37] p. 135 f; [38], 43 f. with further evidence; [39] p. 1167; [40] p. 171 f.

Machine learning approaches would change police methods of suspicion-detection (Verdachtsgenerierung), see also [41] p. 3. The model for data analysis, in the case of Section 4 (2) Nr. 2 FlugDaG - the pattern - would be created (fully or partially) automatically. Such approaches do not rely on theoretical or practical assumptions about causal relationships. Accordingly, they are also not restricted by such, see also [12] p. 17. Instead, machine learning approaches rely on data - correlations within data sets are the basis for algorithmic hypothesis generations, which are then used to construct patterns. The results are thus machine-generated, inductively developed patterns. A pattern generation and the possibility of updating already generated patterns through PNR data analysis is explicitly stated in Section 4 (4) FlugDaG. The scope of the data basis is specified in Section 2 (2) FlugDaG (see also the listing at the beginning of Section 2).

Database. The content of a passenger name record varies depending on the information provided by each passenger. It is likely to be considered containing relatively mundane information but could be a powerful analytical resource [22], p. 4. At the most basic level, it allows checks against police databases of sought persons or objects. As pointed out in [22] p. 4, by using simple forms of link analysis or contact chaining, PNR makes it possible to discover hidden connections between known terrorists and their previously unknown associates. The more sophisticated the analytical method, the more powerful the analytical results can be.

Beyond the use of personal PNR data, non-personal data would also play an essential role in the creation of a predictive model. A model could take into account data about the weather, holidays, or certain events in some countries, as well as other factors that could influence flight and booking behavior (e.g., discounts from hotels or airlines), thereby generating more reliable predictions. For example, such data could allow the model to evaluate short-term or high-volume bookings, bookings untypical for a certain season and multiple rebookings without classifying such behavior as suspicious. It could also allow for a consideration of the seasonal nature of some offenses.

Output. Pattern matching should be able to output a *suspicion* or the *lack of suspicion* regarding the offenses listed in Section 4 (1) FlugDaG. The offenses must be punishable with a maximum term of at least three years of imprisonment in order to fall under the scope of the German PNR Act. The list includes serious crimes such as illicit trafficking in cultural goods, drugs-, arms-, organ-, human-trafficking, fraud, cyber and environmental crime and murder but also terrorist offenses such as the formation of criminal organizations, aircraft-hijacking and the financing of terrorism (for a full list see Annex II of the PNR Directive). These are crimes that are largely characterized by fairly inconspicuous behavior. The complexity of the criminal background structures, which may involve seemingly everyday activities such as a flight booking or a financial transaction, can make pattern recognition difficult or even impossible for an individual, see also [42] p. 278. Some crimes are hardly perceptible. The planning and committing of offenses such as money laundering (Section 4 (1), Nr. 6 FlugDaG, i.c.w. EU-RL

2016/681, Appendix II, Nr. 8) or the financing of terrorism (Section 4 (1), Nr. 4 FlugDaG, i.c.w. Section 89c StGB) thrives on the possibility that multiple behaviors of multiple people pass by multiple control instruments, be it institutions or individuals, unnoticed. The aim is to be inconspicuous to the highest degree possible. While such behaviors may successfully speculate what an individual would perceive, this could be more difficult if the control instrument is a machine learning model that is explicitly designed to place the inconspicuousness of a behavior in a conspicuous context.

Modeling. Various machine learning approaches can be considered for the process of *pattern creation*. Unsupervised approaches could identify anomalies within the database and segment passenger data into several clusters. The different clusters could then be analyzed to interpret the reasons for the specific segmentation choice, decide what the anomalies are and whether they are significant enough to be selected as criteria of patterns. Unsupervised learning could make it easier to identify criteria with particularly high predictive power.

The use of supervised learning for pattern creation would be possible as long as the German PIU has a sufficient amount of high-quality data on the flight behavior of offenders that can be used as training data. Based on such data, supervised learning algorithms can be trained to determine how criteria from the PNR data set will be considered in certain patterns. For example, information on the status of frequent flyers or baggage information could have particularly high predictive power for trafficking offences. If this were the case, a supervised machine learning algorithm would learn to weigh such criteria accordingly in subsequent classifications. Based on ongoing feedback, such algorithms further refine the arrangement or the weights of pattern criteria. It is not clear how much data of offenders is already available to the German PIU. It has been stated that there are generally fewer data available about terrorist offenses than about other criminal phenomena, which could, supposedly, render supervised predictive models unsuitable in the field of terrorism prevention, see [43] p. 133 with further evidence. In view of recent developments in terrorism-related databases, information and analysis, this does not necessarily have to be the case. For an overview of terrorism-related European databases, see [44] with further information about the Europol analysis project "Travellers" (33.911 data points, 5.877 of verified foreign terrorist fighters) and also the INTERPOL Database (48.700 data points on foreign terrorist fighters).[13] Moreover, in supervised learning, the quality of the training data is generally more important than the quantity. Still, in case of insufficient training data, a combination of several learning approaches, both supervised and unsupervised, would be more effective.

For an increase in the amount of training data, data exchange with member states, Europol and third countries, as stipulated by the PNR Act in Sections. 7, 9 and 10 FlugDaG, must also be taken into consideration. Scholars discussing former initiatives on PNR data processing have pointed to the transfer of terrorist intelligence obtained by the USA from the analysis of passenger data to Europol, Eurojust and the security authorities of the Member States [3] p. 129. Currently, there is majoritarian support within the Working Party on Information Exchange and Data Protection (DAPIX) regarding the

---

[13] https://tinyurl.com/yyd27n2x, last accessed on 30.1.2021.

involvement of Europol and cooperation between the Member States in the development of patterns.[14] At a more global level, similar supporting initiatives by the United Nations can be observed, announcing future enhancements of Member States' PNR-Systems, including extending the use of artificial intelligende algorithms to facilitate the identification of still unknown suspects (i.e., pattern matching).[15]

Experts can also generate synthetic PNR data in order to achieve sufficiently large numbers of training or test samples. Such approaches have proven to be an effective source of data in the context of PNR data analysis, as demonstrated by [25] in the context of terrorism prevention and by [26] in the context of customer segmentation and nationality prediction. A "Data Injector Tool", which generates test data, has already been implemented by the Netherlands and is being discussed in European level working group meetings (IWG PNR).[16] Lastly, a transfer learning approach may allow for the creation of a classification model, which could be trained on different personal data (e.g., consumer data, voter data). The architecture of such a model could be adopted for a classification model for flight passengers, as long as it can be assumed that the models can, in principle, solve similar problems in a similar way. For examples of the use of transfer learning by law enforcement agencies, see [45] p. 264.

While *pattern matching* can be automated via supervised models, neither the context of use nor the wording of Section 4 (3) FlugDaG allows for matching results to be directly used as training samples without prior verification. Therefore, while a basic function of machine learning, real-time optimization of patterns does not seem like a feasible option in this case. Instead, the patterns would likely be re-trained over time.

Once a machine learning model is built, it is tested for performance in the same way as theory-based models – based on its ability to reproduce known results. The degree of complexity of learning models and the way in which patterns are constructed often means they can generate more accurate predictions than theory-based models but at the expense of the comprehensibility of their overall functionality and of the reasoning behind the output. In this respect working with machine learning means working with some degree of ignorance.

4   Conclusion

This paper illustrates two technological approaches to pattern creation and pattern matching applicable for the purposes the German PNR Act. Both approaches have their advantages and disadvantages and can and should be combined to ensure promising results. While theory-based patterns may be more well known and explainable, machine learning approaches can be used to confirm or refute them and also serve as a basis for the development of new, more elaborate patterns. The possibilities of machine learning approaches to PNR data analysis have been illustrated in some technical papers, see [21–26]. Such research is important, but its current state barely scratches the surface of this topic. It could provide researchers of different fields, including the legal field, with important

---

[14] EU Council 6300/19, 15.2.2019, p. 8 ff., see also [5], p. 12.

[15] UN Homepage, https://www.un.org/cttravel/goTravel, last accessed on 30.1.2021.

[16] EU Council 10139/18, 21.6.2018, p. 3.

information to build on, when examining their national legal frameworks, as this paper has hopefully demonstrated. Ever since the adoption of the PNR Directive, there has been a need for more European-level technical research on this topic. A message this paper also hopes to convey.

References

1. Directive (EU) 2016/681 of the European Parliament and of the Council of 27 April 2016 on the use of passenger name record (PNR) data for the prevention, detection, investigation and prosecution of terrorist offenses and serious crime
2. Fiedler, T.N.: Die Einführung eines europäischen Fluggastdatensystems. Konflikt zwischen Datenschutz und Innerer Sicherheit. Baden-Baden, Nomos (2016)
3. Argomaniz, J.: When the EU is the 'Norm-taker': the passenger name records agreement and the EU's Internalization of US border security norms. J. Eur. Integr. **31**(1), 119–136 (2009). https://doi.org/10.1080/07036330802503981
4. Proposal for a Directive of the European Parliament and of the Council on the use of Passenger Name Record data for the prevention, detection, investigation and prosecution of terrorist offenses and serious crime, COM(2011) 32 final
5. Commission Staff Working Document SWD: 128 final, Accompanying the document Report from the Commission to the European Parliament and the Council On the review of Directive 2016/681 on the use of passenger name record (PNR) data for the prevention, detection, investigation and prosecution of terrorist offences and serious crime {COM(2020) 305 final} (2020)
6. Stellungahme des Nationalen Normenkontrollrates gemäß § 6 Absatz 1 NKRG zum Entwurf eines Gesetzes über die Verarbeitung von Fluggastdaten zur Umsetzung der Richtlinie (EU) 2016/681 (NKR-Nummer 3976, BMI)
7. Rademacher, T.: Predictive Policing im deutschen Polizeirecht. AöR **142**(3), 366–416 (2016). https://doi.org/10.1628/000389117X15054009148798
8. Ulbricht, L.: When big data meet securitization. Algorithmic regulation with passenger name records. Eur. J. Secur. Res. **3**(2), 139–161 (2018). https://doi.org/10.1007/s41125-018-0030-3
9. Koc-Menard, S.: Trends in Terrorist Detection Systems. JHSEM **6**(1) Article 4, 1–13 (2009). https://doi.org/10.2202/1547-7355.1474
10. Deutscher Bundestag 18. Wahlperiode, Innenausschluss, Wortprotokoll der 114. Sitzung, 24 April 2017
11. NZK: Information on Predictive Policing. https://www.nzkrim.de/synthese/zeige/approach-predictive-policing. Accessed 30 Jan 2021
12. Knobloch, T.: Vor die Lage kommen: Predictive Policing in Deutschland. Chancen und Gefahren datenanalytischer Prognosetechnik und Empfehlungen für den Einsatz in der Polizeiarbeit. Bertelsmann-Stiftung (2018)
13. Wischmeyer, T.: Predictive Policing. Nebenfolgen der Automatisierung von Prognosen. In: Kulick, A., Goldhammer, M. (eds.) Der Terrorist als Feind?, pp. 194–213. Tübingen, Mohr Siebeck, Personalisierung im Polizei- und Völkerrecht (2020)
14. Hildebrandt, M.: Smart Technologies and the End(s) of Law. Novel Entanglements of Law and Technology. Edward Elgar, Cheltenham (2016)
15. LaFree, G., Freilich, J.D. (eds.): The Handbook of the Criminology of Terrorism. Wiley-Blackwell, Chichester (2017)
16. LaFree, G., Freilich, J.D.: Bringing criminology into the study of terrorism. In: LaFree, G., Freilich, J.D. (eds.) The Handbook of the Criminology of Terrorism, pp. 1–14. Wiley-Blackwell, Chichester (2017)

17. Rusteberg, B.: Wissensgenerierung in der personenbezogenen Prävention. Zwischen kriminalistischer Erfahrung und erkenntnistheoretischer Rationalität. In: Münkler, L. (ed.) Dimensionen des Wissens im Recht, Tübingen, Mohr Siebeck, pp. 233–264 (2019)
18. Filstad, C., Gottschalk, P.: Knowledge management in the police force. In: Örtenblad, A. (ed.) Handbook of Research on Knowledge Management. Adaption and Context, pp. 69–86. Edward Elgar, Cheltenham (2015)
19. Hüttemann, A.: Ursachen, 2nd revised edition. De Gruyter, Berlin (2018)
20. Selbst, A.D., Barocas, S.: The intuitive appeal of explainable machines. Fordham L. Rev. **87**(3), 1085–1139 (2018)
21. Romero Morales, D., Wang, J.: Forecasting cancellation rates for services booking revenue management using data mining. Eur. J. Oper. Res. **202**(2), 554–562 (2010). https://doi.org/10.1016/j.ejor.2009.06.006
22. Sales, N.A.: Big Data at the border. Balancing visa-free travel and security in a digital age. Syracuse University College of Law (2015). https://perma.cc/WK8G-C95V
23. Ariyawansa, C.M., Aponso, A.C.: Review on state of art data mining and machine learning techniques for intelligent Airport systems. In: ICIM, Proceedings of the International Conference on Information Management, pp. 134–138. IEEE, Piscataway (2016)
24. Domingues, R., Buonora, F., Senesi, R., Thonnard, O.: An application of unsupervised fraud detection to passenger name records. In: 46th Annual IEEE/IFIP International Conference on Dependable Systems and Networks Workshop, pp. 54–59. IEEE (2016)
25. Zheng, Y.-J., Sheng, W.-G., Sun, X.-M., Chen, S.-Y.: Airline passenger profiling based on fuzzy deep machine learning. IEEE Trans. Neural Netw. Learn. Syst. **28**(12), 2911–2923 (2017). https://doi.org/10.1109/TNNLS.2016.2609437
26. Mottini, A., Lheritier, A., Acuna-Agost, R.: Airline passenger name record generation using generative adversarial networks. In: ICLM workshop on Theoretical Foundations and Applications of Deep Generative Models (2018)
27. Korff, D., Georges, M.: Passenger name records, data mining & data protection: the need for strong safeguards, Council of Europe T-PD 11 (2015)
28. Adensamer, A., Klausner, L. D.: Ich weiß, was du nächsten Sommer getan haben wirst, juridikum **31**(3), 419–431 (2019). https://arxiv.org/ftp/arxiv/papers/1907/1907.00934.pdf. Accessed 30 Jan 2021
29. Arzt, C.: Das neue Gesetz zur Fluggastdatenspeicherung. Einladung zur anlasslosen Rasterfahndung durch das BKA. DÖV **24**, 1023–1030 (2017)
30. Broemel, R., Trute, H.-H.: Alles nur Datenschutz? Zur rechtlichen Regulierung algorithmenbasierter Wissensgenerierung. BDI **27**(4), 50–65 (2016)
31. Hoffmann-Riem, W.: Artificial intelligence as a challenge for law and regulation. In: Wischmeyer, T., Rademacher, T. (eds.) Regulating Artificial Intelligence, pp. 1–29. Springer, Cham (2020). https://doi.org/10.1007/978-3-030-32361-5_1
32. Djeffal, C.: Normative Leitlinien für Künstliche Intelligenz in Regierung und öffentlicher Verwaltung. In: Mohabbat-Kar, R., Thapa, B.E.P., Parycek, P. (eds.) (Un)berechenbar?, pp. 493–515. Kompetenzzentrum Öffentliche IT, Algorithmen und Automatisierung in Staat und Gesellschaft, Berlin (2018)
33. Price, W.N., II., Rai, A.K.: Clearing opacity through machine learning. SSRN J. (2020). https://doi.org/10.2139/ssrn.3536983
34. Martini, M.: Blackbox Algorithmus – Grundfragen einer Regulierung Künstlicher Intelligenz, Springer, Heidelberg (2019).https://doi.org/10.1007/978-3-662-59010-2
35. Meyer, S.: Künstliche Intelligenz und die Rolle des Rechts für Innovation. Rechtliche Rationalitätsanforderungen an zukünftige Regulierung. ZRP **8**, 221–252 (2018)
36. Hermstrüwer, Y.: Die Regulierung der prädiktiven Analytik: eine juristisch-verhaltenswissenschaftliche Skizze. In: Hoffmann-Riem, W. (ed.) Big Data - Regulative Herausforderungen, pp. 99–116. Baden-Baden, Nomos (2018)

37. Dreyer, S.: Predictive Analytics aus der Perspektive von Menschenwürde und Autonomie. In: Hoffmann-Riem, W. (ed.) Big Data - Regulative Herausforderungen, pp. 135–143. Baden-Baden, Nomos (2018)

38. Wischmeyer, T.: Regulierung intelligenter Systeme. AöR **143**(1), 1–66 (2018)

39. Coglianese, C., Lehr, D.: Regulating by robot: administrative decision making in the machine-learning era. Penn Law Legal Scholar. Rep. **15**(6), 1147–1223 (2017)

40. Gless, S.: Predictive policing und operative Verbrechensbekämpfung. In: Wolter, J., Herzog, F., Schlothauer, R., Wohlers, W. (eds.) Rechtsstaatlicher Strafprozess und Bürgerrechte. GS für Edda Weßlau, pp. 165–180. Duncker & Humblot, Berlin (2016)

41. Singelnstein, T.: Predictive Policing: Algorithmenbasierte Straftaprognosen zur vorausschauenden Kriminalintervention. NStZ **2**, 1–9 (2018)

42. Baur, A.: Maschinen führen die Aufsicht. Offene Fragen der Kriminalprävention durch digitale Überwachungsagenten. ZIS **15**(6), 275–284 (2020)

43. Pravica, S.: Variablen des Unberechenbaren. Eine Epistemologie der Unwägbarkeiten quantitativer Voraussageverfahren in Sicherheit und Militär. In: Friedrich, A., Gehring, P., Hubig, C., Kaminski, A., Nordmann, A. (eds.) Technisches Nichtwissen, pp. 123–146. Nomos, Baden-Baden (2017)

44. Monroy, M., Busch, H.: Umfangreiche Wunschzettel - EU-Datenbanken und Terrorismusbekämpfung. CILIP **112** (2017). https://www.cilip.de/

45. Sherer, J.A., Sterling, N.L., Burger, L., Banaschik, M., Taal, A.: An investigator's christmas carol: past, present, and future law enforcement agency data mining practices. In: Jahankhani, H. (ed.) Cyber Criminology. ASTSA, pp. 251–273. Springer, Cham (2018). https://doi.org/10.1007/978-3-319-97181-0_12

Migration-Related Semantic Concepts for the Retrieval of Relevant Video Content

Erick Elejalde[1], Damianos Galanopoulos[2(✉)], Claudia Niederée[1], and Vasileios Mezaris[2]

[1] L3S Research Center, Leibniz-University, Hannover, Germany
{elejalde,niederee}@l3s.de
[2] CERTH-ITI, Thermi-Thessaloniki, Greece
{dgalanop,bmezaris}@iti.gr

Abstract. Migration, and especially irregular migration, is a critical issue for border agencies and society in general. Migration-related situations and decisions are influenced by various factors, including the perceptions about migration routes and target countries. An improved understanding of such factors can be achieved by systematic automated analyses of media and social media channels, and the videos and images published in them. However, the multifaceted nature of migration and the variety of ways migration-related aspects are expressed in images and videos make the finding and automated analysis of migration-related multimedia content a challenging task. We propose a novel approach that effectively bridges the gap between a substantiated domain understanding - encapsulated into a set of Migration-related semantic concepts - and the expression of such concepts in a video, by introducing an advanced video analysis and retrieval method for this purpose.

Keywords: Migration · Semantic concept · Video analysis · Conceptualization

1 Introduction

Migration is a complex process, where decisions are driven by a multitude of factors, including the perceptions about migration routes and target countries [29]. Media, and especially social media, with their powerful use of images and videos from multiple sources, plays an essential role in forming and manipulating such perceptions and misperceptions [1], e.g., via misinformation campaigns. A better understanding of the media and its impact, thus, can help in anticipating possible migration-related risks at the border and in transit countries.

With the vast amounts of media and media channels from a wide variety of sources, automated content analysis is necessary. However, the multifaceted nature of migration and the range of ways related aspects are expressed in images and videos make the finding and automated analysis of migration-related content very challenging.

© Springer Nature Switzerland AG 2021
S. Yildirim Yayilgan et al. (Eds.): INTAP 2020, CCIS 1382, pp. 404–416, 2021.
https://doi.org/10.1007/978-3-030-71711-7_34

To address some of these challenges, we propose a novel method, which effectively combines a top-down with a bottom-up approach. We leverage the substantial theoretical understanding that has been achieved on migration factors and migration decisions [24,26,28]. For this, we define a domain conceptualization in close collaboration with experts, resulting in a set of Migration-Related Semantic Concepts (top-down). This is combined with an advanced video analysis method that captures and retrieves the different ways these semantic concepts are expressed in videos and images (bottom-up). Since the Migration-Related Semantic Concepts (MRSCs) are often abstract definitions (e.g. *'ethnic identity'*, *'law enforcement'*, etc.), it is very challenging to find and annotate video exemplars with these concepts.

Typical concept annotation and retrieval methods use image/video exemplars as training materials to develop pre-defined concept detectors [20–22]. However, these methods suffer from scalability limitations because it is difficult to collect and annotate large enough datasets. Moreover, it is very time and effort consuming to integrate new concepts due to the manual annotation and training phases. To overcome these limitations, we aim at associating MRSCs with visual content without using any training visual exemplars. We adopt a state-of-the-art approach for Ad-hoc Video Search (AVS) that directly transforms visual and textual content into a common feature space, in which a straightforward comparison is feasible. AVS is a type of cross-modal retrieval problem, in which video shots are recovered when the query is a complex textual sentence. Similarly, our MRSCs retrieval problem is to identify and annotate images or video shots with MRSCs, starting from the textual definition of the MRSCs.

Early attempts on the AVS problem have relied on large sets of pre-trained visual concept detectors and NLP techniques for query analysis to find relevant visual concepts in the query. In [19], the association between visual concepts and the textual queries was reached by using complex NLP rules and a vast set of pre-trained deep neural networks for video annotation. More recently, the problem has been addressed using deep neural networks to transform both the textual queries and the visual content in a new shared space [15]. The dual encoding network proposed in [9] uses multiple levels of encoding to transform videos and queries into a common dense representation using an improved loss function [11]. An extension of the above was presented in [12], where state-of-the-art results were achieved using rich representations and attention-based layers of encoding for both the text and the visual modalities. We build on this method to address the identification of visual content that could be associated with MRSCs.

2 Migration-Related Semantic Concepts (MRSCs)

A semantic concept is understood here as a meaningful entity or a comprehensive idea formed in the person's mind from the information perceived and the person's background. Moreover, a semantic concept is intrinsically linked to a context [10]. Based on an in-depth study of migration theories and discussions with domain experts, we have collected semantic concepts that will help specialists to express the migration aspects they are interested in and to identify relevant visual information to be later interpreted and analyzed.

The collection of concepts has resulted in a set of 106 Migration-Related Semantic Concepts (MRSCs), i.e., concepts relevant in the context of migration. These are organized in five general categories (see Sect. 2.2).

The advantages of basing our video retrieval process in MRSCs are many-fold. First, it provides a substantiated and diverse common language (with ground definitions of concepts), which can be used to express information needs; and be used in later expert analysis of the retrieved information. Also, by critically relying on theoretically founded categories and discourses of migration, we minimize distorted or biased views of the subject under study and foster the consideration of a wide variety of aspects.

2.1 Migration Theories

We base our analysis mostly on three popular theoretical approaches used to study migration-related issues: the Neo-classical economic equilibrium perspective, Historical-structural approach, and Migration systems theory [13,16]. We took these models into account to create a hierarchical definition of the concepts. However, as these models (for most purposes) are orthogonal to each other, our concepts and their classification are not tied to one particular theory. Instead, in combination, they help us to better identify concepts in the context of migration.

In essence, the *Neo-classical theory* centers on the imbalanced conditions between the country/region of origin and that of destination. It assumes that individuals in the process of migration will try to maximize their benefit in composition with other external constraints. Alternatives are compared, and from the gathered information, the potential migrant will decide if it is more 'profitable' to stay or leave [2]. Related to the Neo-classical theory is the *Push-Pull framework* [17], which continues to emphasize the drivers of the flow of people. The underlying assumption of this theory is that negative factors at the origin push people away, while positive factors at the destination pull people toward them. The Push-Pull model has been adapted and extended in various ways [16]. For example, in [24], the author suggests to include the mooring dimension (referred to as the Push-Pull-Mooring (PPM) theory). The mooring factors are equivalent to moderating variables in that they can either potentiate migration or dissuade the migrants from leaving their current country.

The *historical-structural approach* provides an alternative to explain the migration processes. It also stresses the unequal distribution of economic and political influence in the world's economy but is mostly based on the Marxist view of the political economy [6,28]. The historical-structuralist accounts shift the focus away from voluntary migration (as suggested by push-pull models) to a global scale recruitment of labor by capital [13]. Here, migration is presented as a means of mobilizing cheap labor for capital, which, in turn, preserves the existing uneven development.

Both the neo-classical perspective and the historical-structuralist approach have faced criticism [14,26,27]. The former is accused of overlooking historical antecedents of movements, and underestimating the role of the state, while the latter attributes to the interests of capital most of the weight in the migration process, and pays almost no attention to the personal motivations [13]. As a response to these criticisms, comes up the third model considered in our study, i.e., *Migration systems* [3,26]. The migration systems approach proposes a more holistic analysis that examines the origin and the destination by considering all the linkages between the two places. This approach suggests that the migratory process can be represented as the result of interacting macro-, meso- and microstructures [3]. Macro-structures are represented by large institutional factors (mostly out of the control and independent from the migrant - e.g., the political economy of the world market). Micro-structures are understood as the pattern of relations between essential elements of the social life that cannot be further divided and have no social structure of their own (e.g., cultural capital). Finally, meso-structures are located in the space between micro and macro-structures. These act as obstacles or facilitators in the migratory process. Even when they are related to the individual, they are not entirely under her/his control (e.g., technology, migration industry, etc.). All these structures are interconnected and help to describe the entire process from the migration decision to settlement and community formation [13].

2.2 Factors Classification

Semantic concepts can be combined to form meaningful templates, containing several aspects and, in turn, specifying further semantics. For example, the aspects 'family' and 'war' can be combined in a template as 'Families in war'. These templates can then also be used as a semantic concept. Based on these patterns, and similar to comparable works such as the World bank theme taxonomy[1], we have defined the MRSCs as a hierarchical structure. This tree-style classification further allows annotating information at different aggregation levels and contributes to the definition of each concept's context.

The identified concepts are grouped into five categories: economic, social, demographic, environmental, and political. These classes are consistent across the migration literature [3,13,26]. We identified 106 MRSCs that we organized on two levels: 20 on the first level and the other 86 under them (see Table 1).

As expected, many social factors are related to migration. One crucial definition in this category is that of 'Ethnicity'. The concept of ethnicity is relevant in more than one of the sub-classes. However, we have specifically identified a class called 'Ethnicity', which refers to a real process of historical individuation by linguistic and cultural practices that give a sense of collective identity [5].

Another important category identified concerning MRSCs is 'Demographic'. This category comprises concepts such as 'Target-earners', 'Gender', and 'Refugees'. Identifying gender-specific perceptions and expectations during the migration process is critical in the analysis of media content. Many gender-related misperceptions lead to conflicts and security issues[2]. This is why one

---

[1] http://pubdocs.worldbank.org/en/275841490966525495/Theme-Taxonomy-and-def
initions.pdf.

[2] https://migrationdataportal.org/themes/gender-and-migration.

Table 1. Dataset of MRSCs organized in five general categories and in two hierarchical levels. In the second level column we are including only a subset of the complete list.

Category	1st Level	2nd Level (examples)
Economic	Labour market	Working conditions, Labor movements, Job segmentation
	Migrant groups infrastructure	Migration industries, Family labor, Socio-spatial texture
	Capital flows	Investment, Informal economic activities, International trade
Social	Ethnic minority formation	Others-definition, Self-definition, Ethnic identity
	Ethnic community formation	Cohesion, Access to community, Access to information and services
	Ethnicity	Xenophobia, Racism, Language
	Interpersonal relationships	Radicalization, Rumors, Cultural interaction
	Cultural capital	Adaptability, *Education*, Knowledge of other country
	Social capital	Informal social activities, Opinion formers
Demographic	Target-earners	Remittances, Relative success/failure in target country
	Gender	Marriage, Domestic service, Caretaking
	Skilled professionals	Brain drain
	Refugees	*War*, *Political instability*, Persecution
Environmental	*Urbanization*	Global cities, Stopgaps, Ethnic footholds, *Access to medical care*
	Ecology	Climate change, Pollution, Natural disasters
Political	Settlement	Citizenship, Laws, Nation
	Immigration policies	Representation of immigrants in policies, Change of policies over time
	Crime	Acculturation problems, Ethnic tensions, Cultural predispositions
	Organized crime	Human trafficking, Document fraud, Money laundering
	Politics	Corruption, Policymakers, Regulatory hoops/their avoidance

essential class of issues to be analyzed relates explicitly to 'Gender'. This group of concepts will deal with terms such as 'Marriage', 'Care-taking', and 'Domestic service' (all of which are disproportionately associated with women). Another relevant concept in this category is 'Refugees'. This, in turn, can be contextualized in terms of more specific concepts such as 'War' or 'Political instability', which are identified as factors influencing forced migration.

Environmental factors are becoming more and more relevant when it comes to migration. Environmental migrants or climate refugees are forced to leave their home region due to sudden or long-term changes to their local environment. These changes compromise their well-being or their secure livelihood. Such changes may include increased droughts, desertification, sea-level rise, and disruption of seasonal weather patterns. Other environmental factors that bring people to migrate are those related to an increasing tendency toward urbanization. This includes topics such as 'Global cities', 'Stopgaps', 'Ethnic footholds', and other factors like better 'access to medical care' that drive migrants looking to improve their quality of life.

It is crucial to notice that our list of MRSCs is defined based on the specific interests of our current research, and they do not constitute a comprehensive list of all the concepts related to migration. Also, despite the tree-style hierarchical classification of the concepts, these are not necessarily mutually exclusive. For example, 'remittances' is a concept that can be associated with economic factors such as 'Capital flow', but also is strongly related to demographic factors as one of the main drivers for 'Target-earners' (i.e., economically active people who want to save enough in a higher-wage economy to improve conditions at home).

3   MRSC-Based Video Retrieval

We address the MRSC-based video retrieval problem by adapting a previously developed state-of-the-art method for the AVS problem [12]. This approach's overall idea is to train a deep neural network (DNN) by using video-caption pairs. This DNN is then used as a video retrieval system by inputting MRSCs to recover the most related video shots. Since the MRSCs are typically high-level abstractions of concepts, we choose to enrich them so that we have an information-rich input to the video retrieval system. For this, each MRSC is manually complemented (i.e., augmented) with a small set of complex sentences that describe it. For instance, for the MRSC 'Education', sentences like "students in a classroom attend a lecture" are added. This approach is closely related to the training procedure for our network. The MRSC (with its descriptions) and video shots from the target dataset are used as input to our system. They are encoded into the common feature space, and for every MRSC, a ranked list with the most related media items within the given image/video dataset is generated. An overview of the proposed method is illustrated in Fig. 1.

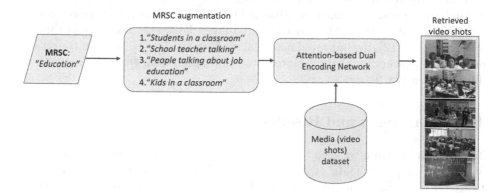

Fig. 1. An overview of the MRSC retrieval method

For MRSCs-related video retrieval, we adjust the attention-based dual encoding network presented in [12]. This network utilizes two similar modules, each consisting of multiple encoding levels, for the visual and textual content respectively, along with a text-based attention component for more efficient textual representation. The network translates a media item (e.g. an entire video or a video shot) $\mathbf{V}$ and a textual item (e.g. a video shot caption or a text query) $\mathbf{S}$ into a new shared feature space $\phi(\cdot)$, resulting in two new representations $\phi(\mathbf{V})$ and $\phi(\mathbf{S})$ that are directly comparable.

More specifically, each video shot is encoded into a three-level representation $[\phi(V_1), \phi(V_2), \phi(V_3)]$. Firstly, the video shot is decoded into a fixed number of n keyframes and fed into a pre-trained DCNN, from where a feature vector v_n is produced for every keyframe. $\mathbf{V} = \{v_1, v_2, \ldots, v_n\}$ is the collection of keyframe feature vectors for the shot and $\phi(V_1) = \frac{1}{n}\sum_{i=1}^{n} v_i$ is considered as the first-level video representation. The keyframes vectors are fed in a sequence of bidirectional Gated Recurrent Units (bi-GRUs) [4], and their output $\mathbf{H_v} \in \mathbb{R}^{n \times 2*h}$, where h is the output size of a GRU cell, is forwarded into a self-attention mechanism [12] resulting in a weight matrix $\mathbf{A_v} \in \mathbb{R}^{n \times n}$. Then, the matrix $\overline{\mathbf{H}}_\mathbf{v} = \mathbf{A_v}\mathbf{H_v}$ is calculated. $\phi(V_2)$ is calculated as $\phi(V_2) = \frac{1}{n}\sum_{t=1}^{n} \overline{h}_t$, where $\overline{h}_t$ is the tth row of $\overline{\mathbf{H}}_\mathbf{v}$. Finally, $\overline{\mathbf{H}}_\mathbf{v}$ is forwarded into a 1-d convolutional layer resulting in the third-level representation $\phi(V_3)$ of the shot. The overall video shot representation is the concatenation of these three representations, which is forwarded into a trainable fully connected layer.

Similar to the visual encoding module, a three-level representation $[\phi(S_1), \phi(S_2), \phi(S_3)]$ is built for every textual item S. Considering a text sentence S as a set of m words $\mathbf{S} = \{w_1, w_2, \ldots, w_m\}$, the first-level $\phi(S_1)$ is created by averaging individual one-hot-vectors of these words. Then, for every word, a deep network-based word embedding vector c_m is created, and is used as input for the bi-directional GRU module. The output of GRU $\mathbf{H_s} \in \mathbb{R}^{m \times 2*h}$, is forwarded into the text-based attention mechanism resulting in a matrix $\overline{\mathbf{H}}_\mathbf{s} = \mathbf{A_s}\mathbf{H_s}$, where $\mathbf{A_s} \in \mathbb{R}^{m \times m}$. Analogous to $\phi(V_2)$, $\phi(S_2) = \frac{1}{m}\sum_{t=1}^{m} \overline{h}_t$, where $\overline{h}_t$ is the tth row of $\overline{\mathbf{H}}_\mathbf{s}$. Finally, $\overline{\mathbf{H}}_\mathbf{s}$ is fed to a 1-d convolutional layer resulting in the textual third-level representation $\phi(S_3)$. Similar to the visual module, the overall textual representation is the concatenation of these three representations, which is forwarded into a trainable fully connected layer. Following the state of the art approach [9,11,12], the improved marginal ranking loss is used to train the entire network. The overview of the adapted attention-based dual encoding network is illustrated in Fig. 2.

4   Experiments and Results

To train our network, we used the combination of two large-scale video datasets: MSR-VTT [30] and TGIF [18]. As initial keyframe representations, we use a ResNet-152 (trained on the ImageNet-11k dataset). Also, two different word embeddings are utilized: i) the Word2Vec model [23] trained on the English tags of 30K Flickr images, provided by [8]; and, ii) the pre-trained language representation BERT [7], trained on Wikipedia content. To evaluate the performance

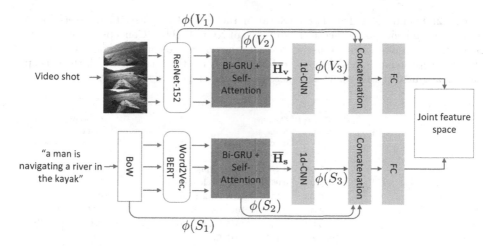

Fig. 2. An overview of the attention-based dual encoding network

of our network for MRSCs retrieval, since there is no available dataset for this, we use the evaluation datasets of the TRECVID Semantic Indexing task (SIN) for the years of 2013 and 2015[3]. The goal is to retrieve the most related video shots by inputting the names of a set of visual concepts. In our analysis, these concepts take over the position of the MRSCs for evaluation purposes. A good performance on these datasets will document the merit of the proposed approach for the needs of the MRSC-based retrieval problem. The mean extended inferred average precision (MXinfAP) is used as an evaluation measure, as is usually the case with these datasets [25].

We compare our proposed model with conventional concept retrieval methods that use predefined sets of visual concepts, positive exemplars for every concept, and are trained on these sets. The goal is to highlight the performance of our approach that does not require concept-annotated training videos. This gives our model a practical advantage over the supervised learning methods.

Table 2 presents the results on the SIN'13 and SIN'15 datasets for the detection of 38 and 30 different concepts, respectively. The results of Table 2 show that the use of additional information (i.e., "augmentations") for every concept (see Sect. 3) leads to a significantly improved performance. Examples of substantial improvements are the concepts *"Telephones"* in both datasets, and *"Bicycling"* and *"Demonstration Or Protest"* in the SIN'15 dataset. The *"Telephones"* concept was described as *"speaking on a telephone"* and *"talking on a telephone"*, and its XinfAP went from 0.0 to 0.3151 and from 0.0 to 0.308 in the SIN'13 and SIN'15 datasets, respectively. Similarly, *"Bicycling"* which was described as *"a man riding a bike"*, *"people riding bicycles"* and *"a woman on a bike"* achieved 0.373 XinfAP, compared to 0.0569 when only the word "bicycling" was used.

---

[3] https://www-nlpir.nist.gov/projects/tv2015/index.html#sin.

Table 2. Results of video shot retrieval in the SIN'13 and SIN'15 datasets for 38 and 30 visual concepts, respectively, in terms of XinfAP. The "Concept name" column presents the results when we use as textual input only the concept label. In contrast, the "Concept name + descriptions" column stands for the setup in which the concept label is augmented with short sentences describing the concept further.

SIN'13 dataset	Concept name	Concept name + descriptions	SIN'15 dataset	Concept name	Concept name + descriptions
1003 Airplane	0.1928	0.2789	1003 Airplane	0.3254	0.5055
1005 Anchorperson	0.0128	0.0646	1005 Anchorperson	0.0067	0.0145
1006 Animal	0.0253	0.1748	1009 Basketball	0.0134	0.1814
1010 Beach	0.4648	0.515	1013 Bicycling	0.0569	0.373
1015 Boat Ship	0.3653	0.4443	1015 Boat Ship	0.4804	0.5998
1016 Boy	0.0601	0.1279	1017 Bridges	0.085	0.1615
1017 Bridges	0.0268	0.0688	1019 Bus	0.1215	0.1382
1019 Bus	0.0657	0.112	1022 Car Racing	0	0.0647
1025 Chair	0.0309	0.1207	1027 Cheering	0.0004	0.0687
1031 Computers	0.112	0.2982	1031 Computers	0.148	0.362
1038 Dancing	0.0242	0.1503	1038 Dancing	0.0002	0.1239
1049 Explosion Fire	0.1884	0.2582	1041 Demonstration Or Protest	0	0.2574
1052 Female Human Face Closeup	0.1017	0.1459	1049 Explosion Fire	0.104	0.1739
1053 Flowers	0.1035	0.1661	1056 Government Leader	0.0003	0.1677
1054 Girl	0.0388	0.1271	1071 Instrumental Musician	0.0002	0.3458
1056 Government Leader	0	0.2767	1072 Kitchen	0.0805	0.34
1059 Hand	0.0904	0.1025	1080 Motorcycle	0.1303	0.236
1071 Instrumental Musician	0.0031	0.3305	1085 Office	0.0546	0.2425
1072 Kitchen	0.0745	0.1537	1086 Old People	0.0473	0.1993
1080 Motorcycle	0.2042	0.2581	1095 Press Conference	0.0001	0.0219
1083 News Studio	0.0206	0.0609	1100 Running	0.0008	0.0178
1086 Old People	0.0854	0.2108	1117 Telephones	0	0.3088
1089 People Marching	0	0.0626	1120 Throwing	0.0001	0.0485
1100 Running	0.0059	0.1494	1261 Flags	0.0685	0.156
1105 Singing	0.0008	0.1057	1297 Hill	0.0319	0.0675
1107 Sitting Down	0.0001	0.0084	1321 Lakes	0.0577	0.2033
1117 Telephones	0	0.3151	1392 Quadruped	0.0017	0.2311
1120 Throwing	0	0.125	1440 Soldiers	0.2436	0.3709
1163 Baby	0.2991	0.4707	1454 Studio With Anchorperson	0.0021	0.0393
1227 Door Opening	0.0177	0.0377	1478 Traffic	0.1372	0.2046
1254 Fields	0.0192	0.1578			
1261 Flags	0.1274	0.2687			
1267 Forest	0.1026	0.1939			
1274 George Bush	0	0.44			
1342 Military Airplane	0.0001	0.1062			
1392 Quadruped	0.0214	0.2928			
1431 Skating	0.2684	0.424			
1454 Studio With Anchorperson	0.0047	0.0419			
Mean XinfAP	0.0831	**0.2012**		0.0733	**0.2075**

Table 3. Comparison with SIN Task-specific methods in the SIN'13 and SIN'15 datasets, in terms of XinfAP.

	SIN 2013	SIN 2015
Proposed AVS approach (concept name + descriptions; no training exemplars)	0.2012	0.2075
[21] (using annotated exemplars for training)	0.2504	–
[22] (using annotated exemplars for training)	0.1580	–
[20] (using annotated exemplars for training)	–	0.263

To highlight the performance of our approach, we compare our results with different methods that were designed to solve the SIN task, using training video samples. For the SIN'13 dataset, we compared with the work presented in [21] and the CERTH participation in the TRECVID SIN task in 2013 [22]. For the SIN'15 dataset, we offer a comparison with the CERTH participation in the TRECVID SIN task in 2015 [20]. Table 3 shows that our approach is very competitive, even though the baselines are explicitly designed for the SIN task. Even though our MRSCs detection approach does not outperform the baseline methods on the SIN task, these results are strong evidence that our approach is suitable for the MRSCs retrieval problem where, as opposed to the TRECVID SIN task used for this evaluation, no training data (annotated visual exemplars) are available for the MRSCs.

As mentioned before, there is no MRSC-specific dataset to evaluate our approach's performance empirically. For this reason, we only presented results on the TRECVID SIN datasets. However, to further illustrate our approach's performance, we give some visual examples of the retrieved video shots when we use the MRSCs as input to our method. In Fig. 3, the top-5 retrieved shots are

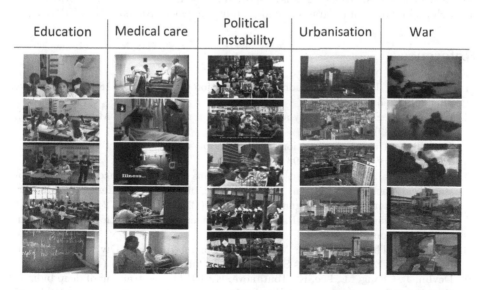

Fig. 3. Example results, for five MRSCs (shown on the top of the figure). The top-5 retrieved shots for each MRSC are shown.

presented for a subset of the available MRSCs. These selected MRSCs include representatives of multiple categories and both levels of the hierarchical classification (see highlighted concepts in Table 1). Although preliminary, results further point to the potential of our approach as a valid and effective solution in finding shots related to MRSCs.

5   Conclusions and Future Work

In this paper, we presented an approach that combines two needs for a better understanding of migration decisions and the migration situation: a) a multi-faceted view on the migration process, and b) practical automated support for collecting and analyzing relevant video content for this multifaceted perspective. The theoretically founded MRSCs foster a broad view of the migration topic and a common language for analysis. The presented AVS approach can retrieve videos related to abstract MRSC concepts without requiring the time-consuming task of manual video annotation (for training), thus bridging the gap between concepts and video content. The experimental evaluation showed the effectiveness of the proposed approach. Such an approach can be used by border agencies to enrich their analysis of migration contexts and situations with appropriate video coverage. Future research could focus on three aspects: i) fully automated pipeline through automatic MRSCs creation via efficient web harvesting, ii) further performance improvement by AVS method enhancement with better encoding and improved visual and text representations, and iii) further experimentation with domain-specific datasets.

Acknowledgments. This work was supported by the European Union's Horizon 2020 research and innovation programme under grant agreement No. 832921 (MIRROR).

References

1. Bakewell, O., Jolivet, D.: Broadcasting Migration Outcomes, pp. 183–204. Palgrave Macmillan, London (2016)
2. Borjas, G.J.: Economic theory and international migration. Int. Migr. Rev. **23**(3), 457–485 (1989)
3. Castelli, F.: Drivers of migration: why do people move? J. Travel Med. **25**(1), 1–7 (2018). https://doi.org/10.1093/jtm/tay040
4. Cho, K., et al.: Learning phrase representations using RNN encoder-decoder for statistical machine translation. In: Proceedings of the 2014 Conference on Empirical Methods in Natural Language Processing (EMNLP), pp. 1724–1734 (2014)
5. Cohen, P., Bains, H.S.: Multi-Racist Britain. Macmillan International Higher Education, London (1988)
6. Cohen, R.: The New Helots: Migrants in the International Division of Labour (Research in Ethnic Relations Series). Gower Pub Co, Farnham (1987)
7. Devlin, J., Chang, M., Lee, K., Toutanova, K.: BERT: pre-training of deep bidirectional transformers for language understanding. arXiv preprint arXiv:1810.04805 (2018)

8. Dong, J., Li, X., Snoek, C.G.M.: Predicting visual features from text for image and video caption retrieval. IEEE Trans. Multimedia (TMM) **20**(12), 3377–3388 (2018)
9. Dong, J., et al.: Dual encoding for zero-example video retrieval. In: Proceedings of IEEE Conference on CVPR 2019, pp. 9346–9355 (2019)
10. Eriksson, K.: Concept determination as part of the development of knowledge in caring science. Scand. J. Caring Sci. **24**, 2–11 (2010)
11. Faghri, F., Fleet, D.J., Kiros, J.R., Fidler, S.: VSE++: improving visual-semantic embeddings with hard negatives. In: Proceedings of the British Machine Vision Conference (BMVC) (2018)
12. Galanopoulos, D., Mezaris, V.: Attention mechanisms, signal encodings and fusion strategies for improved ad-hoc videosearch with dual encoding networks. In: Proceedings of the ACM International Conference on Multimedia Retrieval (ICMR 2020). ACM (2020)
13. de Haas, H., Castles, S., Miller, M.: The Age of Migration, 6th edn. International Population Movements in the Modern World. Guilford Publications, New York (2019)
14. de Haas, H.: The determinants of international migration. IMI Working Papers (2011)
15. Habibian, A., Mensink, T., Snoek, C.G.: Video2vec embeddings recognize events when examples are scarce. IEEE Trans. Pattern Anal. Mach. Intell. **39**(10), 2089–2103 (2017)
16. Hear, N.V., Bakewell, O., Long, K.: Push-pull plus: reconsidering the drivers of migration. J. Ethnic Migr. Stud. **44**(6), 927–944 (2018)
17. Lee, E.S.: A theory of migration. Demography **3**(1), 47–57 (1966)
18. Li, Y., et al.: TGIF: a new dataset and benchmark on animated GIF description. In: Proceedings of IEEE CVPR 2016, pp. 4641–4650 (2016)
19. Markatopoulou, F., Galanopoulos, D., Mezaris, V., Patras, I.: Query and keyframe representations for ad-hoc video search. In: Proceedings of the 2017 ACM International Conference on Multimedia Retrieval, (ICMR 2017), pp. 407–411. ACM (2017)
20. Markatopoulou, F., Ioannidou, A., Tzelepis, C., et al.: ITI-CERTH participation to TRECVID 2015. In: Proceedings of the TRECVID 2015 Workshop, Gaithersburg, MD, USA, November 2015
21. Markatopoulou, F., Mezaris, V., Patras, I.: Deep multi-task learning with label correlation constraint for video concept detection. In: Proceedings of the 24th ACM International Conference on Multimedia (MM 2016), pp. 501–505 (2016)
22. Markatopoulou, F., Moumtzidou, A., Tzelepis, C., et al.: ITI-CERTH participation to TRECVID 2013. In: Proceedings of the TRECVID 2013 Workshop, Gaithersburg, MD, USA, November 2013
23. Mikolov, T., Corrado, G., Chen, K., Dean, J.: Efficient estimation of word representations in vector space. In: 1st International Conference on Learning Representations, Workshop Track Proceedings. ICLR 2013 (2013)
24. Moon, B.: Paradigms in migration research: exploring 'moorings' as a schema. Prog. Hum. Geogr. **19**(4), 504–524 (1995)
25. Over, P., Awad, G., Fiscus, J., Sanders, G., Shaw, B.: TRECVID 2013-an introduction to the goals, tasks, data, evaluation mechanisms, and metrics. In: Proceedings of the TRECVID 2013 Workshop, Gaithersburg, MD, USA (2013)
26. Portes, A., Böröcz, J.: Contemporary immigration: theoretical perspectives on its determinants and modes of incorporation. Int. Migr. Rev. **23**(3), 606–630 (1989)

27. Portes, A., Rumbaut, R.G.: Immigrant America: A Portrait, 4th edn. University of California Press, Berkeley (2014)
28. Sassen, S.: The Mobility of Labor and Capital. Cambridge University Press, New York (1988)
29. Timmerman, C., De Clerck, M.L., Hemmerechts, K., Willems, R.: Imagining Europe from the Outside: the Role of Perceptions of Human Rights in Europe in Migration Aspirations in Turkey, Morocco, Senegal and Ukraine, pp. 220–247. Palgrave Macmillan, London, January 2014
30. Xu, J., Mei, T., Yao, T., Rui, Y.: MSR-VTT: a large video description dataset for bridging video and language. In: Proceedings of IEEE CVPR 2016, pp. 5288–5296 (2016)

Correction to: Intelligent Technologies and Applications

Sule Yildirim Yayilgan, Imran Sarwar Bajwa, and Filippo Sanfilippo

Correction to:
S. Yildirim Yayilgan et al. (Eds.): *Intelligent Technologies and Applications*, **CCIS 1382,**
https://doi.org/10.1007/978-3-030-71711-7

The original version of the book's subtitle was revised: the conference city was corrected from Grimstad, Norway, to Gjøvik, Norway.

The updated version of the book can be found at
https://doi.org/10.1007/978-3-030-71711-7

Author Index

Printed in the United States
by Baker & Taylor Publisher Services